General Engineering

General Engineering

R L Timings

Longman
Scientific &
Technical

Longman Scientific & Technical
Longman Group Limited
Longman House, Burnt Mill, Harlow
Essex, CM20 2JE, England
and Associated Companies throughout the world

© Longman Group Limited 1995

First published 1995

British Library Cataloguing in Publication Data
A catalogue entry for this title is available from the British Library

ISBN 0-582-08805-4

Set by 4 in 10/12 pt Times
Printed in Malaysia

Contents

Preface

General Engineering has been written to cover the following City and Guilds of London Institute (CGLI) Basic Engineering Competence units:

201-2-21	Industrial studies	(Element 01)
201-2-22	Basic engineering processes	(Elements 02−07)
201-2-23	Material removal	(Element 08)
201-2-24	Joining	(Element 09)
201-2-25	Assembly and dismantling	(Element 10)

It has also been written to cover the 'Underpinning Knowledge and Understanding' elements of the Engineering Training Authority's (EnTra) basic training specifications. The author and the Publishers are grateful to EnTra for allowing the reproduction and adaptation of some of their illustrations and material in this text. Since most students studying for a CGLI certificate in Basic Engineering Competences will also be undergoing practical skill training to EnTra standards, they should find the commonality of subject matter and approach particularly helpful. This joint approach also provides the knowledge required for the National Vocational Qualification in Engineering Manufacture (Foundation) at Level 2.

Those students who wish to progress to CGLI main competences will require certification in endorsement 201-2-32 Science Background to Engineering. A companion text entitled *Science Background to Engineering* and covering this endorsement is in preparation and is intended to be used as a complement to *General Engineering*.

It should be noted that students progressing to CGLI main competences will also require certification in one or more appropriate occupational endorsements.

Finally, the text has been written in a less formal style than that normally adopted for technical texts and the author hopes that, as a result, the reader will find it more enjoyable.

1994   R. L. Timings

Acknowledgements

The author is grateful to the following for permission to reproduce copyright material:

Silvaflame Ltd for Fig. 2.10; Colchester Lathe Company for Fig. 2.11; Myford Ltd for Fig. 4.35 from *Series 7 Manual, No. S723W*; Neill Tools Ltd for Figs 5.14, 5.15 & 6.3; Tucker Fasteners Ltd for Fig. 9.7(b) & (c); International Tin Research Institute for Fig. 9.11; W. Bolton for Table 9.4 from Table 8.1 in *Materials Technology 4* published by Butterworth-Heinemann Ltd.

EnTra Publications for permission under a reciprocal agreement to reproduce and adapt some of their material.

Extracts from British Standards are reproduced with the permission of BSI. Complete copies can be obtained by post from BSI Sales, Linford Wood, Milton Keynes, MK14 6LE.

1 Industrial studies

1.1 The development of the engineering industry

During the seventeenth century social and economic changes were taking place in Britain. Trade at home and abroad was expanding, capital was being accumulated, and social and political change was taking place. As a result there was not only a rapidly increasing demand for goods but the wealth to pay for them.

At that time our economy was based largely on agriculture. The blacksmith provided the basic metal working services required by the local farming community, and craftsmen such as jewellers and silversmiths in the larger towns produced fine metal products. There were also clock and instrument makers. Skilled as these persons were, their resources were limited and hand-crafted goods produced with loving care in small workshops were not only expensive, their production methods could not meet the demands of expanding trade. Great changes were about to occur.

The eighteenth century saw many important developments and inventions that were to give rise to the Industrial Revolution. For example:

1708 Abraham Derby (I) found that iron ore could be smelted using coal instead of charcoal. This was very important because coal was much more plentiful and it avoided the cutting down of Britain's forests. Coal had been tried before without success but Abraham Derby used coal that had been turned into coke and this produced iron that was as good as that produced using charcoal and a lot cheaper.

1708 Thomas Newcomen developed the first steam pumping engine for mines. This enabled mines to be dug deeper without fear of flooding. With steam, a new source of energy had been harnessed.

It was the mechanisation of the spinning and weaving industries which were to produce the greatest changes. Cottage industries gave place to the factory system. Mill owners wanted ever bigger and better spinning machines and looms. They also wanted energy sources that could drive their mills all the year round, unlike waterwheels which ceased to turn at times of drought. The early inventors and metal workers did not let them down. Let's look at some of the highlights of what was to follow.

1769 Richard Arkwright invented and manufactured the first spinning machine (driven by water power).

1774 John Wilkinson produced the first power driven and practical horizontal boring machine for boring out the barrels of cannons. James Watt was soon to adapt this machine to boring out his steam engine cylinders.

1779 James Watt produced the first, practical, rotary steam engine that could drive machines.

1785 Richard Arkwright and James Watt got together and developed the first steam powered spinning mill.

However, there were limitations to the achievements of these early engineers. They lacked machine tools and they lacked high strength materials. Mostly they had to work with cast iron and wrought iron. Small quantities of crucible cast steel, which could be hardened, were available for cutting tools. This was to change in the nineteenth century as the industrial revolution gathered momentum.

1800 Henry Maudslay produced the first *sliding, surfacing and screw-cutting lathe* with most of the features of a modern centre lathe.

1818 Joseph Clement produced the first planing machine for metal.

But it was no good producing goods by machinery if the raw materials could not be transported to the factory and the goods produced could not be delivered to the customer. It must be remembered that all goods were moved by horse drawn carts travelling over primitive roads in those days. Alternatively, goods could be sent by horse-drawn barges on the canal system or by small coastal sailing ships. But this was soon to change with the coming of the railways. The earliest railways were associated with quarries and mines where it was found that horses could pull heavier loads if the trucks ran on smooth rails. The next step was to replace horse power with steam power. Various names were associated with the first experiments in this form of transport, but it was George Stephenson who was responsible for the first commercial steam railway between Stockton and Darlington. Largely self-taught, George Stephenson soon became a national figure with a genius for building railways.

1821 George Stephenson developed the first commercial railway between Stockton and Darlington in the North of England. He not only built the railway but the locomotives and rolling stock as well. His next project was the Liverpool—Manchester railway. This was a major achievement and a competition was held at Rainhill to find the best locomotives for the railway.

1829 The famous *Rocket* locomotive built jointly by George Stephenson and his son Robert Stephenson won the trials convincingly and established the principles of modern steam locomotive design. From then on George Stephenson was in demand by many railway companies to survey and build railways for them. Robert Stephenson set up a locomotive building business which was to survive until the end of steam traction on British railways.

From then on, developments in engineering materials and products not only continued to accelerate but engineers put new scientific discoveries — such as electromagnetism — to practical use. Some of the more important developments which have influenced the engineering industry during the nineteenth and twentieth centries up to today are:

1829 Henry Maudslay built the first bench micrometer for making fine linear measurements.

1831 Michael Faraday established the laws of electromagnetism and laid the foundations of the electrical engineering industry. The first practical dynamo for generating electricity was built in 1844 and used for electroplating.

1856 Henry Bessemer produced mild steel using his famous 'converter', and laid the foundations for the modern steel industry. The development of mild steel, which has superior properties to wrought iron for most engineering purposes, stimulated even greater achievements in engineering.

1861 William Siemens developed the open hearth process for producing higher quality plain carbon steels and low alloy steels.

During this period the engineers had not been idle and, between 1830 and 1860, men such as Maudsley, Naysmyth, Whitworth and others had produced metal cutting machines as we would know them today. For example: lathes, drilling machines, planing, shaping and slotting machines, milling machines, gear cutting machines and steam hammers for forging. Whitworth had standardised screw threads and introduced the concept of using standardised components. This led to the founding of the British Standards Institution (BSI). Across the Atlantic, in the USA, Brown and Sharpe applied the vernier principle to the vernier caliper, and the micrometer principle to the micrometer caliper.

1872 Nicholas Otto (Germany) developed the first practical internal combustion engine.

1886 Gottlieb Daimler (Germany) had developed Otto's engine to run on petrol.

1888 Carl Benz (Germany) had put the Daimler engine into the first motor car.

1893 Charles Parsons developed the first commercial steam turbine.

1901 Marconi made the first transatlantic radio transmission.

1903 The Wright brothers (USA) made the first flight in a power driven aircraft at Kittihawk.

1912 Henry Ford (USA) laid down the first production assembly line and the low-cost popular car became a reality. Until then, each car was individually hand built.

1944 The first electronic computer was built at Harvard University

1947 J. Bardsen and W. H. Brattain made the first transistor in the USA. This was to lead the way to the development of solid-state electronics which is at the heart of all modern electronic developments such as: the micocomputer, computer controlled machine tools, industrial robots, artificial satellites. Other scientists and engineers have given us lasers for accurate measurement and metal cutting and the polymeric materials on which the plastics industry is based, as well as high strength adhesives which are being increasingly used as an alternative to welding for bonding together highly stressed metal components.

These are only some of the more important developments that have taken place and many important experimenters and engineers have not been mentioned, otherwise the list would have filled this book. At least I hope that the inventions and developments which I have mentioned have been sufficient to show you how the industry you are working in has developed from small beginnings. The dates and events listed above are the first recorded commercial application of each device or process. In many instances much experimental work had gone on prior to these dates and many false starts had been made.

1.2 The trade unions

Such rapid and profound developments could not take place without a corresponding upheaval in the social structure of this country. The industrial revolution led to the accumulation of great wealth in the hands of the landowners as they exploited the mineral rights of their estates and, later, the accumulation of great wealth in the hands of the factory owners. In many cases this led to the exploitation of the working classes. The change from cottage industries to the factory system resulted in the development of the industrial towns and the building of much sub-standard housing to accommodate the work-force. Working conditions were poor, wages were low and long hours were the norm even for women and young children. Social deprivation was widespread.

The trade union movement grew up to try and counter-balance the power of the employers and the movement fought hard for better working conditions, shorter hours, a decent wage, and better social conditions for its members. It must be remembered that at this time social unrest was rife on the Continent of Europe. The ruling classes, who dominated Parliament, were fearful of the consequences of the masses banding together in Britain. They feared that the industrial revolution might lead to a full-scale revolution such as had happened in France. Thus legislation called the Combination Acts was passed in 1799 and 1800. These Acts made it illegal for workers to combine together and form unions.

These Acts of Parliament were repealed in 1824. In 1825 Parliament gave trade unions the bare right to exist. In 1859 an amending measure gave workers the right of peaceful picketing. These rights remained in force until 1871, when the existing arrangements were swept away by the Trade Union Act and the Criminal Law Amendment Act. This legislation was retrogressive. It put limits on workers' rights to take strike action and removed the right to peaceful picketing. The Criminal Law Amendment Act was replaced in 1875 by the Conspiracy and Protection of Property Act. This reinstated the right to strike and the right to peaceful picketing. Various legislation has been enacted at intervals up to the present day. Such legislation has extended or curtailed the rights of workers and their unions depending upon the political complexion of the government of the day. Individual unions still fight for their members' working conditions and wages both locally and nationally. They have links with unions in other countries through the international labour organisations. For many years workers had sought representation in Parliament through their own members, rather than have to depend upon the good offices of sympathetic members of the established political parties. However, before we can consider the birth of the Labour Party, we must first consider the formation and role of the Trades Union Congress (TUC).

The Trades Union Congress came into being in Manchester in 1868. Its membership was based on the northern unions. Other areas had separate conferences of locally amalgamated unions. This continued until 1871, when the repressive measures of the legislation of that date (discussed above) made it necessary for these local amalgamations to be swept away and replaced by a national body. The Trades Union Congress took over the responsibility for coordinating the unions' fight for better working conditions on a national basis. The structure of the TUC remained unchanged until its general council was called upon to organise the general strike of 1926. This strike was defeated and the general council of the TUC tried to become more conciliatory in its approach to industrial relations (Mond—Turner conversations). Arrangements were made for regular consultations with the employers' organisations, but this was not successful. During the Second World War the government itself set up various consultative bodies with the employers and the unions, as represented by the TUC, equally represented. This was done in an endeavour to foster good industrial relations and increase productivity. The exercise was not particularly successful. The TUC is now generally recognised as representing wide-ranging working-class interests. However, it does not have any enforceable authority over the unions who comprise its membership and it can only exert moral pressure. In fact some unions are not members of the TUC.

The British Labour Party came into existence in 1900 and was known, at first, as the Labour Representation Committee. This committee was set up as a sequel to a resolution passed at the Trades Union Congress of 1899. It fought its first election in 1900 in 13 seats and returned 2 members to Parliament. The aim of this political party was to give working people a voice of their own in Parliament. After the general election of 1906, the Labour Representation Committee changed its name to the Labour Party and formed itself into a separate party in the House of Commons. The unions continued to sponsor members to stand as prospective Labour Members of Parliament at every election, and still do to this day. They are also the major source of funding for that party.

1.3 Employers' organisations

Just as the power and influence of the employers resulted in their employees banding together into unions, so the growing power of the unions resulted in the employers banding together as a counterforce. The National Federation of Associated Employers was founded in 1870, and from 1890 there was a considerable growth in powerful combinations amongst both employers and employees. In fact, by 1936, some 1820 employers' organisations had been registered and were dealing with wage bargaining and labour matters in general. This may seem a very large number compared with the number of unions registered, but it must be remembered that the employers' organisations each represented a different trade or sector of the industry. On the other hand, the unions were often common to, and spread across, many different sectors of the industry.

These employers' organisations not only concerned themselves with negotiations with the trade unions, but they also offered a useful forum for the exchange of information and ideas concerned with technical developments. Like the unions, they also became pressure groups hoping to encourage favourable legislation. Employers' organisations can be divided into two main categories:

(a) Trade-based organisations with common interests in the organisation of their sector of the industry and in the advance of technology. Such an organisation is the Engineering Employers' Federation. This organisation has its headquarters in London and coordinates, at a national level, the Engineering Employers' Associations operating at the local level. Amongst their many activities on behalf of their members, the local associations are concerned with local wage bargaining, with training and with representing employers' interests in the local community, as well as promoting technological advance.

(b) General groupings of employers such as the Confederation of British Industries (CBI), the Chambers of Commerce, and the Institute of Directors. These balance the role of the TUC and also act as pressure groups to encourage favourable legislation which promotes the requirements of British industry at home and abroad.

There are also technical development associations such as the Copper Development Association (CDA), the Cast Iron Research Association (CIRA), and the Motor Industry Research Association (MIRA). Bodies such as these provide a forum for the exchange of technical information as well as carrying out fundamental research and testing on behalf of their members.

1.4 Basic commercial concepts

Wealth creation

Wealth is created by producing something which somebody else wants to buy. You won't create any wealth if you don't produce anything, and you won't create any wealth if nobody wants to buy your products. Production, in this sense, means more than making cars and motor cycles and washing machines, it also means the growing of food, the extraction of mineral resources from the ground, and the provision of services such as transport, banking and insurance.

Less obvious, but vitally important to the creation of wealth, is the work of teachers and college lecturers who educate the next generation of producers so that they have the knowledge and ability to compete in the world's markets. We not only depend upon the doctors, nurses and other health workers who keep the workforce healthy and active, we also need the armed services who keep open our trade routes and protect the nation's interests worldwide. Our consulates and embassies also help by fostering good relations with those countries upon whom our export markets depend. They also have commerce departments which can alert our manufacturers to the changing needs of our overseas customers.

So you can see that wealth creation is a cooperative national effort requiring the talents, skills and knowledge of the whole community. One way or another we are all involved. Some in the production of goods and services which can be exchanged and to which value is added at each step in the chain, and some as customers to purchase those goods and services. Without customers there would be no trade, and with no trade there would be no wealth creation. The main factors which influence the commercial viability of a manufacturing unit can be summarised as follows.

(a) The production of the right product at the right price at the right time.
(b) The ability to produce products of a satisfactory quality, where quality is defined as 'fitness for purpose'. The product must perform to the satisfaction of the purchaser who will expect it to have a reasonable service life with the minimum of breakdowns and maintenance. In short, it must give value for money.
(c) Products must not only be delivered on time, but the time taken must be less than that taken by the manufacturer's competitors.
(d) Customer loyalty must be maintained not only by the points raised above, but also by manufacturers providing efficient after-sales service and customer liaison in order to ensure a market for the next generation of their products.

Supply and demand

We have already seen that, as engineers, we have to produce products that our customers will buy, in order to create wealth. Our production is governed by the economic law of *supply and demand*. That is, we supply goods to satisfy a demand. No matter how efficiently and cheaply we manufacture our goods we will create no wealth if there are no customers to buy them or, if the demand is so small, we cannot recover the manufacturing costs.

This brings us nicely to the difference between marketing and selling. Marketing and selling are often confused. Marketing is the analysis of customer requirements and changing trends. This enables new products to be developed, and accurate

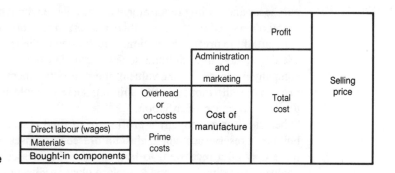

Fig. 1.1 Cost structure

production forecasts to be made, so that the goods the customers want will hit the market at the correct moment. Hopefully, our marketing experts will be better at making these forecasts than those of our competitors so that we get a bigger market share.

Having identified the market and produced the product the sales staff then go out and sell the products. Sometimes a manufacturer may have a good idea for a product for which no market exists. In this case the market can often be created by clever advertising.

Costs and profits

It is no good producing a product to satisfy a demand unless we make a profit. That is, cost of producing and selling the product must be substantially less than the customer is prepared to pay for that product. Figure 1.1 shows how the costs are built up to arrive at the selling price of the product. The prime costs are the labour and materials costs which can be directly allocated to a particular job. The overheads (on-costs) are the general costs of running the factory and include such things as the rent, rates, telephones, gas, water and electricity, office workers' salaries, managers' salaries, etc. How to identify these costs and allocate them fairly across all the products made by a firm is a difficult accounting problem and many systems have been developed. Customers always want value for money and, since your competitors will always be trying to make a better product at a lower price, it is essential to review your costs constantly in order to see if you can reduce them whilst maintaining or improving the quality of your product.

Why do we have to make a profit? Well, there are a number of reasons and we'll now look at some of the more important ones.

(a) If you draw your savings out of the bank to start your first company then, unless you make more profit than the interest you were getting on the money whilst it was in the bank, there is no point in starting your business in the first place.

(b) If you have to borrow money from the bank or a machinery leasing company then your profit must not only be greater than the interest you were getting on your savings (your capital) it must also cover the loan repayments (capital and interest) to your bank or whoever you borrowed the money from.

(c) Big companies borrow money from the stock market to finance their equipment purchases and trading requirements. The people who lend the money are called shareholders and they receive their interest in the form of dividends which are paid out of the profits. Sometimes the dividends are less than what the investor could get, say, in a building society. This is often acceptable because, if the company is successful, the value of the shares will increase (capital gain), whilst the value of the money in the building society would have remained static, or declined, because of inflation.

(d) Other uses for a company's profits are to fund research and development, to build up a reserve account against unforeseen expenses or against the time when there may be a recession, to buy up other businesses in order to expand the company's trading base, and to replace plant as it becomes worn out or obsolete.

Inflation

Inflation occurs when the economy is over-stimulated so that demand outstrips supply. This increase in demand enables suppliers to increase their prices and widen their profit margins (a seller's market). Because you can then buy fewer goods for the same amount of money, the value of your money has fallen. It has less purchasing power. Inflation is the name we give to this loss of purchasing power. The sequence of events goes like this:

(a) Since the value of money has diminished, the selling price of each product sold must include an allowance for the increased cost of the materials required to make its replacement.

(b) Since you will want to maintain your standard of living you will want a pay rise so that you can buy the same number of goods as you did before the prices went up. Assuming you get your rise then the cost of this will have to be included in the selling price as well. But you are not alone, everyone in the country will try and keep pace with the increase in the cost of living.

(c) Everything a company pays for will go up, the rent, rates, lighting, heating, maintenance, telephones, transport, plant, tools, etc. All these increases must be reflected in the selling price if the company is to remain profitable.

(d) So another round of price rises occurs and the cycle starts all over again. This results in a rising spiral of inflation and money continues to diminish in value.

Eventually prices rise to a level where demand is reduced or ceases altogether as it becomes cheaper to import goods from abroad where inflation may be lower and pricing policies are more stable. This leads to recession at home, the closure of businesses and increasing unemployment. It is very easy to start the inflationary cycle, but extremely difficult and painful to stop it once it has started. This is why it is so important to keep inflation as low as possible. It must not equal or exceed the inflation in those countries with whom we trade or with those countries which make the same goods as we do, our competitors.

Environment

At the start of the industrial revolution nobody worried particularly about environmental issues. The main aim was ever increasing wealth creation by ever increasing production. The chimney stacks of the steam-powered cotton and woollen mills of Lancashire and Yorkshire belched out smoke and soot to blacken the surrounding towns and countryside. Their dye-houses polluted the rivers beside which they stood. The blast furnaces of the Midlands were open topped and the smoke, dust and sulphurous fumes made living conditions terrible, resulting in ill-health and an early grave for those who lived and worked in the local manufacturing communities. The green fields became blackened to such an extent that the whole area became known as the 'Black-country'.

It soon became evident that the country was being destroyed and whilst manufacturing and the extractive production of minerals is essential for the economic well-being of the country it must not be allowed to destroy the environment and the quality of life of the community. Unfortunately, cleaning up industry is expensive and we have just considered what happens when production costs and selling prices increase, so manufacturing industry has always resisted doing more than the minimum necessary to keep in line with environmental legislation. It must be remembered that in a country which exists, economically, by trading in the world markets, we are in competition with countries who are not necessarily as environmentally aware as we are. It is difficult to maintain a balance between the needs of industry and the needs of the environment, but great strides have been made in recent years as the importance of the environment has been more widely appreciated. Visual pollution has been reduced by in-filling disused quarries, removing the spoil heaps of disused mines, often by filling them in again, siting factories so that they are hidden by the natural contours of the land, and landscaping them with quick growing trees. Legislation is frequently passed by Parliament and directives are issued by the European Community to increase the control that can be exercised over effluent discharged into the air and into the rivers by industrial plants. It is also now appreciated that pollution is not a local matter but the uncontrolled emission of waste substances by industry and transport can endanger the environment on a world-wide scale, for example: global warming, damage to the ozone layer, and the destruction caused by acid rain.

1.5 The products and structure of the engineering industry

Products

Typical products and services provided by the engineering industry can be grouped as follows.

Components

Nuts, bolts, washers, dowels, taper pins, rivets, springs, circlips, oil seals, pipe fittings, conduit fittings, electrical and electronic components, etc.

Sub-assemblies

Coolant pumps, hydraulic pumps, oil and fuel pumps, gear boxes, shock absorbers, gas valves, water-valves, steam-valves, brake-cylinders, circuit boards for electronic devices, etc.

Assemblies

Machine tools, internal combustion engines, road vehicles, consumer durables, steam turbines, alternators, transformers, locomotives and rolling stock, ships, aircraft, computers, etc.

Fabrications

Oil rigs, bridges, chemical plant, storage tanks, steam boilers, electricity pylons, etc.

Instrumentation

Micrometer and vernier callipers, vernier height gauges, bubble levels, dial gauges, ammeters, voltmeters, wattmeters, oscilloscopes, etc.

Cutting tools

Grinding wheels, milling cutters, lathe tools, drills, files, hacksaw blades, chisels, taps and dies, etc.

Tooling equipment

Drilling jigs, welding jigs, milling fixtures, assembly fixtures, die-sets, robot end-effectors, etc.

Spares and maintenance

Oil filters, exhaust systems, bearings, belts, clutch plates, brake shoes, etc.

These are just a few of the enormous range of goods made by the engineering industry. It follows, therefore that the industry itself is equally widespread and complex and we will now consider its general structure.

Structure

There are various ways of grouping the main elements of the engineering industry. Figure 1.2 shows one such grouping. This figure tends to over-simplify the structure of the industry. In reality the elements are by no means so clear cut and there is much overlapping of trades and services. Just consider a motor car. It combines mechanical engineering, electrical/electronic engineering, sheet metal fabrication, upholstery and trim, and painting. Across all the fields of engineering there is a need for servicing and maintenance engineering if complex plant and equipment is to be kept working efficiently so as to give an adequate return on the capital invested in them. Servicing and maintenance engineering is also important in ensuring that machinery, plant and equipment work safely and do not cause accidents or pollute the environment. Let's now look at the different types of company to be found within the engineering industry.

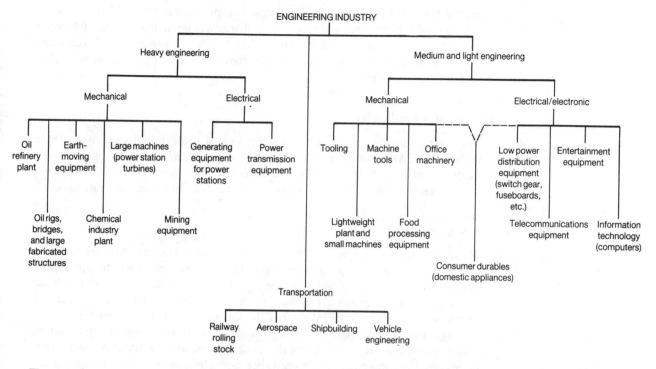

Fig. 1.2 Structure of the Engineering Industry

Companies

Private companies

These are companies which are wholly owned by a single person, a family or a small group of invidiuals. These persons own the company outright and none of the shares are available for sale to the general public. Such companies can be further subdivided into proprietorships, partnerships and private companies with limited liability.

Public limited companies

These are large companies whose scale of operation and financing is beyond the resources of even the most wealthy private individuals. Such companies are funded by the sale of stocks and shares to the general public, and the investment institutions such as the insurance companies. The stocks and shares in public limited companies (plc) are bought and sold through the stockbroking companies who, in turn, operate through the stock markets. Public companies pay interest on the money borrowed in this way. In the case of stock, a fixed rate of interest is paid. This may be less that the interest paid on ordinary shares and there is no capital growth. However, stocks have preference over shares in the event of the company failing and can be considered a safer investment.

The interest paid on shares is called a dividend and it is paid out of the profits of the company. When the profits go up, the dividend is raised and the shareholders get a higher rate of return on their investment. If profits fall, the dividend may have to be reduced. If the company prospers its shares will be in demand and, following the law of supply and demand, the price of the shares will rise and the shareholders will make a *capital gain* if they sell their shares at a higher price than what they paid for them originally.

Nationalised industries

These are companies owned by the state because of strategic and social importance to the nation. Many of the *public utilities* (gas, water and electricity) were among the first companies to be nationalised in Britain after the Second World War. These were closely followed by such industries as the coal mines and the railways.

Monopolies

These are companies who are free from competition because they are the only companies operating in a particular market. This is most likely due to the specialised nature of the service they offer and the high level of capital investment involved. A group of companies acting together to reduce competition and to keep prices and profits artificially high is called a *cartel*. If monopolies and cartels raise their prices too high, then it eventually becomes worthwhile for other companies to be set up despite the high level of investment involved. This breaks the monopoly and brings prices down to a more reasonable level. For example British Telecom is now having to compete with Mercury Communications.

Cooperatives

These are companies owned by the workforce, the management and, in some instances by the customers as well. For all practical purposes they operate as limited companies with the shares owned exclusively by the members. The idea is to eliminate the profit element demanded by the more usual sources of capital funding. Any profits which are made are retained and reinvested in the business after an agreed dividend has been paid to the members. Such companies are registered under the Industrial and Provident Societies Act.

We have now seen how the engineering industry is structured, and we have discussed some of the different types of company to be found in the industry. Now we need to look at the structure of an individual company.

1.6 The structure, management and personnel of a company

The free flow of information between the departments of an engineering company is essential to the well-being of that company. In a small company consisting of the proprietor and two or three employees this is no problem. However, in large companies, information flow becomes more complex and companies have failed when the channels of information have broken down.

In a large company it is impossible for one person to solve all the problems, make all the decisions, and carry out all the management duties. There comes a time in the development of the company when management has to be delegated. Figure 1.3

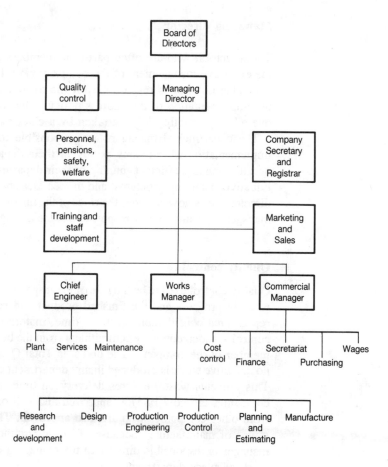

Fig. 1.3 Typical company organisation structure

shows a typical management structure and the inter-relationships between the departments. This is the most common form of management 'tree' but there are others. Let's now look at the function of the various elements of the company.

Board of directors

The directors are appointed to the board because of their technical and commercial experience, and/or because they have influential contacts which are beneficial to the company. They are usually professionally qualified in technology, accountancy, law, banking, insurance and marketing. They plan the strategy of the company and ensure that their policy is carried out efficiently. They sanction large scale capital expenditure and they are responsible to the shareholders for ensuring that the company's finances are soundly managed. In a public company the shareholders have the ultimate power to vote individual directors off the board. In fact they have the power to vote the whole board out of office if they are not satisfied with the running of the company. This rarely happens in practice.

Managing director

The directors, who are often part-time members of the board, communicate with the executive management of the company via a full-time managing director. The managing director is responsible for the overall running of the company and for the implementation of the board's policy. Alternatively, in some companies, this overall responsibility is undertaken by a chief executive.

The departmental managers are responsible to the managing director for the implementation of company policy in their departments and for the day-to-day organisation and efficient running of their departments. They are expected to show initiative in solving problems, and to feed ideas back to the board via the managing director. Let's now consider the roles of the major departments and the departmental managers who are directly responsible to the managing director as shown in Fig. 1.3.

Quality control

Quality control used to be the role of the inspection department. They would inspect work in progress and the finished product and reject faulty items. This rejection represented considerable waste of time, materials and money. Nowadays quality control is a total company commitment from the board of directors to the most junior member of the company. The object is Total Quality Management (TQM) so that no defective work is produced in any department or by any person in the company. This prevents waste, ensures delivery on time, and customer satisfaction. Many companies are now BS5750 approved and will only purchase goods and services from other companies who are also approved. This ensures product quality at all stages of manufacture. Because of the importance of quality control, the quality manager is responsible directly to the managing director and has oversight of the work of every department.

Company secretary and registrar

The company secretary often has a legal background and will also be a member of the Institute of Company Secretaries. The company secretary and his/her office are responsible for advising the managing director and the board on day-to-day legal matters; ensuring that the legal obligations of company legislation are met with; ensuring that the statutory documents are kept and that the necessary returns are made to the appropriate government agencies. As registrar, he/she is responsible for the issue of share certificates, the keeping of the share register, and the issuing of dividend cheques. Sometimes, in very large companies, the work of the registrar is sub-contracted out to firms specialising in this work.

Personnel manager

The personnnel manager and his/her staff are responsible for implementing the employment policy of the company. As its name suggests, the personnel department is concerned with all aspects of the personnel employed by the company at all levels. Its main activities are as follows:

(a) appointments, discipline and dismissals
(b) records of all employees at all levels
(c) wage bargaining
(d) employees' personal development
(e) employees' personal performance
(f) employees' welfare
(g) pensions

Training manager

This is an important department and, in the larger companies, there is often a director with a special responsibility for training to support the training manager and his/her staff. Training covers a wide range of activities. For example:

(a) training graduate apprentices (technical and management)
(b) training commercial apprentices
(c) training technician apprentices
(d) training craft apprentices
(e) training operatives
(f) staff development programmes for existing employees at all levels particularly where new technology is concerned

Chief engineer

The chief engineer's department is concerned with the installation and maintenance of the plant, the installation and maintenance of factory services such as gas water and electricity, and the maintenance of the fabric of the premises.

Commercial manager

The commercial manager is responsible for all the non-technical aspects of the company. For example:

(a) company finance
(b) payment of wages and salaries
(c) cost control and costing
(d) secretarial services
(e) purchasing

Sales and marketing manager

This is a very important department, for unless the goods manufactured can be sold, the company cannot remain in business. As described in section 1.4, marketing is a research activity to find out what the customers want in time for new products to be developed and produced, and to organise a programme of advanced publicity to prepare the market for the new products. Once this has been done and the new products are available, the work of the sales team is to go out into the market place and obtain firm orders for the products. The marketing division of the department is also concerned with finding new markets and predicting the size of those markets. It must also be able to predict when the demand for a product is coming to an end so that the company is not left with surplus and unsaleable stocks on its shelves.

Works manager

The works manager's department can be sub-divided into a number of divisions. Let's now consider the more important of these divisions.

Research and development

This division is responsible for the development of new products and services to satisfy future customer requirements as identified by the marketing and sales departments. It is also responsible for investigating new materials, new developments in technology, and new manufacturing techniques, particularly if they lead to improved quality at reduced cost. All this is necessary to keep the company ahead of its competitors.

Design

This division is responsible for the design of new products and the design of the tooling necessary for making those products. This not only involves the production of detail and assembly drawings but also the styling of the product so that it looks attractive to the purchaser. This is particularly important when the product is for sale to the general public, for example: cars, washing machines and television sets. Companies often sub-contract the styling to specialist studios.

Inspection and testing

This division is most important in maintaining product quality. It not only tests the finished products but also the incoming materials, components and sub-assemblies in order to ensure that the company's suppliers are maintaining the required standards. Further, it is no use waiting until the product is complete before finding out that it has been made from inferior materials. The inspection and testing division is also responsible for approving the prototypes of all new designs before they are put into production.

Planning and production

This division is concerned with planning the manufacturing programme so that the correct goods are available at the correct price at the correct time. The division must ensure that the plant and the work force are kept fully employed with a uniform work load and that production flows smoothly.

Manufacturing

This division of the department is closely associated with the planning and production division and is responsible for the actual manufacture of the company's products in the workshops. It is also responsible for manufacturing any jigs, fixtures and special tools required in production.

Product support

This division of the works manager's department has three areas of responsibility, all of which are directly concerned with customer satisfaction and in giving technical back-up to the sales staff.

(a) After-sales service and commissioning.
(b) Applications engineering. That is, providing advice to customers on the most effective way of using the company's products.
(c) Training the customer's workforce in the use of the company's products.

Supervisors

Supervisors are responsible to the departmental managers for the efficient running of their sections and divisions. They are responsible for the direct supervision of the workforce in order to ensure that the policy of the department is being properly carried out and the workforce is profitably employed.

1.7 Technical personnel—their work, education and training

The persons filling the posts and heading the departments, divisions and sections described above may come from a variety of backgrounds and have a wide range of qualifications. In addition there will be technicians, craftspersons and operatives concerned with the actual making of the company's products in the workshops. Let's now look at the technical background, education and training of some of these persons.

Chartered engineers

These are technologists who hold a degree in engineering and possibly higher degrees which they will have obtained through study at a university or a polytechnic. This will have been supplemented by a post-graduate apprenticeship or pupillage. They will also have a number of years' experience in their chosen branch of the engineering profession in a responsible position. Some older chartered engineers may have academic qualifications other than a first or higher degree. Chartered engineers fill some of the most senior technical and managerial posts in the company. The chief engineer and the works manager will most certainly be chartered engineers, as will the technical directors on the board.

Technician engineers

Also known as *technical engineers*, they may also have a degree in engineering from a university or polytechnic, or they may have a Higher National Certificate or Diploma (HNC or HND) in their chosen branch of engineering. HNC and HND qualifications are usually awarded after study at a polytechnic or at a college of higher education. In a medium or large company, technician engineers will work under the direction of a chartered engineer and, in all possibility become chartered engineers in their own right when they have gained the necessary experience and responsibility. They will have undertaken an engineering apprenticeship and they will hold posts as assistant managers heading the subdivisions of the works manager's department and the chief engineer's department. In smaller companies the technician engineer may be the most senior engineer on site.

Engineering technicians

They usually have an national certificate or diploma in engineering and will have studied at a college of further education. They will also have undergone a technician apprenticeship. They may also be studying part-time for a higher certificate in engineering. They will work under the direction of a chartered engineer or a technician engineer and, in turn, may have craftspersons and operatives working for them. As well as being qualified technicians, the company will be looking for qualities of initiative and leadership in their technicians. This is because many technicians become section leaders and supervisors as they improve their qualifications and start to climb the management ladder.

Craftspersons

They will have received some form of practical training either through one or other of the government training schemes or through a company scheme. A few large companies still offer craft apprenticeships. Trainee craftspersons will also attend colleges of further education on a part-time basis in order to study for City and Guilds and National Vocational qualifications. Craftspersons will have also acquired considerable manual skills and experience. Again, companies will be on the lookout for signs of initiative and leadership, since many craftspersons move on to become chargehands, foremen and forewomen. Bridging courses are also available allowing persons with higher craft qualifications to bridge across to technician qualifications. They may become technicians in research and development departments and in work study where their background of practical experience is of great importance.

Operatives

They will usually have undergone limited skill training on a 'need-to-know' basis. Some may also attend a college of further education to take a course leading to a City and Guilds operative certificate. Where suitable personal qualities are shown some operatives may be trained as chargehands and machine setters. A few may take further qualifications by evening classes at a college of further education.

1.8 Educational institutions, examining boards, and training

Having looked at the sort of qualifications and training the various categories of personnel in the engineering industry are likely to have, it is now necessary to consider where these qualifications can be obtained and who sets the patterns and standards. Remember, we are only looking at courses which are of interest to engineers. The institutions described below also offer a very wide range of courses in other areas of study.

Universities

The term 'university' covers a range of institutions. There are the old, traditional universities; the more recent 'red-brick' universities and, very recently the redesignation of the polytechnics as universities. These institutions all offer degree courses, higher degrees and research degrees. The degree courses offered by the redesignated polytechnics are still supervised by the Council for National Academic Awards (CNAA), whilst their higher technician qualifications (HNC and HND) are still organised and supervised by the Business and Technician Education Council (BTEC).

Colleges of higher education

These offer a range of degree courses in association with their local universities. They also offer the HND and HNC courses.

Colleges of further education

These offer BTEC courses at the intermediate (ONC and OND level). Some may also offer BTEC courses at the HNC level in special cases. They also offer the wide range of City and Guilds qualifications at the craft, operative and, in some subject areas, technician level. They also offer the specialist City and Guilds courses at higher levels, for example in computing, and computer-aided engineering. National Vocational Qualifications (NVQs) are increasingly replacing traditional technical and commercial qualifications.

Training

An appreciation of practical engineering skills often forms part of degree and full-time technician courses. This practical experience is often provided by cooperation between the universities and their local colleges of further education. Some courses are called 'sandwich courses' and the student spends part of his or her time in their sponsoring companies and part in the university or college which is providing the associated academic qualification.

Practical skill training in industry is provided by the training departments of the larger engineering companies and organisations who specialise in providing training services for the smaller engineering companies offering self-accredited or NVQ certificates. They work in conjunction with the local Training and Enterprise Councils (TECS). Training standards and training programmes are provided by the Engineering Training Authority (EnTra). Various training schemes are sponsored by the government under its Youth Training Programme. Also the government provides training and re-training for the adult unemployed.

Finally it must be mentioned that, for those who are not fortunate enough to be able to get to one of the educational institutions mentioned above, it is possible to study for a wide range of qualifications by 'open-learning' schemes organised by local colleges, or by correspondence courses and, for higher qualifications, through the Open University.

Exercises

1 Early in the industrial revolution most industries were owned by
    (a) private land-owners and entrepreneurs
    (b) the nation
    (c) finance corporations
    (d) the banks

2 One of the earliest and most important factors in the development of the engineering industry was the development of the
    (a) internal combustion engine
    (b) gas turbine
    (c) the steam engine
    (d) electric motor

3 Standardisation has resulted in
    (a) uninteresting designs
    (b) reduced costs and improved reliability
    (c) reduced costs and poor quality goods
    (d) high cost, high quality products.

4 In public companies the shares are
    (a) owned by one private individual or family
    (b) owned by the government
    (c) bought directly from the company by the general public
    (d) quoted on the stock market

5 A company which does not have any competition for its goods or services is
    (a) called a cooperative
    (b) called a cartel
    (c) said to have a monopoly
    (d) said to be a public utility

6 A group of companies which band together to fix the price of their goods and services rather than competing with each other is called a
    (a) cooperative
    (b) cartel
    (c) public utility
    (d) quango

7 The Combination Acts of 1799 and 1800
    (a) prevented the setting up of trade unions
    (b) allowed trade unions to be set up on a limited scale
    (c) made the trade unions accountable to the TUC
    (d) gave trade unions unlimited rights

8 The Trade Union Act and Criminal Law Amendment Act of 1871
    (a) allowed peaceful picketing for the first time
    (b) allowed the right to strike and the right to peaceful picketing
    (c) imposed limits on strike action but removed the right to peaceful picketing
    (d) allowed unlimited strike action but removed the right to peaceful picketing

9 The Conspiracy and Protection of Property Act of 1875
    (a) removed the right to strike and the right to peaceful picketing
    (b) reinstated the right to strike and the right to picket peacefully
    (c) made strike action and picketing a criminal offence
    (d) made strike action and picketing a capital offence

10 The Trades Union Congress originated in Manchester in 1868 for the purpose of
    (a) replacing the various conferences of amalgamated unions with a single, national conference
    (b) dominating the unions in the northern manufacturing centres
    (c) dominating the unions in the southern and midland manufacturing centres
    (d) providing a more conciliatory approach to industrial relations (Mond– Turner conversations)

11 Employers' organisations (e.g. the Engineering Employers' Federation) grew up
    (a) to help in developing export trade
    (b) to represent engineering employers at the British Standards Institution
    (c) as a forum for the exchange of technical information
    (d) as a counterforce to the growing power of the unions

12 It is a basic concept of economics that
    (a) wealth is created by production which satisfies needs
    (b) the creation of wealth is unrelated to production
    (c) wealth is created by production alone and is unrelated to need
    (d) production refers only to manufactured goods

13 Supply, demand and cost are economic concepts and
    (a) all three are wholly unrelated
    (b) all three are closely related
    (c) only supply and cost are related
    (d) only demand and cost are related

14 Inflation, in the economic sense, results in
    (a) increased competitiveness
    (b) increased purchasing power
    (c) decreased purchasing power
    (d) a reduction in the cost of living

15 The profit made by the sale of a manufactured product is
    (a) the whole of the difference between the prime costs and the selling price
    (b) the remainder of the selling price after deducting prime costs, factory overheads, administration and marketing costs
    (c) the 'mark-up' on the cost of manufacture
    (d) the VAT added to the selling price

16 The cost of manufacture refers to
    (a) material and labour costs only
    (b) labour and overhead costs only
    (c) prime and overhead costs only
    (d) the capital cost of the plant only

17 In a typical public limited company, the departmental managers are directly responsible to the
    (a) managing director
    (b) company secretary
    (c) board of directors
    (d) shareholders

18 Figure 1.4 shows
    (a) the cost structure for a company
    (b) the structure of a company department
    (c) the structure of the engineering industry
    (d) the management organisation chart for a company

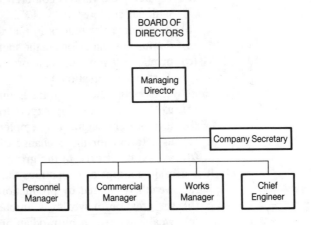

Fig. 1.4

19 An employee possessing CGLI basic and main craft competency certificates will most likely have studied at
    (a) a sixth form college
    (b) a college of further education
    (c) a college of higher education
    (d) a university

20 An employee possessing a BTEC national certificate in engineering will most likely be a
    (a) craftsperson
    (b) technician
    (c) technologist
    (d) chartered engineer

2 Safety

2.1 Health and Safety at Work etc., Act

It is essential to observe safe working practices not only to safeguard yourself, but also to safeguard the people with whom you work. The Health and Safety at Work etc., Act provides a comprehensive and integrated system of law for dealing with the health, safety and welfare of workpeople and the general public as affected by industrial, commercial and associated activities. The Act has six main provisions:

(a) To completely overhaul and modernise the existing law dealing with safety, health and welfare at work.
(b) To put *general duties* on employers ranging from providing and maintaining a safe place to work, to consulting on safety matters with their employees.
(c) To create a Health and Safety Commission.
(d) To reorganise and unify the various government inspectorates concerned with industrial safety.
(e) To provide powers and penalties for the enforcement of safety laws.
(f) To establish new methods of accident prevention, and new ways of operating future safety regulations.

The Act places the responsibility for safe working equally upon:

(a) the employer
(b) the employee (that means you)
(c) the manufacturers and suppliers of materials, goods, equipment and machinery

2.2 Health and Safety Commission

The Act provides for a full-time, independent chairman and between six and nine part-time commissioners. The commissioners are made up of three trade union members appointed by the TUC, three management members appointed by the CBI, two local authority members, and one independent member.

The commission has taken over the responsibility previously held by various government departments for the control of most occupational health and safety matters. The commission is also responsible for the organisation and functioning of the Health and Safety Executive.

2.3 Health and Safety Executive

This unified inspectorate combines together the formerly independent government inspectorates such as the Factory Inspectorate, the Mines and Quarries Inspectorate, and similar bodies. Since 1975 they have been merged together into one body known as the Health and Safety Executive Inspectorate. The inspectors of the HSE have wider powers under the Health and Safety at Work, etc., Act than under previous legislation and their duty is to implement the policies of the commission.

Should an inspector find a contravention of one of the provisions of earlier Acts or Regulations still in force, or a contravention of the Health and Safety at Work etc., Act, the inspector has three possible lines of action available.

Prohibition notice

If there is a risk of serious personal injury, the inspector can issue a prohibition notice. This immediately stops the activity giving rise to the risk until the remedial action specified in the notice has been taken to the Inspector's satisfaction. The prohibition notice can be served upon the person undertaking the dangerous activity, or it can be served upon the person in control of the activity at the time the notice is served.

Improvement notice

If there is a legal contravention of any of the relevant statutory provisions, the inspector can issue an improvement notice. This notice requires the infringement to be remedied within a specified time. It can be served on any person on whom the responsibilities are placed. The latter person can be an employer, employee or a supplier of equipment or materials.

Prosecution

In addition to serving a prohibition notice or an improvement notice, the inspector can prosecute any person (including an employee — *you*) contravening a relevant statutory provision. Finally the inspector can *seize, render harmless* or *destroy* any substance or article which the inspector considers to be the cause of imminent danger or personal injury.

Thus every employee must be a fit and trained person capable of carrying out his or her assigned task properly and safely. Trainees must work under the supervision of a suitably trained, experienced worker or instructor. By law, every employee must:

(a) obey all the safety rules and regulations of his or her place of employment
(b) understand and use, as instructed, the safety practices incorporated in particular activities or tasks
(c) not proceed with his or her task if any safety requirement is not thoroughly understood, *guidance must be sought*
(d) keep his or her working area tidy and maintain his or her tools in good condition
(e) draw the attention of his or her immediate supervisor or the safety officer to any potential hazard
(f) report all accidents or incidents (even if injury does not result from the incident) to the responsible person
(g) understand emergency procedures in the event of an accident or an alarm
(h) understand how to give the alarm in the event of an accident or an incident such as fire
(i) cooperate promptly with the senior person in charge in the event of an accident or an incident such as fire

Fig. 2.1 Causes of industrial accidents

Therefore, safety health and welfare are very personal matters for a young worker, such as yourself, who is just entering the engineering industry. This chapter sets out to indentify the main hazards and suggests how they may be avoided. Factory life, and particularly engineering, is potentially dangerous and you must take a positive approach towards safety, health and welfare.

2.4 Accidents

Accidents do not happen, they are caused. There is not a single accident which could not have been prevented by care and forethought on somebody's part. Accidents can and must be prevented. They cost millions of lost man-hours of production every year, but this is of little importance compared with the immeasurable cost in human suffering.

In every eight-hour shift nearly one hundred workers are the victims of industrial accidents. Many of these will be blinded, maimed for life, or confined to a hospital bed for months. At least two of them will die. Figure 2.1 shows the main causes of accidents.

2.5 Personal protection

Clothing

For general workshop purposes a *boiler suit* is the most practical and safest form of clothing. However, to be completely effective certain precautions must be taken as shown in Fig. 2.2.

Long hair

(a) Long hair is liable to be caught in moving machinery such as drilling machines and lathes. This can result in the hair and scalp being torn away which is

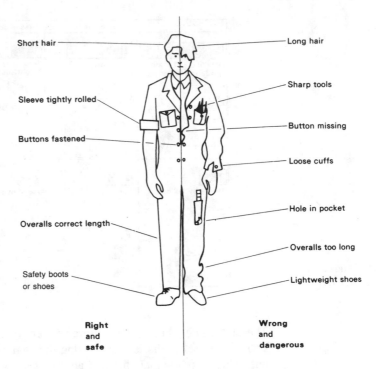

Short hair — Long hair

Sharp tools

Sleeve tightly rolled — Button missing

Buttons fastened — Loose cuffs

Hole in pocket

Overalls correct length — Overalls too long

Safety boots or shoes — Lightweight shoes

Right and safe — **Wrong and dangerous**

Fig. 2.2 Correct dress

extremely dangerous and painful. Permanent disfigurement will result and brain damage can also occur.

(b) Long hair is also a health hazard, as it is almost impossible to keep clean and free from infection in a workshop environment. Head protection is dealt with further in section 2.6.

Sharp tools

Sharp tools protruding from the breast pocket can cause severe wounds to the wrist. Such wounds can result in paralysis of the hand and fingers.

Buttons missing

Since the overalls cannot be fastened properly, it becomes as dangerous as any other loose clothing and liable to be caught in moving machinery.

Loose cuffs

Not only are loose cuffs liable to be caught up like any other loose clothing, they may also prevent you from snatching your hand away from a dangerous situation.

Hole in pocket

Tools placed in a torn pocket can fall through onto the feet of the wearer. Although this may not seem potentially dangerous, nevertheless it could cause an accident by distracting your attention at a crucial moment.

Overalls too long

These can cause you to trip and fall, particularly when negotiating stairways.

Lightweight shoes

The possible injuries associated with lightweight and unsuitable shoes are:

(a) puncture wounds caused by treading on sharp objects
(b) crushed toes caused by falling objects
(c) damage to your achilles tendon due to insufficient protection around the heel and ankle

Suitable footwear for workshop use is discussed in section 2.8.

2.6 Head protection

As has already been stated, long hair is a serious hazard in a workshop. If it becomes entangled in a machine, as shown in Fig. 2.3, the operator can be scalped. If you wish to retain a long hair style in the interests of fashion, then your hair must be contained in a close fitting cap. This also helps to keep your hair and scalp clean and healthy.

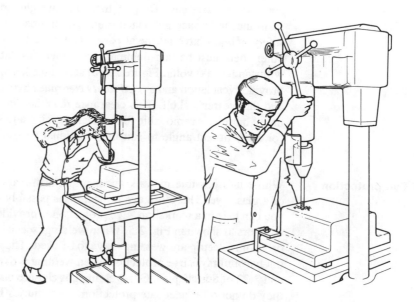

Fig. 2.3 The hazard of long hair

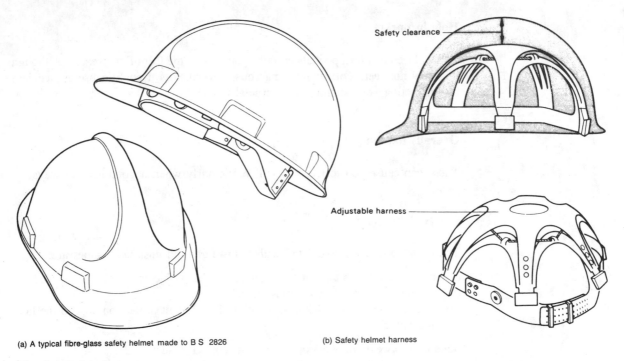

(a) A typical fibre-glass safety helmet made to B S 2826

(b) Safety helmet harness

Fig. 2.4 Safety helmet

When working on site, or in a heavy engineering erection shop involving the use of overhead cranes, all persons should wear a safety helmet complying with BS 2826. Even small objects such as nuts and bolts can cause serious head injuries when dropped from a height. Figure 2.4(a) shows such a helmet. Safety helmets are made from high impact resistant plastics or from fibre glass reinforced polyester mouldings. Such helmets can be colour coded for personal identification and are light and comfortable to wear. Despite their lightweight construction, they have a high resistance to impact and penetration. To eliminate the possibility of electric shock, safety helmets have no metal parts. The materials used in the manufacture of the outer shell must be non-flammable and their insulation resistance must be able to withstand 35000 volts. Figure 2.4(b) shows the harness inside a safety helmet. This provides ventilation and a *fixed safety clearance* between the outer shell of the helmet and the wearer's skull. This clearance must be maintained at 32 millimetres. The entire harness is removable for regular cleaning and sterilising. It is fully adjustable for size, fit and angle to suit the individual wearer's head.

2.7 Eye protection

Whilst it is possible to walk about on an artificial leg, nobody has ever seen out of a glass eye. Therefore eye protection is possibly the most important precaution you can take in a workshop. Eye protection is provided by wearing suitable goggles or visors as shown in Fig. 2.5. When welding, special goggles (oxy-fuel gas welding) or visors (electric arc welding) have to be used. These have coloured lenses to filter out harmful rays. Eye protection when welding is discussed further in sections 2.21 and 2.22 of this chapter. Gas-welding goggles are not suitable for arc welding since they do not offer adequate protection. Eye injuries fall into three main categories:

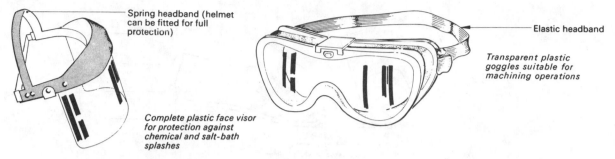

Spring headband (helmet can be fitted for full protection)

Elastic headband

Transparent plastic goggles suitable for machining operations

Complete plastic face visor for protection against chemical and salt-bath splashes

Fig. 2.5 Safety goggles and visors

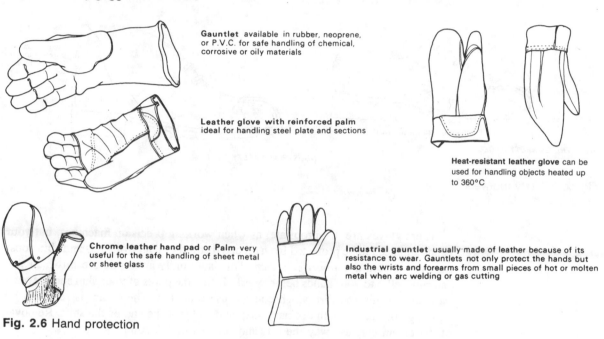

Gauntlet available in rubber, neoprene, or P.V.C. for safe handling of chemical, corrosive or oily materials

Leather glove with reinforced palm ideal for handling steel plate and sections

Heat-resistant leather glove can be used for handling objects heated up to 360°C

Chrome leather hand pad or Palm very useful for the safe handling of sheet metal or sheet glass

Industrial gauntlet usually made of leather because of its resistance to wear. Gauntlets not only protect the hands but also the wrists and forearms from small pieces of hot or molten metal when arc welding or gas cutting

Fig. 2.6 Hand protection

(a) pain and inflammation due to abrasive grit and dust getting between the lid and the eye;

(b) damage due to exposure to ultraviolet radiation (arc welding) and high intensity visible light. Particular care is required when using laser equipment;

(c) loss of sight due to the eyeball being pierced or the optic nerve cut by flying splinters of metal (swarf), or by the blast of a compressed air jet.

2.8 Hand protection

Your hands are in constant use and, because of this, they are constantly at risk handling dirty, oily, greasy, rough, sharp, hot and possibly corrosive and toxic materials. Gloves and 'palms' of a variety of styles and types of materials are available to protect your hands whatever the nature of the work. Some examples are shown in Fig. 2.6. In general terms, plastic gloves are impervious to liquids and should be worn when handling oils, greases and chemicals. However, they are unsuitable and even dangerous for handling hot materials. Leather gloves should be used when handling sharp, rough and hot materials.

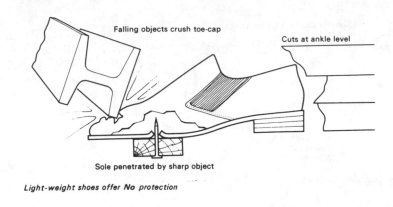

Falling objects crush toe-cap

Cuts at ankle level

Sole penetrated by sharp object

Light-weight shoes offer No protection

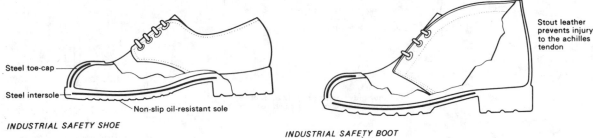

Stout leather prevents injury to the achilles tendon

Steel toe-cap

Steel intersole

Non-slip oil-resistant sole

INDUSTRIAL SAFETY SHOE

INDUSTRIAL SAFETY BOOT

Fig. 2.7 Safety footwear

Where gloves are inappropriate, as when working precision machines, but your hands still need to be protected from oil and dirt rather than from cuts and abrasions, then you should use a *barrier cream*. This is a mildly antiseptic cream which you can rub well into your hands before work. It fills the pores of your skin and prevents the entry of oils and dirt which could cause infection. The cream is removed by washing your hands with ordinary soap and water at the end of the shift. Removal of the cream carries away the dirt and sources of infection.

2.9 Foot protection

The dangers associated with wearing unsuitable shoes in a workshop have already been discussed. The injuries which you can suffer when wearing lightweight, casual shoes are shown in Fig. 2.7. This figure also shows some examples of safety footwear as specified in BS 1870. Such safety footwear is available in a variety of styles and prices. It looks as smart as normal footwear and is equally as comfortable.

2.10 Health hazards

Noise

Excessive noise can be a dangerous pollutant of the working environment. The effects of noise can result in:

(a) fatigue leading to careless accidents
(b) mistaken communications between workers leading to accidents
(c) ear damage leading to deafness
(d) permanent nervous disorders

The level at which a noise becomes dangerous depends upon its frequency (pitch) and the length of time you are exposed to it. Noise is energy and it represents waste since it does not do useful work. Ideally it should be suppressed at source to avoid waste of energy and to improve the working environment. If this is not possible then you should be insulated from the noise by sound absorbant screens and/or ear-protectors (ear-muffs or ear-plugs).

Narcotic (anaesthetic) effects

Exposure to small concentrations of narcotic substances causes headaches, giddiness and drowsiness. Under such conditions you are obviously prone to accidents since your judgement and reactions are adversely affected. A worker who has become disorientated by the inhalation of narcotics is a hazard to himself or herself and a hazard to other workers. Prolonged or frequent exposure to narcotic substances can lead to permanent brain damage and permanent damage to other organs of the body, even in relatively small concentrations. Exposure to high concentrations can result in rapid loss of consciousness and death. Examples of narcotic substances are to be found amongst the many types of solvent used in industry. Solvents are used in paints, adhesives, polishes and degreasing agents. Careful storage and use is essential and should be carefully supervised by qualified persons. Fume extraction and adequate ventilation of the work-place must be provided when working with these substances. Suitable respirators should be available for use in emergencies.

Irritant effects

Many substances cause irritation to the skin both externally and internally. They may also sensitise your skin so that it becomes irritated by substances not normally considered toxic.

External irritants can cause industrial dermatitis by coming into contact with your skin. The main irritants met with in a workshop are oils (particularly cutting oils and coolants), adhesive and degreasing solvents, and electro-plating chemicals.

Internal irritants are the more dangerous as they may have long-term and deep-seated effects on the major organs of the body. They may cause inflammation, ulceration, internal bleeding, poisoning and the growth of cancerous tumours. Internal irritants are usually air pollutants in the form of dusts (e.g. asbestos fibres), fumes and vapours. As well as being inhaled, they may also be carried into your body on food handled without washing or from storing noxious substances in discarded soft-drinks bottles without proper labelling. Many domestic tragedies happen this way.

Systemic effects

Toxic substances, also known as systemics, affect the fundamental organs and bodily functions. They affect your brain, heart, lungs, kidneys, liver, your central nervous system and your bone marrow. Their effects cannot be reversed and thus lead to chronic ill-health and, ultimately, early death. These toxic substances may enter the body in various ways.

(a) Dust and vapour can be breathed in through your nose. Observe the safety codes when working with such substances and wear the respirator provided no matter how inconvenient or uncomfortable.

(b) Liquids and powders contaminating your hands can be transferred to the digestive system by handling food or cigarettes with dirty hands. Always wash before eating or smoking. Never smoke in a prohibited area. Not only may there be a fire risk, but some vapours change chemically and become highly toxic (poisonous) when drawn in through a cigarette.

(c) Liquids, powders, dusts and vapours may all enter the body through the skin:
- directly through the pores;
- by destroying the outer tough layers of the skin and attacking the sensitive layers underneath;
- by entering through undressed wounds.

Regular washing, use of a barrier cream, use of suitable protective (plastic or rubber) gloves, and the immediate dressing of cuts (no matter how small) is essential to proper hand care.

2.11 Personal hygiene

As already stated above, personal hygiene is most important. There is nothing to be embarrassed about in rubbing a barrier cream into your hands before work, about washing thoroughly with soap and water after work, or about changing your overalls regularly so that they can be cleaned. Personal hygiene can go a long way towards preventing skin diseases, both irritant and infectious.

2.12 Behaviour in workshops

In an industrial environment horseplay infers reckless, foolish and boisterous behaviour such as pushing, shouting, throwing things, and practical joking by a person or a group of persons. This cannot be tolerated. There is no place for such foolish behaviour in an industrial workplace. Such actions can distract a worker's attention and break his or her concentration. This can lead to scrapped work, serious accidents and even fatalities.

Horseplay observes no safety rules. It has no regard for safety equipment. It can defeat safe working procedures and undo the painstaking work of the safety officer by the sheer foolishness and thoughtlessness of the participants.

The types of accident caused by horseplay depend largely on the work of the factory concerned and the circumstances leading to the accident. Generally such accidents are caused when:

(a) A person's concentration is disturbed so that they incorrectly operate their machine or inadvertently come into contact with moving machinery or cutters.

(b) Someone is pushed against moving machinery or factory transport.

(c) Someone is pushed against ladders and trestles upon which people are working at heights.

(d) Someone is pushed against and dislodges heavy, stacked components.

(e) Electricity, compressed air or dangerous chemicals are involved.

2.13 Lifting and carrying

As was shown in Fig. 2.1, the movement of materials is the single biggest cause of factory accidents. Therefore, this topic area is allocated a complete chapter of its own. The safe and correct lifting and movement of loads is dealt with in detail in Chapter 3 of this book.

2.14 Hazards associated with hand tools

Newcomers to industry often overlook the fact that, as well as machine tools, badly maintained and incorrectly used hand tools can also represent a serious safety hazard. Unfortunately the newcomer can be influenced by more experienced men and women — who should know better — misusing hand tools. The time and effort taken to fetch the correct tool from the stores or to service a worn tool is considerably less than the time taken to recover from injury. Figure 2.8 shows some badly maintained and incorrectly used hand tools.

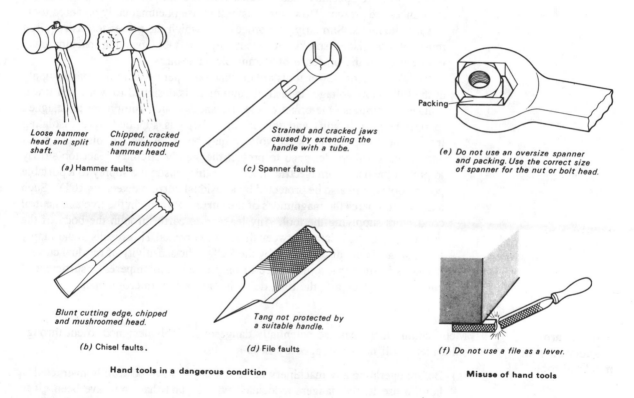

Loose hammer head and split shaft.   *Chipped, cracked and mushroomed hammer head.*

(a) Hammer faults

Strained and cracked jaws caused by extending the handle with a tube.

(c) Spanner faults

Packing

(e) Do not use an oversize spanner and packing. Use the correct size of spanner for the nut or bolt head.

Blunt cutting edge, chipped and mushroomed head.

(b) Chisel faults.

Tang not protected by a suitable handle.

(d) File faults

(f) Do not use a file as a lever.

Hand tools in a dangerous condition   **Misuse of hand tools**

Fig. 2.8 Dangers in the use of hand tools

2.15 Hazards associated with portable power tools

In addition to maintaining portable power tools in good order, it is imperative that the equipment and, particularly the power lead, is electrically sound or a fatal electric shock can occur to the user. It is equally important that the compressed air hose supplying pneumatic tools is also in good order. When using electrically powered tools the following points should be observed.

(a) Be sure that the tool is correctly earthed or that it is 'double-insulated'. Earthing will be considered further in section 2.17.

(b) Do not attempt to use faulty equipment. Faults in electrical equipment must be corrected by a qualified electrician. You must report the following unsafe conditions:

   (i)   defective or broken insulation (tool and supply cable)
   (ii)   broken or defective plug
   (iii) improperly or badly made connections to terminals
   (iv) loose or broken control switch
   (v)   incorrect voltage for the supply available

(c) Do not overload the motor, the heat generated will damage the insulation and cause excessive sparking at the brushes.

(d) Do not use portable power tools in the presence of flammable vapours and gases. Sparks from the equipment can cause a serious explosion and fire. Some electrical power tools are specially made so that they are safe to use when flammable substances are present. However, it is best to use pneumatically powered tools in such situations. Similarly, the process for which the power tool is required must not give rise to sparks. For example, a portable grinding machine must not be used in the presence of flammable substances.

(e) Although domestic power tools are designed to operate from the mains supply at the full mains voltage, industrial equipment is designed to work at a lower voltage to minimise the effect of electric shock. Such equipment is designed to operate at 110 volts and this lower voltage is supplied by an isolating transformer. For site work the voltage may be as low as 55 volts. The fuses and circuit breakers designed to protect the supply circuitry react too slowly to protect the user from electric shock. For this reason the supply to a portable power tool should also be protected by a residual current detector (RCD). Such a device compares the magnitudes of the current flowing in the live and neutral conductors supplying the tool. Any leakage to earth through the body of the user will upset the balance between these two currents. This results in the supply being immediately disconnected by the RCD. The sensitivity of residual current detectors is such that a difference of only a few milliamperes is sufficient to cut off the supply and the time delay is only a few microseconds.

2.16 Hazards associated with machine tools

Metal cutting machines are potentially dangerous. Tools designed to cut through solid metal will not be stopped by flesh and bone.

(a) Before operating any machinery be sure that you have been fully instructed in how to use it, the dangers associated with it, and that you have been given permission to use it.

(b) Do not operate a machine unless all the guards and safety devices are in position and are operating correctly.

(c) Make sure you understand any special rules and regulations applicable to the *particular machine* you are about to use, even if you have been trained on machines in general.

(d) Never clean or adjust a machine whilst it is in motion. Stop the machine and isolate it from the supply.

(e) Report any dangerous aspect of the machine you are using, or are about to use, immediately and do not use it until it has been made safe by a suitably qualified and authorised person.

(f) A machine may have to be stopped in an emergency. Learn how to make an emergency stop without having to pause and think about it and without having to search for the emergency stop switch.

Transmission guards

By law, no machine can be sold or hired out unless all gears, belts, shafts and couplings making up the power transmission system are guarded so that they cannot be touched whilst they are in motion. Sometimes guards have to be removed in order to replace, adjust or service the components they are covering. Before removing guards or covers, you must:

(a) Stop the machine.
(b) Isolate the machine from its energy supply.
(c) Lock the isolating switch so that it cannot be turned on again whilst you are working on the exposed equipment and keep the key in your pocket.
(d) If it is not possible to lock off the supply, remove the supply fuses for the machine and keep these in your pocket until you have finished and the guards or covers are back in position.

If an 'interlocked' guard is opened or removed, an electrical or mechanical trip will stop the machine from operating. This trip is only provided in case you forget to isolate the machine. It is no substitute for full isolation.

Cutter guards

The machine manufacturer does not normally provide cutter guards because of the wide range of work a machine may have to do.

(a) It is the responsibility of the owner or the hirer of the machine to supply their own cutter guards.
(b) It is the responsibility of the setter and/or the operator to make sure that the guards are fitted and working correctly before operating the machine, and to use the guards as instructed. It is an offence in law for the operator to remove or tamper with the guards provided.
(c) If ever you are doubtful about the adequacy of a guard or the safety of a process, consult your instructor or your safety officer without delay.

The simple drilling machine guard shown in Fig. 2.9(a) only covers the chuck and is only suitable for jobbing work when small diameter drills are being used. The drill chuck shown in Fig. 2.9(b) is used for larger drills and for drills which are mounted directly into the drilling machine spindle. It covers the whole length of the drill and telescopes up as the drill penetrates into the workpiece.

Figure 2.10 shows some horizontal milling machine guards. They are suitable for jobbing work where the setting of the guard has to be changed frequently and the machine is being used by a skilled operator. For production work the cutting zone is frequently totally enclosed, particularly when the operator is not fully skilled.

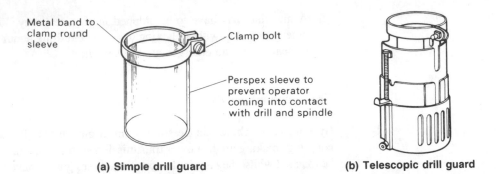

Metal band to clamp round sleeve

Clamp bolt

Perspex sleeve to prevent operator coming into contact with drill and spindle

Fig. 2.9 Drill guards   **(a) Simple drill guard**   **(b) Telescopic drill guard**

Fig. 2.10 Milling cutter guards

Fig. 2.11 Lathe chuck guard

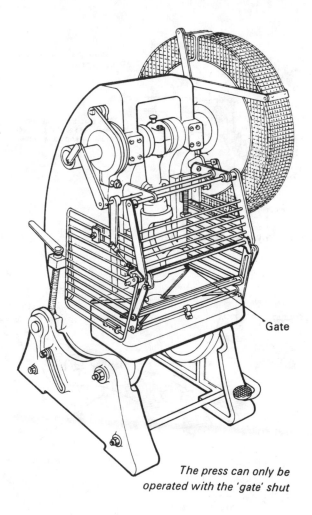

Gate

Fig. 2.12 A
mechanically
interlocked guard

*The press can only be
operated with the 'gate' shut*

Figure 2.11 shows a chuck guard for a centre lathe. This not only prevents the operator coming into contact with the revolving chuck, it also prevents coolant being thrown out by the chuck jaws. Since the guard will not close unless the chuck key has been removed, it is also a reminder to the operator to remove the key before starting the machine. Failure to do this is a frequent cause of accidents and damage to the machine.

Figure 2.12 shows a fully guarded power press. Not only is the transmission mechanism and the flywheel fully guarded, but the work zone is also fully guarded. The guard fitted to the work zone has to be opened so that the tools can be loaded and unloaded. To achieve this safely an interlocked guard is used. This guard is interlocked with the clutch so that the machine cannot be started whilst the guard is open. It is also interlocked with a positive brake so that if a fault in the control mechanism causes the clutch to engage accidentally, the machine will stall and will not trap the operator.

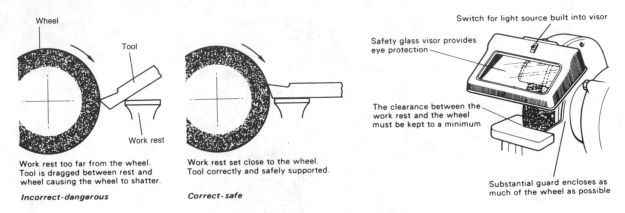

Wheel

Tool

Work rest

Work rest too far from the wheel. Tool is dragged between rest and wheel causing the wheel to shatter.

Incorrect-dangerous

Work rest set close to the wheel. Tool correctly and safely supported.

Correct-safe

Switch for light source built into visor

Safety glass visor provides eye protection

The clearance between the work rest and the wheel must be kept to a minimum

Substantial guard encloses as much of the wheel as possible

Fig. 2.13 Grinding wheel guard and work rest adjustment

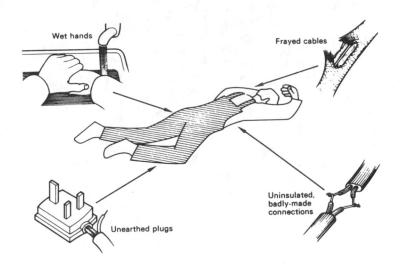

Wet hands

Frayed cables

Unearthed plugs

Uninsulated, badly-made connections

Fig. 2.14 Causes of electric shock

Use of grinding wheels

Because of its apparent simplicity, the double-ended off-hand grinding machine comes in for more than its fair share of abuse. A grinding wheel does not 'rub off' the metal; a grinding wheel is a precision multi-tooth cutting tool in which each grain has a definite cutting geometry. Therefore a grinding wheel must be selected, mounted, dressed and used correctly if it is to cut efficiently. Further, a grinding wheel which is damaged, incorrectly mounted or is unsuitable for the machine, may burst at speed and cause serious damage and injury. Thus the guard for a grinding wheel not only stops the operator coming into contact with the wheel, but it must also provide *burst containment* in case the wheel shatters or bursts in use. That is, the broken pieces of the wheel must be contained within the guard and are not thrown out of the machine at high speed. For this reason grinding wheel guards are made very much stronger than most cutter guards. Figure 2.13 shows a grinding machine with the wheel guard, tool rest and visor all correctly adjusted. The mounting of

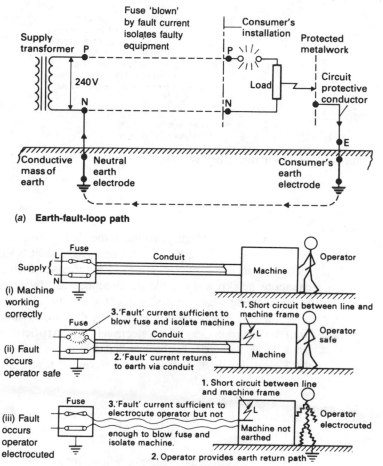

(a) **Earth-fault-loop path**

(b) **The need for earthing metal clad equipment**

Fig. 2.15 The need for earthing

grinding wheels, except by a trained and registered person, is prohibited under the Abrasive Wheel Regulations 1970.

2.17 Electrical hazards

The most common causes of electrical shock are shown in Fig. 2.14. The installation and maintenance of electrical equipment must be carried out by a fully trained and registered electrician. An electric shock from a 240 volt single-phase supply (lighting and office equipment) or a 415 volt three-phase supply (most factory machines) can easily kill you. Even if the shock is not sufficiently severe to cause death, it can still cause serious injury. The sudden convulsion caused by the shock can throw you from a ladder or against moving machinery. To reduce the risk of shock all electrical equipment should be earthed or double insulated. The reason for earthing is shown in Fig. 2.15. Further, portable power tools should be fed from a low-voltage transformer at 110 volts as shown in Fig. 2.16. The machine must be suitable for operating at such a voltage. The transformer should be protected by a circuit breaker containing a residual current detector (see section 2.14).

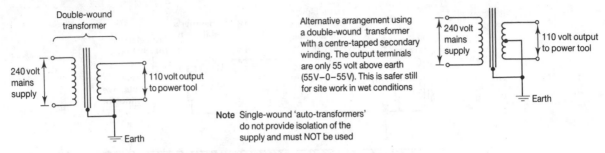

Fig. 2.16 Low voltage supply for portable power tools

In the event of rendering first aid to the victim of electrical shock, great care must be taken when pulling the victim clear of the fault which caused the shock. The victim can act as a conductor and thus, in turn, electrocute the rescuer. If the supply cannot by quickly and completely disconnected, always pull the victim clear by his or her clothing which, if dry, will act as an insulator. If in doubt, hold the victim with a plastic bag or cloth known to be dry. *Never* touch the victim's bare flesh until the victim is clear of the electrical fault. Artificial respiration must be started immediately the victim has been pulled clear of the fault or the live conductor. Figure 2.17 gives details of how to treat a victim of severe electrical shock.

2.18 Fire protection legislation

The purpose of this legislation is to protect lives rather than property and employers are required by law to:

(a) Obtain a local authority fire certificate for premises where more than 20 persons are employed. (Where the premises are not at ground level the number of persons is reduced to 10.)
(b) Ensure that the premises have unobstructed escape routes and that these are clearly indicated and known to all persons using the premises.
(c) Provide adequate and suitable extinguishers and alarms.
(d) Hold regular fire drills and keep a log of the dates and the time taken to evacuate the premises.
(e) Provide training in any fire fighting equipment provided, the use of alarms, and the procedures for summoning the public fire services.
(f) Inspect and test fire alarms and fire fighting equipment regularly, and log the findings of such inspections and tests and any remedial action that has to be taken.

Remember, in an emergency you have no time to read the regulations and instructions. As a result of fire drills, you must know what to do and remember what procedures to follow and, if you have to use equipment, how to use it correctly. Further, this equipment must be kept in proper working order and must not fail you. Extinguishers must be recharged and other equipment checked immediately after use so that it is ready for the next emergency.

Order of action

1 Switch off current
Do this immediately. If not possible do not waste time searching for the switch.

2 Secure release from contact
Safeguard yourself when removing casualty from contact. Stand on non-conducting material (rubber mat, DRY wood, DRY linoleum). Use rubber gloves, DRY clothing, a length of DRY rope or a length of DRY wood to pull or push the casualty away from the contact.

3 Start artificial respiration
If the casualty is not breathing artificial respiration is of extreme urgency. A few seconds delay can mean the difference between success or failure. Continue until the casualty is breathing satisfactorily or until a doctor tells you to stop.

4 Send for doctor and ambulance
Tell someone to send for a doctor and ambulance immediately and say what has happened. Do not allow the casualty to exert himself by walking until he has been seen by a doctor. If burns are present, ask someone to cover them with a dry sterile dressing.

If you have difficulty in blowing your breath into the casualty's lungs, press his head further back and pull chin further up. If you still have difficulty, check that his lips are slightly open and that the mouth is not blocked, for example, by dentures. If you still have difficulty, try the alternative method, mouth-to-mouth, or mouth-to-nose, as the case may be.

Method - mouth-to-mouth

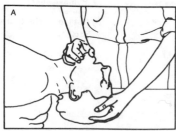

1. Lay casualty on back; if immediately possible, on a bench or table with a folded coat under shoulders to let head fall back. Kneel or stand by casualty's head. Press his head fully back with one hand and pull chin up with the other.

Fig. 2.17 Treatment for electric shock

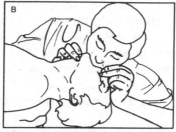

2. Breathe in deeply. Bend down, lips apart and cover casualty's mouth with your well open mouth. Pinch his nostrils with one hand. Breathe out steadily into casualty's lungs. Watch his chest rise.

3. Turn your own head away. Breathe in again.

Repeat 10 to 12 times per minute.

If the patient does not respond proceed as follows:

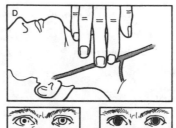

4. Check carotid pulse, pupils of eyes and colour of skin (see Fig. D)

5. Pulse present, pupils normal - continue inflations until recovery of normal breathing (Figs A, B and C)

6. Pulse absent, pupils dilated, skin grey - strike smartly to the left part of breast bone with edge of hand (see Fig. E)

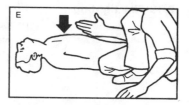

7. Response of continued pulse, pupils contract - continue inflations until recovery of normal breathing

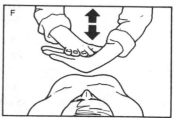

8. No response of continued pulse, pupils unaltered, skin grey - commence external heart compression (see Fig. F)*

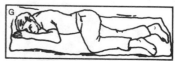

9 When normal breathing commences, keep warm, place casualty in the recovery position (see Fig. G)

* Method - external heart compression (Fig. F)

1. Place yourself at the side of the casualty

2. Feel for the lower half of the breastbone

3. Place the heel of your hand on this part of the bone, keeping the palm and fingers off the chest

4. Cover this hand with the heel of the other hand

5. With arms straight, rock forwards pressing down on the lower half of the breastbone (in an unconscious adult it can be pressed towards the spine for about one and a half inches (4 cm))

6. The action should be repeated about once a second

Continue as above until a continued pulse is felt and pupils contract

Continue inflations until recovery of normal breathing

2.19 Fire fighting

Fire fighting is a highly skilled operation and most medium and large firms have properly trained teams who can contain the fire locally until the professional service arrives. The best way you can help is to learn the correct fire drill; both how to give the alarm and how to leave the building. It only requires one person to panic and run in the wrong direction to cause a disaster.

In an emergency never lose your head and panic.

Smoke is the main cause of panic. It spreads quickly through a building, reducing visibility and increasing the risk of falls down stairways. It causes choking and even death by asphyxiation. Smoke is less dense near the floor: as a last resort crawl. To reduce the spread of smoke and fire, keep fire doors closed at all times but *never locked*. The plastic materials used in the finishes and furnishings of modern buildings give off highly toxic fumes. Therefore it is best to leave the building as quickly as possible and leave the fire fighting to the professionals who have breathing apparatus. Saving human life is more important than saving property.

If you do have to fight a fire there are some basic rules to remember. A fire is the rapid oxidation (burning) of flammable materials at relatively high temperatures. Remove the air (oxygen) or the flammable materials (fuel) or lower the temperature as shown in Fig. 2.18 and the fire goes out. It can be seen from Fig. 2.18 that different fires require to be dealt with in different ways. The normally available fire extinguishers and the types of fire they can be used for are as follows.

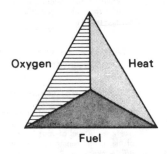

Oxygen   Heat

Fuel

These are the three 3 essentials to start a fire

Note : *Once the fire has started it produces sufficient heat to maintain its own combustion reactions and sufficient surplus heat to spread the fire.*

When solids are on fire remove heat by applying water.

(a) **Remove heat**

Liquids, such as petrol etc. on fire can be extinguished by removing oxygen with a foam or dry powder extinguisher.

(b) **Remove oxygen (air)**

Electrical or gas fires can usually be extinguished by turning off the supply of energy.

(c) **Remove energy source (fuel, gas, electricity etc.)**

Fig. 2.18 Fire fighting

Water

Used in large quantities, water reduces the temperature and puts out the fire. The steam generated also helps to smother the flames as it displaces the air and therefore the oxygen essential to the burning process. However, for various technical reasons, water should only be used on burning solids such as wood, paper and some plastics. A typical hose point and a typical pressurised water extinguisher is shown in Fig. 2.19.

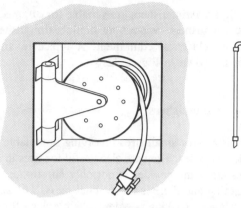

(a) Hose point   (b) Pressurized water extinguisher

Fig. 2.19 Hose point and pressurised water extinguisher

Fig. 2.20 Foam extinguisher

Foam extinguishers

These are used for fighting oil and chemical fires. The foam smothers the flames and prevents the oxygen in the air from reaching the burning materials at the seat of the fire. Water alone cannot be used because oil floats on the water and this spreads the area of the fire. A typical foam extinguisher is shown in Fig. 2.20.

Note: Since both water and foam are electrically conductive, do not use them on fires associated with electrical equipment or the person wielding the hose or the extinguisher will be electrocuted.

Carbon dioxide (CO_2) extinguishers

These are used on burning gases and vapours. They can also be used for oil and chemical fires in confined places. The carbon dioxide gas replaces the air and smothers the fire. It can only be used in confined places, where it cannot be displaced by draughts.

Note: If the fire cannot breathe neither can you, so care must be taken to evacuate all living creatures from the vicinity before operating the extinguisher. Back away from the bubble of CO_2 gas as you operate the extinguisher, do not advance towards it. Figure 2.21 shows a typical CO_2 extinguisher.

Vaporising liquid extinguishers

These include CTC, CBM and BCF extinguishers. The heat from the fire causes rapid vaporisation of the liquid sprayed from the extinguisher, and this vapour displaces the air and smothers the fire. Since a small amount of liquid produces a very large amount of vapour, this is a very efficient way of producing the blanketing vapour. Any vapour which will smother the fire will also smother all living creatures which must be evacuated before using such extinguishers. As with CO_2 extinguishers always back away from the bubble of vapour, never advance into it.

Fig. 2.21 CO_2 extinguisher

Fig. 2.22 Vaporising liquid extinguisher

Vaporising liquid extinguishers are suitable for oil, gas, vapour and chemical fires. Like CO_2 extinguishers, vaporising liquid extinguishers are safe to use on fires associated with electrical equipment. A typical example of a vaporising liquid extinguisher is shown in Fig. 2.22.

Dry powder extinguishers

These are suitable for small fires involving flammable liquids and small quantities of solids such as paper. They are also useful for fires in electrical equipment, offices and kitchens since the powder is not only non-toxic, it can be easily removed by vacuum cleaning and there is no residual mess. The active ingredient is powdered sodium bicarbonate (baking powder) which gives off carbon dioxide when heated. A typical example of a dry powder extinguisher is shown in Fig. 2.23.

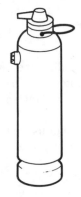

Fig. 2.23 Dry powder extinguisher

General rules governing the use of portable extinguishers

Since fire spreads quickly, a speedy attack is essential if the fire is to be contained. Sound the alarm and send for assistance before attempting to fight the fire. Remember:

(a) extinguishers are only provided to fight small fires
(b) take up a position between the fire and the exit, so that your escape cannot be cut off
(c) DO NOT continue to fight the fire if:
  - it is dangerous to do so
  - there is any possibility of your escape route being cut off by fire, smoke, or collapse of the building
  - the fire spreads despite your efforts
  - toxic fumes are being generated by the burning of plastic furnishings and finishes
  - there are gas cylinders or explosive substances in the vicinity of the fire

If you have to withdraw, close windows and doors behind you wherever possible, but not if such actions endanger your escape. Finally, ensure that all extinguishers are recharged immediately after use.

2.20 Fire prevention

Prevention is always better than cure, and fire prevention is always better than fire fighting. Tidiness is of paramount importance in reducing the possibility of outbreaks of fire. Fires have small beginnings and it is usually amongst accumulated rubbish that many fires originate. So you should make a practice of constantly removing rubbish, shavings, offcuts, cans, bottles, waste paper, oily rags, and other unwanted materials to a safe place at regular intervals. Discarded foam plastic packing is not only highly flammable, but gives off highly dangerous toxic fumes when burnt.

Highly flammable materials should be stored in specially designed and equipped compounds away from the main working areas. Only minimum quantities of such materials should be allowed into the workshop at a time, and then only into *non-*

smoking zones. The advice of the local fire prevention officer should also be sought.

It is good practice to provide metal containers with air-tight hinged lids with proper markings as to the type of rubbish they should contain since some types of rubbish will *ignite spontaneously* when mixed. The lids of the bins should be kept closed so that, if a fire starts, it will quickly use up the air in the bin and go out of its own accord without doing any damage.

Liquid petroleum gases (LPG) such as propane and butane are being used increasingly for process heating and for space heating in workshops and on site. Full and empty cylinders should be stored separately in isolated positions away from the working area and shielded from the sun's rays. The storage area should be well ventilated with plenty of space between the cylinders. The cylinders should also be protected from frost. Where bulk storage cylinders and spheres are used, not only must the above precautions be observed, but the containers must be securely fenced and defended against damage by passing vehicles. Pipe runs, joints and fittings associated with LPG installations must be regularly inspected by a suitably qualified and registered person. Flexible tubing (hoses) used in connection with gas cylinders must be regularly inspected for cuts and abrasions and replaced as necessary. The storage of oxygen and acetylene cylinders as used for welding require special treatment and are dealt with in section 2.19

2.21 Gas-welding hazards

The hazards associated with *oxy-acetylene welding* can be summarised as follows.

(a) *Eye injuries* resulting from the glare of the incandescent (white-hot) weld pool and splatter from molten droplets of metal. Eye injuries can be prevented by the use of proper welding goggles as shown in Fig. 2.24. It is essential to use goggles with the correct filter glasses, for the particular combination of the metals being joined and the flux used affect the type of radiation. Note that the goggles used for gas welding offer no protection from the radiations associated with arc welding.

(b) *Burns and fire hazards* resulting from the careless use of the torch and careless handling of hot metal. Sparks are also a hazard. Ensure that all rubbish and

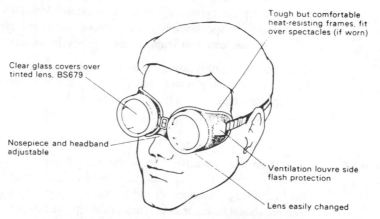

Tough but comfortable heat-resisting frames, fit over spectacles (if worn)

Clear glass covers over tinted lens, BS679

Nosepiece and headband adjustable

Ventilation louvre side flash protection

Lens easily changed

Fig. 2.24 The essential features of gas-welding goggles

Note: GOGGLES WITH LENSES SPECIFIED FOR USE WHEN GAS WELDING OR CUTTING MUST NOT BE USED FOR ARC WELDING OPERATIONS

flammable materials are removed from the working area. Fire-resistant overalls should be worn and cuffs avoided as these present traps for sparks and globules of hot metal. For the same reason overalls should be fastened at the neck. A leather apron and leather spats should be worn. In very hot conditions leather gloves should also be worn.

(c) *Explosions* resulting from the improper storage and use of compressed gases and use of gas mixtures. These can occur when acetylene gas is present in air in any proportion between 2% and 82%. It will also explode spontaneously at high pressure even without air or oxygen being present. The working pressure of acetylene should not exceed 620 millibars. Explosions in the welding equipment itself may result from *flashbacks* due to improper use or lighting up procedures, incorrect setting of the equipment, and faulty equipment. For this reason flashback arrestors (hose-protectors) must be fitted and regularly inspected. An exploding acetylene cylinder is equivalent to a large bomb. It can demolish a building and kill the occupants. Great care must be taken in their use. Copper pipes and fittings must not be used for acetylene as copper reacts with acetylene to form an explosive substance.

(d) *Gas cylinders* are themselves not dangerous as they are regularly inspected to government standards. However, their contents can be dangerous and the following safety precautions should be observed.

- Cylinders must be protected from mechanical damage during storage, transportation and use. *Acetylene cylinders must always be kept upright*.
- Cylinders must be kept cool. On no account should the welding torch be allowed to play on the cylinder or on any part of the welding equipment. Cylinders must also be protected from sunlight and frost.
- Cylinders must be sited in well ventilated surroundings to prevent the build up of explosive mixtures of gases in the event of leakage. Even slight oxygen enrichment can cause the spontaneous ignition of clothing and other flammable materials leading to fatal burns. As stated earlier, the presence of only 2% acetylene in air can result in an explosion.
- Automatic pressure regulators must be fitted to all cylinders prior to use. The cylinder valve must always be kept closed when the welding equipment is not in use or whilst changing a cylinder or equipment.
- Keep the cylinders free from contamination. Oils and greases can ignite or explode spontaneously in the presence of pure oxygen. Similarly oily or dirty clothes can also ignite spontaneously in an oxygen enriched atmosphere.

The above notes only cover the barest outlines of the safety precautions which must be observed when gas welding. The suppliers of welding gases provide a number of important booklets on the safe storage and use of welding gases and the safe use of the associated equipment.

2.22 Arc-welding hazards

The main hazards arising from the use of mains-operated electric arc welding equipment are set out in Table 2.1. To eliminate these hazards as far as possible, the following precautions should be taken. These are only the basic precautions and a check should be made as to whether the equipment, process and working conditions require special additional precautions.

Table 2.1 Arc-welding electrical hazards

Circuit — high voltage — primary

Fault:	*Hazard:*
1. Damaged insulation	Fire — loss of life and damage to property
	Shock - severe burns and loss of life
2. Oversize fuses	Overheating — damage to equipment and fire
3. Lack of adequate earthing	Shock — if fault develops — severe burns and loss of life

Circuit — low voltage — secondary (very heavy current)

Fault:	*Hazard:*
1. Lack of welding earth	Shock — if a fault develops — severe burns and loss of life
2. Welding cable — damaged insulation	Local arcing between cable and any adjacent metalwork at earth potential causing fire
3. Welding cable — inadequate capacity	Overheating leading to damaged insulation and fire
4. Inadequate connections	Overheating — severe burns — fire
5. Inadequate return path	Current leakage through surrounding metalwork — overheating — fire

(a) Make sure that the equipment is fed from the mains via an isolating switch fuse and a circuit breaker containing a residual current detector (RCD). This device was described in section 2.14. Easy access to the isolating switch and protection equipment must be provided at all times.

(b) Make sure that the trailing, high-voltage, primary cable is armoured against mechanical damage as well as being heavily insulated against a supply potential of 415 volts. The cable should be routed so that it cannot be tripped over, cut on the sharp edges of metal objects, or run over by factory trucks.

(c) Make sure that all cable insulation and armouring is undamaged and in good condition, and that all terminations and connecting plugs and sockets are also secure and undamaged. If in doubt, do not operate the equipment until it has been checked and made safe by a qualified electrician.

(d) Make sure that all the equipment and the work is adequately earthed with conductors capable of carrying the heavy currents used in welding.

(e) Make sure that the welding current regulator has an 'OFF' position so that in the event of an accident, or the need to make adjustments, the welding current can be stopped without having to trace the supply cable back to its isolating switch.

(f) Make sure that the cables of the secondary or 'external welding circuit' are adequate for the heavy currents they have to carry.

For all arc welding operations it is essential to protect the welder's head, face and eyes from the radiation, spatter and hot slag, and for this reason a helmet or hand shield is used. Examples of such shields are shown in Fig. 2.25. They protect the welder from heat rays (infra-red) and the even more dangerous ultraviolet rays of the electric arc. Without such protection the welder would suffer serious skin and eye damage.

The obvious precaution is to prevent these harmful radiations from the welding arc and the weld-pool from reaching unprotected skin and from reaching your eyes.

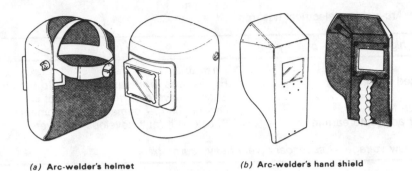

Fig. 2.25 Arc-welding eye and head protection

(a) Arc-welder's helmet   *(b)* Arc-welder's hand shield

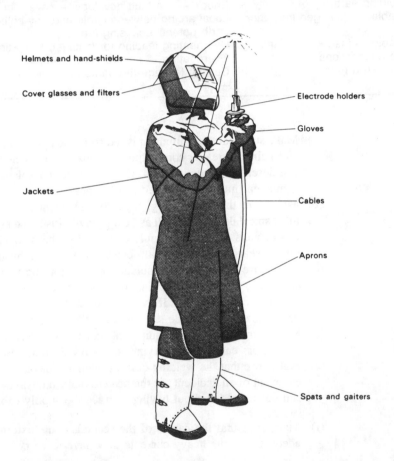

Helmets and hand-shields

Cover glasses and filters

Jackets

Electrode holders

Gloves

Cables

Aprons

Spats and gaiters

Fig. 2.26 Fully protected arc welder

In the latter case special glass filters of a suitable colour and density are used in the face mask or helmet. These filter glasses not only absorb the harmful radiation but also reduce the intensity of the visible light and so prevent the glare from the white-hot metal causing eye strain. The expensive filter glass is protected by a cover glass on the outside. The cover glass is clear and toughened.

The slag left by the flux used when arc welding has to be chipped away when the weld has cooled down. Clear goggles should be worn whilst chipping as the slag breaks away in glass-like splinters. Protective chipping screens should be provided so that adjacent workers are not put at risk.

The welder's body and clothing must also be protected from radiation and burns. Figure 2.26 shows a welder wearing full protective clothing whilst working overhead.

People working in the vicinity of a welding arc, including other welders, can be exposed to stray radiation from the arc, and can be caused considerable discomfort. Wherever possible each arc welding work area should be screened off in such a way as to keep stray radiations to a minimum. This can be achieved by the use of either cubicles or portable screens. Looking at an unscreened welding arc for only a few seconds, even from a distance, can cause 'arc-eye'. The painful effects of exposure will not be felt immediately, but some four to twelve hours later. The symptoms of 'arc-eye' include a feeling of 'sand in your eyes' , soreness, burning and watering. If you are exposed to an arc flash, the effects of 'arc-eye' can be

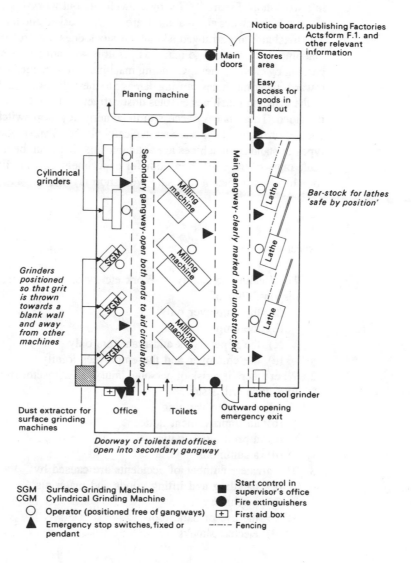

Fig. 2.27 Machine shop layout

minimised by the immediate use of a special lotion which should be available in the first-aid box.

Unlike gas-welding filler rods, arc welding electrodes are flux coated and give off fumes as welding proceeds. You are not likely to suffer any ill effects from welding fumes providing that adequate ventilation is available. Localised ventilation can be provided by a suction fume extractor. This not only removes the fumes but also helps to keep down the temperature and adds to your comfort and efficiency whilst welding. Extraction should be at a 'low-level' so that the fumes are not drawn up past your face.

2.23 Workshop layout Much can be done to prevent accidents by the layout of the machines and equipment in a workshop. Figure 2.27 shows a well laid out workshop. You can see that there are ample gangways and that these are clearly marked and left free from obstructions. The machines are arranged so that bar stock does not protrude into gangways. The machines are arranged so that the operators will not be distracted by other workers passing by close to them. Grinding machines are arranged so that grit is not thrown towards other machines causing damage to their slideways and bearings. The position of the grinding machines enables dust extraction from the working area to be easily provided. There is easy access to the emergency stop switches for the whole shop and the fire extinguishers are strategically placed. Scale models of the more common types of standard machines are available and these can be used in conjunction with scale plans of the workshop floor for experimenting with different layouts in order to achieve an efficient and safe workshop layout.

Exercises

1 The Health and Safety at Work etc., Act makes safety in the workplace the responsibility of
   (a) the employer only
   (b) the employees only
   (c) the supervisors and managers only
   (d) the employer and the employees jointly
2 Where there is a risk of personal injury, an inspector from the Health and Safety Executive will issue
   (a) a written warning
   (b) an improvement notice
   (c) a prohibition notice
   (d) a summons
3 The greatest number of accidents are caused by
   (a) handling and lifting goods and materials
   (b) machinery
   (c) the use of hand tools
   (d) electric shocks

4 Almost all accidents could be prevented by
    (a) increased legislation
    (b) more inspectors
    (c) more supervisors
    (d) greater care and forethought by employers and employees

5 The best clothing to wear for fitting and machining in an engineering workshop is a
    (a) tracksuit and trainers
    (b) T-shirt, jeans and trainers
    (c) boiler suit and industrial safety shoes
    (d) leather apron and industrial safety shoes

6 Appropriate safety glasses should be worn
    (a) only when welding
    (b) only when machining
    (c) only when grinding
    (d) whenever there is danger to the eyes

7 For site work a safety helmet should be worn to
    (a) protect you from falling objects
    (b) keep your hair clean
    (c) prevent your hair becoming entangled in a machine
    (d) keep you warm

8 In a workshop long hair is a hazard because
    (a) it is difficult to keep clean and can result in a scalp infection
    (b) it can become entangled in a machine
    (c) it can be distracting
    (d) of all the above

9 A barrier cream is used to
    (a) keep your skin soft
    (b) prevent dirt from entering the pores of your skin
    (c) save having to use soap when you are washing
    (d) act as an antiseptic when you cut yourself

10 The solvents used in paints and adhesives can be a hazard because
    (a) their fumes have a narcotic effects when inhaled
    (b) they remove the natural oils from your skin and can cause irritation
    (c) prolonged contact may cause chronic ill-health
    (d) all the above

11 'There are hazards associated with hand tools.' This statement is
    (a) true
    (b) not true
    (c) true only if the tools are in bad condition
    (d) true only when used by an untrained person

12 Portable power tools must be supplied from an isolating transformer at a low voltage
    (a) to prevent damage to the equipment if it is overloaded
    (b) to protect the supply cables
    (c) at all times to prevent the possibility of severe electric shock
    (d) only when working on exposed sites

13 Portable electric power tools should be protected by the use of circuit breakers containing residual current detectors (RCD)
    (a) in case there is any residual charge after the tool is disconnected
    (b) to make them easier to control
    (c) to prevent them being overloaded
    (d) so that the tool is immediately isolated from the supply if there is the slightest leak of current to earth

14 The purpose of a fuse is to
    (a) protect a circuit from excess current flow in the event of a fault developing
    (b) prevent an appliance from breaking down whilst it is connected to an electrical supply
    (c) avoid the need for an isolating swaitch
    (d) save the cost of an RCD

15 Double insulated power tools
    (a) do not need to be earthed
    (b) must be earthed
    (c) can only be battery powered
    (d) are unsuitable for maintenance work on site

16 All metal-clad electrical equipment must be earthed to prevent
    (a) electrical interference
    (b) the fuses blowing repeatedly
    (c) the possibility of electrical shock
    (d) radio interference

17 In the event of severe electric shock
    (a) commence artificial respiration immediately
    (b) leave the victim alone whilst you fetch expert help
    (c) remove the victim from contact with the supply and seek expert help
    (d) remove the victim from contact with the supply and commence artificial respiration immediately

18 The main reason for providing guards on machines and machine tools is to
    (a) contain the coolant
    (b) prevent accidental damage to precision mechanisms
    (c) prevent swarf (chips) from entering and damaging the mechanism
    (d) prevent any person from coming into contact with any dangerous or moving parts

19 Guards can be removed or adjusted
    (a) by the operator if they are inconvenient
    (b) only by a trained and authorised person for maintenance and setting purposes
    (c) by the owner if they are reducing production
    (d) only by the manufacturer when carrying out repairs

20 The manufacturer, importer or supplier of a machine
    (a) must ensure that all transmission mechanisms are fully guarded so that they cannot be touched whilst they are in motion
    (b) must supply both transmission and cutter guards
    (c) need not supply any guards as this is the responsibility of the owner or hirer of the machine
    (d) need only supply cutter guards

21 The owner or hirer of the machine is responsible for providing
    (a) the transmission guards
    (b) the cutter guards
    (c) both the cutter and the transmission guards
    (d) none of the guards

22 The most important reason for not using a pressurised water extinguisher on a fire in electrical equipment is because
    (a) the equipment will be damaged
    (b) the person operating the extinguisher can receive a severe or even lethal shock
    (c) the electrical supply to the equipment will become overloaded and damaged
    (d) water will aggravate this type of fire

23 Which of the following types of extinguisher must *not* be used on fire involving flammable liquids such as oil and petrol?
    (a) Foam
    (b) Carbon dioxide
    (c) Vaporising liquid
    (d) Pressurised water

24 Regular fire drills must be held and the following data must be logged
    (a) the time and date of the drill
    (b) the time taken to evacuate the premises
    (c) the date of the drill and the time taken to successfully evacuate the premises
    (d) the date and the number of persons on the premises when the drill took place

25 The most important reason for using visors with special filter glasses when electric arc welding is
    (a) to prevent electric shock
    (b) to provent the welder's face from becoming uncomfortably hot
    (c) to protect the welder's eyes and face from ultraviolet radiation
    (d) to protect the welder's eyes and face from gamma radiation

26 Oxygen and acetylene cylinders must be used in well-ventilated surroundings because
    (a) they smell unpleasant when mixed
    (b) they are highly toxic
    (c) they are dangerously explosive when mixed
    (d) they are highly corrosive

27 Oxy-acetylene welding goggles must not be used when arc welding because
    (a) they do not provide adequate protection for your eyes
    (b) they are too dark and you cannot see
    (c) the lenses would be melted by the heat radiated from the arc
    (d) the lenses would react with the fumes from the electrode flux coating

28 Automatic pressure regulators must be fitted to the gas cylinders
    (a) to prevent the cylinders exploding
    (b) to prevent you running out of gas part way through a job
    (c) to save you having to make any adjustments when setting up
    (d) to maintain a constant flow of gas at the pressure selected by the welder

29 Hoses should be fitted with flashback arrestors to prevent
 (a) explosions due to improper use or lighting up procedures
 (b) too much gas being delivered to the welding torch
 (c) air being drawn back into the cylinders when closing down the equipment
 (d) explosions caused by nearby thunder storms

30 You should report
 (a) serious accidents only
 (b) no incidents until you are fully trained
 (c) only incidents which affect you personally
 (d) all hazards and potentially dangerous incidents

3 Moving loads

3.1 Loads and safety

In the engineering industry, loads are defined as heavy and cumbersome objects such as machines, large castings and forgings, heavy bar, sheet and plate materials, etc., which have to be loaded onto vehicles, unloaded from vehicles and moved within the factory itself. The movement of heavy loads involves careful planning and the anticipation of potential hazards before they arise. When moving such loads it is important that you use the correct handling techniques and observe the appropriate safety precautions and codes of practice at all times.

3.2 Manual lifting (Individual)

In the engineering industry it is often necessary to lift fairly heavy loads. As a general rule, loads lifted manually should not exceed 20 kg. Mechanical lifting equipment should be used for loads in excess of 20 kg. However, even lifting loads less than 20 kg can cause strain and lifting loads incorrectly is one of the major causes of back trouble. The risk of personal injury and damage to equipment can be reduced by taking simple precautions *before* the lifting or handling operations begin. For example, if the load is obviously too heavy or bulky for one person to handle, you should ask for assistance. Even a light load can be dangerous if it obscures your vision as shown in Fig. 3.1. All moveable objects which form hazardous obstructions should be moved to a safe place before movement of the load commences.

As has already been stated, it is important to use the correct lifting technique. This is because the human spine, as shown in Fig. 3.2, is not an efficient lifting device. If it is subjected to heavy strain, or incorrect methods of lifting, the lumbar discs may be damaged causing considerable pain. This is often referred to as a 'slipped-disc' and the damage (and pain) can be permanent.

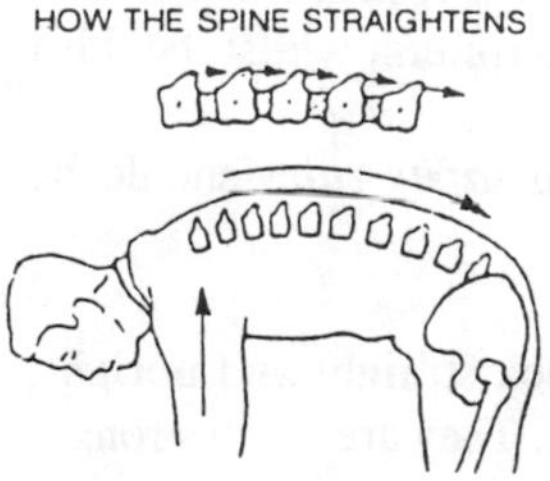

The correct way to lift a load manually is shown in Fig. 3.3. You should start the lift in a balanced squatting position with your legs at hip width apart and one foot slightly ahead of the other. The load to be lifted should be held close to your body. Make sure that you have a safe and secure grip on the load. Before taking the weight of the load, your back should be straightened and as near to the vertical as possible. Keep your head up and your chin drawn in, this helps to keep your spine straight and rigid as shown in Fig. 3.3(a). To raise the load, first straighten your legs. This ensures that the load is being raised by your powerful thigh muscles and bones, as shown in Fig. 3.3(b), and not by your back. To complete the lift, raise the upper part of your body to a vertical position as shown in Fig.3.3(c). To carry the load, keep your body upright and hold the load close to your body as shown in Fig. 3.4(a). Wherever possible hold the load so that the bone structure of your body supports the load as shown in Fig. 3.4(b). If the load has jagged edges wear protective gloves and if hazardous liquids are being handled wear the appropriate protective clothing as shown in Fig. 3.5.

CLEAR MOVABLE OBJECTS

Fig. 3.1 Obstructions to safe movement must be removed

HOW THE SPINE STRAIGHTENS

Fig. 3.2 The human spine

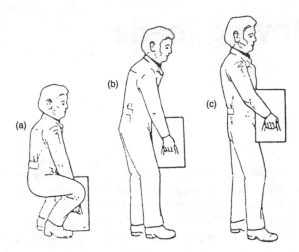

Fig. 3.3 Correct manual lifting

3.3 Manual lifting (team)

Fig. 3.4 Correct carrying

Rubber or plastic gloves

Rubber or plastic apron

Rubber or plastic boots

Fig. 3.5 Wear appropriate protective clothing

When a lifting party is formed in order to move a particularly large or heavy load, the team leader is solely responsible for the safe completion of the task. The team leader should not take part in the actual lifting but should ensure that:

(a) Everyone understands what the job involves and the method chosen for its completion.

(b) The area is clear of obstructions and that the floor is safe and will provide a good foothold.

(c) The members of the lifting party are of similar height and physique, and that they are wearing any necessary protective clothing. Each person should be positioned so that the weight is evenly distributed.

(d) He or she takes up a position which gives the best all round view of the area and will permit the development of any hazardous situation to be seen so that the appropriate action can be taken in time to prevent an accident.

(e) Any equipment moved in order to carry out the operation is put back in its original position when the task has been completed. This sequence of events is shown in Fig. 3.6.

Loads which are too heavy to be lifted or carried can still be moved manually by using a crowbar and rollers as shown in Fig. 3.7. The rollers should be made from thick walled tubes so that there is no danger of trapping your fingers if the load should move whilst positioning the rollers. Turning a corner is achieved by placing the leading roller at an angle. As the load clears the rearmost roller, this roller is moved to the front, so that the load is always resting on two rollers, whilst the third roller is being positioned.

When lifting and moving loads manually, the following *safety rules* should be observed.

(a) Use the correct lifting technique — maintain your back straight and upright; bend your knees and let your legs and thighs do the work. They are much stronger than your back.

(b) Keep your arms straight and close to your body.

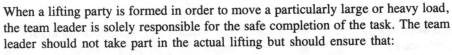

(c) Balance the load using both hands.

(d) Avoid sudden movements and any twisting of your spine.

(e) Take account of the centre of gravity of the load when lifting.

(f) Clear all obstructions from the area where the lifting and movement of loads is taking place.

(g) Take care to avoid injury to other people, particularly when moving long loads.

(h) Use gloves to protect your hands when moving loads with sharp or jagged edges.

(i) Use appropriate protective clothing when moving containers holding hazardous and toxic substances.

(j) Take particular care when moving materials which are wrapped and greased, they may slip through your grasp — wear safety shoes.

(k) Plan all stages of the move to avoid unnecessary lifting.

(l) Move all loads by the simplest method — *simple is safe*.

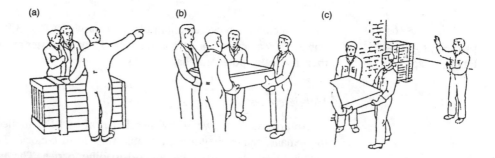

(a) (b) (c)

Fig. 3.6 Team lifting

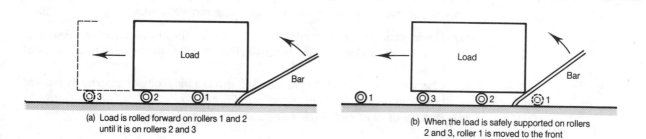

(a) Load is rolled forward on rollers 1 and 2 until it is on rollers 2 and 3

(b) When the load is safely supported on rollers 2 and 3, roller 1 is moved to the front ready for the next move

Fig. 3.7 Use of rollers

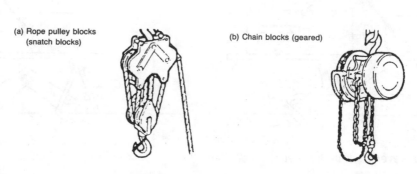

(a) Rope pulley blocks (snatch blocks)

(b) Chain blocks (geared)

Fig. 3.8 Manual lifting equipment

3.4 Mechanical lifting equipment

Mechanical lifting equipment can be classified according to the motive power used to operate it.

Manual (muscle power)

Examples of this type of equipment are shown in Fig. 3.8. Rope pulley blocks (snatch blocks) are light and easily mounted. However, the tail rope has to be tied off to prevent the load falling when the effort force is removed. Some rope blocks have an automatic brake which is released by giving the tail rope a sharp tug before lowering the load. They are suitable for loads up to 250 kg. Chain pulley blocks are portable and are used for heavier loads from 250 kg to 1 tonne. They also have the advantage that they do not run back (overhaul) when the effort raising the load is removed.

Powered

An example of a powered chain block is shown in Fig. 3.9. Such devices may be powered by electricty or compressed air. They are faster and can raise greater loads than manually powered chain blocks.

Fig. 3.9 Powered lifting equipment

Mobile cranes

These are usually powered by diesel, petrol or LPG fuelled engines. Because of the exhaust fumes they are unsuitable for use in factories but are widely used on erection sites and for loading and off-loading lorries. The engine is coupled to the crane or hoist mechanically or, increasingly, by hydraulic transmission systems. Special precautions must be taken when using mobile cranes.

(a) Never stand under suspended loads — this applies to all types of hoist.
(b) Never work under a suspended load (Fig. 3.10) — this applies to all types of hoist.
(c) Check the condition of the ground. Soft ground and faulty or incorrectly inflated tyres can have a destabilising effect (Fig. 3.11).
(d) Beware of overhead, high-voltage cables (Fig. 3.12).

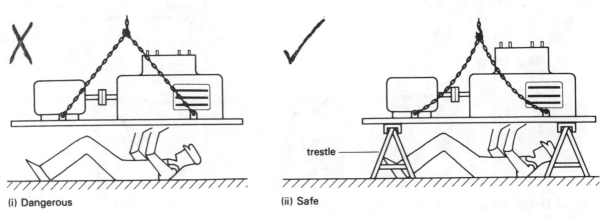

(i) Dangerous

(ii) Safe

trestle

Fig. 3.10 Never work under a suspended load

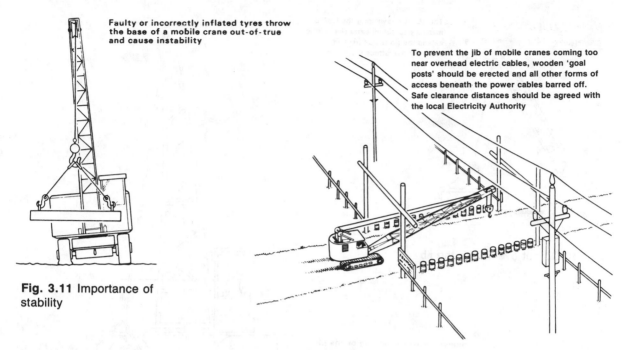

Faulty or incorrectly inflated tyres throw the base of a mobile crane out-of-true and cause instability

To prevent the jib of mobile cranes coming too near overhead electric cables, wooden 'goal posts' should be erected and all other forms of access beneath the power cables barred off. Safe clearance distances should be agreed with the local Electricity Authority

Fig. 3.11 Importance of stability

Fig. 3.12 Care when working near overhead cables

(e) Do not swing the load to increase the reach of the jib. Loads should only be lifted vertically. It is a hazard to swing the load out manually to gain additional radius for, in so doing, the effect is to extend the effective length of the jib (Fig. 3.13) and throw stresses on the crane for which it was not designed. The crane could also become unstable and overturn.

(f) A similar problem arises if the load is swung sideways. Again the jib is overstressed and the crane is destabilised and in danger of overturning (Fig. 3.14).

(g) Mobile cranes should not be moved with the jib in its minimum radius position, particularly if moving up an incline. The jib can whip back and overturn the crane (Fig. 3.15).

Safety

Only fully competent persons (i.e. trained and authorised) are permitted to operate mechanical lifting equipment. Trainees can only use such equipment under the close supervision of a qualified and authorised instructor. Even after you have been instructed in the use of lifting equipment, always make the following checks before attempting to raise a load.

(a) Check that the lifting equipment is suitable for the load being raised. All lifting equipment should be clearly marked with its *safe working load* (*SWL*).

(b) Never leave a load unattended whilst it is supported by lifting equipment and ensure that, before it is released from the lifting equipment, it is resting in a stable condition on a suitable support.

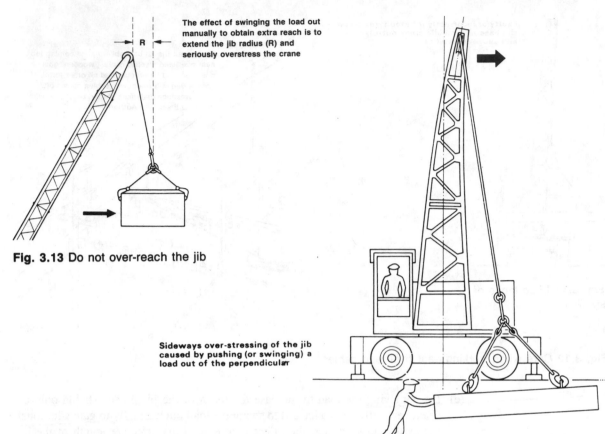

The effect of swinging the load out manually to obtain extra reach is to extend the jib radius (R) and seriously overstress the crane

Fig. 3.13 Do not over-reach the jib

Sideways over-stressing of the jib caused by pushing (or swinging) a load out of the perpendicular

Fig. 3.14 Do not swing the load

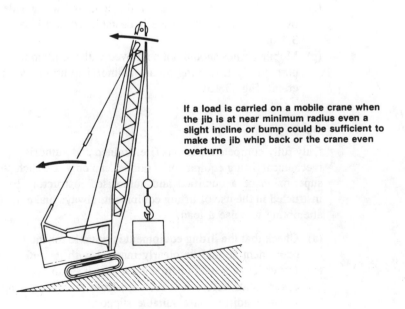

If a load is carried on a mobile crane when the jib is at near minimum radius even a slight incline or bump could be sufficient to make the jib whip back or the crane even overturn

Fig. 3.15 Care when moving the load

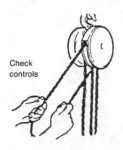

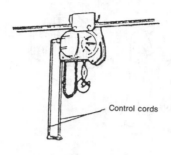

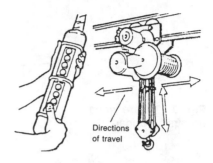

(a) Manual chain blocks. Check which way the chain has to be pulled to raise or lower the load

(b) Power hoist. Check which cord raises and which lowers the load

(c) Power hoist with power traverse. Check all the pendant controls to raise, lower and move the load

Fig. 3.16 Check the operating procedure to raise, lower and move the load

    (c) Hand chain: check the direction in which the chain must be pulled to raise or to lower the work as shown in Fig. 3.16(a).

    (d) Cord control: when using cord-controlled power-operated hoists, check which cord raises the load and which cord lowers it as shown in Fig. 3.16(b).

    (e) Pendant switch control: if the pendant switch controls a travelling hoist, check the direction of travel as well as which press buttons raise and lowers the load as shown in Fig. 3.16(c).

3.5 Lifting a load

Before lifting a load using a mechanical lifting device you should:

    (a) warn everyone near the load and anyone approaching the load to keep clear

    (b) check that all slings and ropes are safely and securely attached both to the load and to the hook

    (c) take up the slack in the chain, sling or rope gently

    (d) raise the load slowly and steadily so that it is just off the ground

    (e) check that the load is stable and that the sling has not become accidentally caught on a part of the load incapable of sustaining the lifting force

    (f) stand well back from the load and lift steadily

3.6 Traversing a load on a travelling crane

Before traversing a load on a travelling crane:

    (a) make sure the load will not pass over anyone (Fig. 3.17)

    (b) check that there are no obstacles in the way of the crane and its load

    (c) keep well clear of the load and move it steadily

    (d) stop the crane immediately if anyone moves across the path of the load

3.7 Lowering a load

Before lowering a load:

    (a) check that the ground is clear of obstacles and is capable of supporting the load;

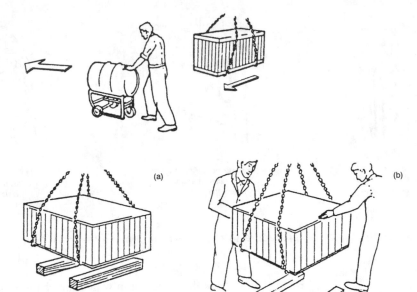

Fig. 3.17 Care when traversing a load

Fig. 3.18 Care when lowering a load

(b) place runners under the load as shown in Fig. 3.18(a) so that the sling will not be trapped and damaged. This will also facilitate its removal.

Lower the load until it is close to the ground and then gently ease it onto the runners until the strain is gradually taken off the lifting equipment. It may be necessary to manually guide the load into place as shown in Fig. 3.18(b), in which case safety shoes and protective gloves should be worn.

3.8 Hand signals

If the hoist operator cannot clearly see the load, then the assistance of a signaller should be obtained. The signaller should be positioned so as to see the load clearly and so that he or she can be clearly seen by the hoist operator. Both must be familiar with the standard code of hand signals as shown in Fig. 3.19.

3.9 Accessories for lifting gear

Hooks

These are made from forged steel and are carefully proportioned so that the load will not slip from them whilst being lifted. The hooks of lifting gear are frequently painted bright yellow to attract attention and to prevent people walking into them.

Slings

These are used to attach the load to the hook of the lifting equipment. There are four types in common use. They must all be marked with tags stating their *safe working load* (SWL).

(a) Chain slings (Fig. 3.20(a)): as well as general lifting, only this type of sling is suitable for lifting loads having sharp edges or for lifting hot materials.

Fig. 3.19 Standard code of hand signals for crane control

Raise load   Move load to my right   Travel towards me   Stop

Lower load   Move load to my left   Travel away from me   Emergency stop

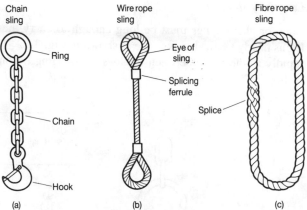

Fig. 3.20 Types of sling

Chain sling

Wire rope sling

Fibre rope sling

Ring

Chain

Hook

Eye of sling

Splicing ferrule

Splice

(a)   (b)   (c)

(b) Wire rope slings (Fig. 3.20(b)): these are widely used for general lifting. They should not be used for loads with sharp edges, nor for sharp edged loads, nor should they be allowed to become rusty. Further, they should not be bent round a diameter of less than 20 times the diameter of the wire rope itself.

(c) Fibre rope slings (Fig. 3.20(c)): fibre rope slings may have eyes spliced into them or, more usually, they are endless as shown. They are used for general lifting, and are particularly useful where machined surfaces and paintwork have to be protected from damage.

(d) Belt or strap slings: because of their breadth they do not tend to bite into the work and cause damage to the surface finish of the work. Rope and belt slings themselves must be protected from sharp edges as shown in Fig. 3.21.

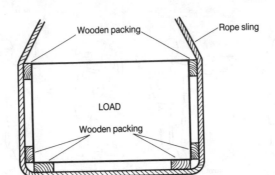

Fig. 3.21 Protecting the sling from sharp corners

Care of slings

Wire rope and fibre rope slings must not be shortened by knotting since this twists and kinks the fibres causing them to fracture. Chain slings must not be shortened by bolting the links together.

Condition of slings

All slings must be checked before use for cuts, wear, abrasion, fraying and corrosion. Damaged slings must never be used and the fault must be reported.

Length of slings

Rope or chain slings must be long enough to carry the load safely and with each leg as nearly vertical as possible as shown in Fig. 3.22. The load on a sling increases rapidly as the angle between the legs of the sling becomes greater. This is shown in Fig. 3.23.

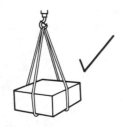

Fig. 3.22 Correct length of sling

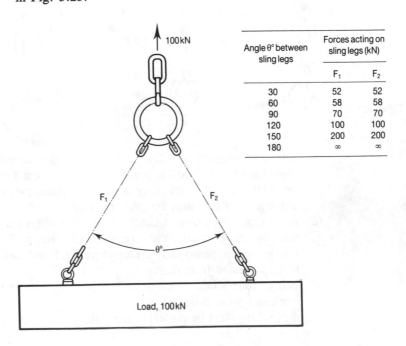

Angle $\theta°$ between sling legs	Forces acting on sling legs (kN)	
	F_1	F_2
30	52	52
60	58	58
90	70	70
120	100	100
150	200	200
180	∞	∞

Fig. 3.23 Effect of angle on the load

Rings

These are used for ease of attachment of the sling to the crane hook. They also prevent the sling being sharply bent over the hook. Figure 3.24(a) shows a chain sling fitted with a suitable ring at one end. Figure 3.24(b) shows how a ring is used in conjunction with a rope sling.

(a) Use of a ring with a two leg chain sling

(b) Use of a ring with a chain sling

Fig. 3.24 Use of rings

Eyebolts

Forged steel eyebolts to BS 4278 are frequently provided for lifting equipment and assemblies such as electric motors, gear boxes, and small machine tools. An example of the correct use of an eyebolt is shown in Fig. 3.25(a), whilst Fig. 3.25(b) shows how eyebolts must never be used.

Shackles

Forged steel shackles are used to connect lifting accessories together. In the example shown in Fig. 3.25(c), the eye of a wire rope sling is connected to an eyebolt using a shackle.

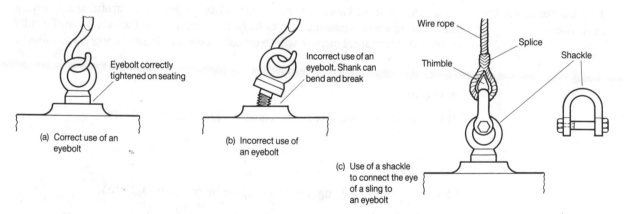

Fig. 3.25 Use of eyebolts

Special purpose equipment

Figure 3.26(a) shows how claws are used for lifting heavy barrels and drums. Particular care has to be taken when moving barrels or drums which are only partly filled. The movement of the barrel or drum can cause the liquid to surge about. This, in turn, changes the position of the centre of gravity and can cause the container to slip from the lifting equipment. If possible, completely fill or completely empty containers so that surging cannot take place. Figure 3.26(b) shows how plate hooks and a spreader are used. Spreaders are also used for lifting long loads such as bundles of tubing, girders, etc. Finally, Fig. 3.26(c) shows a plate hook in greater detail.

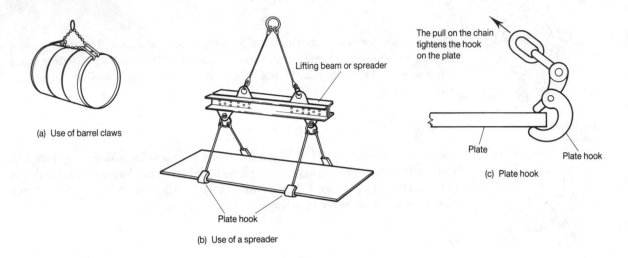

(a) Use of barrel claws

Lifting beam or spreader

The pull on the chain tightens the hook on the plate

Plate

Plate hook

(c) Plate hook

Plate hook

(b) Use of a spreader

Fig. 3.26 Special purpose equipment

3.10 Useful knots for fibre ropes

A knowledge of the knots that can be tied in fibre ropes can be useful when moving and securing loads. Knots must never be tied in wire ropes as they are not sufficiently flexible and permanent damage will be caused. Some widely used knots are as follows.

Reef knot

This is used for joining ropes of equal thickness (Fig. 3.27(a)).

Clove hitch

This is used for attaching a rope to a pole or bar (Fig. 3.27(b)).

Single loop

This is used to prevent fibre ropes from slipping off crane hooks (Fig. 3.27(c)).

Half hitches

Two half hitches can be used to secure a rope to a solid pole or for securing a rope to a sling (Fig. 3.27(d)).

Bowline

This is used to form a loop which will not tighten under load (Fig. 3.27(e)).

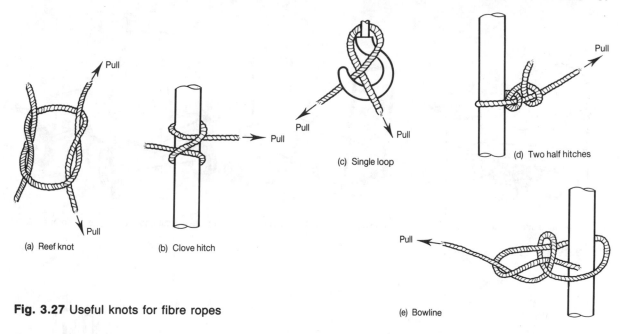

Fig. 3.27 Useful knots for fibre ropes

(a) Reef knot

(b) Clove hitch

(c) Single loop

(d) Two half hitches

(e) Bowline

3.11 Transporting loads (trucks)

Various types of truck are used for transporting loads around workshops and factory sites. Only manually propelled trucks will be considered as power-driven trucks are beyond the scope of this chapter. The simplest sort of truck is the *hand truck* (*sack-truck*) shown in Fig. 3.28. It uses the principle of levers to raise the load ready for wheeling it away. Quite heavy loads can be moved quite easily with this type of truck.

Platform or flat trucks are used with various wheel arrangements so that they can be steered.

The type shown in Fig. 3.29(a) requires the load to be placed over the wheels so that the truck is balanced for ease of movement. The type shown in Fig. 3.29(b) has a wheel at each end and the load does not have to be so carefully balanced. Only one end wheel is in contact with the ground at any one time. Also the end wheels can slide. This facilitates steering. A heavier duty 'turntable' truck is shown in Fig. 3.29(c). This has four wheels in the conventional position and the front wheels can be turned so that the truck can be steered.

Figure 3.30(a) shows a truck with a manually operated elevating table. The table is raised hydraulically by means of a double acting hand pump. This type of truck removes the need for lifting the load, for example, from a bench down onto the truck or from the truck up onto a bench. Finally, Fig. 3.30(b) shows a manually operated stacking truck for warehouse use. The load should always be lowered before the truck is moved. This lowers the centre of gravity of the truck and load and renders it stable and safe. Whatever type of truck you use there are two safety points you should observe.

(a) Stack the load on the trolley so that you can see where you are going in order to avoid a collision, particularly if people are working on ladders or steps in the vicinity

(b) Balance the load so that it will not topple off the truck or overturn the truck when you are turning a corner.

Fig. 3.28 Hand truck (sack truck)

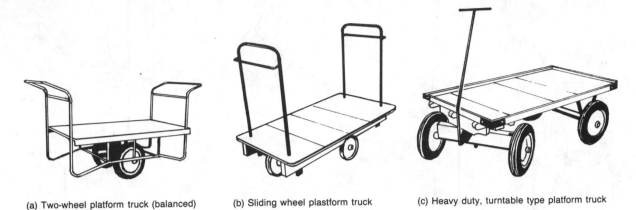

(a) Two-wheel platform truck (balanced)   (b) Sliding wheel plastform truck   (c) Heavy duty, turntable type platform truck

Fig. 3.29 Types of platform truck

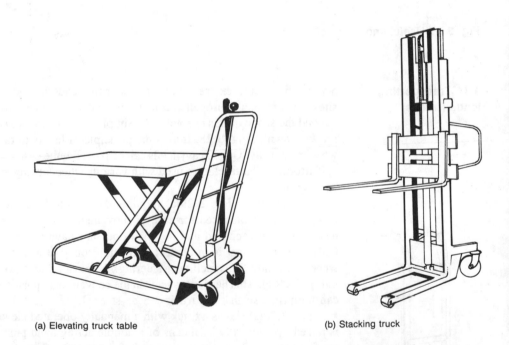

Fig. 3.30 Elevating
table truck

(a) Elevating truck table   (b) Stacking truck

3.12 Inspection

It is a legal requirement under the Health and Safety at Work etc., Act that all lifting equipment is regularly inspected by qualified engineers specialising in such work and that the results of such inspections are recorded in the register provided. If an inspector condemns any item of equipment it must be taken out of service immediately and either rectified or destroyed. If rectified, it must be re-inspected and approved by a qualified inspector before being taken back into service. The inspector will, on each visit, also confirm the safe working load (SWL) markings for each piece of equipment. No new item of lifting equipment must be taken into service until it has been inspected and certificated.

Exercises

1 When you lift a load manually you should
    (a) keep your back straight and upright, bend your knees and let your leg and thigh muscles do the work
    (b) keep your knees straight, bend your back and let your back muscles do the work
    (c) bend both your back and your legs and let your arm muscles do the work
    (d) keep your legs and back straight and only use your arms

2 Platform-trucks and sack-trucks should not be loaded more than chest high so that
    (a) they are not overloaded
    (b) the person pushing them is not strained
    (c) you can avoid collisions by seeing where you are going
    (d) they can be easily unloaded

3 It is generally accepted that mechanical lifting gear should be used for loads over
    (a) 10 kg
    (b) 20 kg
    (c) 100 kg
    (d) 200 kg

4 The letters SWL stand for safe working load. This is
    (a) the minimum load for which the equipment should be used
    (b) the average load for which the equipment is suitable
    (c) the maximum load for which the equipment is suitable
    (d) the only load for which the equipment is suitable

5 When you have to work under equipment it should be
    (a) supported by at least two slings
    (b) centralised under the crane hook
    (c) supported on suitable trestles or stands
    (d) jacked up only

6 You should position a crane hook so that it is
    (a) at the centre of gravity of the load
    (b) above the centre of gravity of the load
    (c) below the centre of gravity of the load
    (d) to one side or the other of the centre of gravity of the load

7 When you use a crane to traverse a heavy load
    (a) it is safe to pass over other people providing the load does not exceed the SWL
    (b) it is safe to pass over other people providing they are wearing safety helmets
    (c) it is always permissible to pass over persons working below
    (d) it is never permissible to pass over persons working below under any circumstances

8 The slingers' signal shown in Fig. 3.31 indicates
    (a) come forward
    (b) go back
    (c) raise the load
    (d) lower the load

Fig. 3.31

(a) Use of barrel claws

Fig. 3.32

9 The barrel shown in Fig. 3.32 is being lifted by means of
    (a) a two-leg chain sling with barrel claws
    (b) a two-leg chain sling with standard hooks
    (c) a continuous chain sling with standard hooks
    (d) a continuous chain sling with barrel claws

10 The forces acting on each leg of the sling shown in Fig. 3.33 is
    (a) $F_1 = F_2 = 5.0$ kN
    (b) $F_1 = F_2 = 5.8$ kN
    (c) $F_1 = F_2 = 7.0$ kN
    (d) $F_1 = F_2 = 10.0$ kN

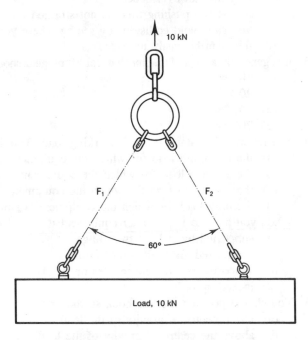

Fig. 3.33

11 If the angle between the legs of the sling shown in Fig. 3.33 is made less than the angle shown, the loads acting on the legs will
    (a) remain the same
    (b) be increased
    (c) become zero when the angle becomes zero
    (d) be decreased

12 The device shown in Fig. 3.34 is a
    (a) shackle
    (b) ring
    (c) eyebolt
    (d) thimble

13 Figure 3.35 shows a
    (a) reef knot
    (b) bowline
    (c) clove hitch
    (d) splice

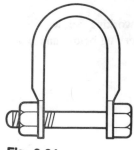

Fig. 3.34

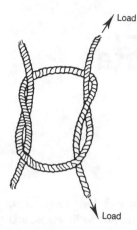

Fig. 3.35

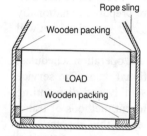

Fig. 3.36

14 You use the knot shown in Fig. 3.35 for
   (a) joining two ropes of equal thickness
   (b) fastening a rope to a pole
   (c) making a loop which will not tighten
   (d) preventing a rope from slipping off a hook

15 The wooden packing shown in Fig. 3.36 is used to
   (a) protect the load
   (b) increase the radius of the corner so as not to stretch the rope fibres
   (c) take up any slack in the sling
   (d) allow the rope sling to be removed when the load is resting on the floor

16 It is a legal requirement of the Health and Safety at Work Act that lifting gear must be
   (a) inspected only if accidentally overloaded
   (b) inspected occasionally
   (c) inspected when first taken into use
   (d) inspected regularly by a qualified engineer

17 When using a mobile crane near overhead electric supply cables, the safe working clearance distance must be agreed with
   (a) the site manager
   (b) the works electrician
   (c) the owner of the crane
   (d) the local electricity authority

18 The ends of fibre or wire ropes are joined to make continuous slings by means of a
   (a) reef knot
   (b) ferrule
   (c) high strength synthetic adhesive
   (d) splice

19 When an item of lifting equipment fails its inspection a note must be entered in the log and the equipment must be
   (a) repaired as soon as it is convenient
   (b) taken out of service immediately
   (c) used on lighter loads
   (d) taken out of service as soon as a replacement can be obtained

20 The minimum number of rollers on which a load can be moved is
   (a) two
   (b) three
   (c) four
   (d) five

4 Interpreting drawings, specifications and data

4.1 Purpose of technical drawings and specifications

Technical information has to be transmitted between such people as design engineers, manufacturing engineers, sales engineers, maintenance and service technicians, and craftspersons. This information has to be transmitted without it being misunderstood or misinterpreted. For this reason drawings and specifications are used rather than written descriptions and these drawings and specifications are prepared to nationally and internationally accepted standards. Technical drawings and specifications will vary depending upon for whom they are intended.

For example, the craftsperson will require detail drawings and operation schedules, the customer will require installation drawings and operational data. The service engineer will require exploded views and schedules of assembly and dismantling procedures for the equipment being maintained. These different methods of transmitting information will be considered in more detail later in this chapter. For example, technical drawings and specifications should provide the following information.

General arrangement drawing

(a) A list of all the components in an assembly (manufactured parts, bought-in parts, fastenings).
(b) The detail drawing reference numbers for the manufactured parts.
(c) The relationship between the associated components in an assembly.

Detail (manufacturing) drawing

(a) The size and shape of the component.
(b) The position, size and shape of holes, slots and other features.
(c) The material to be used.
(d) The finish (decorative, corrosion resistant, self-colour etc.).

Operation sequence planning

The sequence of operations required to manufacture the component, together with a list of the tooling required and the speeds and feeds for machining operations.

Assembly drawing

This is often an 'exploded' drawing and it shows the correct procedure and sequence for assembly and dismantling.

Installation drawings

(a) Foundation and installation drawings and specifications.
(b) Commissioning and operational information.

Performance specifications

Quality and performance data compared with competing equipment for the benefit of sales engineers and customers.

Most people have a natural instinct for appearance and proportion. They know when a product looks right and they probably know the old saying: 'If a design looks right, it is right'. The designer must not only consider function and 'fitness for purpose' he or she must also have a flair for styling so that the product is attractive to the customer as well as providing value for money. This is particularly the case when designing consumer durables and motor vehicles for the general public.

4.2 Standards in technical communication

 It has already been stated that various types of drawing are required to transmit technical information. Technical drawings prepared to internationally accepted standards are less likely to cause confusion than written descriptions, particularly if such descriptions have to be translated from one language into another. At some time or another you have most likely read the instruction book for some imported product and found that the translation ranged from the unintentionally humorous to the frustratingly incomprehensible but at least, thank goodness, the drawings made sense.

At the start of the industrial revolution, standardisation was unheard of. Each and every component was made individually. Every nut and bolt was made as a matched pair and they could not be interchanged with any other nut or bolt. Obviously this was highly inconvenient and you have already read in Chapter 1 that screw threads and screwed fastenings were the first manufactured goods to be standardised.

The benefits of such standardisation were so great, that the standardisation of many other manufactured goods and materials were quickly added to an ever-growing list. One such standard with which we are concerned in this chapter is BS 308: *Engineering Drawing Practice*. Many editions of this standard have been produced over the years as the requirements of technical drawings have become more exacting and also to harmonise the Standard with international practice.

Initially standards were developed on a national basis, and the body responsible for standardisation in the UK was, and still is, the British Standards Institution. Since 1947 the International Organisation for Standardisation (ISO) has been steadily harmonising national standards throughout the world to encourage and ease international trade. The British Standards Institution (BSI), as a major member of the ISO, has cooperated closely with that body and with the various committees of the European Community to ensure that our national standards for goods and services satisfy the requirements of world trade. The BSI summarises the main aims of standardisation as follows.

(a) The provision of communication amongst all interested parties.
(b) The promotion of economy in human effort, materials and energy in the production and exchange of goods.
(c) The protection of consumer interests through adequate and consistent quality of goods and services.
(d) The promotion of international trade by the removal of barriers caused by differences in national practices.

To achieve these aims the BSI publishes the following:

Standard specifications

These specify the requirements for particular materials, products or processes, and they also specify the method for checking that the requirements of the standard have been met.

Codes of practice, guides, etc.

As their names imply, these are recommendations for good practice. They aim to assist in ensuring the provision of goods and services which are safe and of consistently high quality.

Glossaries

To ensure that the standards are correctly interpreted, glossaries are available. These are lists of specialist and technical words and phrases together with their meanings. They are grouped according to the particular materials, products, processes and services to which they apply.

Five categories of standardisation apply to engineers, technicians and craftspersons, and these assist in the understanding of technical drawings, specifications and published data. The five categories are:

(i)   terminology and symbols (e.g. drawing conventions)
(ii) classification and designation
(iii) specifications for materials, standard products, and processes
(iv) methods of measuring, testing, sampling and analysing
(v)   recommendations on product or process applications and codes of practice

The standard specifications published by the BSI and the ISO are the result of consultation and agreement between all the interested parties. They are only recommendations and they are not legally binding unless they form part of a legal contract, or if a claim of compliance is made, or if they are included in legislation.

4.3 Methods of communicating technical information

Technical drawings and operation sheets

These are drawings providing the technical information you require in order to manufacture, assemble, install and maintain items of mechanical or electrical equipment. These drawings have to show a three-dimensional object on a two-dimensional, flat sheet of paper. To do this various standard drawing techniques are used and these will be considered later in this chapter. Figure 4.1 shows a typical detail drawing for a simple turned component and its associated operation sheet.

The purpose of the operation sheet, or operation schedule, or operation planning sheet (all different names for the same thing) is to provide you with the following information.

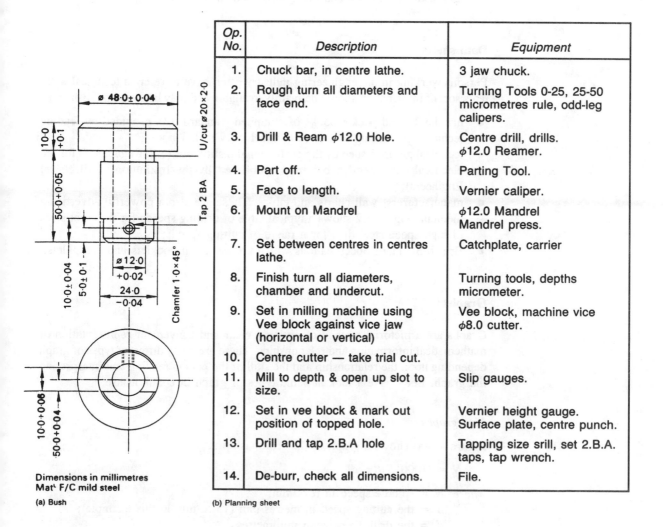

Op. No.	Description	Equipment
1.	Chuck bar, in centre lathe.	3 jaw chuck.
2.	Rough turn all diameters and face end.	Turning Tools 0-25, 25-50 micrometres rule, odd-leg calipers.
3.	Drill & Ream ϕ12.0 Hole.	Centre drill, drills. ϕ12.0 Reamer.
4.	Part off.	Parting Tool.
5.	Face to length.	Vernier caliper.
6.	Mount on Mandrel	ϕ12.0 Mandrel Mandrel press.
7.	Set between centres in centres lathe.	Catchplate, carrier
8.	Finish turn all diameters, chamber and undercut.	Turning tools, depths micrometer.
9.	Set in milling machine using Vee block against vice jaw (horizontal or vertical)	Vee block, machine vice ϕ8.0 cutter.
10.	Centre cutter — take trial cut.	
11.	Mill to depth & open up slot to size.	Slip gauges.
12.	Set in vee block & mark out position of topped hole.	Vernier height gauge. Surface plate, centre punch.
13.	Drill and tap 2.B.A hole	Tapping size srill, set 2.B.A. taps, tap wrench.
14.	De-burr, check all dimensions.	File.

Dimensions in millimetres
Mat^L F/C mild steel

(a) Bush

(b) Planning sheet

Fig. 4.1 Detail drawing and planning sheet

(a) A drawing number so that you can check that the correct drawing for the job has been issued.

(b) The job number for the craftsperson to book his or her time against for costing purposes.

(c) The date required.

(d) The batch size (number required).

(e) The material size and type to be used.

(f) Any special remarks concerning finish, etc.

(g) The person authorising manufacture.

(h) The sequence of operations, any special tooling required, cutting speeds and feed rates.

The amount of detail provided will vary from firm to firm and will also depend upon the complexity of the job and the system of quality control employed.

Data sheets

Persons working in the engineering industry often have to refer to technical data. This sort of information should be readily available and may be found published in:

- handbooks and pocket books of compiled standard data provided by leading technical publishing houses (e.g. Machinery's Handbook);
- technical guides issued by the professional institutions (e.g. Regulations for the electrical equipment in buildings: published by the Institution of Electrical Engineers);
- manufacturers' wall charts and tables. These are also a powerful advertising medium. Figure 4.2 shows a typical table of drilling speeds for different sizes of high speed steel drill for a range of cutting speeds;
- British Standard Specifications which are issued in booklets and pamphlets.

Graphs

Graphs are a pictorial method of giving a clear and convenient representation of mathematical information and relationships. There are many different types of graph depending upon the relationship and the skill of the person reading and interpreting the graph. Let's have a look at some types of graph in common use.

Line graphs

Figure 4.3(a) shows a graph of the relationship:

$$N = (1000 . S)/(\pi . d)$$

where: N = spindle speed in revs/min;
S = the cutting speed in metres/min (15 m/min in this example);
d = the drill diameter in millimetres

In this instance it is in order to use a continuous flowing curve through the points.

Metric series	CUTTING SPEEDS Approximate							Metric series
ft/min	30	40	50	60	70	80	90	100
m/min	9	12	15	18	21	24	27	30
diam/ mm	Revolutions per minute							
·5	5817	7756	9695	11634	13573	15512	17451	19390
1·0	2909	3878	4847	5817	6786	7756	8725	9695
1·5	1942	2589	3237	3884	4532	5179	5826	6474
2·0	1456	1942	2427	2912	3397	3883	4369	4854
3·0	970	1294	1617	1940	2264	2587	2911	3234
4·0	728	970	1213	1455	1698	1940	2183	2425
5·0	582	777	970	1164	1359	1553	1747	1941
6·0	485	647	808	970	1132	1294	1455	1617
7·0	416	555	693	832	970	1109	1248	1386
8·0	364	485	606	728	849	970	1091	1213
9·0	324	431	539	647	755	962	970	1078
10·0	291	388	485	582	679	776	873	970
11·0	265	353	441	529	617	706	794	882
12·0	243	324	404	485	566	647	728	808
13·0	234	299	373	448	522	597	672	746
14·0	208	277	346	416	485	554	623	693
15·0	194	259	323	388	453	517	582	647
16·0	182	243	303	364	424	485	546	606
17·0	171	228	285	342	399	456	513	571
18·0	162	216	269	323	377	431	485	539
19·0	153	204	255	306	357	408	459	511
20·0	146	194	242	291	340	388	436	485
21·0	139	185	231	277	323	370	416	462
22·0	133	177	220	265	309	353	397	441
23·0	127	169	211	253	295	337	380	422
24·0	121	162	202	242	283	323	364	404
25·0	117	155	194	233	272	310	349	388

Fig. 4.2 Typical data sheet

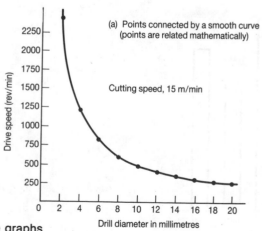

(a) Points connected by a smooth curve (points are related mathematically)

Cutting speed, 15 m/min

Drive speed (rev/min)

Drill diameter in millimetres

Fig. 4.3 Line graphs

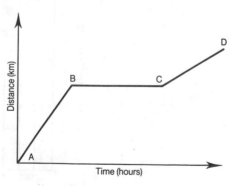

(b) Points connected by straight lines

This is because the points plotted are related by a mathematical expression. Also every value of N and d lying between the given points, and which can be calculated from the equation, will also lie on the curve.

This is not true in every instance as shown in Fig. 4.3(b). This graph connects time and distance. From A to B the distance travelled is proportional to the elapsed time. That is, when the vehicle is moving with uniform velocity. Fom B to C there is no increase in distance with time. The vehicle is stationary. From C to D the vehicle continues its journey, again with uniform velocity. In this graph the points are correctly connected with straight lines because each stage of the journey is represented by linear equations and each stage of the journey is unrelated to the previous stage or the next stage.

Histograms

Figure 4.4 shows the number of notifiable accidents which occur each year in a factory over a number of years. The points cannot be joined by a smooth curve as this would imply that they follow some sort of mathematical equation, which they do not. Neither can they be connected by a series of straight lines. This would imply that, although the graph does not follow a mathematical equation, the number of accidents increased or decreased continuously between one year and the next. In fact, the accidents are scattered throughout the year in a random manner and the annual total is independent of the previous year and the subsequent year. The correct way to present this type of information is by a *histogram*.

Bar charts

These are frequently used for indicating work in progress and are used for production planning. An example is shown in Fig. 4.5.

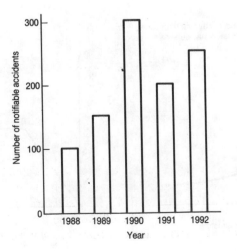

Fig. 4.4 Histogram

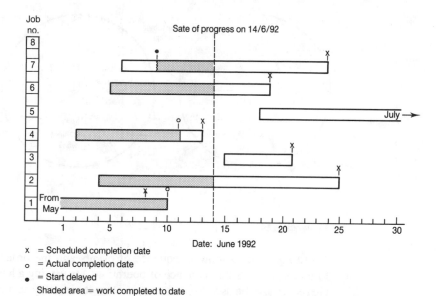

Fig. 4.5 Bar chart

x = Scheduled completion date
o = Actual completion date
• = Start delayed
Shaded area = work completed to date

Ideographs (pictograms)

These are frequently used for presenting statistical information to the general public or other people who may not be expert in interpreting graphical information. In Fig. 4.6 each symbol represents 1000 cars. Therefore, in 1990, the number of cars using the visitors' carpark at a company was 3000 (1000 cars for each symbol), in 1991 the number of cars was 4000, and in 1992 the number of cars was 6000.

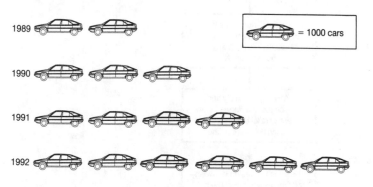

Fig. 4.6 Ideograph (pictogram)

Number of cars using a car park each month

Pie charts

These are used to show how a total quantity is divided into its individual parts. Since a complete circle is 360°, and this represents the total, then a 60° sector would represent 60/360 = 1/6 of the total. This is shown in Fig. 4.7(a). The total number of castings produced by a machine tool company's foundry is divided up between the various machines manufactured as shown in Fig. 4.7(b).

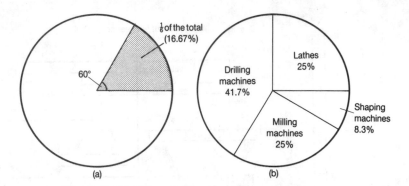

Fig. 4.7 Pie-chart

(a)   (b)

Flow charts

These are used to show a sequence of events and the order in which they occur. Figure 4.8 shows the sequence of operations for turning a hexagon head bolt. Flow charts can also be used for indicating a correct assembly sequence. Figure 4.9 shows the sequence for assembling a flanged pipe joint. It has been assumed that the flanges are already welded to the ends of the pipes to be connected.

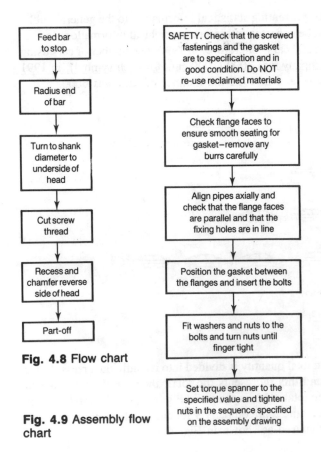

Fig. 4.8 Flow chart

Fig. 4.9 Assembly flow chart

Data storage

Traditionally engineering drawings were, and still are, produced on tracing paper or tracing cloth. The working drawings sent out from the drawing office are prints taken from the tracing by a dyeline printing process. Although not strictly a photographic process the tracings are often referred to as negatives and the prints as positives. Originally a process was used which produced white drawings on a blue background, hence the name 'blue prints'. The process has long since given way to the dyeline process currently used, but the name still persists.

Tracings take up a lot of space and are relatively easily torn and discoloured. Nowadays *microfilm* is increasingly used to store drawings on 16 mm or 35 mm film by photographic reduction. Prints are made when required by photographic enlargement of the microfilm negative. This saves an enormous amount of space in the drawing office library.

Company records (archives) and stores data is often recorded on *microfiche* systems. The data is recorded photographically in grid frames on a large rectangular transparent film. Individual frames can be selected and projected onto the screen of a desktop viewer. The enlarged frame can be easily read.

Electronic data storage is also increasingly being used. The data is 'read' or 'scanned' by an electronic encoding device and the original data is digitised so that it can be stored on a computer disk. The data can then be called up as required on computer screens anywhere on the system.

Video tapes are also widely used for training and sales presentations. Not only is it easier for an export sales team to take a video tape presentation to a customer than to ship out a large sample piece of equipment, the tape can also be dubbed into any language required.

4.4 Interpretation of technical drawings

Craftspersons are rarely called upon to produce formal technical drawings, although they may have to make sketches of parts for maintenance replacements. However, a detail knowledge of the types of drawings, the projections used, and the standard conventions, is essential to the correct interpretation of drawings in order to manufacture the parts shown. Firstly we will consider the types of drawing and how these are presented.

To save time in the drawing office, most companies adopt a standardised and pre-printed drawing sheet as shown in Fig. 4.10. The layout and content will vary from company to company but, generally, such sheets will provide the following information.

(a) The drawing number and title.
(b) The projection used (first angle or third angle).
(c) The scale.
(d) The material specification.
(e) Warning notes.
(f) Any corrections or revisions and the zone where they occur.
(g) Special notes concerning heat treament, decorative, corrosion resistant or other surface finishes.

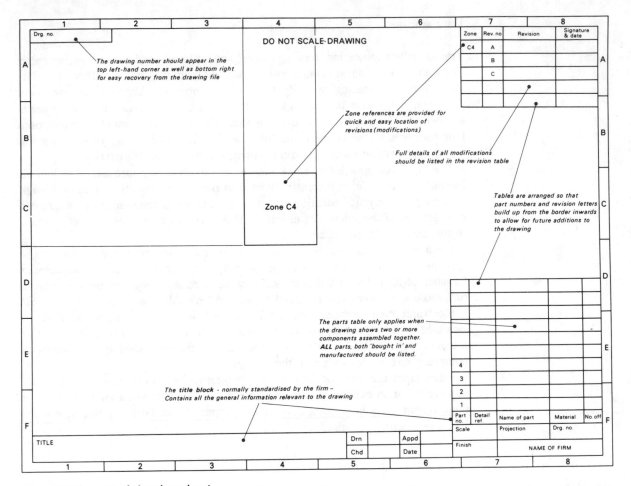

Fig. 4.10 Layout of drawing sheet

General arrangement drawings

An example of a general arrangement (GA) drawing is shown in Fig. 4.11. It shows all the components correctly assembled, and lists all the parts required. For those parts to be made in the factory, the detail drawing numbers will be provided together with the material specification and the quantity of parts required. For those components which will be 'bought in', it will state the maker and catalogue reference for the benefit of the purchasing department. General arrangement drawings no not usually carry dimensions except, occasionally, overall dimensions for reference.

Detail drawings

These provide all the details to make a component and an example is shown in Fig. 4.12. It not only shows the shape of the component but also its size and the tolerances within which it has to be manufactured. It states the materials to be used, and the

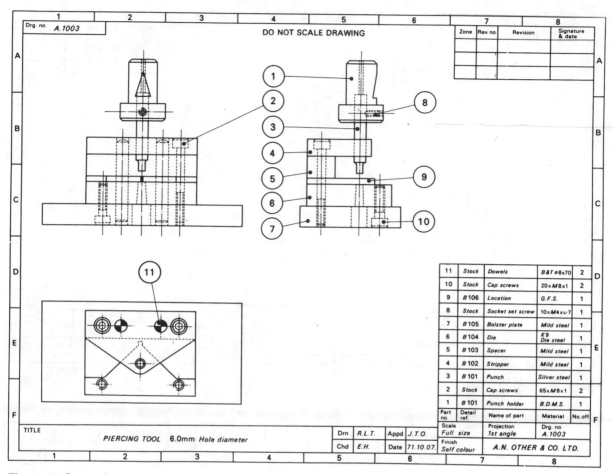

Part no.	Detail ref.	Name of part	Material	No.off
11	Stock	Dowels	B&T ⌀8x70	2
10	Stock	Cap screws	20×M8x1	2
9	B 106	Location	G.F.S.	1
8	Stock	Socket set screw	10×M4×υ·7	1
7	B 105	Bolster plate	Mild steel	1
6	B 104	Die	K9 Die steel	1
5	B 103	Spacer	Mild steel	1
4	B 102	Stripper	Mild steel	1
3	B 101	Punch	Silver steel	1
2	Stock	Cap screws	65×M8x1	2
1	B 101	Punch holder	B.D.M.S.	1

TITLE

PIERCING TOOL   6.0mm Hole diameter

Drn	R.L.T.	Appd	J.T.O.
Chd	E.H.	Date	71.10.07.

Scale *Full size* · Projection *1st angle* · Drg. no *A.1003*

Finish *Self colour* — *A.N. OTHER & CO. LTD.*

Drg. no. *A.1003* — DO NOT SCALE DRAWING

Zone	Rev.no.	Revision	Signature & date

Fig. 4.11 General arrangement drawing

heat treatment of the punch. Similar detail drawings would be required for all the other components shown in the general arrangement drawing.

Block diagrams

These are used to show the relationship between the main subassemblies. Figure 4.13(a) shows the drive train for a milling machine, whilst Fig. 4.13(b) shows the drive train for a lathe.

Exploded (assembly) drawings

These are largely found in the service manuals for machines and show the various components in the correct relationship to each other and the stock reference number

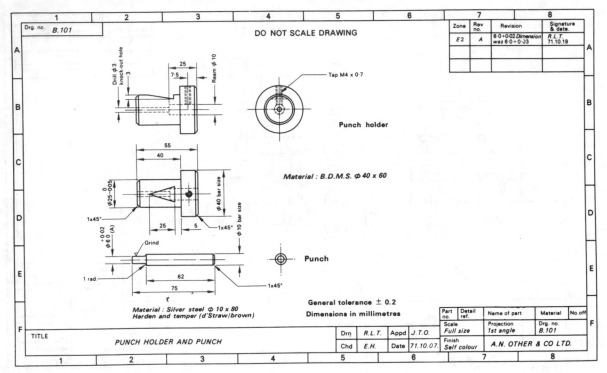

Fig. 4.12 Detail drawing

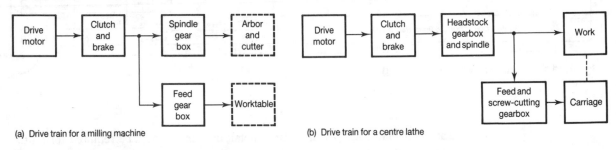

(a) Drive train for a milling machine

(b) Drive train for a centre lathe

Fig. 4.13 Block diagrams

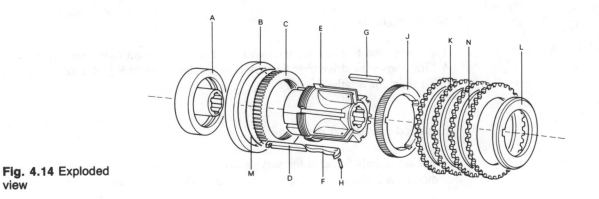

Fig. 4.14 Exploded
view

of each component to facilitate the ordering of spare parts. An example is shown in Fig. 4.14.

Location (installation) drawings

These are used to show the correct layout of the various major items of a plant installation. It may also include details of any foundations which may have to be prepared and any service ducts for electrical, hydraulic, pneumatic and fuel links and services. An example is shown in Fig. 4.15.

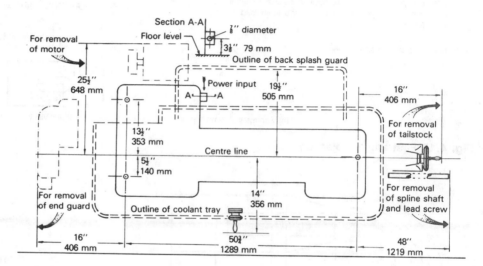

Fig. 4.15 Installation drawing

4.5 Orthographic projection

This is a technique which enables you to draw three-dimensional solid objects on a flat, two-dimensional sheet of paper without the need for artistic skills. It enables all the views to be drawn to their true shape and size. Figure 4.16 shows a simple clamp drawn pictorially. It is then shown in *first angle projection* in Fig. 4.17 and in *third angle projection* in Fig. 4.18 to show you how a three-dimensional solid can be drawn on a flat sheet of paper. Orthographic drawing is used for detail and general arrangement drawings. These drawings will be read by engineers, technicians and craftspersons who are skilled in their interpretation.

Auxiliary views

The use of an auxiliary view enables an inclined surface to be shown with true size and shape. Figure 4.19 shows a bracket with an inclined face. When it is drawn in first-angle projection it can be seen that the features in the plan view and end view are heavily distorted. To overcome this distortion a projection is made of an extra view at right-angles to the inclined surface. This true view of the inclined surface is the *auxiliary view*.

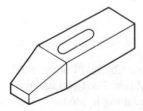

Fig. 4.16 Clamp

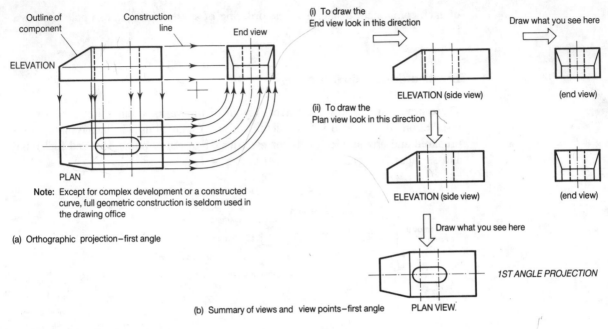

(a) Orthographic projection–first angle

Note: Except for complex development or a constructed curve, full geometric construction is seldom used in the drawing office

(b) Summary of views and view points–first angle

Fig. 4.17 First angle projection

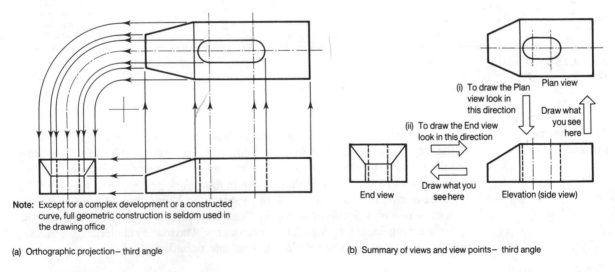

(a) Orthographic projection– third angle

Note: Except for a complex development or a constructed curve, full geometric construction is seldom used in the drawing office

(b) Summary of views and view points– third angle

Fig. 4.18 Third angle projection

Section views

These are used to show the inside (hidden details) of hollow objects. Figure 4.20 shows how you can draw sections of components and assemblies. First you imagine that the cutting plane actually cuts through the component, splitting it into two parts. Secondly, and still in your imagination, you remove the unwanted portion so as to

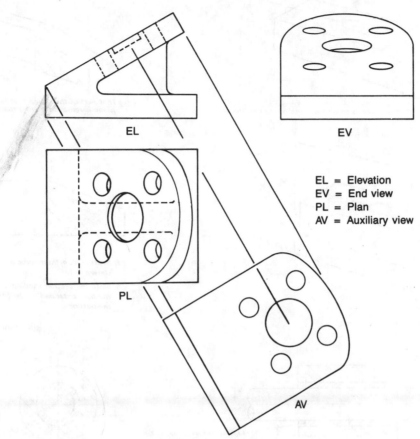

EL = Elevation
EV = End view
PL = Plan
AV = Auxiliary view

Fig. 4.19 Auxiliary view

leave the required section view. Note that the 'cut' surfaces are shaded by fine sloping lines. This is called *hatching*. Where an assembly of two components come together, the direction of the section shading lines is reversed to show the boundary between the components. You can also see from Fig. 4.20 that such features as shafts and webs are not sectioned. Further, you will come across half-sections, part (scrap) sections and revolved sections as shown in Fig. 4.21.

4.6 Drawing conventions

Figure 4.22 compares a pictorial representation of a screw thread with the current British Standard convention. Given a drawing with a lot of screw threads that you have got to produce quickly which method of drawing a screw thread would you prefer to use? Engineering drawings are not works of art. They are not ends in themselves. They are a costly but necessary inconvenience for relaying the designer's intentions to the craftsperson who is going to make the design a reality. If a cheaper and quicker method of relaying that information could be found, then engineering drawings would disappear. Therefore, as shown with the screw thread, engineering drawings use a form of 'short-hand' called *conventions* to speed up the drawing of

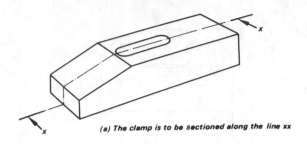

(a) The clamp is to be sectioned along the line xx

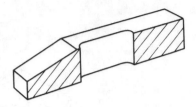

(c) That part of the clamp that lies in front of the cutting plane is removed leaving the sectioned component

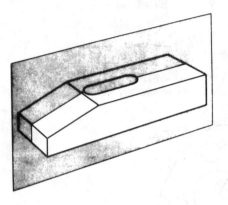

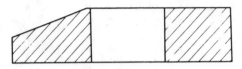

(d) Sectioned, orthographic elevation of the clamp shown in (a).

Note the section shading lines lie at 45° to the horizontal and are half the thickness of the outline.

(a) Principle of section drawing

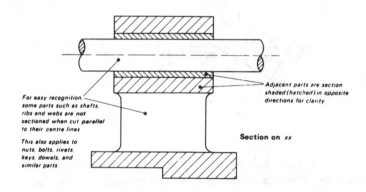

For easy recognition, some parts such as shafts, ribs and webs are not sectioned when cut parallel to their centre lines

This also applies to nuts, bolts, rivets, keys, dowels, and similar parts.

Adjacent parts are section shaded (hatched) in opposite directions for clarity

Section on xx

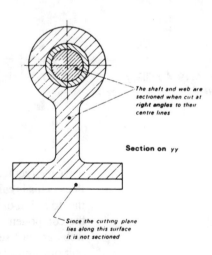

The shaft and web are sectioned when cut at right angles to their centre lines

Section on yy

Since the cutting plane lies along this surface it is not sectioned

1ST ANGLE PROJECTION

(b) Sectioning an assembly

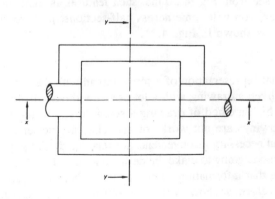

Fig. 4.20 Section drawing

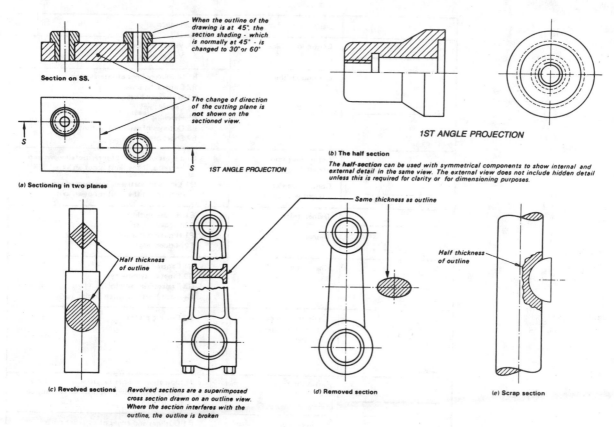

When the outline of the drawing is at 45°, the section shading - which is normally at 45° - is changed to 30° or 60°

Section on SS.

The change of direction of the cutting plane is not shown on the sectioned view.

1ST ANGLE PROJECTION

(a) Sectioning in two planes

1ST ANGLE PROJECTION

(b) The half section

The half-section can be used with symmetrical components to show internal and external detail in the same view. The external view does not include hidden detail unless this is required for clarity or for dimensioning purposes.

Same thickness as outline

Half thickness of outline

Half thickness of outline

(c) Revolved sections   Revolved sections are a superimposed cross section drawn on an outline view. Where the section interferes with the outline, the outline is broken

(d) Removed section

(e) Scrap section

Fig. 4.21 Further examples of sectioning

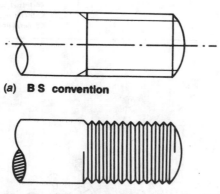

(a)   **B S convention**

Fig. 4.22 Need for conventions

(b)   **Pictorial representation**

frequently used component features. Such conventions may be company standards, national standards, or international standards. The conventions generally used in the UK are those specified in BS 308: *Engineering Drawing Practice*. These are internationally accepted and are harmonised with ISO and EC directives. Examples of standard lines and their uses are shown in Fig. 4.23. Examples of other conventions for common features are shown in Fig. 4.24.

Line	Description	Application
A	Continuous thick	A1 Visible outlines A2 Visible edges
B	Continuous thin	B1 Imaginary lines of intersection B2 Dimension lines B3 Projection lines B4 Leader lines B5 Hatching B6 Outlines of revolved sections B7 Short centre lines
C	Continuous thin irregular	C1 Limits of partial or interrupted views and sections, if the limit is not an axis
D	Continuous thin straight with zigzags	D1 Limits of partial or interrupted views and sections, if the limit is not an axis
E	Dashed thick	E1 Hidden outlines E2 Hidden edges
F	Dashed thin	F1 Hidden outlines F2 Hidden edges
G	Chain thin	G1 Centre lines G2 Lines of symmetry G3 Trajectories and loci G4 Pitch lines and pitch circles
H	Chain thin, thick at ends and changes of direction	H1 Cutting planes
J	Chain thick	J1 Indication of lines or surfaces to which a special requirement applies (drawn adjacent to surface)
K	Chain thin double dashed	K1 Outlines and edges of adjacent parts K2 Outlines and edges of alternative and extreme positions of movable parts K3 Centroidal lines K4 Initial outlines prior to forming K5 Parts situated in front of a cutting plane K6 Bend lines on developed blanks or patterns

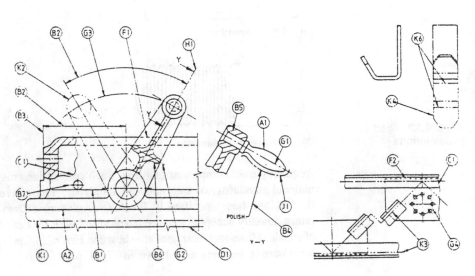

Fig. 4.23 Types of line and their applications

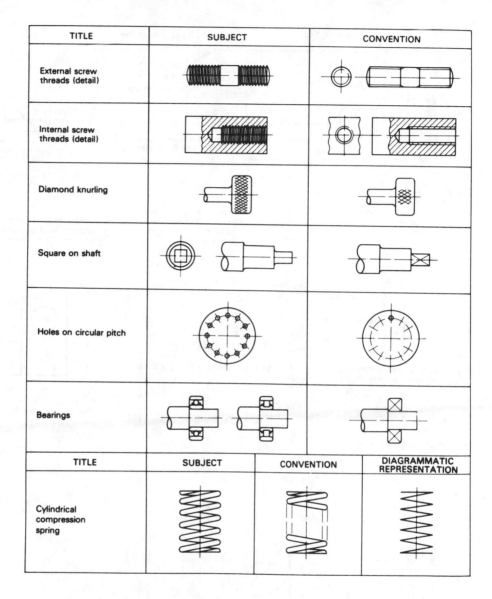

Fig. 4.24 Typical conventions for some common features

4.7 Dimensioning

Having drawn the correct outline of the component using either first- or third-angle projection, we now know what the component looks like, but we do not know how big it is, so the next stage is to add the dimensions. The dimension lines and projection lines should be thin, continuous lines that are half the thickness of the drawing outline. This helps us to avoid confusing the dimension and projection lines with the outline. Further, we also leave a short gap between the projection lines and the outline of the component. The arrow heads of the dimension lines should touch the projection lines, and the dimensions should be positioned so that they can be read from the bottom right-hand corner of the drawing. They should also be kept outside the outline of the drawing wherever possible. Figure 4.25 shows the basic principles of

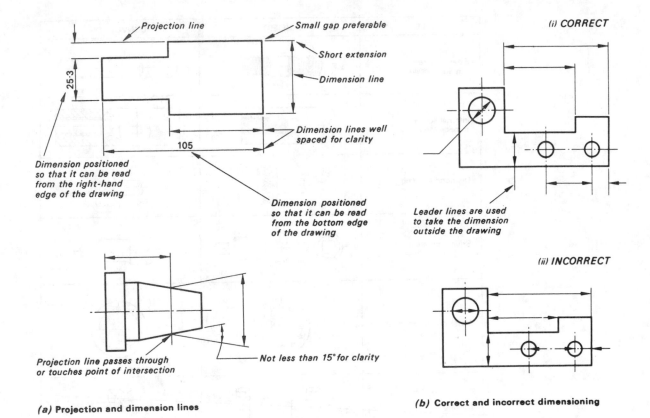

(a) **Projection and dimension lines**

(b) **Correct and incorrect dimensioning**

Fig. 4.25 Dimensioning

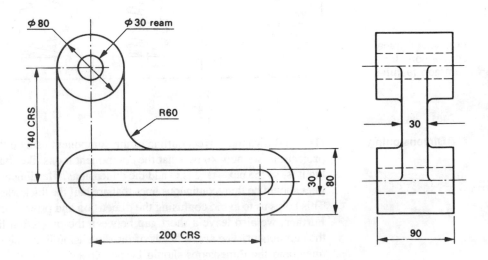

Dimensions in millimetres

Fig. 4.26 Correct positioning of dimensions

Dimensions should be placed in the view which shows the feature in clear outline

dimensioning and Fig. 4.26 shows the correct positioning of dimensions. The advantages and limitations of chain and absolute dimensioning will be compared and discussed in section 5.8.

4.8 Pictorial views (oblique)

This is the simplest of the techniques used by engineers to show a pictorial representation of a solid object and an example is shown in Fig. 4.27. The component is positioned so that you can draw one face true to size and shape. The lines running 'into' the page are called *receding* lines and these are drawn at 45° to the front face as shown. To improve the proportions of the drawing, You draw the receding lines half their true length. For ease of drawing and realism you should observe the following rules.

(a) Any curve or irregular face should be drawn true shape. For example, a circle on a receding face would have to be constructed as an ellipse, whereas if it were positioned on the front face it could be drawn true shape with compasses.

(b) Wherever possible the longest side should be shown on the front, true view. This prevents violation of perspective and gives a more realistic appearance.

(c) For long objects of circular cross-section, such as a shaft, the above two rules conflict. In this instance the circular shape should be the true view even though this results in the long axis receding.

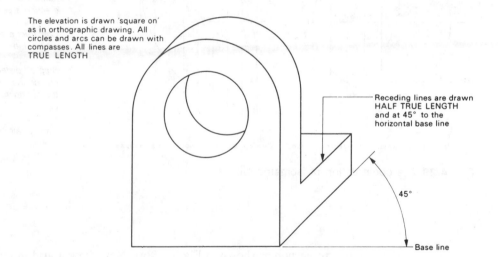

The elevation is drawn 'square on' as in orthographic drawing. All circles and arcs can be drawn with compasses. All lines are TRUE LENGTH

Receding lines are drawn HALF TRUE LENGTH and at 45° to the horizontal base line

45°

Base line

Fig. 4.27 Oblique drawing

4.9 Pictorial views (isometric)

The bracket shown in Fig. 4.28 is drawn in isometric projection. The isometric axes are at 30° to the base line. To be strictly accurate these receding lines should be drawn to isometric scale and only the vertical lines should be true length. However, for all practical purposes, all the lines are made true length to save time.

Although isometric drawing produces a more pleasing representation than oblique drawing, it has the disadvantage that no curved profiles such as arcs, circles, radii, etc., can be drawn with compasses and all curved profiles have to be constructed. You can do this by erecting a grid over the feature concerned in orthographic

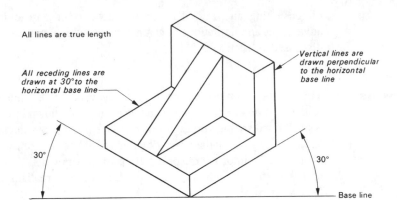

All lines are true length

All receding lines are
drawn at 30° to the
horizontal base line

Vertical lines are
drawn perpendicular
to the horizontal
base line

30°

30°

Base line

Fig. 4.28 Isometric
drawing

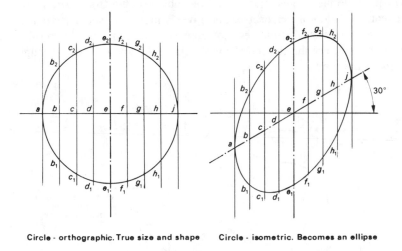

Circle - orthographic. True size and shape

Circle - isometric. Becomes an ellipse

30°

1. *Construct a grid over the true circle by
   dividing its centre line into an equal
   number of parts, a b c ... j, and
   erecting a perpendicular at each point*

2. *Construct a similar grid on the isometric
   centre line*

3. *Step off distances b_1–b–b_2, c_1–c–c_2
   etc. on the isometric grid by transferring
   the correponding distances from the true
   circle*

4. *Draw a fair curve through the points
   plotted*

Fig. 4.29 The construction of isometric curves

projection as shown in Fig. 4.29(a). Now draw a grid of equal size where it is to
appear on the isometric drawing. The points where the circle cuts the grid in the
orthographic drawing are transferred to the isometric grid as shown in Fig. 4.29(b).
A smooth curve is drawn through these isometric points and the circle appears as
an ellipse. An example of a fully dimensioned component in isometric projection
is shown in Fig. 4.30.

4.10 Sketching

Sketching implies the freehand drawing of engineering components. These may be
in orthographic or pictorial form depending upon the purpose for which they are
required.

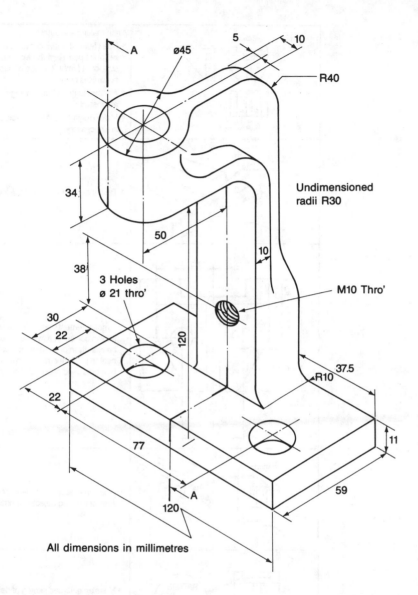

Fig. 4.30 Fully dimensioned component in isometric projection

All dimensions in millimetres

Orthographic sketching

Figure 4.31 shows a bracket which is to be made and fitted to the end of a machine tool bed. Figure 4.32 shows the procedure for making a freehand orthographic sketch for the bracket.

(a) Use a sheet of clean, good quality paper of adequate size and an 'H' pencil
(b) Paper ruled with squares is helpful as it gives you a guide for lines at right-angles to each other.
(c) Now make outline sketches of the views you require using faint lines.
(d) When you are satisfied with your initial sketches, draw in the outline more heavily and add any necessary details.

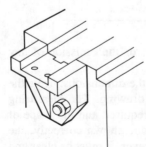

Fig. 4.31 Bracket

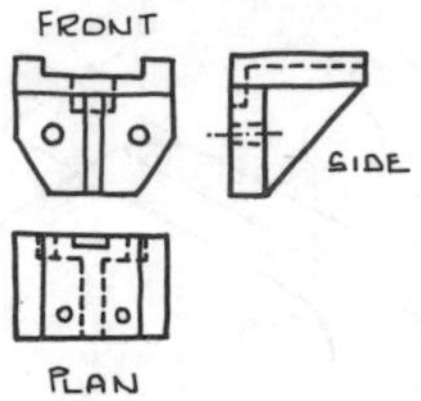	When making a sketch: • Use cleanest paper available and a sharp pencil or ballpoint pen. Rest the work on a flat surface or support it firmly. The use of paper ruled with squares is helpful. • Attempt to keep the drawing as clean and clear as possible. • Make rough sketches to decide what views are necessary.
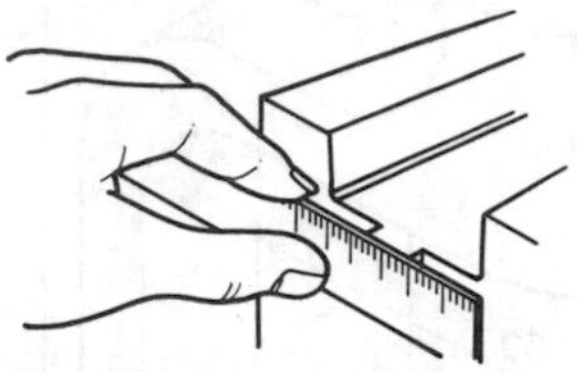	• Take measurements and mark on sketch.
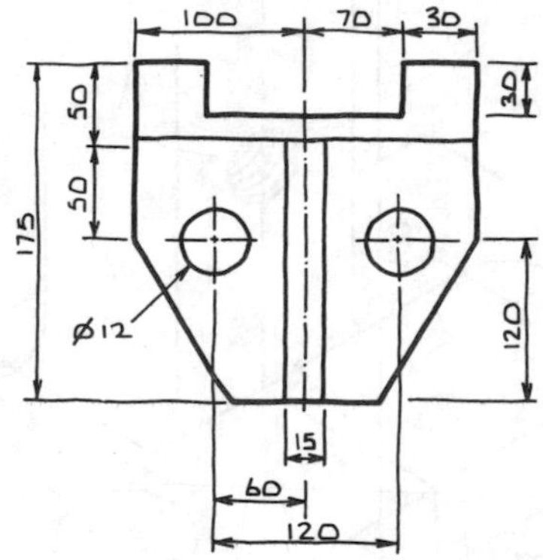	• If measurements are taken accurately, and shown correctly, a freehand sketch need not be exactly in proportion. It must be clear and neat to prevent error in reading from it. Symbols used should adhere to BS 308.
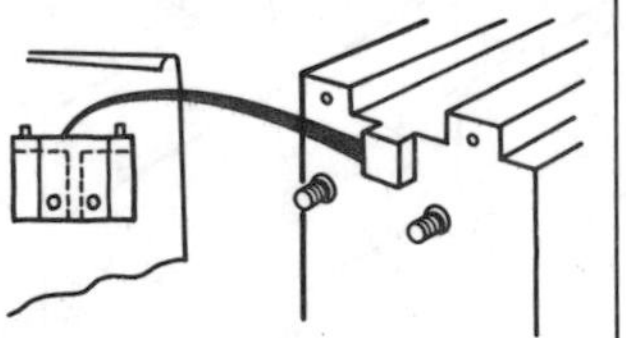	• When shapes are complete, check carefully against existing objects for omissions.
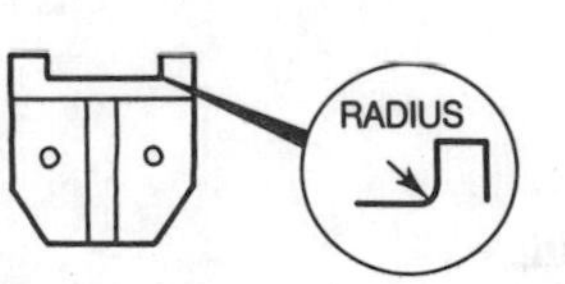	• Make an enlarged sketch of detail where necessary.

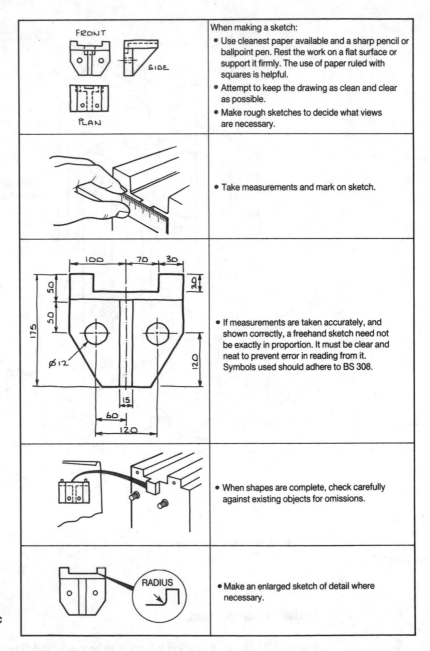

Fig. 4.32 Orthographic sketching

(e) When the basic sketch is complete, check carefully for the omission of any essential details.

(f) Having completed the outline, now you have to add the dimensions. Take the measurements you require and transfer them to the drawing. The measuring instruments you use will depend upon the accuracy required and the shape of the details. If the dimensions are taken accurately, and shown correctly, the freehand sketch need not be in exact proportion. However, it must be clear and neat to prevent errors when reading from it. Symbols used should be to BS 308.

(g) Make an enlarged sketch of any small details where necessary.

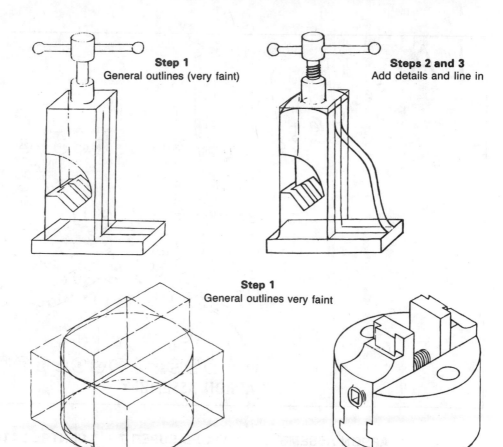

Fig. 4.33 Pictorial sketching (oblique)

Fig. 4.34 Pictorial sketching (isometric)

Pictorial sketching

Pictorial sketches can be in oblique or isometric projection. Figure 4.33 shows you how to sketch a vice in *oblique* projection.

(a) First sketch a 'box' to contain the outline of the finished drawing. Faint lines should be used.
(b) Next lightly sketch in the details of the component or assembly being drawn.
(c) Go over the outline more heavily to make it stand out from the construction lines.
(d) Finally, add dimensions as required.

Figure 4.34 shows you how to sketch a chuck in *isometric* projection.

(a) The technique is similar to that for the previous, oblique sketch. However, the initial, outline 'box' is drawn in isometric projection.
(b) Now sketch in the curves using faint lines. Remember that in isometric projection these will be ellipses or parts of ellipses.
(c) Add any details that are required.
(d) Finally line in the outline and details more heavily so that they stand out from the construction lines.
(e) Add dimensions as required.

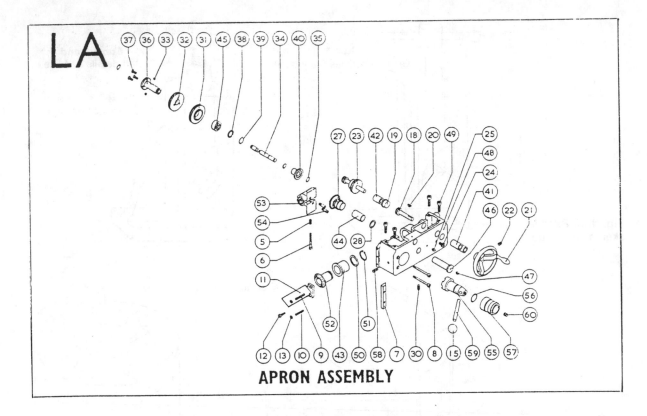

APRON ASSEMBLY — MYFORD SUPER 7 $3\frac{1}{2}$″ CENTRE LATHE

Drg. Ref.	Part No.	Description	No. Off/Mc.	Drg. Ref.	Part No.	Description	No. Off/Mc.
LA5	A4729	Spring—Leadscrew Nut	1	LA38	A9782	Washer—Drive Shaft	1
LA6		Cap Hd. Screw—Leadscrew Nut (2 B.A. × $1\frac{3}{4}$″)	1	LA39		Circlip—Drive Shaft (Anderton 1400—$\frac{5}{8}$″)	1
LA7	A2082	Gib Strip—Leadscrew Nut	1	LA40	A9208	Knob Operating Spindle	1
LA8	A9193	Ch. Hd. Screw—Strip Securing	2	LA41	A9210	'Oilite' Bush	2
LA9	A9194	Adjusting Screw—Gib Strip	1	LA42	A9211	'Oilite' Bush	1
LA10	A9195	Adjusting Screw-Gib Strip	1	LA43	A9212/1	'Oilite' Bush—Flanged	1
LA11	A9196	Leadscrew Guard	1	LA44	A7595	'Oilite' Bush	1
LA12		Hex. Hd. Set Screw (2 B.A. × $\frac{1}{2}$″)	1	LA45	A9220	Clutch Insert	1
LA13		Hex. Locknut (2 B.A.)	2	LA46	A9203/1	Stud—Gear Cluster	1
LA15	80002	Ball Knob (KB5/100)	1	LA47	65001	Oil Nipple (Tecalemit NC6057)	1
LA18	A9198	Hand Traverse Pinion	1	LA48	10025/1	Apron Assembly (includes LA41, LA42, LA43)	1
LA19	65004	Sealing Plug—Apron (AQ330/15)	1	LA49		Cap Screw (M6 × 1 × 25 mm)	4
LA20	70002	Woodruff Key (No. 404)	1	LA50	10217	Thrust Washer	1
LA21	A2087	Handwheel Assembly	1	LA51	10431	Circlip	1
LA22		Socket Set Screw ($\frac{1}{4}$″ B.S.F. × $\frac{1}{4}$″) (Knurled Cup Point)	1	LA52	A9200/1	Bevel Pinion	1
				LA53	A1975/3	Leadscrew Nut set	1
LA23	A9199	Rack Pinion Assembly	1	LA54	10508	Cam Peg	2
LA24	A2531	Oil Level Plug	1	LA55	10528	Cam	1
LA25	65000	Oil Nipple (Tecalemit NC6055)	1	LA56	65007	'O' Ring (BS/USA115)	1
LA27	A9201	Bevel Gear Cluster Assembly (includes LA44)	1	LA57	10529	Eccentric Sleeve	1
LA28	A9202	Thrust Washer	1	LA58		Socket Set Screw ($\frac{5}{16}$″ B.S.F. × $\frac{5}{8}$″, Half Dog Point)	1
LA30		Socket Set Screw ($\frac{1}{4}$″ B.S.F. × $\frac{1}{2}$″) (Knurled Cup Point)	1	LA59	10530	Lever	1
LA31	A9204	Clutch Gear Assembly (includes LA45)	1	LA60		Socket Set Screw (2 B.A. × $\frac{1}{4}$″, Cup Point)	1
LA32	A9205	Drive Gear	1	LA61	10424	Guard Plate (not illustrated)	1
LA33	73010	Ball—Clutch (5 mm ϕ)	2				
LA34	A9206	Operating Spindle	1				
LA35		Circlip (Anderton 1400—$\frac{3}{4}$″)	3				
LA36	A9207	Drive Shaft	1				
LA37		C's'k Hd. Socket Screw (2 B.A. × $\frac{3}{4}$″)	3				

Fig. 4.35 Exploded view and parts list

4.11 Identification of components

As well as being able to read drawings so that you can make the component shown, you also have to be able to identify components that you can obtain from the stores ready made. Such components may be such standard items as bolts, studs, nuts, washers, dowels, etc. You may have a reference code which you can quote exactly as it is stated on the drawing or you may have to write down all the details as you pick them out from the various views of the drawing. For example, consider a simple metric screwed fastening. You would need to specify:

(a) The type of fastening (bolt, set screw, cap screw, stud, etc.).
(b) The material from which it is made (if not steel).
(c) Details of the thread (fine or coarse series, diameter, and pitch).
(d) Length.

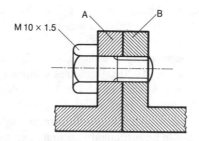

Sizes in mm				ISO-METRIC COARSE THREADS							Sizes in mm	
Nominal size and symbol	Pitch	Major diameter	Effective diameter	Minor diameters				Section at minor diameter 'd'	Tensile stress area 'e'	Depth of external thread 0·6134p	Tapping drills		Clearance drills
				Ext. thds. (bolts) 'a'			Int. thds. (nuts) 'b' 5H,6H,7H				Recom-mended	Alter-native	
				Class 4h	6g	8g							
M1	0·25	1·000	0·838	0·693	0·675	—	0·729	0·377	0·460	0·1534	0·75	0·78	1·05
M1·1	0·25	1·100	0·938	0·793	0·775	—	0·829	0·494	0·588	0·1534	0·85	0·88	1·15
M1·2	0·25	1·200	1·038	0·893	0·875	—	0·929	0·626	0·732	0·1534	0·95	0·98	1·25
M1·4	0·30	1·400	1·205	1·032	1·014	—	1·075	0·937	0·982	0·1840	1·10	1·15	1·45
M1·6	0·35	1·600	1·373	1·170	1·151	—	1·221	1·08	1·27	0·2147	1·25	1·30	1·65
M1·8	0·35	1·800	1·573	1·370	1·351	—	1·421	1·48	1·70	0·2147	1·45	1·50	1·85
M2	0·40	2·000	1·740	1·509	1·490	—	1·567	1·79	2·07	0·2454	1·60	1·65	2·05
M2·2	0·45	2·200	1·908	1·648	1·628	—	1·713	2·13	2·48	0·2760	1·75	1·80	2·25
M2·5	0·45	2·500	2·208	1·948	1·928	—	2·013	2·98	3·39	0·2760	2·05	2·10	2·60
M3	0·50	3·000	2·675	2·387	2·367	—	2·459	4·47	5·03	0·3067	2·50	2·55	3·10
M3·5	0·60	3·500	3·110	2·764	2·743	—	2·850	6·00	6·78	0·3681	2·90	2·95	3·60
M4	0·70	4·000	3·545	3·141	3·119	—	3·242	7·75	8·78	0·4294	3·30	3·40	4·10
M4·5	0·75	4·500	4·013	3·580	3·558	—	3·688	10·1	11·3	0·4601	3·70	3·80	4·60
M5	0·80	5·000	4·480	4·019	3·995	3·995	4·134	12·7	14·2	0·4908	4·20	4·30	5·10
M6	1·00	6·000	5·350	4·773	4·747	4·747	4·917	17·9	20·1	0·6134	5·00	5·10	6·10
M7	1·00	7·000	6·350	5·773	5·747	5·747	5·917	26·2	28·9	0·6134	6·00	6·10	7·20
M8	1·25	8·000	7·188	6·466	6·438	6·438	6·647	32·8	36·6	0·7668	6·80	6·90	7·20
M9	1·25	9·000	8·188	7·466	7·438	7·438	7·647	43·8	48·1	0·7668	7·80	7·90	9·20
M10	1·50	10·000	9·026	8·160	8·128	8·128	8·376	52·3	58·0	0·9202	8·50	8·60	10·20
M11	1·50	11·000	10·026	9·160	9·128	9·128	9·376	65·9	72·3	0·9202	9·50	9·60	11·20
M12	1·75	12·000	10·863	9·853	9·819	9·819	10·106	76·2	84·3	1·0735	10·20	10·40	12·20

For example, an M10 × 1.50 ISO metric coarse thread bolt, the clearance hole in part A needs to be 10·20 mm diameter and the tapping size in part B needs to be 8·50 mm diameter.

Fig. 4.36 Interpreting tables of data

Sometimes you have to identify parts that have to be replaced when maintaining or reconditioning assemblies. Manufacturers of engineering machinery and equipment issue service manuals in which the assemblies and subassemblies are shown as exploded pictorial views. The individual parts are given a drawing reference number and they are indexed to a list in which the parts are named. The list also contains the part number for ordering purposes. The drawing shows the the relationship between the parts as a guide to assembly and dismantling. A typical example is shown in Fig. 4.35.

4.12 Interpreting tables and graphs

Consider the simple assembly shown in Fig. 4.36(top). The two components are joined by an M10 coarse series hexagon head bolt 25 millimetres long. The hole in part 'A' needs a clearance hole and the hole in part 'B' needs to be 'tapping size' so that the screw thread can be cut in it. You can obtain this sort of information from screw thread tables and an example is shown in Fig. 4.36(bottom). The table shows all the details of the thread. The columns at the righthand side of the table show that the tapping drill size should be 8.50 millimetres diameter and the clearance size drill should be 10.20 millimetres diameter.

As well as showing data in tabular form it can also be shown in graphical form. Figure 4.37(a) shows a graph relating bar sizes in inch and metric dimensions. Note that although 1 inch = 25.4 mm, this graph approximates 1 inch as 25 mm. In this instance this would be sufficiently accurate because if you rang up a steel stockholder for a length of 3 inch × 1 inch bar or a length of 75 mm × 25 mm bar you would get the same bar. This is a straight line graph in which the two variables are mathematically related. It is safe therefore to find intermediate sizes by *interpolation*

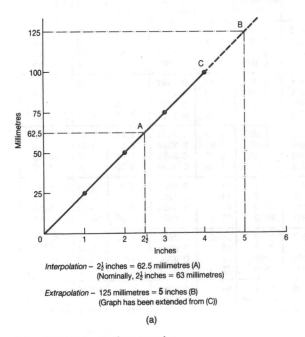

Interpolation – 2½ inches = 62.5 millimetres (A)
(Nominally, 2½ inches = 63 millimetres)

Extrapolation – 125 millimetres = **5** inches (B)
(Graph has been extended from (C))

(a)

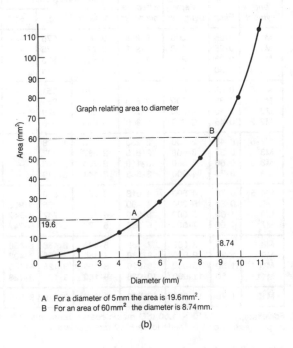

A   For a diameter of 5 mm the area is 19.6 mm².
B   For an area of 60 mm² the diameter is 8.74 mm.

(b)

Fig. 4.37 Interpreting graphs

as shown. In this case you could extend the graph and *extrapolate* values as shown as well. However, this is not always the case and great care has to be taken before extrapolating values from a graph.

Early in this chapter (Fig. 4.3 to be precise) you were introduced to a graph connecting twist drill diameters and spindle speeds for a cutting speed of 15 m/min. Because the graph was a curve and, since it followed a mathematical law, it was safe to *interpolate* values from graph. Figure 4.37(b) shows a similar graph and derives some values from the graph by interpolation.

Table 4.1 Colour coding for gas cylinders. (Based upon BS 349)

If a cylinder has no neck band its contents are neither poisonous nor flammable.
If a cylinder has a red neck band or it is wholly coloured red or maroon its contents are flammable.
If a cylinder has a yellow neck band its contents are poisonous.
If a cylinder has both a red and a yellow neck band its contents are both flammable and poisonous.
Full details can be found in BS 349 *Identification of the Contents of Industrial Gas Containers*.

Whilst on site the cylinders should be kept clean so that they can be easily identified. On no account must the colour of any cylinder be changed by any person either on site or in the workshop. Acetylene cylinders must never be stacked horizontally. Here are some examples of colour coding.

Gas	Ground colour of cylinder	Colour of neck bands
Acetylene	Maroon	None
Air	French grey	None
Ammonia	Black	Signal red and golden yellow
Argon	Peacock blue	None
Carbon monoxide	Signal red*	Golden yellow
Helium	Middle brown	None
Hydrogen	Signal red*	None
Methane	Signal red*	None
Nitrogen	French grey	Black
Oxygen	Black	None

*The name of the contents is also painted clearly on the cylinder in a contrasting colour.

Table 4.2 Identification of electrical cables

Service	Cable	Colour
Single phase Flexible	Live	Brown
	Neutral	Blue
	Earth	Green/yellow
Single phase Non-flexible	Live	Red
	Neutral	Black
	Earth	Green/yellow
Three phase Non-flexible	Line (live) [colour denotes phase]	Red or white or blue
	Neutral	Black
	Earth	Green/yellow

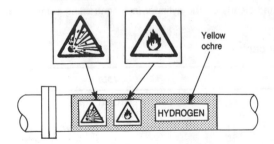

Dimensions in mm (approx.)

Basic identification This is placed at junctions, both sides of valves, service appliances, bulkhead and wall penetrations and other places where identification is necessary. Pipes may be banded as shown left, or the whole pipeline may be painted with the basic identification colour.

Safety colours

- Red for fire-fighting
- Yellow for warning
- Auxiliary blue with green basic colour for fresh water both potable and non-potable,

Pipe contents	Basic identification colour name
Water	Green
Steam	Silver grey
Oils and combustible liquids	Yellow ochre
Gases and liquefied gases (other than air)	Yellow ochre
Acids and alkalis	Violet
Air	Light blue
Other liquids	Black
Electrical services and ventilation ducts	Orange

Fresh water

Fire-extinguishing water

Information Use the following systems singly or in combination to identify the contents of pipes:

- Name in full, abbreviation of name or chemical symbol.
- Refrigerant number as specified in BS 4580.
- Appropriate colour code as above: whole pipeline painted, colour bands, self-adhesive tapes or colour clips.
- Hazard signs and/or data panels as appropriate.

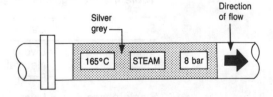

Examples of the use of hazard signs — risk of explosion and/or fire

Examples of the use of data panels — marking of pressure and temperature

Fig. 4.38 Identification of pipelines and services (see BS 1710 for detailed information)

4.13 Colour coding   Colour coding is used for identification purposes. Your safety and the safety of the people you work with depends upon your ability to understand and use such codes. Typical applications are:

(a) The identification of gases in cylinders (Table 4.1).
(b) The identification of electrical cables (Table 4.2).
(c) The identification of the contents of pipes and conduits such as gas, water, steam, etc. (Fig. 4.38).
(d) The identification of component values (Fig. 4.39 shows how colour coding is applied to carbon resistors).
(e) The identification of bar stock in material stores. There is no British or ISO standard for such identification. Where used, each firm has its own coding. Learn it and use it but, if you change firms, forget it and start again with the coding used by your new employer. It is not unusual for such coding to vary between different branches of the same company where such branches are on widely separated sites, so take care.

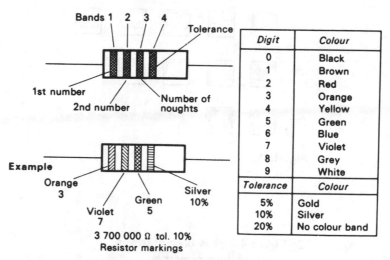

Digit	Colour
0	Black
1	Brown
2	Red
3	Orange
4	Yellow
5	Green
6	Blue
7	Violet
8	Grey
9	White

Tolerance	Colour
5%	Gold
10%	Silver
20%	No colour band

Fig. 4.39 Carbon resistors colour code

Note: small capacitors are marked in the same manner, but the units are picofarads

Exercises

1 To avoid translation errors and misunderstanding, technical information should be transmitted wherever possible by
   (a) written specifications through the post
   (b) written specifications by fax
   (c) technical drawings
   (d) word of mouth

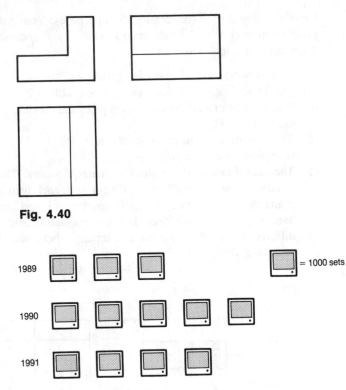

Fig. 4.40

Fig. 4.41

2 Figure 4.40 has been drawn in
    (a) oblique projection
    (b) isometric projection
    (c) first-angle orthographic projection
    (d) third angle orthographic projection
3 Figure 4.41 shows the output of a television manufacturing company presented by means of a histogram. The number of television sets produced in 1990 was
    (a) 2000 sets
    (b) 3000 sets
    (c) 4000 sets
    (d) 5000 sets
4 Figure 4.42 shows a typical
    (a) pie chart
    (b) pictogram
    (c) histogram
    (d) bar chart

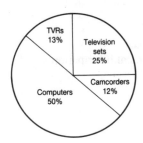

Fig. 4.42

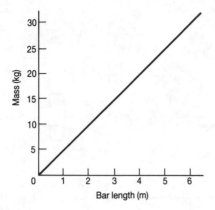

Fig. 4.43

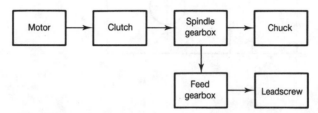

Fig. 4.44

5   Figure 4.43 shows the relationship between the length of a steel bar and its mass
    in kilogrammes: The mass of a bar 5 metre long is
    (a) 15 kg
    (b) 20 kg
    (c) 25 kg
    (d) 30 kg

6   From Fig. 4.43, it can be seen that the length of the bar whose mass is 15 kg is
    (a) 3 m
    (b) 4 m
    (c) 5 m
    (d) 6 m

7   Figure 4.44 shows a machine tool transmission train. This type of diagram is
    called a
    (a) flow chart
    (b) block diagram
    (c) general arrangement drawing
    (d) pictogram

8   Figure 4.45 shows some of the simplified drawing details specified in BS 308:
    Part 1. These are called
    (a) conventions
    (b) standards
    (c) abbreviations
    (d) symbols

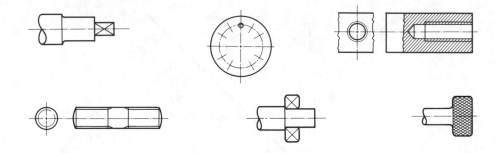

Fig. 4.45

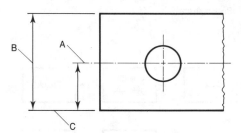

Fig. 4.46

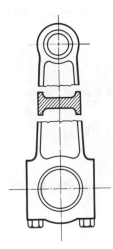

Fig. 4.47

9 In Fig. 4.46 the line A is called a
   (a) dimension line
   (b) centre line
   (c) leader line
   (d) projection line

10 In Fig. 4.46 the line B is called a
   (a) dimension line
   (b) centre line
   (c) leader line
   (d) projection line

11 In Fig. 4.46 the line C is called a
   (a) dimension line
   (b) centre line
   (c) leader line
   (d) projection line

12 The shaded portion of Fig. 4.47 is a
   (a) revolved section
   (b) simple section
   (c) scrap section
   (d) pocket section

13 A metal pipe coloured orange will contain
   (a) natural gas
   (b) water
   (c) electric cables
   (d) compressed air

14 The insulation colours of a three core flexible electric cable for live, neutral and earth are respectively
   (a) red, black and green
   (b) red, blue and green
   (c) brown, black and green/yellow striped
   (d) brown, blue and green/yellow striped

15 A compressed gas cylinder coloured black with no neck band will contain
   (a) acetylene
   (b) oxygen
   (c) propane
   (d) carbon dioxide

16 A compressed gas cylinder coloured maroon with no neck band will contain
   (a) acetylene
   (b) oxygen
   (c) propane
   (d) carbon dioxide

17 Technical drawings should be prepared in accordance with an internationally accepted standard such as BS 308 in order to
   (a) avoid import tariffs
   (b) avoid errors of interpretation
   (c) reduce postal costs
   (d) make it possible to transmit drawings by fax

18 A general arrangement drawing usually shows a three dimensional solid object by means of
   (a) isometric projection
   (b) oblique projection
   (c) an exploded view
   (d) orthographic projection

19 The information required for manufacturing a component is usually shown on
   (a) an assembly drawing
   (b) a detail drawing
   (c) a general arrangement drawing
   (d) a block diagram

20 Figure 4.48 has been drawn in
   (a) oblique projection
   (b) isometric projection
   (c) first-angle orthographic projection
   (d) third-angle orthographic projection

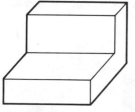

Fig. 4.48

5 Measurement and dimensional control

5.1 Measurement as a comparator process

When you measure the length, width, thickness or any other feature of a component you compare the size of that feature with the size of a measuring device. For example, Fig. 5.1(a) shows the width of a step being measured with a steel rule. Figure 5.1(b) shows a hole being checked with a plug gauge to see if it is the correct diameter. In the first example the width of the step is being compared with the scale of the rule. In the second example the diameter of the hole is being compared with the diameter of the plug gauge. Thus we can say that measurement is a *comparator process*.

Indicating equipment

When you measure a feature of a component with a rule, you find out the size of the feature. This is because the scale of the rule indicates the actual size of the feature. Measuring equipment possessing scales is called *indicating* equipment. How accurate the measurement will be depends upon the accuracy of the equipment and your skill in using it. Remember, no equipment is perfectly accurate and we all have limitations of sight and feel no matter how skilled we are. It is impossible to work to an exact size and, even if it were possible, you would never know since no one can measure to an exact size.

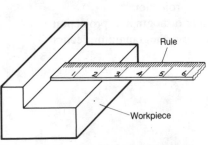

(a) Comparing the width of the step with a steel rule

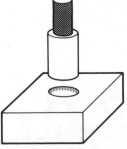

(b) Comparing the diameter of a hole with a plug gauge

Fig. 5.1 Measurement as a comparator process

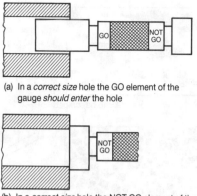

(a) In a *correct size* hole the GO element of the gauge *should enter* the hole

(b) In a *correct size* hole the NOT GO element of the gauge *should not* enter the hole

(c) In an *oversize* hole the NOT GO element of the gauge *will enter* the hole

(d) In an undersize hole neither element of the gauge will enter the hole

Fig. 5.2 Use of a plug gauge

Non-indicating equipment

Gauges do not have scales and cannot indicate the actual size of a feature. All they can do is to determine whether or not the size of a feature lies within the limits of size set by the designer. Figure 5.2 shows how a plug gauge can be used to check whether or not a hole diameter lies within the limits of size set by the designer. It cannot indicate the actual size of the hole. Therefore, as an item of non-indicating equipment it is used for checking and not for measuring.

5.2 Dimensional properties

When checking or measuring a component there are a number of dimensional properties which you have to consider. Let's now consider the more important ones.

Length

When you measure length, you measure the shortest distance in a straight line between two points, lines or faces. It doesn't matter what you call this distance (width, thickness, depth, height, diameter) it is still a measurement of length. The preferred unit for measuring lengths in mechanical engineering is the millimetre. We will consider the measurement of length in greater detail in section 4.5.

Flatness

A flat surface lies in a true plane. When you check the flatness of a component you are measuring how the surface of the component deviates from a true plane. There are various ways of doing this including the use of sophisticated optical equipment. In the workshop it is usually adequate to compare the surface of the component with

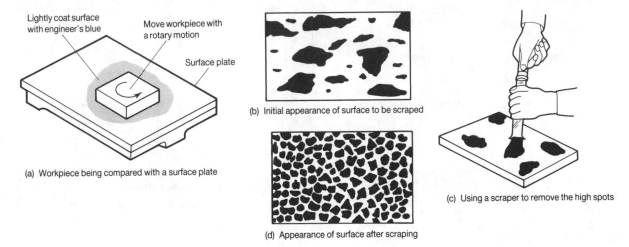

(a) Workpiece being compared with a surface plate

(b) Initial appearance of surface to be scraped

(c) Using a scraper to remove the high spots

(d) Appearance of surface after scraping

Fig. 5.3 Producing a flat surface

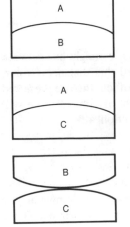

Fig. 5.4 Comparison of three surface plates to achieve flatness

a surface plate. These are available in various grades of accuracy. Figure 5.3 shows how you can compare a component with a surface plate and how you can remove local high spots with a scraper. A little engineer's blue is smeared lightly onto the surface plate. You then slide the component lightly over the surface plate. Any high spots on the component will pick up some of the blue as shown. These high spots are then removed with a scraper and the process is repeated until the component surface is uniformly covered with a fine pattern of high spots as shown.

You may wonder where the first surface plate came from and with what it was compared. In fact a flat surface can be generated by working three surfaces together as shown in Fig. 5.4. For example, surfaces A and B will appear flat when compared with each other using engineer's blue as previously described. Plates A and C could also appear flat if B and C were made using plate A as the standard. However, any deviation from a plane surface will immediately become apparent when plates C and B are compared. The plates are scraped until they show themselves to be flat when compared in any combination. The surfaces of A and B, A and C and B and C will only show overall contact when perfect flatness has been achieved.

Narrow surfaces (edges) can be checked using a straight edge. This can either be used with engineer's blue as previously described, or by checking the light gap as shown in Fig. 5.5.

Parallelism

This is the constancy of distance between two lines or surfaces: in practice, the lack of taper. Parallelism can either be measured using an indicating instrument as shown in Fig. 5.6(a), or checked with a non-indicating instrument as shown in Fig. 5.6(b). When an indicating instrument is used, the component is parallel if the reading is the same at each end. Any difference between the readings shows the lack of parallelism (taper). If a non-indicating instrument is used parallelism is indicated by the same 'feel' at both ends of the component feature.

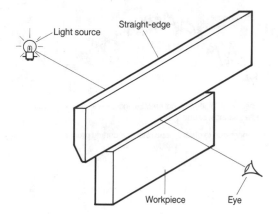

Fig. 5.5 Use of a straight edge

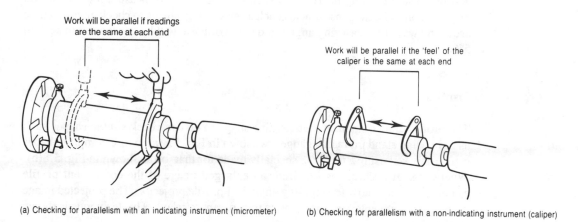

(a) Checking for parallelism with an indicating instrument (micrometer)

(b) Checking for parallelism with a non-indicating instrument (caliper)

Fig. 5.6 Parallelism

Surface roughness

This is the condition of the surface of a component as left by a casting, forming or cutting process. The difference between roughness and waviness is shown in Fig. 5.7. Surface roughness can be assessed by using comparison blocks (non-indicating equipment) or by a surface measuring machine (indicating equipment). Surface comparison blocks come as a boxed set and represent typical surface roughness values as produced by various workshop processes. Comparison is made by drawing your fingernail across the component and then across the test blocks until a match of feel is achieved. This requires a lot of skill and practice and is not very accurate.

The surface measuring machine draws a measuring head across the surface being checked. The stylus of the measuring head (which is similar to a record player pickup head) is deflected by the surface roughness. These deflections are amplified electronically and are printed out on a paper tape. The trace is an enlarged reproduction of the component surface. Knowing the amplification factor of the equipment, the actual value of the peaks and troughs can be scaled and measured.

------- Waviness due to geometrical errors in machine slides,
spindle bearings, or cutter

Roughness due to chatter, feed rate, and cutting process

Fig. 5.7 Roughness and waviness

Angles

An angle is a measure of the inclination of one line or one surface to another. Again, you may use indicating instruments such as protractors to measure angles, or you may use non-indicating instruments such as taper plug gauges to check angles. There are many ways of measuring angles and some of these will be considered in section 5.6.

Profiles

The profile of a component is its outline shape. You can check simple shapes such as radii using standard radius gauges as shown in Fig. 5.8(a). More complex shapes can be checked using a template specially made for that job as shown in Fig. 5.8(b). Where greater accuracy is required, an enlarged image of the component profile can be projected onto a screen using an optical profile projector. The projected image is compared with enlarged templates or transparent overlays. This technique is shown in Fig. 5.8(c).

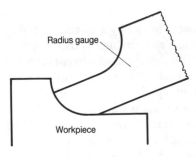

(a) Checking a radius with a radius gauge

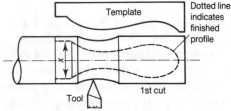

1. The diameter 'x' is easily checked with a micrometer caliper so it is used for the 'control' diameter.
2. A series of cuts are taken, each one deepening the profile until it matches the template throughout its length.
3. The profile is then turned down until the diameter 'x' lies within limits. The rest of the profile will then be dimensionally correct.

(b) Use of a template to turn a profile

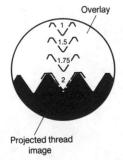

(c) Use of a profile projector to check a screw thread form

Fig. 5.8 Checking a profile

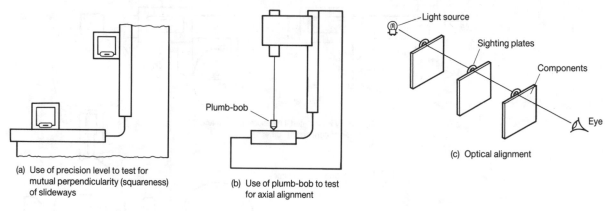

(a) Use of precision level to test for mutual perpendicularity (squareness) of slideways

(b) Use of plumb-bob to test for axial alignment

(c) Optical alignment

Fig. 5.9 Checking for alignment

Relative position

The alignment of the major components and subassemblies prior to final assembly and fixing can be carried out in various ways. Horizontal and vertical planes can be established using precision bubble levels (spirit levels) as shown in Fig. 5.9(a). Alignment in the vertical plane can also be achieved using a plumb-bob as shown in Fig. 5.9(b). A plumb-bob always hangs vertically: that is, it always points towards the centre of the Earth. Since plumb-bobs are radial to the Earth's centre, no two plumb-bobs can be parallel to each other. However, for all practical purposes this lack of parallelism can be ignored over short distances. Spirit (bubble) levels are considered further in section 5.10.

Optical alignment can also be used. Figure 5.9(c) shows how a light source and sights may be used. Whilst equipment such as the alignment telescope, the autocollimator and the laser may be used where greater accuracy is required. Such equipment is beyond the scope of this book but is considered within the main competences.

Roundness and concentricity

A round component is one with a truly circular cross-section. That is, a section through a perfect cylinder or a perfect cone. Roundness implies how closely a cylindrical or conical component approaches this ideal. You can measure the diameter of a circular component using a micrometer or a vernier calliper. Such measurement will also detect out of roundness if ovality has occurred. This is shown in Fig. 5.10(a). Some forms of out of roundness cannot be detected in this way and Fig. 5.10(b) shows the problem presented when measuring a component which has a constant diameter, lobed cross-section. The only way to detect this form of out of roundness is to rotate the component under a dial test indicator (DTI) whilst the component is supported in a V-block as shown in Fig. 5.10(c). You will find out more about dial test indicators in section 5.5.

Concentricity implies a number of diameters having a common axis. For example,

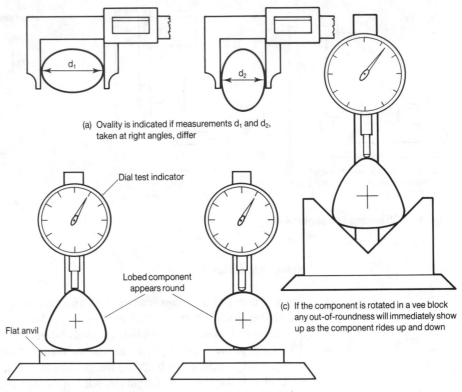

(a) Ovality is indicated if measurements d_1 and d_2, taken at right angles, differ

Dial test indicator

Lobed component appears round

Flat anvil

(c) If the component is rotated in a vee block any out-of-roundness will immediately show up as the component rides up and down

Fig. 5.10 Testing for out of roundness

(b) Some types of lobed cross-section will not show up when checked on a flat anvil

If you draw a number of circles having different diameters on a piece of paper and you don't move the position of the point of your compasses, then all the circles will be concentric. Figure 5.11 shows how you can test the diameters of a turned component for concentricity. Diameters turned at the same setting in a lathe will normally be concentric with each other. Lack of concentricity (eccentricity) is often referred to as 'run-out'.

Accuracy of form

This is the combination of all the dimensional properties we have considered so far. For many components it is only necessary to specify toleranced dimensions as described in section 5.7. The machining process can then be relied upon to provide the required accuracy of form. However, the precision and performance criteria for engineering components is becoming increasingly exacting all the time and accuracy of form cannot always be assumed. For this reason, geometrical as well as dimensional tolerancing is used on the drawings for precision components. Such tolerancing will insure that the component is the correct shape as well as the correct size. This eases the assembly process and ensures uniform performance of engineering products. Geometrical tolerancing is beyond the scope of this book but, if you are interested, you can refer to BS 308: Part 3 in your library.

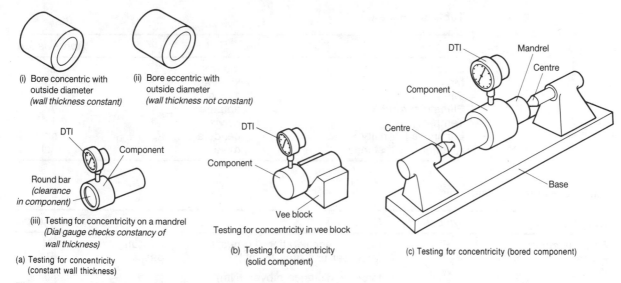

(i) Bore concentric with outside diameter *(wall thickness constant)*

(ii) Bore eccentric with outside diameter *(wall thickness not constant)*

DTI

Component

Round bar *(clearance in component)*

(iii) Testing for concentricity on a mandrel *(Dial gauge checks constancy of wall thickness)*

(a) Testing for concentricity (constant wall thickness)

DTI

Component

Vee block

Testing for concentricity in vee block

(b) Testing for concentricity (solid component)

DTI Mandrel

Centre

Component

Centre

Base

(c) Testing for concentricity (bored component)

Fig. 5.11 Testing for concentricity with dial test indicator (DTI)

5.3 Standards of measurement

Standards of measurement such as weights and lengths are required if trading is to take place in an organised manner and if disputes between traders are to be settled by arbitration. Various physical standards have been pressed into service, over the ages, to represent length and weight.

International standardisation

In order that world trade could flourish it became necessary for national standards to be 'harmonised'. In Britain this is the responsibility of the British Standards Institution (BSI) which works in conjunction with the International Standards Organisation (ISO) and European Community standards committees. Such international standardisation is essential to ensure the interchangeability of components and equipment manufactured in different countries. Standardisation refers to both dimensional accuracy and also quality. *Systeme Internationale (SI)* units are now used throughout the world.

Quantities and units (SI)

The base units of the Systeme International d'Unites (SI) are given in Table 5.1. These can be combined to give the derived units as shown in Table 5.2. Where these units are too large or too small for practical applications, multiples or submultiples of the units are used as shown in Table 5.3.

Dimensional standards

In Britain, length was once defined as the distance between the ends of a rod (yard-

Table 5.1 Base units

Quantity	Unit	Abbreviation
Length	metre	m
Mass	kilogram	kg
Time	second	s
Electric current	ampere	A
Temperature	kelvin	K
Luminous intensity	candela	cd
Amount of substance	mole	mol

Table 5.2 Some derived units

Quantity	Symbol	Derivation	Unit	Unit symbol
Force (weight)	F	mass × acceleration ($kg\ m/s^2$)	newton	N
Pressure (stress)	P	force per unit area (N/m^2)	pascal	Pa
Work	W ⎫			
Energy	E ⎬	force × distance moved (Nm)	joule	J
Power	P	work per unit time (J/s)	watt	W
Velocity	v	distance per unit time (m/s)	—	m/s
Acceleration	a	velocity per unit time (m/s^2)	—	m/s^2
Frequency	f	cycles per unit time (cycles/s)	hertz	Hz

Table 5.3 Multiples and submultiples

Multiple or submultiple	Prefix	Symbol
1 000 000 000 000 = 10^{12}	tera	T
1 000 000 000 = 10^9	giga	G
1 000 000 = 10^6	mega	M
1 000 = 10^3	kilo	k
1 = 10^0	—	—
0.001 = 10^{-3}	milli	m
0.000 001 = 10^{-6}	micro	μ
0.000 000 001 = 10^{-9}	nano	n
0.000 000 000 001 = 10^{-12}	pico	p

Examples
1 kilometre (km) = 1000 m
1 millimetre (mm) = 0.001 m
1 megahertz (MHz) = 1 000 000 Hz
1 microfarad (μF) = 0.000 001 F

stick) or, more recently, the distance between two lines scribed on gold plugs pressed into a bronze bar. The metre was, at that time, defined as the distance between two lines scribed on the central web of an X-shaped bar of platinum-iridium alloy kept in Paris. Unfortunately such physical standards tend to change in length over the years owing to molecular changes in the alloy. It was also difficult to make accurate copies of them for day-to-day use in factories and laboratories. The matter was further complicated by the fact that the American standard yard and the British standard yard were not the same. An attempt was made to overcome this by the adoption of the international standard yard, based on the metre (1 yard = 0.9144 metre), in 1960. At the same time, the Eleventh General Conference of Weights and Measures, held in Paris in 1960, redefined the metre in terms of wavelengths of light from a krypton isotope discharge lamp. The international standard yard was adopted as the British legal standard on 31 January 1964.

However, technology becomes increasingly demanding and an even more accurate standard has become necessary. Currently, the metre is defined as:

the length of the path travelled by laser light in 1/299 792 458 seconds. The light being realised through the use of an iodine stabilised helium-neon laser.

Such length standards can be reproduced to an accuracy of 3 parts in 10^{11}. This is equivalent to measuring the circumference of the world to within one millimetre. Unlike the old physical standards, every major physical laboratory and metrology laboratory can have their own standard of length. (Note: *metrology = science of fine measurement*. This should not be confused with *meteorology = science of climate and weather*).

Optical standards have a number of important advantages over material (metal-bar) standards. For instance:

(a) they do not change in length as a result of temperature changes or changes of molecular structure;
(b) damaged or destroyed standards can be replaced without loss of accuracy;
(c) identical copies can be kept in standards rooms and physical laboratories throughout the world;
(d) it is not only much easier to make comparative measurements with the new optical standards than it was with the old metal-bar standards, but the measurements themselves are to a much higher level of accuracy.

Only the largest companies or companies involved in the manufacture of measuring instruments would have their own laser standards. For the average engineering company their standard would be a set of inspection grade slip or block gauges. These would, in turn, be used to check and calibrate workshop grade slip gauges, dial test indicators, micrometer calipers, vernier calipers, rules, etc.

There is a hierarchy in the use of such standards. The firms specialising in calibration services to the engineering industry would have their equipment calibrated by the National Physical Laboratory (NPL) through the *National Measurement Accreditation Service* (NAMAS) — see Fig. 5.12. The firms offering a calibration service would then calibrate the standards (reference or inspection grade slip gauges) of small and medium-sized precision manufacturing companies. Large companies would have their own metrology departments who would deal direct with the NPL.

Technical terms and symbols

Technical terms, symbols and abbreviations are also standardised to provide a universal language for industry and to prevent errors resulting from misinterpretation

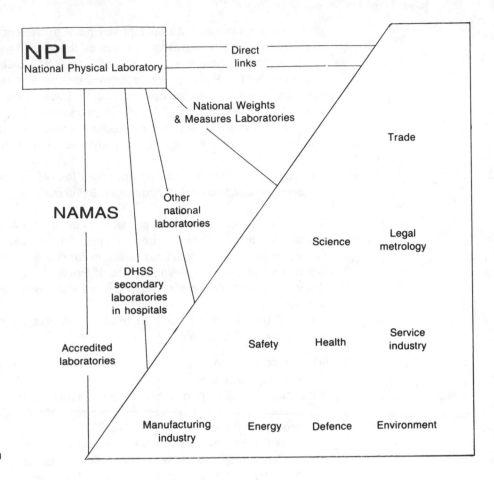

Fig. 5.12 National measurement system

of instructions. Examples of standard terms and symbols can be found in engineering drawings complying with BS 308. This standard was considered in Chapter 4.

Quality control in manufacture

To satisfy a typical product specification it is essential that:

(a) The quality specification for the materials used and the units of measurement have been clearly and accurately specified.
(b) The manufacturing equipment can operate within the accuracy defined.
(c) The measuring equipment available during manufacture and subsequent inspection is also capable of operating within the accuracy specified.
(d) The performance of the product and the performance testing procedure is also specified.

In addition to the quality specifications for the manufactured products, there are also quality specifications for measuring tools and equipment. For example, there are British Standard specifications for rules, micrometers, vernier calipers, slip gauges, dial test indicators, surface plates and a host of other items of measuring equipment.

These standards not only specify the initial quality and accuracy of such measuring devices but also specify recommendations for their testing, care and use.

The accuracy of inspection and testing equipment must be substantially greater than the accuracy of the dimensional feature being measured or gauged. As a general rule, inspection equipment should be ten times more accurate than the feature being measured or gauged.

Environmental standards in measurement

Standards rooms, metrology laboratories and inspection rooms require a controlled environment so that precision measurements can be carried out. The internationally agreed temperature for precision measurements is 20°C. The need for a constant, standard temperature is essential because most materials expand when heated and contract when cooled. This not only affects the linear dimensions of components but also causes distortion. Distortion is most likely to occur in assemblies made up from different materials with different rates of expansion when subject to the same temperature change.

5.4 Advantages of standards

In the early days of engineering each nut and bolt was made as a matched pair and could not be interchanged with any other nut and bolt. This was highly inconvenient and screw threads became the subject of the first steps in standardisation (see section 1.1). Nowadays we expect any M10 × 1.25 mm nut to fit any M10 × 1.25 mm bolt no matter where they are made. This level of interchangeability is only possible with the introduction and acceptance of international standards.

Standardised components can have other advantages. Not only is the quality guaranteed but, because of the increased volume of manufacture, costs are reduced and availability is increased. Further, costs can also be reduced through the interchangeability of standard components allowing non-selective assembly.

5.5 Measurement of length

Rules

These should be made from corrosion resistant spring steel or from matt chrome-plated spring-temper carbon steel. The markings should be engine engraved for clarity and accuracy, and the edges of the rule should be ground so that it can be used as a straight edge. The datum end should be ground square with the edges and should be protected from undue wear, as this will lead to measuring errors. You should never use a rule as a screw-driver or for cleaning out machine tee-slots. A steel rule should be thin to avoid sighting errors (see also section 5.8) and some methods of using a steel rule are shown in Fig. 5.13.

Calipers

You use calipers in conjunction with a rule in order to transfer distances between the edges or faces of a component to a rule in such a way as to reduce sighting errors.

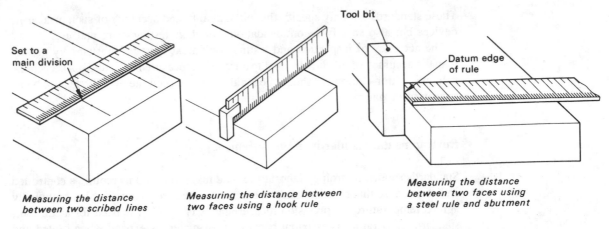

Set to a
main division

Tool bit

Datum edge
of rule

*Measuring the distance
between two scribed lines*

*Measuring the distance between
two faces using a hook rule*

*Measuring the distance
between two faces using
a steel rule and abutment*

Fig. 5.13 Use of the rule

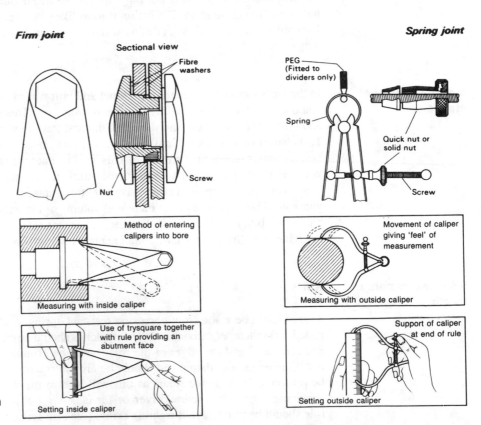

Fig. 5.14 Construction
and use of calipers

Firm joint calipers are used in the larger sizes and spring joint calipers are used for fine work, as in instrument-making and tool-making. Examples of internal and external calipers, both firm joint and spring joint, are shown in Fig. 5.14 together with examples of how to use them.

The accurate use of calipers depends upon a highly developed sense of feel that can only be acquired with practice. When using a caliper you should observe the following rules.

(a) Hold the caliper gently and near the joint.

(b) Hold it square to the work.

(c) No force should be used to 'spring' it over the work. Contact should only just be felt.

(d) The caliper should be handled and laid down gently to avoid disturbing the setting.

(e) When measuring work which is being machined, the machine must be turned off and *stationary* whilst taking measurements. This applies to all types of measuring instruments when measuring work which is being machined. It is essential for *safety* and *accuracy*.

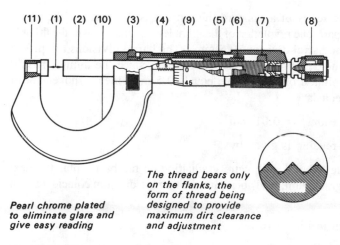

(1) **Spindle and anvil faces** — Glass hard and optically flat, also available with **Tungsten carbide** faces
(2) **Spindle** — Thread ground, and made from alloy steel, hardened throughout, and stabilised
(3) **Locknut** — effective at any position. Spindle retained in perfect alignment
(4) **Barrel** — Adjustable for zero setting. Accurately divided and clearly marked. Pearl chrome plated
(5) **Main nut** — Length of thread ensures long working life
(6) **Screw adjusting nut** — For effective adjustment of main nut
(7) **Thimble adjusting nut** — Controls position of thimble
(8) **Ratchet** — Ensures a constant measuring pressure
(9) **Thimble** — Accurately divided and every graduation clearly numbered
(10) **Steel frame** — Drop forged. Marked with useful decimal equivalents
(11) **Anvil end** — Cutaway frame facilitates usage in narrow slots

Pearl chrome plated to eliminate glare and give easy reading

The thread bears only on the flanks, the form of thread being designed to provide maximum dirt clearance and adjustment

Fig. 5.15 The micrometer caliper

Micrometer calipers

Most engineering work has to be measured to a much greater accuracy than is possible with a rule, even when aided by the use of calipers. To achieve this greater precision, measuring equipment of greater accuracy and sensitivity must be used.

One of the most familiar measuring instruments found in the workshop is the *micrometer caliper* (commonly called a 'micrometer'). The construction of a micrometer and details of its more important parts and features are shown in Fig 5.15. The operation of the micrometer depends upon the principle that the distance a nut moves along a screw is proportional to the number of revolutions made by the nut. Therefore by controlling the number of revolutions and fractions of a revolution made by the nut, the distance it moves along the screw can be accurately controlled. The movements of the screw and nut are relative. The same arguments apply if the nut remains stationary and the screw is rotated.

These principles are used in a micrometer caliper. The screw thread is rotated by the thimble which has a scale to indicate the 'partial' revolutions. The barrel of the instrument has a scale which indicates the 'whole' revolutions. In a standard metric micrometer the screw has a lead of 0.5 mm and the thimble and barrel are graduated as shown in Fig. 5.16.

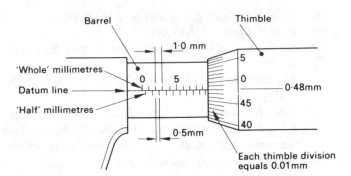

Fig. 5.16 Micrometer scales (metric)

Since the lead of the screw of a standard micrometer is 0.5 mm and the barrel divisions are 0.5 mm apart, one revolution of the thimble and screw moves the thimble along the barrel by one barrel division (0.5 mm). The barrel divisions are placed on alternate sides of the datum line for clarity. Further, since the thimble has 50 divisions and one revolution of the thimble equals 0.5 mm, then a movement of *one thimble division* equals:

(0.5 mm)/(50 divisions) = 0.01 mm

Thus the micrometer reading is given by:

The largest visible 'whole' millimetre graduation on the barrel plus the next 'half' millimetre graduation, if visible, plus the thimble division coincident with the datum line.

So, the reading shown in Fig. 5.16 is as follows:

9 'whole' millimetres	= 9.00
1 'half' millimetre	= 0.50
48 hundredths of a millimetre	= 0.48
Reading	= 9.98 mm

Unless a micrometer caliper is properly looked after it will soon lose its intial accuracy. To maintain this accuracy you should observe the following precautions:

(a) wipe the work and the anvils of the micrometer clean before making a measurement;
(b) do not use excessive measuring pressure, two 'clicks' of the ratchet is sufficient;
(c) do not leave the anvil faces in contact when not in use;
(d) when machining, stop the machine before making a measurement. Attempting to make a measurement with the machine working can ruin the instrument and also lead to a serious accident. This rule applies to all measuring instruments.

From time to time you should check a micrometer caliper and make any necessary adjustment using the special spanner found in its case. The procedures for making the adjustments are as follows:

(a) Any looseness in the screw can be taken up by a slight turn of the screw adjusting nut. (Refer back to item 6 in Fig. 5.15.)

(b) Zero error. Periodically the anvil faces should be wiped clean and carefully closed with normal measuring pressure (two 'clicks' of the ratchet). If the zero graduation of the thimble does not coincide with the datum line on the barrel, turn the barrel in the frame using the 'C' end of the spanner until the datum line does come into line with the zero graduation of the thimble. (Refer back to item 4 in Fig. 5.15.)

Although easy to read and convenient to use, micrometer calipers have two disadvantages:

(i) A limited range of only 25 mm. Thus a range of micrometers are required, for example, 0–25 mm, 25–50 mm, 50–75 mm, and so on.
(ii) Separate micrometers are required for internal and external measurements. The micrometer caliper so far described can only be used for external measurements. Other instruments using the micrometer principle are shown in Fig. 5.17.

Internal micrometer This is shown in Fig. 5.17(a). You can use it for measuring bore diameters and slot widths from 50 mm to 210 mm.

Cylinder gauge This is used for measuring smaller diameter holes to a high degree of accuracy and combines the micrometer principle with a wedge as shown in Fig. 5.17(b).

Depth micrometer This is used measuring the depth of holes and slots. You must take care when using a depth micrometer because its scales are reversed when compared with the familiar micrometer caliper. Also the measuring pressure tends to lift the micrometer off its seating. A depth micrometer is shown in Fig 5.17(c).

Vernier calipers

Although more cumbersome to use and rather more difficult to read, the vernier caliper has two main advantages over the micrometer caliper. First it can be used for both internal and external measurements, and second one instrument can be used for measurements ranging over the full length of its main (beam) scale. Figure 5.18 shows a vernier caliper and some typical applications. Remember that for internal measurements you have to add the combined thickness of the jaws to the scale readings. Unfortunately:

(a) it is difficult to obtain a correct 'feel' with this instrument due to its size and weight
(b) the scales can be difficult to read accurately even with a magnifying glass

All vernier type instruments have two accurately engraved scales. A main scale marked in standard increments of measurement like a rule, and a vernier scale which slides along the main scale. This vernier scale is marked with divisions whose increments are slightly smaller than those of the main scale. Some vernier calipers are engraved with both inch and millimetre scales.

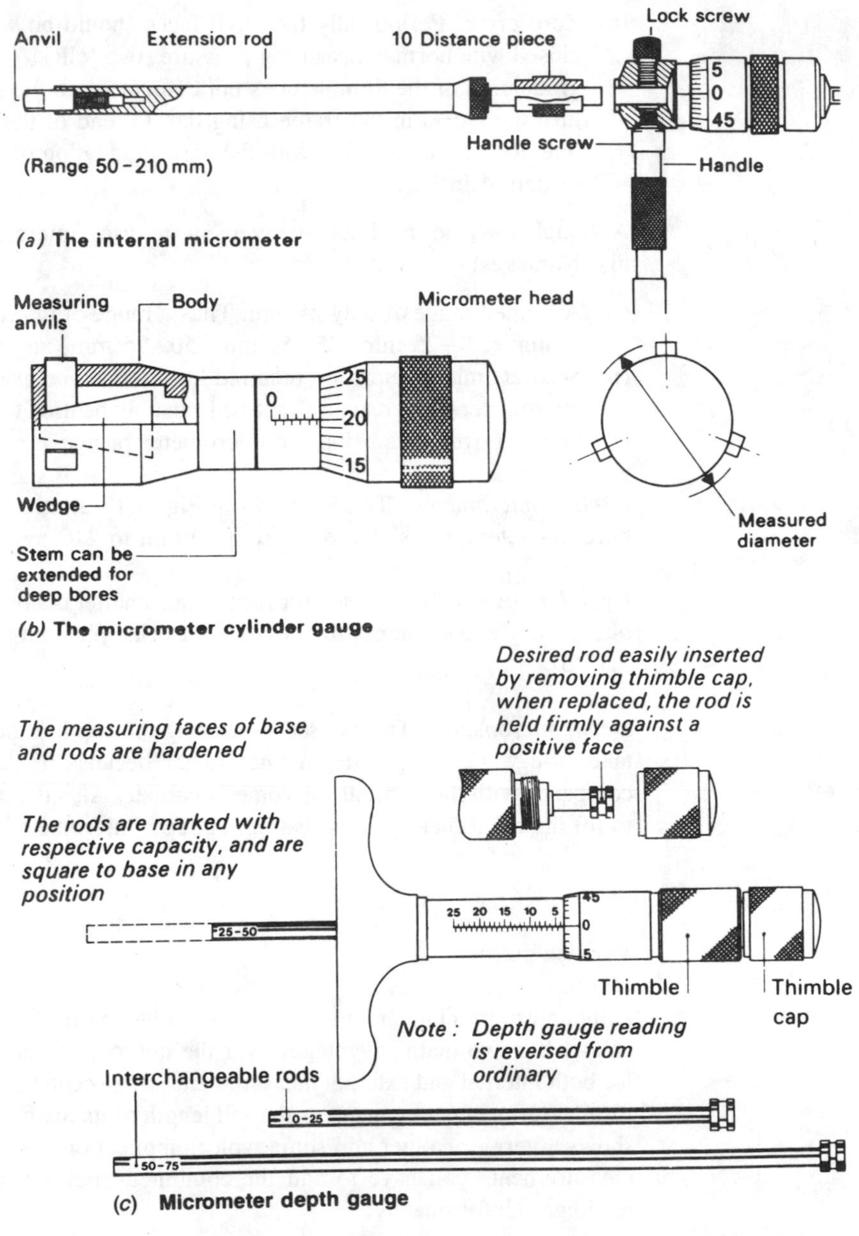

Anvil   Extension rod   10 Distance piece   Lock screw   5 0 45   Handle screw   Handle

(Range 50–210 mm)

(a) **The internal micrometer**

Measuring anvils   Body   Micrometer head   25 0 20 15   Measured diameter

Wedge

Stem can be extended for deep bores

(b) **The micrometer cylinder gauge**

The measuring faces of base and rods are hardened

The rods are marked with respective capacity, and are square to base in any position

Desired rod easily inserted by removing thimble cap, when replaced, the rod is held firmly against a positive face

25–50   25 20 15 10 5 45 0 5   Thimble   Thimble cap

Note : Depth gauge reading is reversed from ordinary

Interchangeable rods   0–25   50–75

Fig. 5.17 Further applications of the micrometer

(c) **Micrometer depth gauge**

In the example shown in Fig. 5.18(c) the main scale is marked off in 1.00 mm increments whilst the vernier scale has 50 divisions marked off in 0.98 mm increments. This enables you to read the instrument to an accuracy of $1.00-0.98 = 0.02$ mm. The reading is obtained as follows:

(a) note how far the zero of the vernier scale has moved along the main scale (32 'whole' millimetres in this example) ;

(b) note the vernier reading where the vernier and main scale divisions coincide (11 divisions in this example). You then multiply the 11 divisions by 0.02 mm which gives you 0.22 mm;

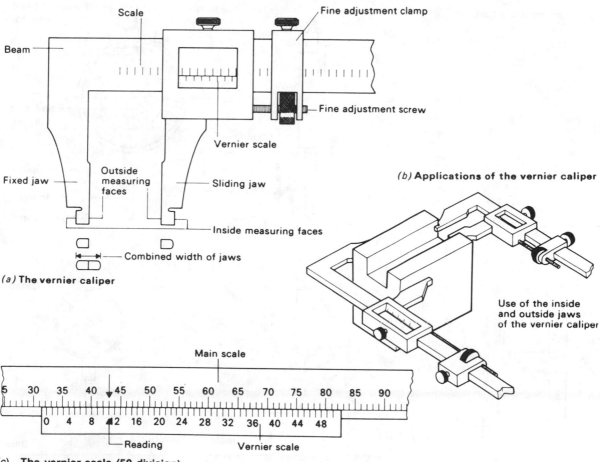

Fig. 5.18 The vernier caliper

(c) add these two readings together:

32 'whole' millimetres	= 32.00
11 vernier divisions	= 00.22
Reading shown in Fig. 5.18(c)	= 32.22 mm

Always check the scales before use as there are other systems available and not all vernier scales have 50 increments. This is particularly the case in some cheap intruments. Also check that the instrument reads zero when the jaws are closed. If not, then the instrument has been strained and will not give a correct reading. Battery operated direct reading digital calipers are also available, However, these tend to be heavier and more bulky and are often not so convenient to use as vernier calipers despite being easier to read. As for all measuring instruments, vernier calipers must be treated with care and cleaned before and after use. They should always be kept in the case provided.

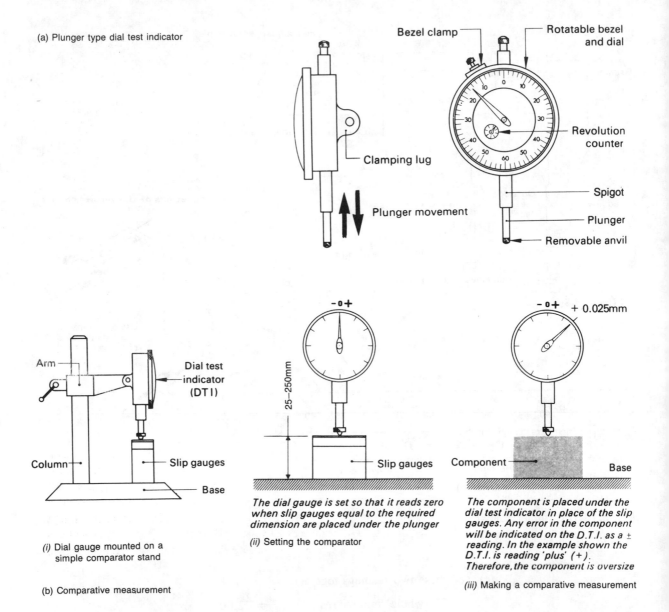

(a) Plunger type dial test indicator

Bezel clamp

Rotatable bezel and dial

Clamping lug

Plunger movement

Revolution counter

Spigot

Plunger

Removable anvil

Arm

Dial test indicator (DTI)

Column

Slip gauges

Base

(i) Dial gauge mounted on a simple comparator stand

(b) Comparative measurement

25–250mm

– o +

Slip gauges

The dial gauge is set so that it reads zero when slip gauges equal to the required dimension are placed under the plunger

(ii) Setting the comparator

– o +   + 0.025mm

Component

Base

The component is placed under the dial test indicator in place of the slip gauges. Any error in the component will be indicated on the D.T.I. as a ± reading. In the example shown the D.T.I. is reading 'plus' (+). Therefore, the component is oversize

(iii) Making a comparative measurement

Fig. 5.19 The plunger type dial test indicator (DTI)

Dial test indicators (DTI)

Dial test indicators are often referred to as 'clocks' because of the appearance of the dial and pointer. They measure the displacement of a plunger or stylus and indicate the magnitude of the displacement on a dial by means of a rotating pointer. There are two main types of dial test indicator.

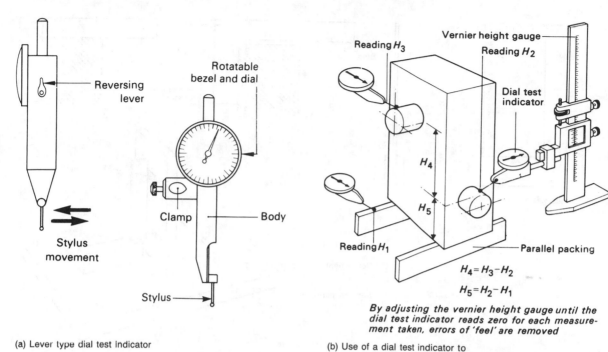

(a) Lever type dial test indicator

(b) Use of a dial test indicator to
ensure uniform measuring pressure

Fig. 5.20 The lever type dial test indicator (DTI)

Plunger type

This type relies upon a rack and pinion mechanism to change the linear (straight-line) movement of the plunger into rotary motion for the pointer. A gear train is used to magnify the movement of the pointer. This type of instrument has a long plunger movement and is, therefore, fitted with a secondary scale to count the number of revolutions made by the main pointer. A large range of dial diameters and markings are available. Figure 5.19(a) shows a typical example of this type of instrument and Fig. 5.19(b) shows how you can use one of these instruments to make comparative measurements.

Lever type

This type of instrument uses a lever and scroll to magnify the displacement of the stylus. Compared with the plunger type, the lever type instrument has only a limited range of movement. However, it is extremely popular for inspection and machine setting because it is more compact and the scale is more conveniently positioned for these applications. Figure 5.20(a) shows a typical example of this type of instrument and Fig. 5.20(b) shows an application of their use. In this example the DTI is mounted on a vernier height gauge. You can read about vernier height gauges in section 6.4. In this application the DTI is ensuring that the measuring, contact pressure over D_1 and D_2 is constant. That is, in each position, the vernier height gauge is adjusted until the DTI reads zero before the height gauge reading is taken.

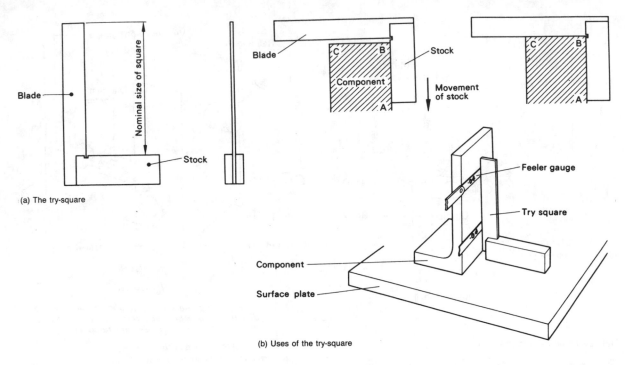

(a) The try-square

Blade

Nominal size of square

Stock

Blade

Stock

C B

Component

A

Movement of stock

C B

A

Feeler gauge

Try square

Component

Surface plate

(b) Uses of the try-square

Fig. 5.21 The try-square

5.6 Measuring angles

Right angles

Figure 5.21(a) shows a typical engineer's try-square and names its more important features. Try-squares are used for marking out and checking lines that are at right angles (90°) to an edge, or for checking that two surfaces are at right angles to each other. Two surfaces or lines at right angles to each other are said to be:

(a) perpendicular to each other;
(b) mutually perpendicular;
(c) 'square' to each other.

All of which mean the same thing. Try squares should comply with BS 939 and are made in three grades of accuracy:

AA = reference squares for standards rooms;
A = precision squares for checking and inspection;
B = general purpose squares for workshop use.

Figure 5.21(b) shows two applications of a try-square. In the first example the stock is placed against the edge AB of the work and slid gently downwards until the blade comes into contact with the edge BC. Any lack of squareness will allow light to be seen between the edge BC and the try-square blade. It is not always convenient to hold large work and a try-square up to the light. The second example shows an alternative method using a surface plate as a datum surface. The squareness

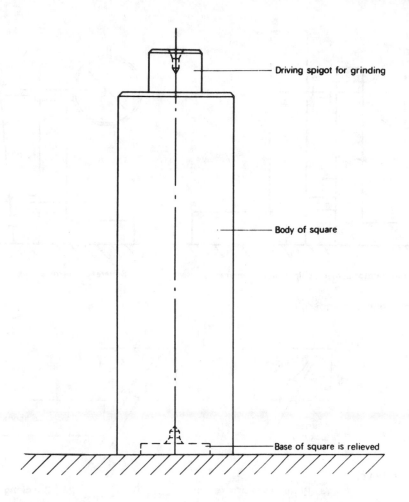

Driving spigot for grinding

Body of square

Base of square is relieved

Fig. 5.22 Cylinder square

of the component face is checked with feeler gauges as shown. If the face is square to the base the gap between it and the try-square blade will be constant.

Try-squares are precision instruments and they should be treated with care if they are to retain their initial accuracy. They should be kept clean and lightly oiled after use. They should not be dropped, nor should they be kept with other bench tools which may knock up burrs on the edges of the blade and stock. They should be checked for squareness at regular intervals.

In addition to try-squares, prismatic squares and cylinder squares (Fig. 5.22) may be used for checking large work. Their design ensures that they make line contact with the work. Figure 5.23 shows a squareness comparator being used in conjunction with a try-square.

Angles other than right angles

Figure 5.24 shows a simple bevel protractor for measuring angles of any magnitude between 0° and 180°. Such a protractor has only limited accuracy (±0.5°). Where

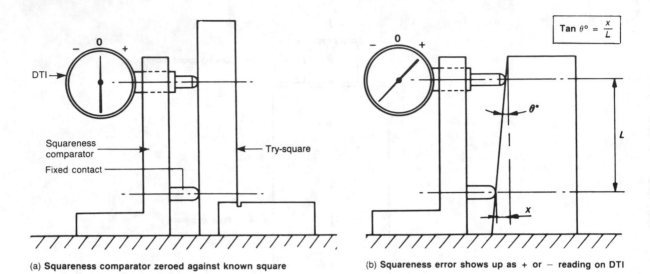

(a) **Squareness comparator zeroed against known square**

(b) Squareness error shows up as + or − reading on DTI

Fig. 5.23 Squareness comparator

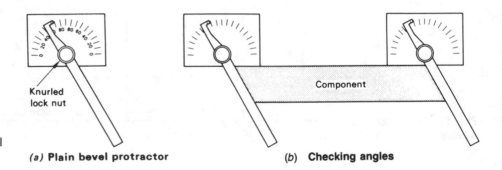

Fig. 5.24 Plain bevel protractor

(a) **Plain bevel protractor**

(b) **Checking angles**

greater accuracy is required the *vernier protractor* should be used. The scales of a vernier protractor are shown in Fig. 5.25. The main scale is divided into degrees of arc, and the vernier scale has 12 divisions each side of zero. These vernier scale divisions are marked 0 to 60 minutes of arc, so that each division is 1/12 of 60, that is 5 minutes of arc. The reading for a vernier protractor is given by the sum of:

(a) the largest 'whole' degree on the main scale as indicated by the vernier zero mark;
(b) the reading of the vernier scale division in line with a main scale division.

Thus the reading for the scales shown in Fig. 5.25. is:

17 'whole' degrees	= 17° 00′
vernier 25 mark in line with main scale	= 00 25′
Total angle	= 17° 25′

Vernier protractors are also available which can be read in degrees and decimal fractions of a degree.

Fig. 5.25 Vernier protractor scales

5.7 Dimensional deviation

In section 5.1 you read that it is impossible to work to an exact size and that it is impossible to measure to an exact size. Therefore allowance has to be made for dimensional deviation. To control this deviation, the designer specifies a range of dimensions within which the component will work satisfactorily. This is explained in Fig. 5.26. The upper and lower sizes are called the *limits* and the difference in size between the limits is called the *tolerance*. The terms associated with limits and fits can be summarised as follows:

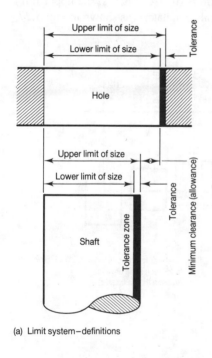

(a) Limit system – definitions

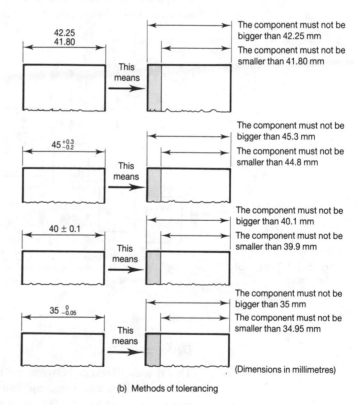

The component must not be bigger than 42.25 mm
The component must not be smaller than 41.80 mm

The component must not be bigger than 45.3 mm
The component must not be smaller than 44.8 mm

The component must not be bigger than 40.1 mm
The component must not be smaller than 39.9 mm

The component must not be bigger than 35 mm
The component must not be smaller than 34.95 mm

(Dimensions in millimetres)

(b) Methods of tolerancing

Fig. 5.26 Toleranced dimensions

Nominal size

This is the dimension by which a feature is identified for convenience. For example, a slot 25.15 mm actual width would be known as the 25 mm wide slot.

Basic size

This is the exact functional size from which the limits are derived by application of the necessary allowance and tolerances. The basic size and the nominal size are frequently the same.

Limits

These are the high and low values of size between which the size of a component feature may lie. For example, if the lower limit of a hole is 25.05 mm and the upper limit of the same hole is 25.15 mm, then a hole which is 25.1 mm diameter is 'within limits' and acceptable.

Tolerance

This is the arithmetic difference between the limits of size. That is, the upper limit minus the lower limit. Tolerances may be bilateral or unilateral as shown in Fig. 5.27.

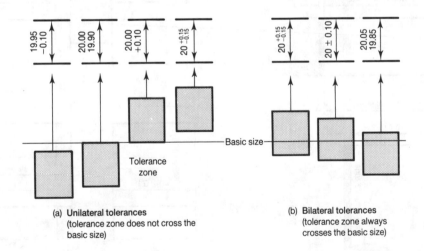

Fig. 5.27 Types of tolerance

(a) **Unilateral tolerances** (tolerance zone does not cross the basic size)

(b) **Bilateral tolerances** (tolerance zone always crosses the basic size)

Deviation

This is the difference between the basic size and the limits. The deviation may be *symmetrical*, in which case the limits are equally spaced above and below the basic size. For example, 50.00 ± 0.15 mm. Alternatively, the deviation may be *asymmmetrical*, in which case the deviation may be greater on one side of the basic size than on the other, e.g. 50.00 mm + 0.25 or −0.05.

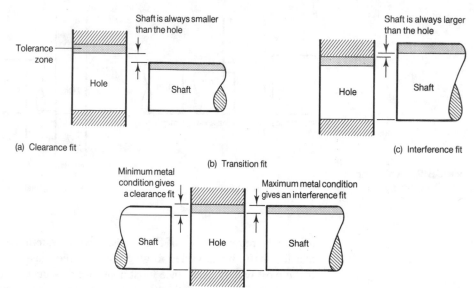

Fig. 5.28 Classes of fit

Mean size

This size lies halfway between the upper and lower limits of size and must not be confused with either the nominal size or the basic size. It is only the same as the basic size when the deviation is symmetrical.

Minimum clearance (allowance)

This is the clearance beween a shaft and a hole under maximum metal conditions. That is the largest shaft in the smallest hole that the limits will allow — the tightest fit between shaft and hole that will function correctly. With a *clearance* fit the allowance is positive. With an *interference* fit the allowance is negative (see Fig. 5.28).

Actual size

The measured size correct at 20°C.

Classes of fit

Figure 5.28 shows the classes of fit that may be obtained between mating components. In the *hole basis* system the hole size is kept constant and the shaft size is varied to give the required class of fit. In an *interference fit* the shaft is always slightly larger than the hole. In a *clearance fit* the shaft is always slightly smaller than the hole. A *transition fit* occurs when the tolerances are so arranged that under maximum metal conditions (largest shaft: smallest hole) an interference fit is obtained, and that under minimum metal conditions (largest hole: smallest shaft) a clearance fit is obtained.

In a *shaft basis* system the shaft size is kept constant and the hole size is varied

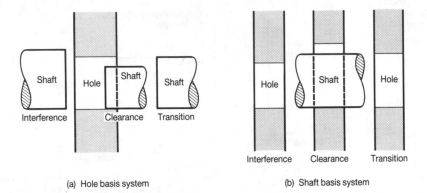

Fig. 5.29 Hole and shaft basis sytems

(a) Hole basis system

(b) Shaft basis system

to give the required class of fit. In a *hole basis* system the hole size is kept constant and the shaft size is varied to give the required class of fit. The hole basis sytem is the most widely used since most holes are produced by using standard tools such as drills and reamers. It is then easier to vary the size of the shaft by turning or grinding to give the required class of fit. Shaft and hole basis systems are shown in Fig. 5.29.

Tables of limits and fits and the instructions for their application to engineering components are set out in BS EN 20286-2 (previously BS 4500). A detailed study of BS EN 20286-2 is beyond the scope of this book, but I have included some typical ISO fits (hole basis) in Table 5.4. An example of the application of these standard limits and fits are shown in Fig. 5.30. Let's see how the system works.

The tables provide for twenty-eight types of shaft designated by lower-case letters, a, b, c, d, etc., and twenty-eight types of hole designated by upper-case letters, A, B, C, D, etc. To each type of shaft or hole the grade of tolerance is designated by a number 01, 0, 1, 2, ... 16, thus giving 18 grades of tolerance in all. The letter indicates the position of the tolerance relative to the basic size and is called the *fundamental deviation*. The number indicates the magnitude of the tolerance and is called the *fundamental tolerance*. A shaft is completely defined by its basic size, letter and number, e.g. 75 mm h6. Similarly a hole is completely defined by its basic size, letter and number, e.g. 75 mm H7 . Figure 5.30(a) shows how a precision

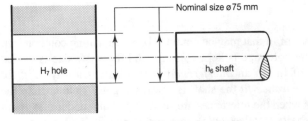

(a) Tolerance specification (precision clearance fit)

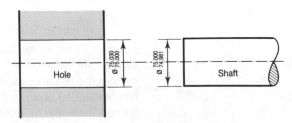

(b) Dimensional limits to give precision clearance fit as derived from BS 4500: 1969 (see text)

Fig. 5.30 Application of limits and fits

Table 5.4 Some selected ISO fits — hole basis. (Abstract from BS Data Sheet 4500A, derived from BS EN 20286-2)

Normal sizes		Loose clearance		Average clearance		Close clearance		Precision clearance		Transition clearance		Interference	
Over mm	Up to mm	H9	e9	H8	f7	H7	g6	H7	h6	H7	k6	H7	p6
—	3	+25 +0	−14 −39	+14 +0	−6 −16	+10 +0	−2 −8	+10 +0	−0 −6	+10 +0	+6 +0	+10 +0	+12 +6
3	6	+30 +0	−20 −50	+18 +0	−10 −22	+12 +0	−4 −12	+12 +0	−0 −8	+12 +0	+9 +1	+12 +0	+20 +12
6	10	+36 +0	−25 −61	+22 +0	−13 −28	+15 +0	−5 −14	+15 +0	−0 −9	+15 +0	+10 +1	+15 +0	+24 +15
10	18	+43 +0	−32 −75	+27 +0	−16 −34	+18 +0	−6 −17	+18 +0	−0 −11	+18 +0	+12 +1	+18 +0	+29 +18
18	30	+52 +0	−40 −92	+33 +0	−20 −41	+21 +0	−7 −20	+21 +0	−0 −13	+21 +0	+15 +2	+21 +0	+35 +22
30	50	+62 +0	−50 −112	+39 +0	−25 −50	+25 +0	−9 −25	+25 +0	−0 −16	+25 +0	+18 +2	+25 +0	+42 +26
50	80	+74 +0	−60 −134	+46 +0	−30 −60	+30 +0	−10 −29	+30 +0	−0 −19	+30 +0	+21 +2	+30 +0	+51 +32
80	120	+87 +0	−72 −159	+54 +0	−36 −71	+35 +0	−12 −34	+35 +0	−0 −22	+35 +0	+25 +3	+35 +0	+59 +37
120	180	+100 +0	−85 −185	+63 +0	−43 −83	+40 +0	−14 −39	+40 +0	−0 −25	+40 +0	+28 +3	+40 +0	+68 +43
180	250	+115 +0	−100 −215	+72 +0	−50 −96	+46 +0	−15 −44	+46 +0	−0 −29	+46 +0	+33 +4	+46 +0	+79 +50
250	315	+130 +0	−110 −240	+81 +0	−56 −108	+52 +0	−17 −49	+52 +0	−0 −32	+52 +0	+36 +4	+52 +0	+88 +56
315	400	+140 +0	−125 −265	+89 +0	−62 −119	+57 +0	−18 −54	+57 +0	−0 −36	+57 +0	+40 +4	+57 +0	+98 +62
400	500	+155 +0	−135 −290	+97 +0	−68 −131	+63 +0	−20 −60	+63 +0	−0 −40	+63 +0	+45 +5	+63 +0	+108 +68

clearance fit is specified using a 75 mm H7/h6 hole and shaft combination. Reference to Table 5.4 shows that the hole dimensions will be:

$$75 \text{ mm} + 0.030$$
$$+ 0.000$$

and the shaft dimension will be:

$$75 \text{ mm} - 0.000$$
$$- 0.019$$

Figure 5.30(b) shows how these dimensions are applied to the component drawing.

Table 5.5 Standard tolerance grades (see BS EN 20286-2, previously BS 4500)

Nominal sizes		Tolerance grades																		
Over (mm)	Up to and including (mm)	IT1†	IT2†	IT3†	IT4†	IT5†	IT6	IT7	IT8	IT9	IT10	IT11	IT12	IT13	IT14*	IT15*	IT16*	IT17*	IT18*
		(μm)											(mm)						
—	3†	0.8	1.2	2	3	4	6	10	14	25	40	60	0.1	0.14	0.25	0.4	0.6	1	1.4
3	6	1	1.5	2.5	4	5	8	12	18	30	48	75	0.12	0.18	0.3	0.48	0.75	1.2	1.8
6	10	1	1.5	2.5	4	6	9	15	22	36	58	90	0.15	0.22	0.36	0.58	0.9	1.5	2.2
10	18	1.2	2	3	5	8	11	18	27	43	70	110	0.18	0.27	0.43	0.7	1.1	1.8	2.7
18	30	1.5	2.5	4	6	9	13	21	33	52	84	130	0.21	0.33	0.52	0.84	1.3	2.1	3.3
30	50	1.5	2.5	4	7	11	16	25	39	62	100	160	0.25	0.39	0.62	1	1.6	2.5	3.9
50	80	2	3	5	8	13	19	30	46	74	120	190	0.3	0.46	0.74	1.2	1.9	3	4.6
80	120	2.5	4	6	10	15	22	35	54	87	140	220	0.35	0.54	0.87	1.4	2.2	3.5	5.4
120	180	3.5	5	8	12	18	25	40	63	100	160	250	0.4	0.63	1	1.6	2.5	4	6.3
180	250	4.5	7	10	14	20	29	46	72	115	185	290	0.46	0.72	1.15	1.85	2.9	4.6	7.2
250	315	6	8	12	16	23	32	52	81	130	210	320	0.52	0.81	1.3	2.1	3.2	5.2	8.1
315	400	7	9	13	18	25	36	57	89	140	230	360	0.57	0.89	1.4	2.3	3.6	5.7	8.9
400	500*	8	10	15	20	27	40	63	97	155	250	400	0.63	0.97	1.55	2.5	4	6.3	9.7
500	630*	9	11	16	22	32	44	70	110	175	280	440	0.7	1.1	1.75	2.8	4.4	7	11
630	800*	10	13	18	25	36	40	80	125	200	320	500	0.8	1.25	2	3.2	5	8	12.5
800	1000*	11	15	21	28	40	56	90	140	230	360	560	0.9	1.4	2.3	3.6	5.6	9	14
1000	1250*	13	18	24	33	47	66	105	165	260	420	660	1.05	1.65	2.6	4.2	6.6	10.5	16.5
1250	1600*	15	21	29	39	55	78	125	195	310	500	780	1.25	1.95	3.1	5	7.8	12.5	19.5
1600	2000*	18	25	35	46	65	92	150	230	370	600	920	1.5	2.3	3.7	6	9.2	15	23
2000	2500*	22	30	41	55	78	110	175	280	440	700	1100	1.75	2.8	4.4	7	11	17.5	28
2500	3150*	26	36	50	68	96	135	210	330	540	860	1350	2.1	3.3	5.4	8.6	13.5	21	33

Note: Values for standard tolerance grades IT01 and IT0 for basic sizes less than or equal to 500 mm are given in ISO 286-1, annex A, table 5

* Values for standard tolerance grades IT1 to IT5 for basic sizes over 500 mm are included for experimental use

† Standard tolerance grades IT14 to IT18 shall not be used for basic sizes less than or equal to 1 mm

5.8 Accuracy

The greater the accuracy demanded by a designer, the narrower will be the tolerance band and the more difficult and costly will it be to manufacture the component within the limits specified. Table 5.5 shows the standard international (IT) tolerance bands. As the tolerance grade number (IT number) gets bigger, the tolerance gets bigger and the dimension becomes less precise and easier to achieve. You will also notice that as the nominal dimension gets bigger, tolerance gets bigger for any given IT number. This is because the larger a dimension becomes, the more difficult it becomes to hold any given level of accuracy. For example, a tolerance of 0.175 mm on a 2250 mm dimension has a greater accuracy than a tolerance 0.084 mm on a 22.5 mm dimension. Therefore, for ease of manufacture at minimum cost, a designer never specifies an accuracy greater than is necessary to ensure the correct functioning of the component. Table 5.6 relates various manufacturing processes to the accuracy (IT number) which can be expected from them under normal workshop conditions.

The method of dimensioning can also affect the overall accuracy of a component. Figure 5.31(a) shows how incremental (chain) dimensioning can cause a progressive error to build up. This is called a *cumulative* error. Figure 5.31(b) shows how dimensioning from a datum (absolute dimensioning) prevents a cumulative error building up.

5.9 Factors affecting accuracy

The more important factors affecting accuracy when measuring components are as follows.

Temperature

All metals and alloys expand when heated and contract when cooled. This is why measuring should take place in a constant temperature environment (see section 5.3). You may have noticed that when you are machining materials in a workshop they often become hot. A component which has been heated by the cutting process will shrink whilst cooling to room temperature. This may result in a component which was within limits when measured on the machine being found to be undersize when it is checked in the temperature contolled inspection room.

Casting patterns and forging dies have to be made oversize to allow for shrinkage so that when the hot metal cools the components will not be undersize. The pattern maker usually works to a *contraction rule*. This has a normal scale on one side and an expanded scale on the other. By working to the expanded scale, the pattern maker automatically allows for the shrinkage that takes place as the casting metal solidifies and cools. Different rules have to be used for different casting metals, the expansion of the scale being matched to a particular metal.

Accuracy of equipment

Since it is not possible to manufacture components to an exact size nor is it possible to measure them to an exact size, it follows that measuring equipment cannot be made to an exact size either. Therefore measuring equipment also has to be

Table 5.6 Process accuracy

IT number	Class of work
16	Sand casting, flame cutting
15	Stamping
14	Die casting, plastic moulding
13	Presswork, and extrusion
12	Light presswork, tube drawing
11	Drilling, rough turning, boring
10	Milling, slotting, planing, rolling
9	Low grade capstan and automatic lathe work
8	Centre lathe, capstan and automatic
7	High quality turning, broaching, honing
6	Grinding, fine honing
5	Machine lapping, fine grinding
4	Gauge making, precision lapping
3	High quality gap gauges
2	High quality plug gauges
1	Slip gauges, reference gauges

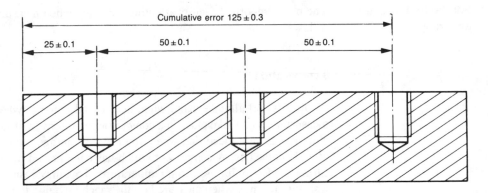

(a) Incremental dimensioning. Cumulative tolerance equals sum of individual tolerances

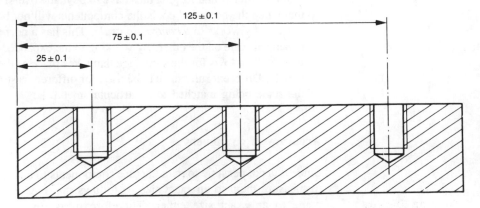

Fig. 5.31 Cumulative error

(b) Absolute dimensioning from one common datum to eliminate the cumulative effect

manufactured to toleranced dimensions. In order that this has the minimum effect upon the measurement being made, the accuracy of a measuring instrument should be about ten times greater than the accuracy of the component being measured.

Measuring equipment should be checked regularly against even more accurate equipment. Where possible any errors should be corrected by adjustment. If this is not possible, and the error has reached significant proportions, the instrument has to be discarded. In the case of standards such as slip gauges, these are checked against even more accurate standards. The actual deviation of size for each slip is charted. This is called calibration and it allows the cumulative error to be calculated, and allowance for this deviation can be made when building up a stack of slip gauges.

Reading errors

There are two main reading errors:

Misreading the instrument scales. Vernier scales are particularly difficult to read unless you have very good eyesight, so it is advisable to use a magnifying glass. When using rules and similar scales, care must be taken to ensure that your eye is over the point of measurement (*parallax* or sighting errors). The use of a solid abutment, as previously shown in Fig. 4.13, avoids you having to sight two points at the same time. Parallax or sighting errors can be minimised by using a rule which is as thin as possible. Reference to Fig 5.32 shows that:

(a) 'M' represents the mark on the work whose position you want to measure by means of a rule laid alongside it. The graduations are on the upper side of the rule, as shown.

(b) If your eye is positioned along the sighting line A−M, which is at right-angles to the work surface, a true reading will be obtained at 'a', for it is then directly opposite 'M',

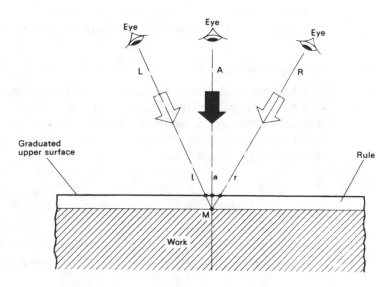

Fig. 5.32 Effect of parallax

(c) If, however, your eye is not on this sighting line but displaced to the right, as at 'R', the division 'r' on the rule scale will appear to be opposite 'M'. This will give you an incorrect reading. Similarly if your eye is displaced to the left, as at 'L' an incorrect reading on the opposite side as at 'l' will result.

Type of equipment

It is possible to measure linear dimensions and angles with a variety of instruments. However, the accuracy of measurement is always lower than the reading accuracy and will depend, largely, upon the skill of the user.

Line and end measurement

Line measurement

As its name suggests, this is the measurement of the distance between two lines or two edges when measured with an instrument such as a steel rule where the distance to be measured is compared directly with an engraved scale. Sighting errors (parallax) makes the measurement of the distance between two lines particularly difficult as datum abutments cannot, in this instance, be used. Dividers can be used to transfer the measurement. When setting the divider points to the lines, one leg of the dividers is 'clicked' into a main division on the rule and only the position on the rule scale of the second leg has to be sighted and read. The difference between the scale positions is the required measurement.

The measurement of the distance between an edge and a line is also difficult when using a line measuring instrument such as a rule. The difficulties of such measurements can be eased by the use of a datum abutment which has already been shown in Fig. 5.13.

The difficulties associated with the measurement of the distance between two edges or across a diameter using a line measuring instrument can be eased with the aid of calipers. The use of calipers has already been shown in Fig. 5.14.

End measurement

This is the preferred method of measurement for the engineer who is mostly concerned with the measurement of distances between faces, edges and across diameters. This measuring technique uses instruments such as micrometer calipers and vernier calipers where the edges or faces to be measured are in contact with the anvils or jaws of the measuring instrument and no sighting is required.

Effect of force

The use of excessive force when closing the measuring instrument on the workpiece being measured can cause distortion of both the workpiece and of the measuring

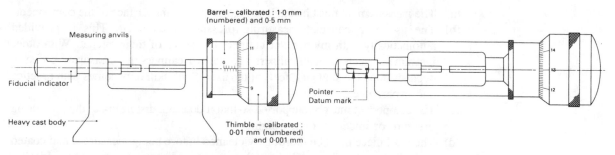

The fiducial indicator removes errors of 'feel'. The micrometer is 'zeroed' with the pointer of the fiducial indicator in line with its datum mark. All subsequent measurements are made with the pointer in this position. This ensures constant measuring pressure

Fig. 5.33 The bench micrometer

instrument resulting in an incorrect reading. In the worst case the distortion is permanent and either the workpiece or the measuring instrument or both become worthless and have to be destroyed.

Some instruments are fitted with devices which ensure a correct and safe measuring pressure automatically. For example, three 'clicks' of the ratchet of a micrometer caliper applies the correct measuring force. The bench micrometer shown in Fig. 5.33 has a measuring force indicator (fiducial indicator) in place of the fixed anvil. When the pointers are in line, the correct measuring pressure is being applied. The force on the plunger of a DTI is limited by the strength of its return spring.

The contact area of the jaws or anvils of the measuring instrument can also influence the measuring pressure. This is because pressure is defined as force per unit area and, for any given measuring force, the contact pressure varies inversely as the contact area. Reduce the area and the measuring pressure is increased. Increase the contact area and the pressure is reduced. A spherically ended stylus will, in theory, result in point contact and this will give rise to an infinitely high measuring pressure. In practice the spherical end on the stylus tends to sink into the surface being measured, thus increasing the contact area. At the same time the spherical end of the stylus tends to flatten and this, again, increases the contact area. Any increase in the contact area results in a decrease in measuring pressure and a balance is automatically achieved between the measuring pressure and the resistance to deformation of the material of the component being measured. Such deformation introduces measuring errors and damage to the finished surfaces of the component being measured. Such effects are marginal where components are made from relatively hard metals but they must be taken into account when measuring components made from softer materials such as some plastics.

Correct use of measuring equipment

No matter how accurately measuring equipment is made, and no matter how sensitive it is, one of the most important factors affecting the accuracy of measurement is the skill of the user. The more important procedures for the correct use of measuring equipment can be summarised as follows.

(a) The measurement must be made at right angles to the surface of the component.

(b) The use of a constant measuring pressure is essential. This is provided automatically with micrometer calipers by means of their ratchet. With other instruments such as plain calipers and vernier calipers the measuring pressure depends upon the skill and 'feel' of the user. Such skill only comes with practice and experience.

(c) The component must be supported so that it does not distort under the measuring pressure or under its own weight.

(d) The workpiece must be thoroughly cleaned before being measured, and coated with oil or a corrosion-inhibiting substance immediately after inspection. Ideally, gloves should be worn so that the acid in your perspiration does not corrode the cleaned surfaces of the instruments and the workpiece.

(e) Measuring instruments must be handled with care so that they are not damaged or strained. They must be cleaned and kept in their cases when not in use. Their bright surfaces should be lightly smeared with petroleum jelly (Vaseline). Measuring instruments must be regularly checked to ensure that they have not lost their intial accuracy. If an error is detected the instrument must be taken out of service immediately.

5.10 Terminology of measurement

Indicated size

This is the size indicated by the scales of a measuring instrument when it is being used to measure a workpiece. The indicated size makes no allowance for any incorrect use of the instrument, such as the application of excessive contact pressure.

Reading

This is the size as read off the instrument scales by the operator. Errors can occur by the user misreading the scales, for example, sighting (parallax) errors can occur when measuring with a rule. Vernier scales are particularly easy to misread in poor light. A magnifying lens is helpful even in good light and even if you have good eyesight. Electronic measuring instruments with digital readouts overcome many of these reading difficulties.

Reading value

Also called the *reading accuracy*, this is the smallest increment of size that can be read directly from the scales of the instrument. It will depend upon the layout of the scales. For example, micrometer calipers normally have a reading value of 0.01 mm, a bench micrometer fitted with a fiducial indicator will have a reading value of 0.001 mm, a vernier caliper with a 50 division vernier scale may have a reading value of 0.02 mm or 0.01 mm.

Measuring range

This is the range of sizes which can be measured by any given instrument. It is the arithmetical difference between the largest size which can be measured and the smallest size which can be measured. For example, a 50 mm to 75 mm micrometer has a measuring range of $75 - 50 = 25$ mm.

Measuring accuracy

This is the actual accuracy expected from a measuring instrument after taking into account all the normal errors of usage as considered in section 4.9. It can never be better than the indicated size and it is defined as the maximum allowable deviation relative to the indicated measurement.

5.11 Miscellaneous measuring equipment

Surface plates and tables

You have already been introduced to the use of surface plates for checking for the flatness of a workpiece surface. You can also use surface plates and tables as a datum when measuring as shown in Fig. 5.34(a). The use of surface plates and tables when marking out will be described in Chapter 6. A typical cast iron surface plate is shown in Fig. 5.34(b) and you can see that the underside of the plate has a heavily ribbed construction. This provides rigidity, yet keeps the overall mass of metal to a minimum. Surface tables are similar but they are very much bigger and are free standing. Surface plates are smaller, portable and are used on a bench. The advantages of using grey cast iron for making surface plates and tables are as follows.

(a) The graphite present in grey cast iron renders it self-lubricating. This enables measuring equipment and marking out equipment to be slid about on the working surface of the plate or the table easily and with a pleasant feel.

(b) The metal is easily cast into complex shapes so that stiffening ribs can be incorporated into the design.

(c) Once it has been rough machined and weathered, the castings become very stable and are unlikely to warp with age. Grey cast iron can be easily machined and scraped flat. It is also relatively inexpensive.

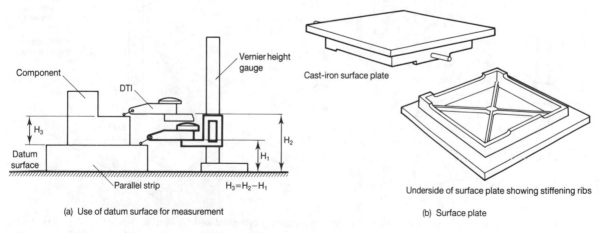

(a) Use of datum surface for measurement

(b) Surface plate

Fig. 5.34 Surface plate and its use for measurement

Granite is also used for large surface tables. This material is also very dense and stable. It has the added advantage that, unlike cast iron, it does not throw up a burr if it is accidentally scratched. Unfortunately, unlike grey cast iron, granite is not self lubricating and does not have such a pleasant feel when sliding measuring instruments about on it.

V-blocks

Figure 5.35(a) shows a pair of V-blocks. They are used to support cylindrical work as shown in Fig 5.35(b), and they may also be used for supporting rectangular section work at 45° to the horizontal as shown in Fig 5.35(c). V-blocks are manufactured in matched pairs so that long cylindrical work may be supported parallel to a datum surface. For this reason V-blocks must always be kept as a pair as initially supplied.

Spirit levels

Figure 5.36 shows the principle of a spirit level. The curved glass tube (the vial) is partly filled with a liquid and sealed. The bubble of air trapped in the tube and the liquid are both acted upon by the force of gravity. Since the liquid has the higher density it is pulled down to the bottom of the tube and the bubble always floats to the top.

The accuracy of the level always depends upon the curvature of the vial. The larger the radius of curvature the greater will be the sensitivity of the level. Curved tubes are sufficiently accurate for carpenters' and builders' levels but they are not accurate enough for engineers' precision levels. For these, the bore of a thick walled glass

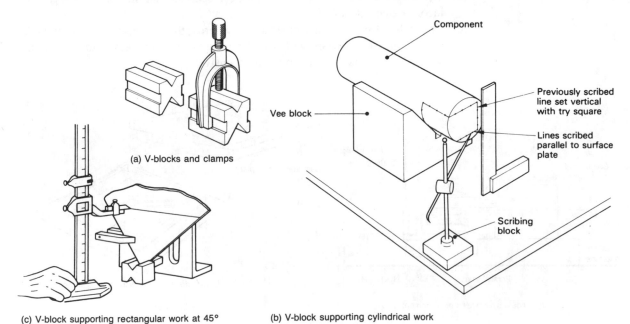

(a) V-blocks and clamps

Component

Vee block

Previously scribed line set vertical with try square

Lines scribed parallel to surface plate

Scribing block

(c) V-block supporting rectangular work at 45°

(b) V-block supporting cylindrical work

Fig. 5.35 V-blocks

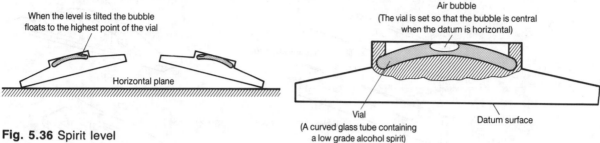

When the level is tilted the bubble floats to the highest point of the vial

Horizontal plane

Fig. 5.36 Spirit level

Air bubble
(The vial is set so that the bubble is central when the datum is horizontal)

Vial
(A curved glass tube containing a low grade alcohol spirit)

Datum surface

tube is ground out to a barrel shape. The ends are sealed after filling. Pecision levels are made to BS 958 and the sensitivity can be expressed in two ways.

(i) The sensitivity can be expressed in seconds of arc. Thus a 10 second level means that tilting the level through an angle of 10 seconds of arc will displace the bubble by one scale division on the vial.

(ii) A level can be said to have a sensitivity of 0.05 mm/m. This means that if such a level is placed on a 1 m long straight edge and if one end of the straight edge is raised through 0.05 mm then the bubble will be displaced by one scale division on the vial.

Spirit or bubble levels, as they are also called, must be carefully handled to prevent damage and they must never be dropped. Before use the ground base must be carefully cleaned and, after use, the bright surfaces must be protected from corrosion by lightly smearing with petroleum jelly (Vaseline).

When a level is used, two readings should always be taken. The level is turned through 180° between the readings and the mean of the readings is the true reading. If there is a difference of more than one scale increment between the readings the level must be adjusted.

Straight edges

These may be rectangular or bevel edged as shown in Fig. 5.37(a) or they may be made from cast iron as shown in Fig. 5.37(b). They can be used for checking straightness and flatness as shown in Fig. 5.37(c) or as an aid to scribing long, straight lines.

Gauges

Plug gauges

These were introduced as non-indicating instruments in section 5.1. Some typical gauges are shown in Fig. 5.38(a). They are used for checking internal dimensions such as toleranced hole diameters. If the hole lies within the design limits, the GO gauge element will enter the hole and the NOT GO element will not enter the hole.

Caliper gauges

Also called *gap gauges* and *snap gauges*, these are used for checking whether an

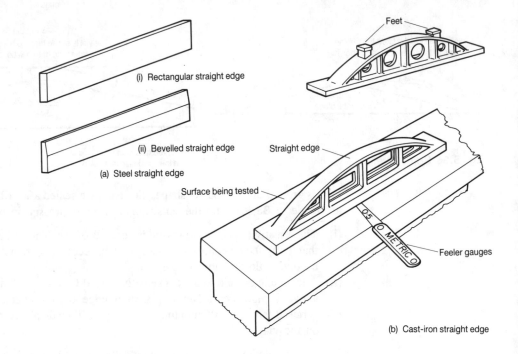

(i) Rectangular straight edge

(ii) Bevelled straight edge

(a) Steel straight edge

Feet

Straight edge

Surface being tested

Feeler gauges

Fig. 5.37 Straight edges

(b) Cast-iron straight edge

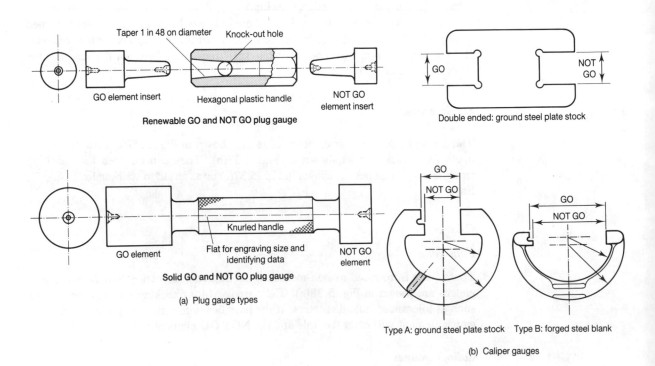

Taper 1 in 48 on diameter

Knock-out hole

GO element insert

Hexagonal plastic handle

NOT GO element insert

Renewable GO and NOT GO plug gauge

GO

NOT GO

Double ended: ground steel plate stock

GO element

Knurled handle

Flat for engraving size and identifying data

NOT GO element

Solid GO and NOT GO plug gauge

(a) Plug gauge types

GO

NOT GO

GO

NOT GO

Type A: ground steel plate stock   Type B: forged steel blank

(b) Caliper gauges

Fig. 5.38 Plug and caliper gauges

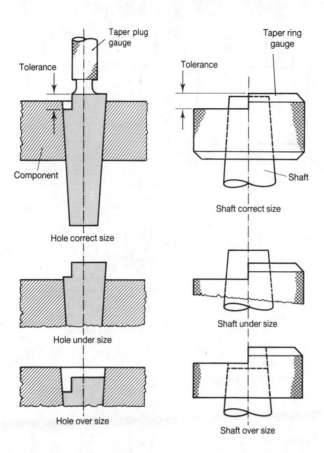

Fig. 5.39 Taper plug and ring gauges

external dimension such as the width of a component or the diameter of a component is within the design tolerance. If the component is correct it will enter berween the GO jaws but will not enter between the NOT GO jaws. Some typical gauges are shown in Fig. 5.38(b).

Taper plug and ring gauges

These are used for checking the size of tapered holes and shafts. Some typical stepped taper gauges are shown in Fig. 5.39. If the taper is the correct size the upper surface of the workpiece lies within the step as shown. A taper plug gauge is only designed to check the size of the taper: it is not designed to measure the angle of taper. However, if a little engineer's blue is smeared down the gauge and the gauge is inserted into the hole some of the blue will be left on the wall of the hole. The taper plug gauge should now be cleaned and inserted once more into the hole. If the angle of taper of the hole is the same as that of the plug, the 'smear' left on the gauge will be parallel as shown in Fig 5.40. If the angle is incorrect the 'smear' will be tapered as shown.

Radius gauges

These are supplied in sets and provide a range of internal and external radii in incremental steps. Figure 5.41(a) shows a typical application.

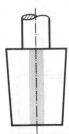  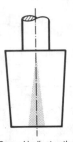

'Smear' indicates that hole has same taper as plug gauge

'Smear' indicates that hole has a **smaller** angle of taper than the gauge

'Smear' indicates that hole has a **larger** angle of taper than the gauge

Fig. 5.40 Checking the angle of taper

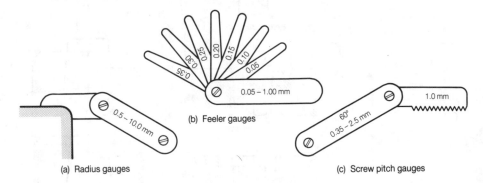

Fig. 5.41 Miscellaneous gauges

(a) Radius gauges   (b) Feeler gauges   (c) Screw pitch gauges

Feeler gauges

These can be used to check and set clearances between components. A typical set is shown in Fig. 5.41(b). The blades are arranged in incremental steps. For example, a typical range could be: 0.05 mm to 1.00 mm thickness in steps of 0.05 mm. In such a set there would be one blade of 0.05 mm and the remaining blades would increase in steps of 0.10 mm. The blades are used singly or in combination.

Screw pitch gauges

These are used for checking the pitch of screw threads. They are available with 55° and 60° included thread angles and in metric and inch pitches. A typical set is shown in Fig. 5.41(c).

5.12 General rules for accurate measurement

This chapter has covered many techniques of measurement and has recommended many procedures for ensuring accurate measurement. The general rules for accurate measurement may be summarised as follows.

(a) Measuring equipment should be between two and ten times as accurate as the dimension being measured (the latter figure being achieved wherever possible). The same rule applies to gauges for checking dimensions.

(b) Accuracy is improved if the measured dimension is as close to the mean dimension as possible.

(c) Accuracy is improved if the setting master used in comparative measurement is as close as possible to the dimension being measured.

(d) Wherever possible the measurement should be taken at the standard temperature of 20°C.

(e) Measuring equipment must be carefully and correctly used. Excessive measuring forces must be avoided so that the equipment is not strained nor the work distorted. Measuring equipment must be cleaned before and after use and wiped over with a corrosion preventative before putting it away. The equipment must be inspected for errors and damage before use and there should be a regular programme of maintenance and recalibration.

(f) Measuring equipment must never be mixed up with other bench tools and cutting tools. After use each item of measuring equipment must be returned to its case. The maker's recommendations for maintaining the equipment in good condition must always be observed.

Exercises

1 A 'go' and 'not go' plug gauge is used to
   (a) determine the exact diameter of a hole
   (b) measure the exact depth of the hole
   (c) check whether the diameter of the hole lies within the design limits
   (d) check whether the depth of the hole lies within the design limits

2 An example of an 'indicating' measuring instrument is a
   (a) caliper (snap) gauge
   (b) taper plug gauge
   (c) vernier height gauge
   (d) slip gauge

3 To avoid errors due to parallax an engineer's rule should be
   (a) as thin as possible
   (b) as thick as possible
   (c) satin chrome finished
   (d) engine engraved

4 The purpose of the metal block in Fig. 5.42 is to
   (a) improve measuring accuracy
   (b) reduce wear on the datum end of the rule
   (c) compensate for wear on the datum end of the rule
   (d) prevent the component from slipping

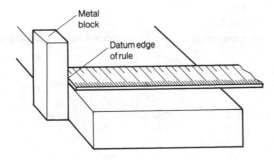

Fig. 5.42

5 If two surfaces are said to be mutually perpendicular, they are
    (a) parallel to each other
    (b) at 180° to each other
    (c) inclined to each other
    (d) at 90° to each other

6 Flatness is the amount by which a surface
    (a) is smooth
    (b) is free from machining marks
    (c) is horizontal
    (d) deviates from a true plane

7 Concentric diameters
    (a) have a common axis
    (b) lack roundness
    (c) are always tapered
    (d) do not have a common axis

8 The ISO standard of length is
    (a) the international standard yard
    (b) the metre
    (c) the kilometre
    (d) the millimetre

9 The ISO standard measuring temperature is
    (a) 18°C
    (b) 65°F
    (c) 20°C
    (d) 70°F.

10 A screw with a thread specification of M12 × 1.25 will have a
    (a) diameter of 1.25 mm and 12 threads per metre
    (b) diameter of 12 mm and a pitch of 1.25 mm
    (c) diameter of 12 mm and 1.25 threads per millimetre
    (d) diameter of 1.25 mm and a pitch of 12 μm

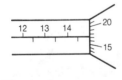

Fig. 5.43

11 The reading of the metric micrometer scales shown in Fig. 5.43 is:
    (a) 14.77 mm
    (b) 14.67 mm
    (c) 14.72 mm
    (d) 15.17 mm

12 When using a micrometer a constant measuring pressure can be obtained by turning the
    (a) thimble
    (b) barrel
    (c) anvil
    (d) ratchet

13 The vernier scale shown in Fig. 5.44 has a reading accuracy of 0.02 mm. The

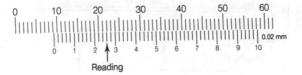

Fig. 5.44

Reading

reading shown is
    (a) 9.00 mm
    (b) 9.23 mm
    (c) 9.26 mm
    (d) 22.23 mm

14 When measuring an internal diameter with a vernier caliper, the jaw thickness should be
    (a) ignored
    (b) divided by the reading
    (c) subtracted from the reading
    (d) added to the reading

15 Figure 5.45 shows a DTI being used to measure the thickness of a component. The measured thickness is
    (a) 24.97 mm
    (b) 25.00 mm
    (c) 25.03 mm
    (d) 25.30 mm

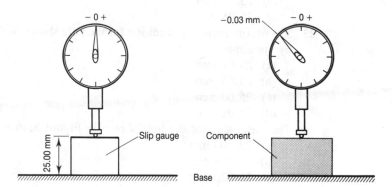

Fig. 5.45

16 The most suitable instrument for measuring an angle of $30° \pm 1°$ is a
    (a) bevel protractor
    (b) vernier protractor
    (c) try-square
    (d) micrometer protractor

17 The wider the tolerance on a dimension, the
    (a) greater will be the accuracy and the lower will be the cost
    (b) lower will be the accuracy and the greater will be the cost
    (c) greater will be the accuracy and the greater will be the cost
    (d) lower will be the accuracy and the lower will be the cost

18 The accuracy of measuring and gauging equipment should be
    (a) less than the accuracy of the dimension being checked
    (b) the same as the accuracy of the dimension being checked
    (c) greater than the accuracy of the dimension being checked
    (d) unrelated to the accuracy of the dimension being checked

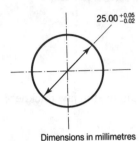

25.00 $^{+0.05}_{-0.02}$

Dimensions in millimetres

Fig. 5.46

19 The nominal size of the hole shown in Fig. 5.46 is
    (a) 25.05 mm
    (b) 25.00 mm
    (c) 24.98 mm
    (d) 0.07 mm

20 The tolerance for the hole shown in Fig. 5.46 is
    (a) 25.05 mm
    (b) 25.00 mm
    (c) 24.98 mm
    (d) 0.07 mm

21 The tolerance for the hole shown in Fig. 5.46 is
    (a) bilaterial
    (b) unilateral
    (c) multilateral
    (d) monolateral

22 The upper limit of size for the hole shown in Fig 5.46 is
    (a) 25.00 mm
    (b) 25.07 mm
    (c) 25.02 mm
    (d) 25.05 mm

23 The maximum metal condition for the hole showr in Fig. 5.46 would be given by the dimension
    (a) 25.07 mm
    (b) 25.05 mm
    (c) 25.00 mm
    (d) 24.98 mm

24 The mean size for the hole shown in Figure 5.46 is
    (a) 25.000 mm
    (b) 25.015 mm
    (c) 25.020 mm
    (d) 25.070 mm

25 A high measuring pressure
    (a) is required to ensure a firm contact with the workpiece
    (b) is liable to cause measuring errors by distorting the workpiece and the instrument
    (c) will have no effect on the measuring accuracy
    (d) will penetrate any dirt on the surface of the workpiece

26 The reading value of a measuring instrument is the
    (a) smallest increment which can be read directly from the scales
    (b) actual size of the feature being measured
    (c) user's interpretation of the indicated size
    (d) same thing as the indicated size

27 The measuring acuracy of a measuring instrument is
    (a) always better than the indicated size
    (b) the same as the indicated size
    (c) unrelated to the indicated size
    (d) never better than the indicated size

28 Surface plates are usually made from granite or
    (a) mild steels
    (b) stainless steel
    (c) cast iron
    (d) cast phophor bronze
29 The gauge shown in Fig. 5.47 is used to
    (a) measure a radius
    (b) measure a diameter
    (c) check a radius
    (d) check a diameter

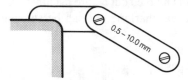

Fig. 5.47

30 The sensitivity of a spirit (bubble) level depends upon
    (a) the length of the vial
    (b) the radius of curvature of the vial
    (c) the diameter of the vial
    (d) the liquid used in the vial

6 Marking out

For most jobbing work, prototype work, small quantity production and toolmaking, the components are usually marked out before manufacture. The purposes, advantages and disavantages of manual marking out can be summarised as follows.

Purposes and advantages

(a) To provide guide-lines which are worked to, and which provide the only control for the size and shape of the finished component. This is only suitable for work of relatively low accuracy.

(b) To indicate the outline of the components to a machinist as an aid to setting and roughing out. The final dimensional control would come, in this instance, from the use of precision measuring instruments in conjunction with the micrometer dials on the machine itself.

(c) To ensure that adequate machining allowances have been left on castings and forgings; that webs, flanges and cores have not been incorrectly positioned or displaced during the casting processes; that holes will be positioned centrally in their bosses after machining (see Fig. 6.1).

Disadvantages

(a) Scribed lines cut into the surface of the workpiece and deface the surface of the metal. Where the surface finish is important, the workpiece must be surface ground to remove the scribing marks. Any marks cut into the surface of the metal are a potential source of fatigue failure and can also lead to cracking during heat treatment.

(b) The above disadvantages cannot be overcome by the use of drawn pencil lines since these are too thick, indistinct, and inaccurate to work to for precision engineering. Drawn lines are used for indicating fold lines when working in tin plate and galvanised steel where penetration of the protective coating by a scribing point would lead to corrosion.

(c) Centre punch marks may not control the drill point with sufficient accuracy unless the metal is heavily indented and, even then, total control cannot be guaranteed. Heavy centre punching can lead to distortion of the component.

When you draw lines on paper you use a sharp pencil. Sometimes this will be used for freehand sketching but, for engineering drawing, guidance is given to your pencil

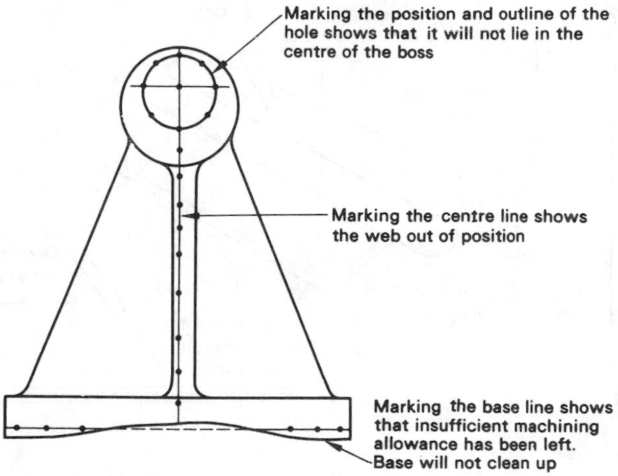

Marking the position and outline of the hole shows that it will not lie in the centre of the boss

Marking the centre line shows the web out of position

Marking the base line shows that insufficient machining allowance has been left. Base will not clean up

Fig. 6.1 Checking a casting

by such devices as T-squares, set squares and templates. Circles and arcs of circles are drawn with compasses or radius templates. You quickly find that accurate drawing and maintaining a uniform line thickness is not easy. The drawing accuracy would certainly not be good enough for producing the component itself. Fortunately you can dimension the drawing and state the required size, so that it does not matter even if your drawing is a bit 'out'.

Marking out on metal in the workshop has to be to a much higher level of accuracy if the lines produced are to provide satisfactory guidance. The lines also have to be much more permanent than a pencil line.

Drawn lines

These are produced by a pencil and are easily wiped off the metal surface. Further, drawing on a hard metal surface quickly blunts the pencil point and prevents a clean, sharp line being drawn. The only time a pencil line is used is to draw the fold lines on tin plate or galvanised plate. The pencil does not cut through the protective coating. Damage to the protective coating allows corrosion to take place.

Scribed lines

For the majority of engineering purposes you use a *scribed* line. This is a fine line cut into the metal surface by means of a scribing tool with a hardened point. A typical scriber is shown in Fig. 6.2(a). The mark left by a scriber is permanent. To make it easier to see the scribed line the surface of the metal being marked out is coated with a thin film of contrasting colour. For example, castings are often whitewashed, whilst bright metal surfaces are usually coated with a thin film of quick-drying layout ink. The correct way to use a scriber is shown in Fig. 6.2(b).

As well as producing scribed lines with a hand held scriber, lines parallel to a datum surface or a datum edge can be produced with a surface gauge (scribing block) as shown in Fig. 6.3 together with some typical applications.

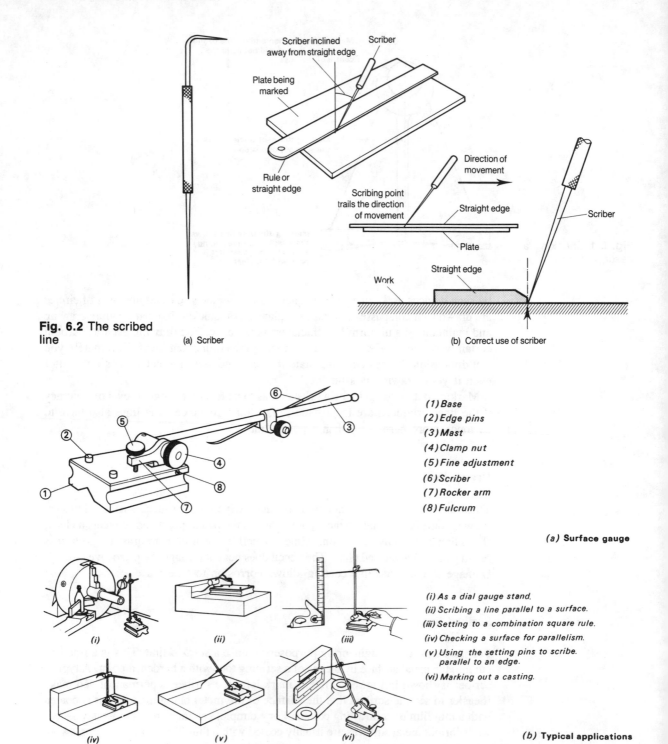

Fig. 6.2 The scribed line

(a) Scriber

(b) Correct use of scriber

(1) Base
(2) Edge pins
(3) Mast
(4) Clamp nut
(5) Fine adjustment
(6) Scriber
(7) Rocker arm
(8) Fulcrum

(a) **Surface gauge**

(i) As a dial gauge stand.
(ii) Scribing a line parallel to a surface.
(iii) Setting to a combination square rule.
(iv) Checking a surface for parallelism.
(v) Using the setting pins to scribe parallel to an edge.
(vi) Marking out a casting.

(b) **Typical applications**

Fig. 6.3 The surface gauge (scribing block)

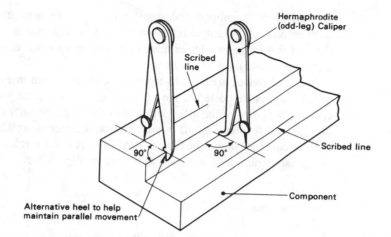

Fig. 6.4
Hermaphrodite
calipers (odd-legs)

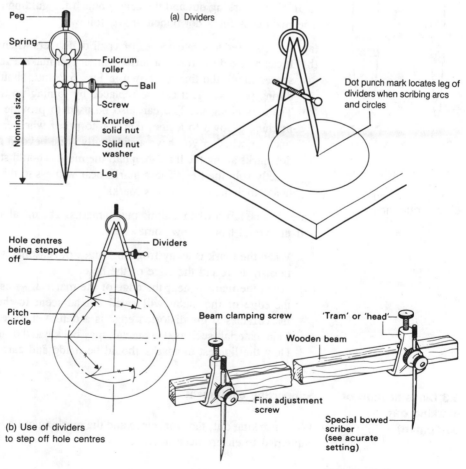

Fig. 6.5 Dividers and
trammels

Hermaphrodite calipers (odd-legs) may also be used to produce lines parallel to a datum edge. An example is shown in Fig. 6.4. This instrument gets its name from the fact that it has one leg similar to that of an external caliper and the other leg similar to those used in dividers.

Arcs and circles are scribed using dividers as shown in Fig. 6.5(a). One leg of the dividers is supported at the centre of the arc or circle and, as the dividers are rotated, the point of the other leg scribes the required arc or circle. Dividers may also be used for stepping off regular distances either along a straight line or around a pitch circle as shown in Fig. 6.5(b). For arcs and circles of larger radii, beam compasses (trammels) are used as shown in Fig. 6.5(c).

Centre marks

Centre marks can be made with either a dot punch as shown in Fig. 6.6(a), or a centre punch as shown in Fig. 6.6(b). You use the dot punch with its 60° point angle as an aid to marking out and the centre punch for guiding the point of a twist drill. The main uses for a dot punch are as follows.

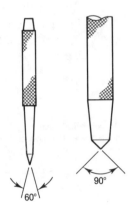

(a) Dot punch (b) Centre punch

Fig. 6.6 Dot and centre punches

(a) It can be used to locate one leg of a pair of dividers when scribing circles and arcs.
(b) It can be used to protect a scribed line. You make a series of fine dots equally spaced along the line as shown in Fig. 6.7 and, should the line be destroyed during processing, it can be replaced by joining up the dots with a new line.
(c) The dots along the line can also be used to provide 'witness marks'. When machining down to a line, there is no proof whether you have just 'split the line', or whether you have accidentally gone beyond it. However, if there are dot marks along the line, then half the marks should still be visible if you have exactly split the line. These marks bear witness to the accuracy of your work, hence their name, 'witness marks'.

Care must be taken when making punch marks. The metal around the mark is spread and this metal has to flow somewhere.

(a) When the mark is away from the edges of reasonably thick material a burr is thrown up round the edge of the hole.
(b) When the mark is near the edge of the material — especially thin material — the edge of the metal will swell out adjacent to the mark. This can cause inaccuracies if the distorted edge is a datum surface.
(c) Thin material, such as sheet metal, may buckle and distort when centre punched. Only the lightest of marks should be made and care must be taken.

6.3 Classification of marking out equipment

Supporting equipment

When marking out, the workpiece and the marking out equipment must be suitably supported to ensure accuracy.

Datum surface

Datum surfaces were introduced in section 5.10. A datum surface was described

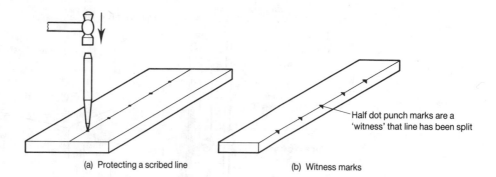

Half dot punch marks are a
'witness' that line has been split

(a) Protecting a scribed line   (b) Witness marks

Fig. 6.7 Protecting a
scribed line

as a common basis for measurement. For example, if the doctor was measuring your height, the floor would not only provide a common basis of measurement for you and the measuring device, but it would also provide support for you and the measuring device as well. In engineering it would not be very convenient or accurate to use the floor as a datum, so you will use surface plates and surface tables instead.

Surface plate

An example of a surface plate was shown in Fig 5.34. It was stated at the time that it can be used for testing flatness and that it can also be used as a datum surface for measuring. It can also be used for supporting the workpiece being marked out as well as providing datum surface for supporting the marking out equipment as shown in Fig. 6.8.

Marking out table

A surface plate is normally supported on a bench and is used when marking out small components. A marking out table is free-standing on its own legs and and can be used when marking out both small and large work.

Angle plates

These are used for supporting work at right angles to a surface plate or a marking out table as shown in Fig. 6.8.

V-blocks

These were introduced in Fig. 5.35 as a means of supporting cylindrical work during measurement. Similarly they may be used to support cylindrical work whilst marking out.

6.4 Measuring equipment

In order to ensure a scribed line is the correct length or in the correct position measuring equipment is required. Such equipment can be classified as those devices from which dimensions are transferred and those devices with which or along which scribed lines are made.

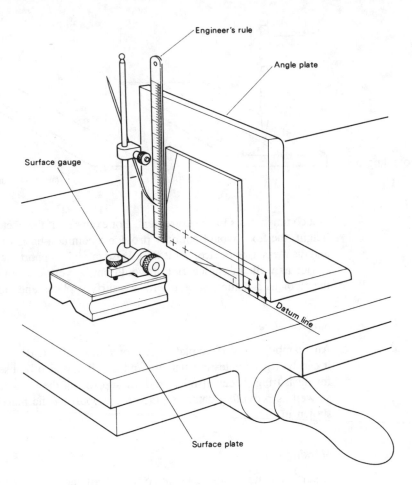

Engineer's rule

Angle plate

Surface gauge

Datum line

Surface plate

Fig. 6.8 Marking out
from a datum surface

Marking out using dimensions taken from a datum

Devices from which dimensions are transferred

The most obvious of these is the steel rule. It can be used:

(a) To make direct measurements as was shown in Fig. 5.13.
(b) For use with a scribing block as shown in Fig. 6.8. The datum end of the rule must be in contact with the surface plate or marking out table on which the work is supported directly. Allowance must be made for the thickness of the parallel strip on which the work is supported if a parallel strip is used.
(c) For setting dividers as shown in Fig. 6.9(right). One leg is 'clicked' into a main division and the other is adjusted to the appropriate scale division.
(d) For setting hermaphrodite (odd-leg) calipers as shown in Fig. 6.9(left). In this instance the datum end of the rule is used. This is why it is important to treat a rule carefully so that this end is not damaged. Never use a rule as a screwdriver or to remove swarf from a machine T-slot.

A *combination set* is shown in Fig 6.10 together with some typical applications.

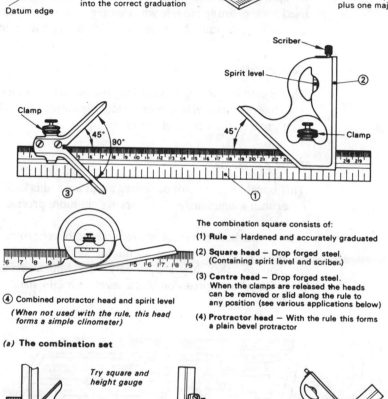

Fig. 6.9 Setting dividers and odd-leg calipers

Rule

Datum edge

The point should be 'clicked' into the correct graduation

Dividers

Rule

Locate one leg in first major division

Adjust the other leg to 'click' into the required division plus one major division

Scriber

Spirit level

②

Clamp

Clamp

45°

90°

45°

③

①

④ Combined protractor head and spirit level

(When not used with the rule, this head forms a simple clinometer)

The combination square consists of:

(1) Rule — Hardened and accurately graduated

(2) Square head — Drop forged steel. (Containing spirit level and scriber.)

(3) Centre head — Drop forged steel. When the clamps are released the heads can be removed or slid along the rule to any position (see various applications below)

(4) Protractor head — With the rule this forms a plain bevel protractor

(a) **The combination set**

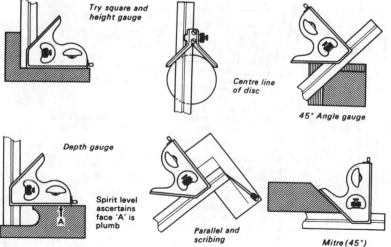

Try square and height gauge

Centre line of disc

45° Angle gauge

Depth gauge

Spirit level ascertains face 'A' is plumb

A

Parallel and scribing

Mitre (45°)

Fig. 6.10 The combination set

(b) **Uses of the combination set**

(Courtesy of Moore and Wright Ltd)

The combination set consists of a strong and relatively thick steel rule onto which can be fitted various sttachments. These can be clamped at any position along the rule.

Mitre square

This can be used as a try-square for marking out angles at 90° or as a mitre gauge for marking out angles at 45° or as a depth gauge for measuring the depths of slots as shown. It can also be used for scribing lines parallel to an edge. It can also be used for supporting the rule when setting a scribing block. In this instance the datum end of the rule must be in contact with the surface plate or marking out table.

Centre square

This is used for finding and marking out the axial centre of circular bars and blanks. Two lines are scribed at approximately right angles to each other and the point where they cross is the centre of the circle.

Bevel protractor

This is a plain protractor of limited accuracy and is used for scribing lines at angles other than a right angle. For marking out more precise angles a vernier protractor should be used.

Note that both the mitre square and the bevel protractor attachments have built in spirit levels. These are useful for setting work in machines but it must be remembered that they are of only very limited accuracy compared with such instruments as a precision block level or a clinometer.

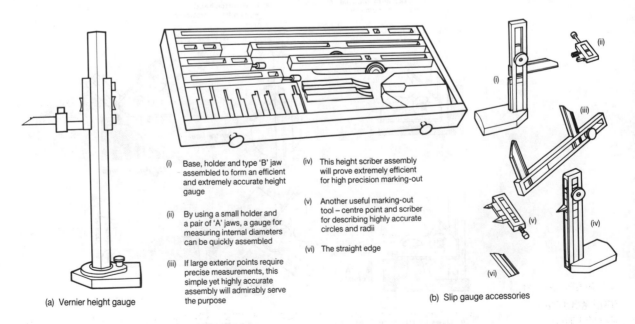

(i) Base, holder and type 'B' jaw assembled to form an efficient and extremely accurate height gauge

(ii) By using a small holder and a pair of 'A' jaws, a gauge for measuring internal diameters can be quickly assembled

(iii) If large exterior points require precise measurements, this simple yet highly accurate assembly will admirably serve the purpose

(iv) This height scriber assembly will prove extremely efficient for high precision marking-out

(v) Another useful marking-out tool – centre point and scriber for describing highly accurate circles and radii

(vi) The straight edge

(a) Vernier height gauge

(b) Slip gauge accessories

Fig. 6.11 Precision marking out equipment

Devices with which or along which scribed lines are made

So far we have only considered marking out to the limited accuracy which can be achieved with a steel rule or with the rule of a combination set. Where greater accuracy is required, the following equipment should be used.

Vernier height gauge

A vernier height gauge is shown in Fig 6.11(a). The scribing point can be set accurately. The height set is the distance from the datum foot of the instrument to the underside of the scribing blade. Thus the foot of the instrument and the workpiece being marked out must both be supported on a common datum surface. If the work has to be raised on a parallel strip, the thickness of the strip must be accurately measured with a micrometer or a vernier caliper and this measurement must be added to the required dimension when setting the height gauge. The scales are read in exactly the same way as the scales of a vernier caliper.

Slip gauges and accessories

Where even greater accuracy is required, slip gauges and slip gauge accessories may be used as shown in Fig. 6.11(b). It is very unlikely you will be called upon to mark out to this level of accuracy.

Straight edges

These were introduced in section 5.11. Straight edges with a bevelled edge can also be used as a guide for your scriber when scribing long straight lines. However, it is more usual to use the edge of a steel rule. This is why you should use a good quality rule with ground edges and why you must look after it carefully and not leave it lying about with other bench tools.

Try-squares

These can be used for guiding your scriber when scribing lines at right angles to a datum edge. They are more accurate than the mitre square attachment of a combination set. This is because the mitre square is adjustable along the rule so that not only can wear take place but dirt can get between the contact faces of the square and the rule.

Box square

This is used for marking out straight lines parallel to the axis of cylindrical components. An example is shown in Fig. 6.12.

6.5 Materials for marking out equipment

Steel

Hardened and tempered medium carbon steels (upper range) are used for rules, straight edges, parallel strips and try-squares. Such steels are also used for centre

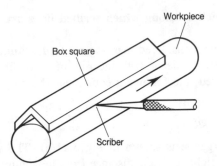

Workpiece

Box square

Scriber

Fig. 6.12 The box square

punches and dot punches. Hardened and tempered high carbon steels are used for all scribing tools which have to maintain a sharp scribing point or edge.

Cast iron

Grey cast iron is used extensively for surface plates, marking out tables, angle plates and the larger sizes of parallel blocks and V-blocks. Cast iron is a dense, stable material which is easily cast to shape and machined. Its graphite content renders it self-lubricating. This latter property allows steel marking out equipment to slide smoothly over a machined or hand scraped cast iron surface.

Carbide

Metal carbides are extremely hard wearing and are being increasingly used for facing the contact points of measuring instruments; for example, the anvils of micrometers. It is also being used increasingly for the scribing points and edges where it retains its sharpness over long periods without having to be re-sharpened. For example, it is used for tipping the blades of vernier height gauges.

6.6 Datum points, lines, edges and surfaces

A datum has already been described as a fixed point, line, edge or surface from which a measurement can be taken. The distance from a datum to some feature of a component such as a hole centre is called an *ordinate*. In practice two such dimensions are required to fix the position of a feature on a flat surface. The two ordinates are called *coordinates*. There are two systems of coordinates in common use.

Coordinates

(a) *Rectangular coordinates*. The feature is positioned by a pair of ordinates (coordinates) lying at right angles to each other and at right angles to the two axes or the two datum edges from which they are measured. This system requires the preparation of two mutually perpendicular datum edges from which the dimensions can be taken before marking out can commence. Figure 6.13(a)

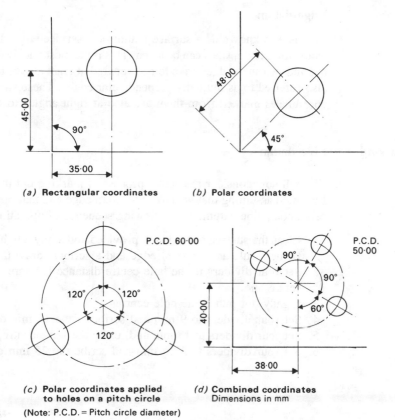

(a) Rectangular coordinates

(b) Polar coordinates

(c) Polar coordinates applied to holes on a pitch circle

(d) Combined coordinates
Dimensions in mm

Fig. 6.13 Coordinates   (Note: P.C.D. = Pitch circle diameter)

shows an example of the centre of a hole dimensioned by means of rectangular coordinates.

(b) *Polar coordinates*. In this instance the coordinates consist of a linear distance and an angular displacement. Dimensioning by this technique is often employed when holes are located around a pitch circle or when machining is taking place on a rotary table. Figure 6.13(b) shows how the centre of a hole can be dimensioned using polar coordinates and Fig. 6.13(c) shows how polar coordinates are applied to a pitch circle. In practice, polar coordinates rarely occur in isolation and are combined with rectangular coordinates as shown in Fig. 6.13(d).

Point datum

This is a single point from which dimensions can be taken when measuring and marking out. For example, the centre point of a pitch circle.

Line datum

This is a single line from which or along which dimensions are taken when measuring and marking out. It is frequently the centre line of a symmetrical component.

Edge datum

This is also known as a surface datum or a service edge. It is a physical surface from which dimensions can be taken. This is the most widely used datum for marking out and two such edges have to be prepared at right angles to each other. They are also referred to as mutually perpendicular edges. These two edges ensure that the coordinates marked from them are also at right angles to each other.

6.7 Use of marking out equipment

Line datum

We will now consider the actual process of marking out the component shown in Fig. 6.14 assuming that we have no datum edge and that we will have to draw and rely upon a line datum. The following sequence of operations refers to Fig. 6.15.

1. Clean the surface of the blank provided and apply a light coating of layout ink. Using a rule as a straight edge and a scriber, draw the centre line.
2. Set your dividers to the hole centre distance (75 mm) and step off along the centre line.
3. Lightly dot punch the hole centres.
4. Set your dividers to 9 mm and scribe in the 18 mm diameter hole.
5. Set your dividers to 18 mm and, using the same centre, scribe the end radius.
6. Set your dividers to 12.5 mm and scribe the 25 mm diameter hole.

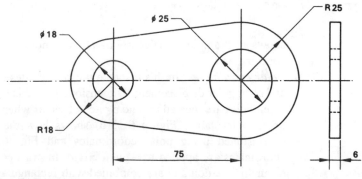

Fig. 6.14 Link

Dimensions in mm

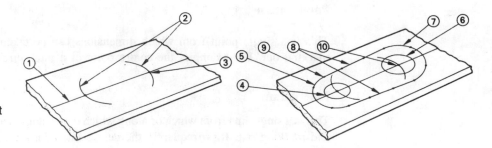

Fig. 6.15 Marking out from a centre line datum

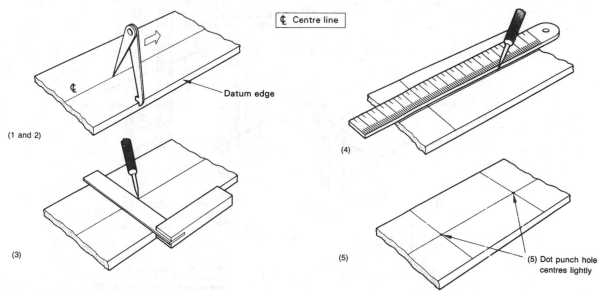

Fig. 6.16 Marking out from a datum edge

7. Set your dividers to 25 mm and, using the same centre, scribe the end radius.
8. Join the 18 mm and 25 mm radii with tangential lines using a rule as a straight edge to guide your scriber.
9. Dot punch the outline of the link.
10. Enlarge the hole centre punch marks with a centre punch ready for drilling. This completes the marking out.

Single edge datum

The following sequence of operations refers to Fig. 6.16.

1. Clean the surface of the blank and apply a light coat of marking out lacquer.
2. Scribe the centre line using odd-leg calipers.
3. Scribe the first hole centre line at right angles to the datum edge using a try-square.
4. Mark off the centre distance to the second hole using your rule and scriber.
5. Scribe the second hole centre line at right angles to the datum edge using a try-square, and dot punch the centre points.
6. The remaining operations are the same as (4) to (10) inclusive in the first example.

Mutually perpendicular datum edges

This time we will assume that the component has been dimensioned as was shown in Fig. 6.13(a). Working from a pair of mutually perpendicular datum edges is the most accurate method of marking out. The general set up is as shown in Fig. 6.17 and the following sequence of operations refers to Fig. 6.18.

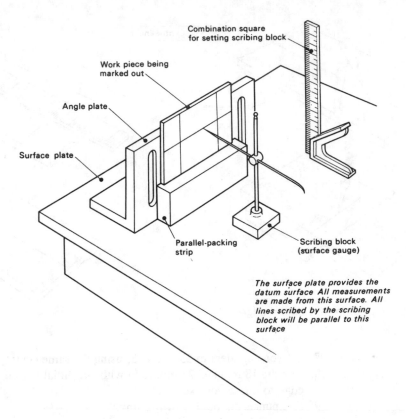

Combination square
for setting scribing block

Work piece being
marked out

Angle plate

Surface plate

Parallel-packing
strip

Scribing block
(surface gauge)

*The surface plate provides the
datum surface All measurements
are made from this surface. All
lines scribed by the scribing
block will be parallel to this
surface*

Fig. 6.17 Marking out
from a datum surface

1. File or machine two edges at right angles to each other and at right angles to the surface being marked out.
2. The blank is placed on its end datum edge on a marking out table as shown. A parallel packing block is used to raise the blank to a convenient height. The thickness of the packing must be measured and allowed for when setting the scribing point. The point of the scriber is set to the combination set rule as shown. The setting is transferred to the blank and a line is scribed parallel to the datum edge. The second hole centre line is then scribed in the same way.
3. The blank is then turned through 90° so that it rests on the other datum edge. This enables the remaining centre line to be scribed at right angles to the first two. The marking out of the link is completed as described in operations (4) to (10) inclusive in the first example.

This final example is mostly used where high levels of precision are required, in which case a vernier height gauge is used in place of the scribing block and rule, or when a very large number of lines has to be scribed parallel to a datum edge, or both.

Marking out on a surface plate or marking out table often involves larger and more awkwardly shaped components. The example in Fig. 6.19 shows how a casting is supported. The casting is clamped to an angle plate and prevented from over balancing by the use of a table jack. Wedges are used to aid the setting up of the casting on the surface plate.

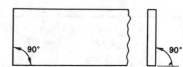

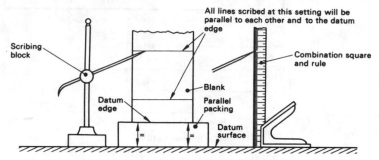

(1) *File or machine up two edges at right angles (perpendicular) to each other and at right angles to the face being marked out*

All lines scribed at this setting will be parallel to each other and to the datum edge

Scribing block

Combination square and rule

Blank

Datum edge

Parallel packing

Datum surface

(2) *Blank is placed on datum edge on surface plate (datum surface). In this example parallel packing is used to raise the blank to a convenient height. The scribing block is set to the combination square and rule. The setting is transferred to the blank. The line so scribed will be parallel to the datum surface and therefore parallel to datum edge of the blank*

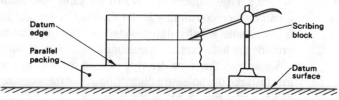

Datum edge

Parallel packing

Scribing block

Datum surface

Fig. 6.18 Marking out procedure when using a datum surface

(3) *Blank is turned through 90° so that it rests on the other datum edge. This enables the remaining centre line to be scribed in at right angles to the first two.*

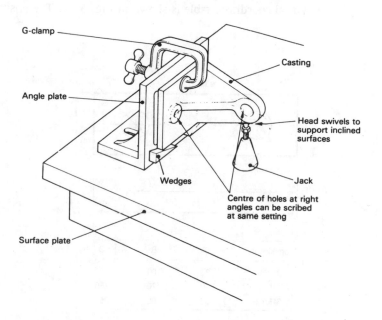

G-clamp

Casting

Angle plate

Head swivels to support inclined surfaces

Jack

Wedges

Centre of holes at right angles can be scribed at same setting

Surface plate

Fig. 6.19 Supporting larger work

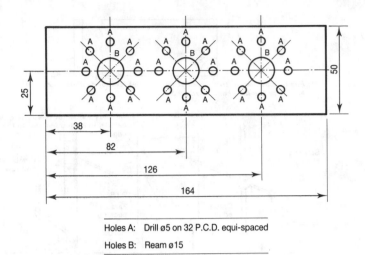

Fig. 6.20 Tabulated data

Holes A: Drill ø5 on 32 P.C.D. equi-spaced

Holes B: Ream ø15

6.8 Hole axes and coordinates

Where a large number of holes of the same size are to be drilled in a component, it can be time consuming in the drawing office and confusing for the craftsperson if every hole is fully dimensioned. In such circumstances it is only necessary to provide the hole centre dimensions and a table of hole sizes as shown in Fig. 6.20.

Sometimes the same drawing is used for similar components of varying size. In this instance the holes are dimensioned but their centre distances are listed in a table as shown in Fig. 6.21.

So far we have only considered positioning holes by centre punching the intersection on scribed centre lines. For many purposes this is not sufficiently accurate. For positioning holes more accurately a coordinate table can be fitted to a drilling machine. A typical coordinate table is shown in Fig. 6.22. The position of the work can be

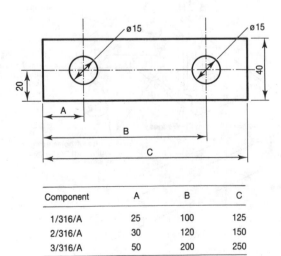

Fig. 6.21 Tabulated dimensions

Component	A	B	C
1/316/A	25	100	125
2/316/A	30	120	150
3/316/A	50	200	250

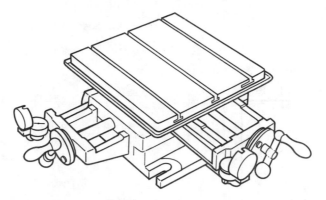

Fig. 6.22 Coordinate table

This co-ordinate table can be set by using the micrometer dials and lead screws (reading accuracy 0.01 mm), or by using slip gauges in the trays provided and the dial gauges as fiducial indicators

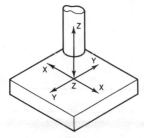

For a drilling machine with a co-ordinated table:

ZZ = Spindle axis
XX = Longitudinal table movement
YY = Lateral (cross) table movement

Fig. 6.23 Labelling axes for coordinate drilling

adjusted by the micrometer controlled lead screws or by slip gauges placed in the trays provided. When slip gauges are used, a constant measuring pressure is ensured by the DTIs which act as fiducial indicators. For even greater accuracy a jig-boring machine can be used and, where a batch of components is required with accurately positioned and drilled or bored holes, a computer numerically controlled (CNC) machining centre could be used. This avoids the need for time consuming marking out. When coordinate drilling and boring, particularly if CNC machines are involved, the axes are labelled as shown in Fig. 6.23. A typical component dimensioned for coordinate drilling is shown in Fig. 6.24(a), and its corresponding operation sheet is shown in Fig. 6.24(b). Since there is no centre punch mark to guide the drill as it starts to cut, it will inevitably run out if an ordinary twist drill is used. To avoid this happening the hole is started with a centre drill. Alternatively, special drills can be used with a point and cutting edge geometry which has been developed to make them self-centring. These latter drills have been developed for use on CNC machine tools.

6.9 Efficient marking out

As for any other engineering operation, efficiency when marking out can be improved by forethought and planning. Before starting to mark out:

(a) Study the dawing carefully and decide what equipment you require, how the work is to be positioned and located whilst marking out and the sequence in which you will proceed. This will ensure that you make the minimum number of moves. For example, to save time, all parallel lines on the same face of the component should be made at the same setting of the workpiece.
(b) Make sure that all the equipment you require is to hand and that it is in good condition. Sharp, clear lines cannot be scribed with blunt equipment.
(c) Make sure that the work is correctly and securely mounted so that it will not move or deflect and also that it is conveniently positioned.
(d) Make sure that your work area is adequately lighted and free from shadows. This will ensure that you will be able to read the instruments easily and accurately and that the scribed lines will be clearly visible.

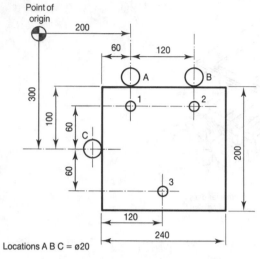

Locations A B C = ø20

(a) Component drawing dimensional for co-ordinate drilling

Item	X	Y	Sequence
⬤	200	300	
A	200	190	Setting
C	130	300	
	–	–	Load workpiece
Hole 1	200	240	Drill ø10
Hole 2	320	240	Drill ø10
Hole 3	260	360	

(b) Operation sheet for co-ordinate drilling

Fig. 6.24 Coordinate drilling

Table 6.1 Faults and inaccuracies when marking out

Fault	Possible cause	Correct
Inaccurate measurement	1 Wrong instrument for tolerance required 2 Incorrect use of instrument	1 Check instrument is suitable for tolerance required 2 Improve your technique
Scribed lines out of position	1 Parallax (sighting) error 2 Rule not square with datum edge	1 Use the scriber correctly 2 Use a datum block (abutment)
Lines not clear	1 Scribing point blunt 2 Work surface too hard 3 Scribing tool lacks rigidity	1 Sharpen the point of the scriber 2 Use a surface coating (spray-on lacquer) 3 Use only good quality tools in good condition
Corrosion along scribed lines	Protective coating (tin plate) cut by using too sharp a scribing point	Use a pencil when marking coated materials
Component tears or cracks along scribed line when bent	1 Scribed line and direction of bend parallel to grain of material 2 Scribed line cut too deeply	1 Bend at right angles to grain of the material 2 Mark bend lines with a pencil
Circles and arcs irregular and not clear	1 Scribing points blunt 2 Instruments not rigid 3 Centre point slipping	1 Resharpen 2 Use only good quality dividers or trammels or correct size for job 3 Use a dot punch to make a centre location
Centre punch marks out of position	1 Incorrect use of punch 2 Scribed lines not sufficiently deep to provide a positive point location	1 Position punch so that point is visible and then move upright when point is correctly positioned 2 Ensure point can click into the junction of the scribed lines

6.10 Avoidance of faults and inaccuracies

Since the main purpose of marking out is to provide guide lines to control the manufacturing process, any inaccuracy in marking out will result in similar inaccuracies in the finished workpiece. Table 6.1 lists some common causes of inaccuracy when marking out and how these inaccuracies may be prevented.

6.11 Care of marking out equipment

Marking out equipment, like the measuring equipment with which it is associated, must be carefully used and maintained.

(a) Scribing points must be kept needle sharp to ensure a clear line. They should be regularly dressed with a small oil-stone (oil-slip) as shown in Fig. 6.25 and they should not be allowed to become so blunt that grinding has to be resorted to. This is because the heat generated by grinding cannot readily escape from the points of scribing equipment and this heat may 'draw the temper' (soften) the points of scribing instruments rendering them useless.

(b) The scribing blades of vernier height gauges have to be ground from time to time to keep them sharp. This should be done as shown in Fig. 6.26 in order to avoid interfering with the datum edge. Take care: some vernier height gauges have carbide tipped scribing blades and these require special treatment.

(c) Like all precision bench equipment, marking out instruments should be kept in the cases in which they were supplied. These cases not only protect the instruments from being damaged, they are also designed to support the instruments so that they do not become distorted. On no account should marking out instruments be mixed with other bench tools. This is to avoid the scribing

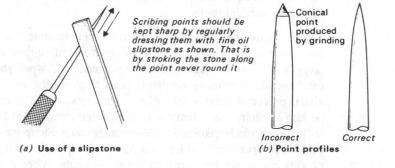

Scribing points should be kept sharp by regularly dressing them with fine oil slipstone as shown. That is by stroking the stone along the point never round it

Conical point produced by grinding

Fig. 6.25 Sharpening scribing points

(a) **Use of a slipstone**

Incorrect   *Correct*

(b) **Point profiles**

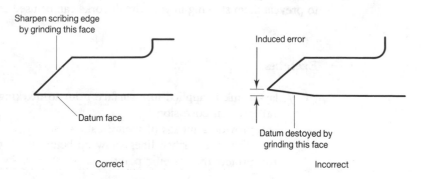

Sharpen scribing edge by grinding this face

Datum face

Induced error

Datum destoyed by grinding this face

Fig. 6.26 Sharpening height gauge scribing blades

Correct   Incorrect

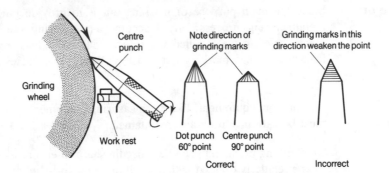

Fig. 6.27 Sharpening centre and dot punches

points being chipped and damaged. It also prevents burrs being knocked up on the edges of marking out equipment such as try-squares and straight edges.

(d) Centre punches and dot punches should be kept sharp by grinding. Again, care must be taken to avoid softening the point by over heating. Both the centre punch and the dot punch must be presented to the grinding wheel as shown in Fig. 6.27 so that the grinding marks run back from the point.

(e) After use all items of equipment must be cleaned and lightly oiled or wiped over with a thin film of petroleum jelly such as Vaseline before returning the equipment to its case in order to prevent corrosion.

6.12 Safety

Most of the hazards associated with marking out are related to:

(a) heavy equipment falling from the surface plate or marking out table
(b) sharp scribing points

Make sure that heavy workpieces are securely mounted so that they cannot fall or over-balance. This also applies to heavy items of equipment such as angle plates, large V-blocks, and jacks. Heavy equipment and work should be lifted onto the marking out table using a suitable hoist to avoid the strain of manual lifting and also to prevent damage to the table. Instruments such as vernier height gauges should be lain on their sides when not in use so that they cannot be knocked over. Better still, they should be returned to their storage cases. Sharp intruments such as scribers, odd-leg callipers and dividers should not be kept in overall pockets. Keeping sharp objects in your pockets can result in serious cuts. When not in use, scribing points should be protected. This is not only to prevent them becoming damaged, but also to prevent them sticking in you. Small corks can be used to protect scribing points.

Exercises

1 A layout ink is applied to a surface prior to marking out in order to
  (a) prevent corrosion
  (b) provide a means of identification
  (c) make the scribed lines show up better
  (d) protect the scribing point

2 Odd-leg (hermaphrodite) calipers are used to scribe
   (a) circular lines
   (b) lines parallel to an edge
   (c) lines perpendicular to an edge
   (d) complex profiles

3 Scribing instruments should be kept sharp with the aid of
   (a) a grinding wheel
   (b) a smooth file
   (c) metal polish
   (d) an oil stone

4 The position of the hole shown in Fig. 6.28 has been dimensioned using
   (a) polar coordinates
   (b) rectangular coordinates
   (c) a centre line datum
   (d) cartesian coordinates

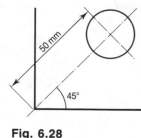

Fig. 6.28

5 A fixed point, line or surface from which a measurement can be taken is known as a
   (a) coordinate
   (b) axis
   (c) datum
   (d) dimension line

6 Dividers are used for scribing
   (a) lines parallel to an edge
   (b) circles and arcs
   (c) lines perpendicular to an edge
   (d) lines inclined to an edge

7 A scribed line can be protected by
   (a) making a series of light dot punch marks along it
   (b) spraying it with marking out ink
   (c) coating it with copper sulphate solution
   (d) covering it with adhesive tape

8 The hole centres shown in Fig. 6.29 have been dimensioned for marking out using
   (a) chain dimensioning
   (b) incremental dimensioning
   (c) absolute dimensioning
   (d) polar coordinates

9 To mark out the hole centres shown in Fig. 6.29, you will first need to have prepared
   (a) mutually parallel datum edges
   (b) point datums
   (c) centre-line datums
   (d) mutually perpendicular datum edges

10 A surface gauge can be used for
   (a) scribing lines perpendicular to a datum surface
   (b) scribing lines parallel to a datum surface to a high degree of accuracy
   (c) scribing lines parallel to a datum surface to rule accuracy only
   (d) checking the surface finish prior to marking out

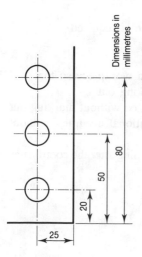

Fig. 6.29

11 To scribe lines parallel to the axis of a cylindrical component you should use a
   (a) box square
   (b) try-square
   (c) centre-finder
   (d) straight edge

12 Figure 6.30 shows two lines D mm apart being scribed using a vernier height gauge. This dimension is equal to height gauge settings of
   (a) $D_1 - D_2$
   (b) $D_2 - D_1$
   (c) $D_1 + D_2$
   (d) $D_2 + D_1$

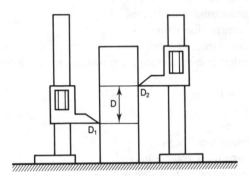

Fig. 6.30

13 One of the disavantages of marking out with a steel scriber is that
   (a) it defaces the surface of the workpiece
   (b) the lines are easily removed
   (c) the lines are thick and unclear
   (d) it cannot be used on non-ferrous metals

14 Marking out is mainly used for
   (a) providing guide lines of limited accuracy to which the fitter or the machinist can work
   (b) dimensional control where very high precision is required
   (c) accurately locating the point of a twist drill
   (d) identification purposes

15 A coordinate table is normally used for positioning a workpiece so that
   (a) polar coordinates can be plotted without marking out
   (b) cartesian (rectangular) coordinates can be plotted without marking out
   (c) holes can be drilled or bored with high positional accuracy without marking out
   (d) holes can be drilled or bored without centre punching after the coordinates have been marked out

7 Work and tool holding

The purpose of workholding is as follows.

(a) To locate the workpiece in the correct position relative to the cutting tool.
(b) To restrain the workpiece so that it is not dislodged by the cutting forces.
(c) To ensure that, in those operations where the workpiece is attached to a moving work table or a chuck, the workpiece moves with the worktable or chuck and that it is restrained so that no slip occurs.

Look at Fig. 7.1, it shows a workpiece set up ready for drilling a hole. In order to do this correctly the following basic objectives must be achieved.

(a) The workpiece must be correctly *located* under the axis and point of the drill. This may be achieved by the use of a centre punch mark or by the use of a coordinate table.
(b) The workpiece must be *restrained* so that it is not pushed downwards by the feed force of the drill. This restraint is achieved in this example by supporting the work on the machine table by the use of parallel strips. The parallel strips prevent the drill from damaging the machine table as it breaks through the bottom of the workpiece. Since the workpiece is in contact with, and restrained by, solid immovable objects this is called *positive restraint*.
(c) The workpiece must be *restrained* so that it is not rotated by the cutting forces exerted by the drill. This restraint is achieved by clamping the workpiece as shown in the Fig. 7.1. Since the workpiece is only retrained by friction, this is called *frictional restraint*. Frictional restraint is quite satisfactory for light machining operations such as drilling small holes. For operations involving greater cutting forces, it is preferable to use positive restraints to resist the cutting forces. Figure 7.2 compares the use of frictional and positive restraints for resisting the main cutting force of a machining operation.

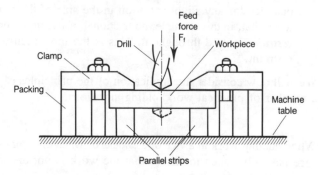

Fig. 7.1 Workpiece set for drilling a hole

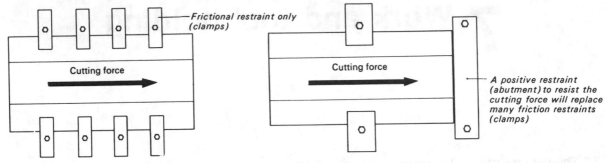

(a) **Excessive clamping is time wasting and bad practice**   (b) **Correctly placed clamps and abutment (stop)**

Fig. 7.2 Positive and frictional restraints (abutments and clamps)

7.2 Principles of workholding

A body in space free of all restraints is able to:

(a) move back and forth along its X axis
(b) move back and forth along its Y axis
(c) move back and forth along its Z axis
(d) rotate about its X axis
(e) rotate about its Y axis
(f) rotate about its Z axis

Thus the metal block shown in Fig. 7.3 has *six degrees of freedom*. To locate the block in any given position, these six degrees of freedom must be retrained. Figure 7.4 shows one way of achieving this objective by the application of suitable fixed and adjustable restraints. Do you remember that in Chapter 5 we said that it is impossible to make anything to an exact size? Well, in planning our locations and restraints, we have to allow for small variations in the size of the block.

(a) The base plate supports the block and locates it in the vertical plane along the Z axis. At the same time it restrains rotation about the X amd.Y axes.
(b) The addition of three pegs adds restraint along the X and Y axes.
(c) Finally, screw clamps are provided to complete the restraint of the block and ensure it is kept securely against the base and the locating pegs. All six of the degrees of freedom have been restrained, and the use of screw clamps compensates for any slight variation in the size of the block. You should be able to see that, in this example, no frictional restraints are employed and that *positive restraint* is used throughout. This is the most secure method of location and restraint.

We will now consider the application of the principles of restraint and location to a number of practical workholding situations.

7.3 Precautions when workholding

When holding work in a vice or a chuck, or when clamping work to a machine table, care has to be taken to ensure that the work is not distorted or broken.

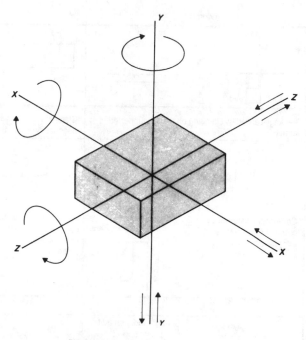

Fig. 7.3 Six degrees of freedom

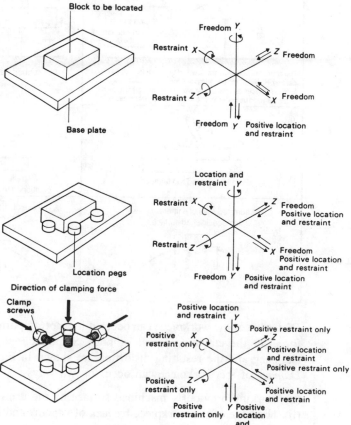

Fig. 7.4 Location and restraint

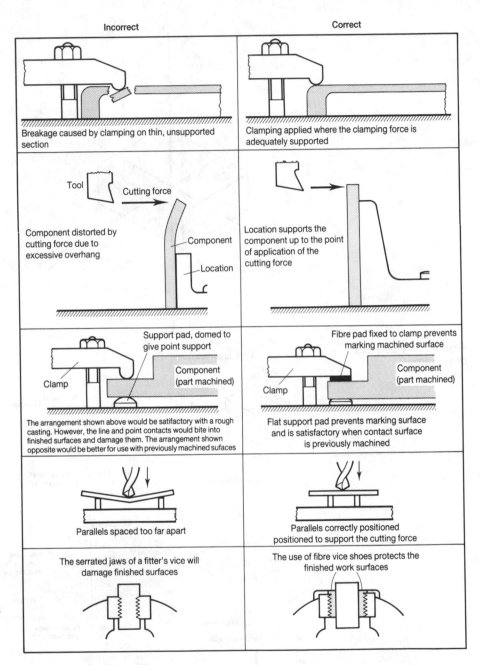

Fig. 7.5 Some causes of distortion and damage when clamping

Distortion of the workpiece can occur if it is not supported so as to resist the cutting forces or the clamping forces or both. Some examples of correct and incorrect clamping and the resulting distortion are shown in Fig. 7.5.

Damage of the workpiece can occur in two ways:

(a) marking previously machined surface by the use of incorrect type of clamps
(b) breakage of the workpiece by lack of support and incorrect positioning of the clamps

Some examples of correct and incorrect clamping and the resulting damage are also shown in Fig. 7.5.

7.4 Workholding applications (vices)

There are many different types of vice used as a quick and convenient way of holding work. The three most common types found in engineering workshops will now be considered.

Fitter's vice

This is also known as a 'parallel-jaw bench vice'. An example is shown in Fig. 7.6 together with the retraints it offers. When you are sawing, filing or chipping work held in a vice, the main cutting force should always be directed towards the fixed jaw so that it offers a positive restraint (abutment). The work should be positioned in the vice so that there is a minimum of overhang. The reason for this is shown in Fig. 7.7. If the cutting force is applied too far from the vice jaws it will have sufficient 'leverage' to cause the work to vibrate so that it emits an irritating squealing

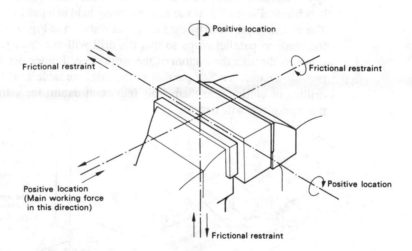

Fig. 7.6 Location in the vice

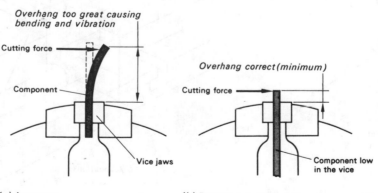

Fig. 7.7 Effect of overhang

noise. In extreme cases the work may even become bent. When the work is supported with the least possible overhang, the cutting force has insufficient 'leverage' to make the work vibrate or bend. The use of vice shoes to prevent the work becoming marked by the serrations on the vice jaws has already been considered in section 7.3. For accurate work the vice must be kept in good condition.

(a) Oil the screw regularly.
(b) Ensure the vice is heavy enough for the job in hand.
(c) Never carry out heavy hammering and bending operations on a vice. For these operations use a blacksmith's anvil.
(d) Never hammer on the top surface of the slide.

Machine vice

You use a parallel-jaw machine vice for holding regularly shaped work for light machining operations. This type of vice is of flatter construction than the bench vice so that it takes up the least space under the machine spindle. It also has smooth jaws so that it does not mark previously machined surfaces. The vice, itself, is bolted to the machine table and the rules for its use and upkeep are the same as for the bench vice. Figure 7.8(a) shows work being held in a machine vice ready for drilling. The restraints provided by the vice are also shown in Fig. 7.8(b). You should support the work on parallel strips so that the drill will not damage the vice slideways as it breaks through the bottom of the workpiece. Remember that the vice slideways provide a datum surface parallel to the machine table and, if they are damaged by drilling or cutting into them, this important datum for setting up and location of the workpiece will be lost.

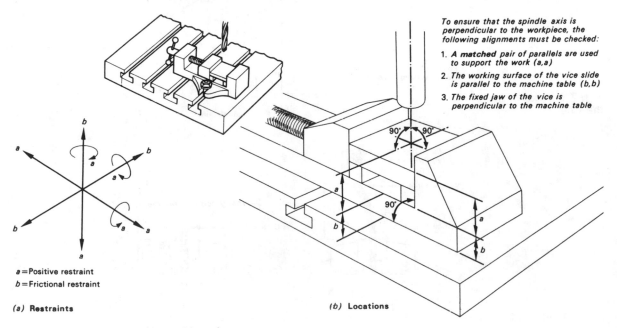

To ensure that the spindle axis is perpendicular to the workpiece, the following alignments must be checked:

1. A *matched* pair of parallels are used to support the work (a,a)
2. The working surface of the vice slide is parallel to the machine table (b,b)
3. The fixed jaw of the vice is perpendicular to the machine table

a = Positive restraint
b = Frictional restraint

(a) **Restraints**

(b) **Locations**

Fig. 7.8 Workholding in a machine vice

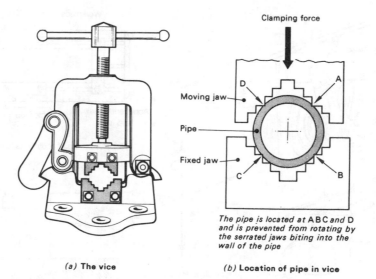

Fig. 7.9 The pipe vice

(a) **The vice**   *(b)* **Location of pipe in vice**

Pipe-vice

The bench vice is unsuitable for holding conduit, tubes and pipes whilst they are being cut to length, threaded and fittings are being screwed home tightly. The force required to keep the pipe from slipping would tend to flatten the pipe. Also, the position of the vice would prevent long lengths of pipe from being held.

For holding pipework, a properly designed pipe vice is required as shown in Fig. 7.9(a). The way in which the jaws are arranged so that the pipe is gripped at a number of points around its circumference is shown in greater detail in Fig. 7.9(b). This multi-point gripping action not only prevents the pipe from twisting in the jaws, it also prevents the pipe from being crushed out of shape as it would be in a parallel-jaw vice. The design of the pipe-vice allows it to accept a large range of pipe sizes.

7.5 Workholding applications (clamps)

You use clamps for securing work directly to the machine table. They are used when the work is too large or the shape is too awkward for it to be held safely in a machine-vice. Figure 7.10(a) shows a large component clamped directly to the table of a milling machine. Clamping to the machine table is also used when heavy cuts have to be taken. Since clamps only provide frictional restraint, you should use additional positive restraints (solid abutments) to resist the main cutting force. This is shown in Fig. 7.10(b). In this example of work being face milled on a vertical milling machine, an end abutment resists the feed force and side abutments prevent the work being spun round by the cutter. Conventional clamping over the work cannot be used in this instance since the whole of the top surface is being machined. Therefore side clamping is incorporated into the front abutment as shown in Fig. 7.10(c). Note how the set pins are inclined so as to pull the work down onto the machine table.

You saw in Fig 7.1 how a workpiece can be clamped directly to a machine table ready for drilling. The hole drilled will be at right angles (perpendicular) to the surface of the workpiece. Figure 7.11 shows work clamped to an angle plate. This enables a hole to be drilled so that its axis is parallel to the datum surface of the workpiece.

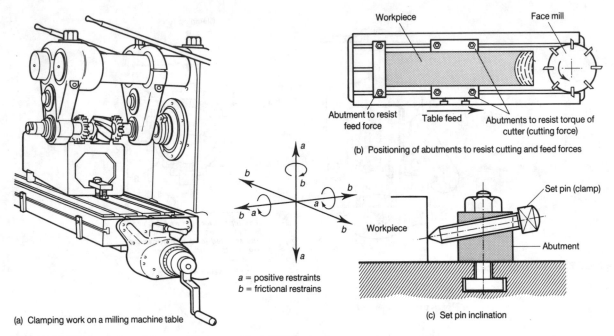

Workpiece

Face mill

Abutment to resist
feed force

Table feed

Abutments to resist torque of
cutter (cutting force)

(b) Positioning of abutments to resist cutting and feed forces

a = positive restraints
b = frictional restrains

(a) Clamping work on a milling machine table

Set pin (clamp)

Workpiece

Abutment

(c) Set pin inclination

Fig. 7.10 Work clamped to a milling machine table

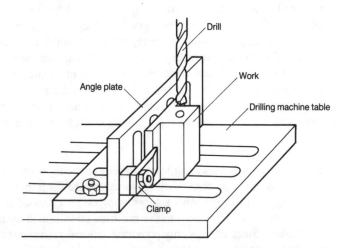

Drill

Angle plate

Work

Drilling machine table

Clamp

Fig. 7.11 Use of an
angle plate

7.6 Workholding applications (V-blocks)

You use these for holding cylindrical work. Figure 7.12(a) shows how a V-block is used in a vice so that the work is held with its axis parallel to the drill axis. That is, the work is held with its axis at right angles to the machine table. Figure 7.12(b) shows how a pair of V-blocks are used to support cylindrical work so that its axis is at right angles (perpendicular) to the spindle and drill axis. You use a pair of *matched V-blocks* in this manner not only for supporting long work, but when a through hole is being drilled. This enables the drill point to clear through the work without catching on and damaging the V-block which would happen if only a single V-block was used.

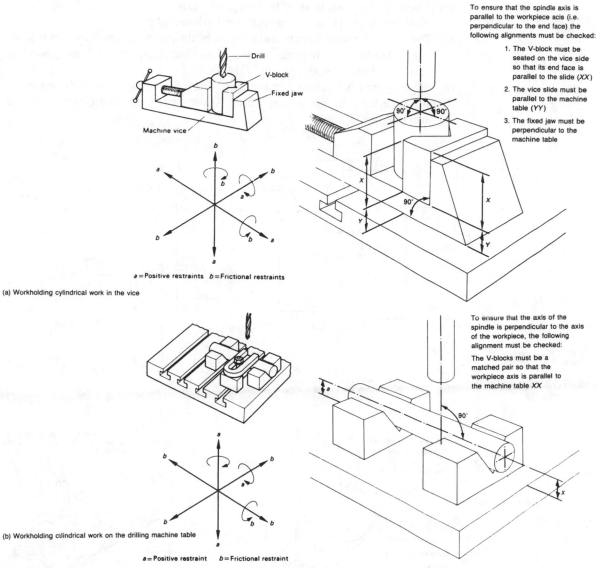

To ensure that the spindle axis is parallel to the workpiece acis (i.e. perpendicular to the end face) the following alignments must be checked:

1. The V-block must be seated on the vice side so that its end face is parallel to the slide (*XX*)

2. The vice slide must be parallel to the machine table (*YY*)

3. The fixed jaw must be perpendicular to the machine table

Drill

V-block

Fixed jaw

Machine vice

a = Positive restraints *b* = Frictional restraints

(a) Workholding cylindrical work in the vice

To ensure that the axis of the spindle is perpendicular to the axis of the workpiece, the following alignment must be checked:

The V-blocks must be a matched pair so that the workpiece axis is parallel to the machine table *XX*

(b) Workholding cylindrical work on the drilling machine table

a = Positive restraint *b* = Frictional restraint

Fig. 7.12 Use of V-blocks

7.7 Workholding applications (between centres)

The general requirement of lathework is that all diameters should be concentric or, if eccentricity is required, the degree of offset is accurately controlled. The most satisfactory way of achieving concentricity is to turn all the diameters at one setting as shown in Fig. 7.13. This is not always possible and a range of workholding methods and devices have been developed for you to use when turning work on a centre lathe. These methods and devices enable you to hold a wide range of workpieces and set them or re-set them to the level of accuracy you require. Such workholding devices must be capable of:

(a) Locating the work relative to the spindle axis.
(b) Rotating the work at the correct speed without slip.
(c) Preventing the work from being deflected by the cutting forces or its own weight. Some slender work requires the use of additional support such as steadies as shown in Fig. 7.14(a) and Fig. 7.14(b).
(d) Holding the work sufficiently rigidly so that it will not spin out of the machine, nor be ejected by the cutting forces, yet not be crushed or distorted by the workholding device.

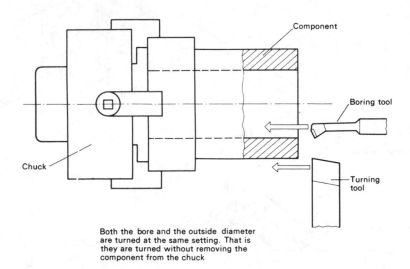

Fig. 7.13 Maintaining concentricity

Both the bore and the outside diameter are turned at the same setting. That is they are turned without removing the component from the chuck

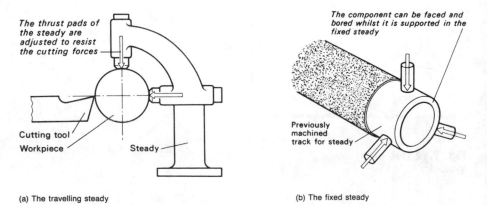

Fig. 7.14 Use of steadies

(a) The travelling steady

(b) The fixed steady

The fundamental method of workholding on the centre lathe, as its name suggests, is between centres and this will now be considered in detail.

Figure 7.15(a) shows how a workpiece is located on centres and is driven by a catch plate, driving pin and carrier. Sometimes the carrier is cranked and engages in a slot in the catch plate. Figure 7.15(b) shows the restraints acting upon a workpiece located between centres and driven as described. Since the driving mechanism can 'float', it has no influence on the accuracy of location. The centres themselves have

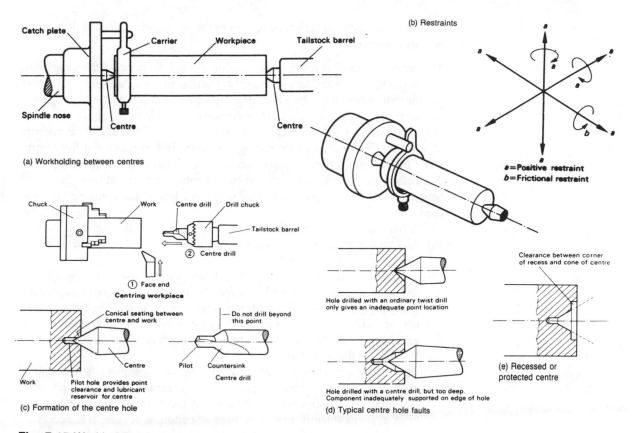

(a) Workholding between centres

(b) Restraints

a=Positive restraint
b=Frictional restraint

(1) Face end
(2) Centre drill
Centring workpiece

(c) Formation of the centre hole

Conical seating between centre and work

Centre

Work

Pilot hole provides point clearance and lubricant reservoir for centre

Do not drill beyond this point

Pilot   Countersink
Centre drill

Hole drilled with an ordinary twist drill only gives an inadequate point location

Hole drilled with a centre drill, but too deep. Component inadequately supported on edge of hole

(d) Typical centre hole faults

Clearance between corner of recess and cone of centre

(e) Recessed or protected centre

Fig. 7.15 Workholding between centres

Morse taper shanks and locate in matching Morse taper bores in the headstock spindle and the tailstock barrel. Providing you keep the tapers clean and in good condition the axes of these components will automatically remain concentric.

Note that in some parts of the UK the terminology is different to that stated here. The headstock is sometimes called a fixed-head because it is fixed to the lefthand end of the machine. The tailstock is sometimes called a loose-head because it is free to be moved along the machine bed. The tail-stock barrel is also sometimes called a poppet. You must become used to the names of engineering equipment changing from place to place.

To ensure that the workpiece is correctly located between the centres it is necessary to drill centre holes in the ends of the workpiece. To do this, the workpiece is held in a chuck (see section 7.8) so that the end of the workpiece can be faced off smooth and the centre hole drilled using a *centre drill* as shown in Fig. 7.15(c). A section through a centre hole with the centre in position is also shown in Fig. 7.15(c). It can be seen that the conical hole in the workpiece *locates on the flanks* of the centre. The point of the centre takes no part in the location of the component. Figure 7.15(d) shows two typical faults in the preparation of centre holes. Finally, Fig. 7.15(e) shows a recessed or 'protected' centre hole. Recessing the centre hole reduces the risk of damage to the centre hole which could result in loss of locational accuracy.

You have to be careful in the use of centres or the work and the centres themselves can be easily damaged.

(a) The headstock centre is rotating with the spindle and, therefore at the same speed as the workpiece. Therefore there is no friction or wear between this centre and the workpiece. It can be a hard or a soft centre and no lubricant is required. A soft centre is sometimes used so that the point can be skimmed up after insertion in the spindle of the machine. This ensures a true running centre. For the majority of work it is not necessary to true up the centre in this manner if the centre, and the bore into which it is inserted, are clean and in good condition.

(b) The tailstock centre is stationary and considerable friction and wear can occur between it and the workpiece if it is not properly adjusted and a suitable lubricant used.

   (i) A hard centre or a rotating centre must be used in this position.

   (ii) An extreme pressure lubricant such as tallow should be used between the work and a fixed centre.

   (iii) The centre must be correctly adjusted. The barrel is wound forward until the work is securely located, but free to rotate. This requires judgement that you will only acquire with practice. Too loose and the location will not be sufficiently accurate for precision work: too tight and the heat generated by the friction will burn out the point of the centre and destroy the hole in the workpiece.

   (iv) As the heat generated by cutting warms up the workpiece it will tend to expand. This will increase the pressure on the centres. Therefore, although they may have been correctly adjusted at the start of the operation, you have to check them from time to time as cutting proceeds. It is necessary to 'ease' the tailstock centre if the expansion of the workpiece due to heating makes the centres too tight. *SAFETY. Stop the machine whilst adjusting the tailstock.*

   (v) When you are using high spindle speeds and/or when you are taking heavy cuts, a rotating centre can be used in the tailstock. Rotating centres overcome the wear and lubrication problems but tend not to be so accurate for fine work. They are also more bulky and sometimes obstruct the cutting tool. You still have to 'ease' the centre from time to time as the work warms up and expands.

For parallel turning, the axis of the spindle centre and the axis of the tailstock centre must be in line with each other and parallel to the bed slideways. To achieve this alignment the tailstock is provided with lateral (sideways) adjustment. When turning between centres, a trial cut should be taken along the component. The component is then checked at each end with a micrometer calliper. If the readings are the same, then the component is parallel (not tapered) and the roughing and finishing cuts may be taken. If the readings are different, then the tailstock has to be adjusted as shown in Fig. 7.16(a). Further trial cuts have to be taken and adjustments made until the diameter is constant along the length of the component.

A more convenient way of bringing the tailstock centre axis into alignment is shown in Fig. 7.16(b). This can only be used if a parallel test bar is available. A mandrel cannot be used as it has a built-in taper and would give false readings. The advantages and limitations of workholding between centres are summarised in Table 7.1.

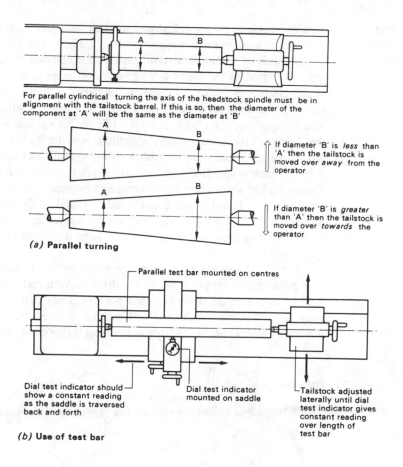

For parallel cylindrical turning the axis of the headstock spindle must be in alignment with the tailstock barrel. If this is so, then the diameter of the component at 'A' will be the same as the diameter at 'B'

If diameter 'B' is *less* than 'A' then the tailstock is moved over *away* from the operator

If diameter 'B' is *greater* than 'A' then the tailstock is moved over *towards* the operator

(a) **Parallel turning**

Parallel test bar mounted on centres

Dial test indicator should show a constant reading as the saddle is traversed back and forth

Dial test indicator mounted on saddle

Tailstock adjusted laterally until dial test indicator gives constant reading over length of test bar

(b) **Use of test bar**

Fig. 7.16 Parallel turning setting the tailstock

Table 7.1 Work holding between centres

Advantages	Limitations
1. Work can be easily reversed without loss of concentricity	1. Centre holes have to be drilled before work can be set up
2. Work can be taken from the machine for inspection and easily re-set without loss of concentricity	2. Only limited work can be performed on the end of the bar
3. Work can be transferred between machines (e.g. lathe and cylindrical grinder) without loss of concentricity	3. Boring operations cannot be performed
4. Long work (full length of bed) can be accommodated	4. There is lack of rigidity
	5. Cutting speeds are limited unless a revolving centre is used. This reduces accuracy and accessibility
	6. Skill in setting is required to obtain the correct fit between centres and work

7.8 Workholding applications (self-centring chuck)

You use this for holding cylindrical work or hexagonal work on a centre lathe. An example of such a chuck is shown in Fig. 7.17(a). The jaws are moved in and out of the chuck by means of a scroll plate in the body of the chuck. The scroll plate itself is rotated by the chuck key by means of bevel gears which form part of each of the chuck key sockets. Providing the chuck is kept in good condition and not strained, the movement of the jaws will be concentric with the axis of the chuck. The backplate of the chuck is made to fit on the spindle nose in such a way that the chuck will run concentrically with the axis of the spindle. It will also be provided with a means of securing the chuck to the spindle and driving the chuck.

Each chuck is supplied with two sets of jaws, an internal set and an external set. Figure 7.17(b) shows how the internal and external jaws are used to hold different types of work. The chucks are numbered 1, 2, and 3. They also bear the same serial number as the chuck body. The jaws are not interchangeable with any other chuck. When changing jaws they must be inserted into the chuck body as numbered starting with number 1.

Figure 7.17(c) shows the restraints provided by a self-centring chuck. These apply to a cylindrical workpiece where the drive is frictional. When a hexagonal bar is held in the chuck the drive becomes positive. Only cylindrical or hexagonal work must be held in the chuck or it will become strained and cease to run true. Since hot-rolled (black) bar is not truly cylindrical it should not be held in a self-centring

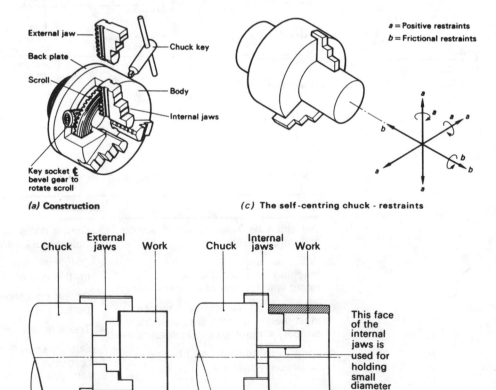

(a) **Construction**

(c) **The self-centring chuck - restraints**

a = Positive restraints
b = Frictional restraints

Fig. 7.17 The three-jaw, self-centring chuck

(b) **Internal and external work holding**

This face of the internal jaws is used for holding small diameter rod

Table 7.2 The self-centring chuck

Advantages	Limitations
1. Ease of work setting	1. Accuracy decreases as chuck becomes worn
2. A wide range of cylindrical and hexagonal work can be held	2. Accuracy of concentricity is limited when work is reversed in the chuck
3. Internal and external jaws are available	3. 'Run out' cannot be corrected
4. Work can be readily performed on the end face of the job	4. Soft jaws can be turned up for second operation work, but this is seldom economical for one-off jobs
5. The work can be bored	5. Only round and hexagonal components can be held

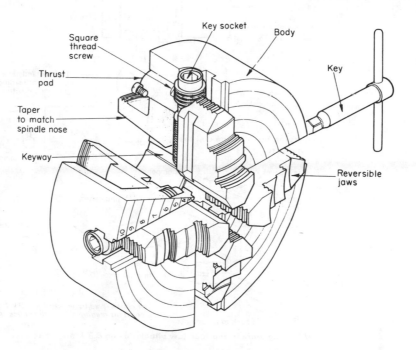

Fig. 7.18 The four-jaw chuck

chuck but in a chuck with independent jaws. Further, the scale from the surface of the hot-rolled bar is extremely abrasive and, if it gets into the body of the chuck, it will cause wear of the scroll plate, the teeth on the backs of the jaws, and the slots that the jaws slide in. This will lead to loss of accuracy. The advantages and limitations of the self-centring chuck are listed in Table 7.2. *SAFETY: Always check that the chuck-key has been removed before starting the machine.*

7.9 The four-jaw independent chuck

This type of chuck, which is shown in Fig. 7.18, is much more heavily constructed than the self-centring chuck and has much greater holding power. Each jaw is moved independently by a square thread screw and is reversible. This type of chuck is used for holding:

(a) irregularly shaped work;

(b) work that must be trued up to run concentrically with a previously machined diameter;

(c) work that must be deliberately offset to run eccentrically.

Eccentrically mounted work must be balanced when using either the four-jaw chuck or a face plate (see section 7.10).

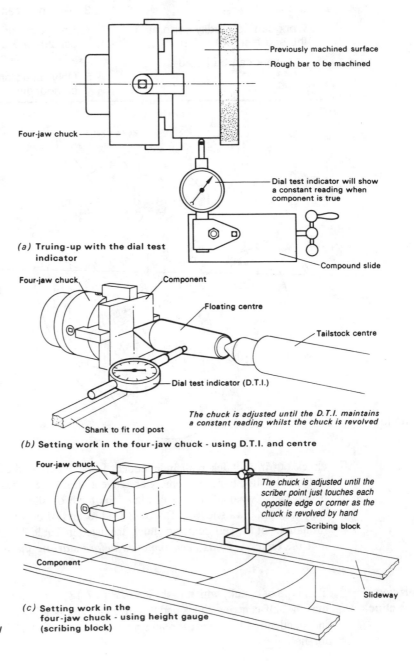

Previously machined surface

Rough bar to be machined

Four-jaw chuck

Dial test indicator will show a constant reading when component is true

(a) **Truing-up with the dial test indicator**

Compound slide

Four-jaw chuck   Component

Floating centre

Tailstock centre

Dial test indicator (D.T.I.)

The chuck is adjusted until the D.T.I. maintains a constant reading whilst the chuck is revolved

Shank to fit rod post

(b) **Setting work in the four-jaw chuck - using D.T.I. and centre**

Four-jaw chuck

The chuck is adjusted until the scriber point just touches each opposite edge or corner as the chuck is revolved by hand

Scribing block

Component

Slideway

(c) **Setting work in the four-jaw chuck - using height gauge (scribing block)**

Fig. 7.19 The four-jaw chuck — work setting

Since the jaws of a four-jaw chuck can be reversed, there is no need for separate internal and external jaws as for the self-centring chuck. The main disadvantage of using a four-jaw chuck is the time taken in setting the work. Since each jaw moves independently, the work has to be set to run concentrically with the spindle axis. If a smooth or previously machined diameter is available, a dial test indicator (DTI) may be used as shown in Fig. 7.19(a). Alternatively, if a centre point is to be picked up for drilling or boring, a floating centre and dial test indicator may be used as shown in Fig. 7.19(b). Rough work may be set as shown in Fig. 7.19(c).

The restraints acting on a component held in a four-jaw independent chuck are shown in Fig. 7.20. The advantages and limitations of this method of workholding are considered in Table 7.3.

7.10 Workholding applications (faceplate)

The centre-lathe workholding devices described so far allow you to machine a diameter true to an existing diameter (chuck), or to an existing axis (centres). The faceplate allows you to turn a diameter parallel or perpendicular to a previously machined flat surface. This flat surface is the datum from which you set the diameter

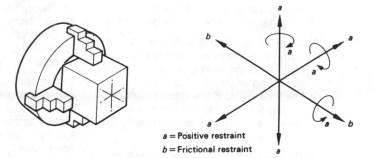

Fig. 7.20 The four-jaw chuck — restraints

a = Positive restraint
b = Frictional restraint

Table 7.3 The four-jaw chuck

Advantages	Limitations
1. A wide range of regular and irregular shapes can be held	1. Chuck is heavy to handle on to the lathe
2. Work can be set to run concentrically, or eccentrically at will	2. Chuck is slow to set up. A dial test indicator (DTI) has to be used for accurate setting
3. Considerable gripping power. Heavy cuts can be taken	3. Chuck is bulky
4. Jaws are reversible for internal and external work	4. The gripping power is so great that fine work can be easily damaged during setting
5. Work can readily be performed on the end face of the job	
6. The work can be bored	
7. There is no loss of accuracy as the chuck becomes worn	

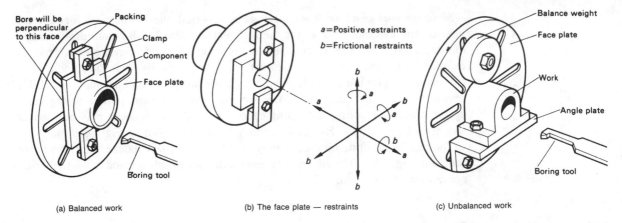

(a) Balanced work   (b) The face plate — restraints   (c) Unbalanced work

Fig. 7.21 The face plate

Table 7.4 The faceplate

Advantages	Limitations
1. A wide range of regular and irregular components can be held	1. The faceplate is slow and tedious to set up. Not only must the workpiece be clocked up to run true, clamps must also be set up on the faceplate to retain the component
2. Work can be set to a datum surface. If the datum surface is parallel to the workpiece axis, it is set on an angle plate mounted on the face plate. If the datum surface is perpendicular to the workpiece axis, the workpiece is set directly on to the faceplate	2. Considerable skill is required to clamp the component so that it is rigid enough to resist both the cutting forces, and those forces that will try to dislodge the work as it spins rapidly round
3. Work on the end face of the job is possible	3. Considerable skill is required to avoid distorting the workpiece by the clamps
4. The work can be bored	4. Irregular jobs have to be carefully balanced to prevent vibration, and the job rolling back on the operator
5. The work can be set to run concentrically or eccentrically at will	5. The clamps can limit the work that can be performed on the end face
6. There are no moving parts to lose their accuracy with wear	
7. The work can be rigidly clamped to resist heavy cuts	

as shown in Fig. 7.21(a), when you want the hole to be *perpendicular* to the datum surface. The restraints acting on the workpiece are shown in Fig. 7.21(b).

Alternatively, when you want to turn a diameter *parallel* to a flat surface, you mount the work on an angle plate which is itself mounted on a face plate. This is shown in Fig. 7.21(c). This time you have to use a balance weight to prevent the out of balance forces from causing vibrations which can not only result in a poor surface finish but which can also damage the spindle bearings. In extreme cases, where heavy work is involved, the out of balance forces can be sufficiently severe for the machine to be rocked on its foundations. Also, even when the machine is

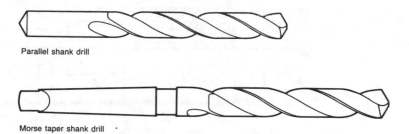

Parallel shank drill

Morse taper shank drill

Fig. 7.22 Drill shanks

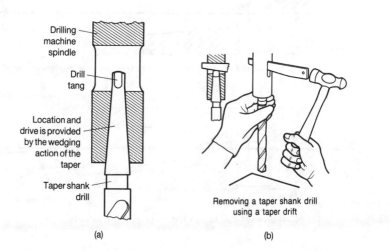

Drilling
machine
spindle

Drill
tang

Location and
drive is provided
by the wedging
action of the
taper

Taper shank
drill

Removing a taper shank drill
using a taper drift

(a)   (b)

Fig. 7.23 Taper
location

stopped whilst taking measurements, lack of balance can cause the work to swing round of its own accord trapping the operator (you). The advantages and limitations of using a faceplate are summarised in Table 7.4.

7.11 Toolholding applications (drills)

Drills are provided with either *parallel* shanks or *taper* shanks, as shown in Fig. 7.22, for their restraint and location. Generally, small diameter drills have parallel shanks, whilst medium and large diameter drills have taper shanks.

Taper shank drills

Taper shank drills are the easiest to locate and restrain in a drilling machine spindle. You can see in Fig. 7.23(a) that the taper shank of the drill fits into a matching taper in the drilling machine spindle. They will both have a standard Morse taper. This type of taper is said to be *self-locking*. That is, the taper will hold the drill in position so that it does not drop out of the spindle under its own weight, and the taper will provide sufficient friction to drive the drill whilst it is cutting. The tang on the end of the drill is for ejection purposes only as shown in Fig. 7.23(b). It is not intended to drive the drill. The taper location also compensates for variations

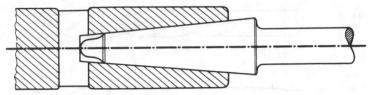

(a) **Spindle and shank maintain axial alignment under maximum metal conditions**

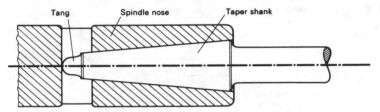

(b) **Spindle and shank maintain axial alignment under minimum metal conditions**

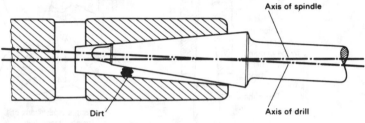

Fig. 7.24 Taper location — alignment error due to dirt

(c) **Misalignment due to dirt between drill and spindle**

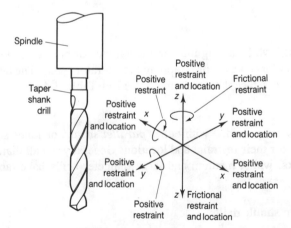

Fig. 7.25 Restraints acting on a taper shank drill

in size due to manufacturing tolerances and a small amount of wear. Figure 7.24(a) shows the fit under maximum metal conditions, whilst Fig. 7.24(b) shows the fit under minimum metal conditions. Figure 7.24(c) shows how even a small amount of dirt can cause considerable misalignment of the drill axis and the machine spindle axis. Further, the dirt will prevent proper contact between the shank and the spindle bore and there will be insufficient friction to drive the drill whilst it is cutting. This will cause the drill to slip and cause considerable damage to both the spindle bore and the drill shank. You must always take care to make sure that both the shank

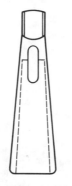

Fig. 7.26 Morse taper adaptor sleeve

of the drill and the bore of the machine spindle are completely clean before inserting the drill. A drill with a worn shank must not be used since this can also slip and damage the machine spindle. It is easier and cheaper to replace a drill than it is to replace a machine spindle. The restraints acting on a taper shank drill located directly in a machine spindle are shown in Fig. 7.25. Sometimes the taper of the drill shank is smaller than the bore in the machine spindle. In this case, an adaptor sleeve has to be used as shown in Fig. 7.26. The restraints acting on the the sleeve and on the drill shank are the same as shown previously.

Parallel shank drills

Parallel shank drills are also known as 'straight shank' and 'plain shank' drills. They have to be held in a self-centring drill chuck. Figure 7.27 shows you how the drill chuck and its arbor make use of a series of concentric tapers to ensure that the drill runs 'true' with the spindle axis. Some small drilling machines and portable, hand held power drills have a spindle with an external taper. This fits directly into the taper of the chuck body without the need for an arbor. Again, cleanliness is essential for true running and lack of wear. The restraints acting upon the chuck are the same as those for a taper shank drill. The restraints acting upon a parallel shank drill held in a chuck are shown in Fig. 7.28.

7.12 Toolholding applications (horizontal milling machine)

A large variety of cutters can be fitted to horizontal milling machines and some examples are shown in Fig. 7.29. These cutters are mounted on an *arbor* which is, itself, attached to the machine spindle.

Unlike the morse taper of a drilling machine spindle, the taper of a milling machine spindle is for location only and does not drive the cutter. This is because the forces

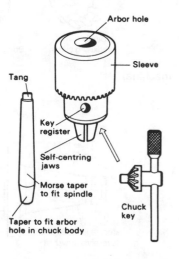

(a) **Typical drill chuck and accessories**

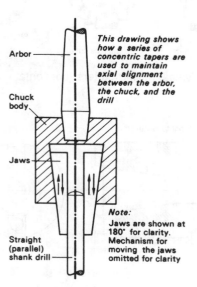

(b) **Principle of the drill chuck**

Fig. 7.27 The drill chuck

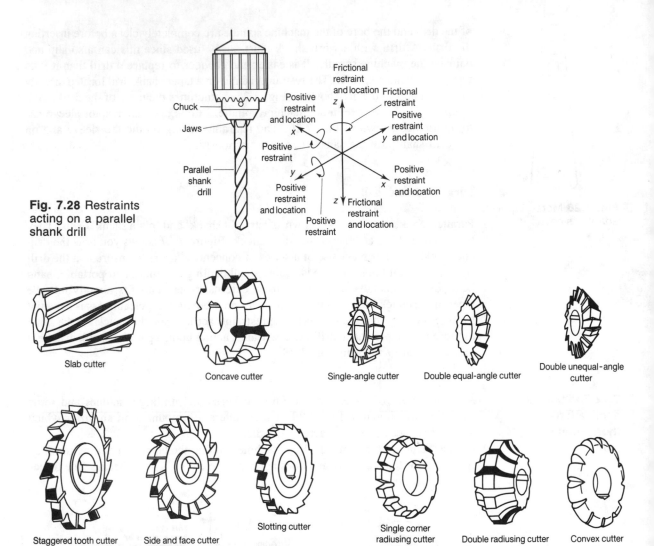

Fig. 7.28 Restraints acting on a parallel shank drill

Chuck

Jaws

Parallel shank drill

Frictional restraint and location

Positive restraint and location

Positive restraint

Frictional restraint

Positive restraint and location

Positive restraint and location

Positive restraint and location

Positive restraint and location

Frictional restraint and location

Positive restraint

Slab cutter

Concave cutter

Single-angle cutter

Double equal-angle cutter

Double unequal-angle cutter

Staggered tooth cutter

Side and face cutter

Slotting cutter

Single corner radiusing cutter

Double radiusing cutter

Convex cutter

Fig. 7.29 Typical milling cutters (horizontal milling machine)

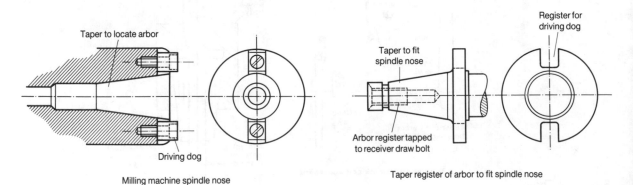

Taper to locate arbor

Driving dog

Milling machine spindle nose

Register for driving dog

Taper to fit spindle nose

Arbor register tapped to receiver draw bolt

Taper register of arbor to fit spindle nose

Fig. 7.30 Milling machine spindle nose and arbor

involved are too great and a positive drive is required. Figure 7.30 shows how this is achieved in a typical milling machine spindle nose and the associated arbor. The tapered end of the arbor is drawn into the spindle nose of the machine by a long bolt passing right through the spindle. The arbor is positively driven by dogs on the spindle nose. These dogs engage in slots in the flange on the end of the arbor. When fitting an arbor to the spindle nose, absolute cleanlinesss is essential to ensure true running. Although, for light work, cutters are frequently driven by friction, this is not good practice since, should the cutter slip, the arbor is damaged and the cutter tooth edge in contact with the work may be broken. It is better to use a key to provide the cutter with a positive drive as shown in Fig. 7.31(a). A cutter mounted on an arbor and the corresponding restraints are shown in Fig. 7.31(b).

The forces acting on a milling cutter, when removing metal rapidly, are very great. Therefore the cutter arbor must be adequately supported and the cutter correctly positioned to avoid inaccuracies and chatter. You are shown how to do this in Fig. 7.32. In Fig. 7.32(a) the cutter is incorrectly positioned so that there is excessive overhang from the points of support. This will allow the arbor to flex, resulting in inaccurate cutting, chatter and a poor surface finish. In extreme cases the cutter teeth may be chipped.

In Fig. 7.32(b) the overarm and the arbor steady bearing have been repositioned to provide support as close to the cutter as possible. Also the cutter, itself, has been mounted as close to the spindle nose as possible. Thus overhang has been reduced to a minimum and the cutter is supported with the maximum rigidity.

Sometimes the shape and size of the work prevents the cutter from being mounted close to the spindle nose. Figure 7.32(c) shows how an additional, intermediate steady can be positioned on the overarm to support the arbor immediately behind the cutter. This again reduces the overhang to a minimum.

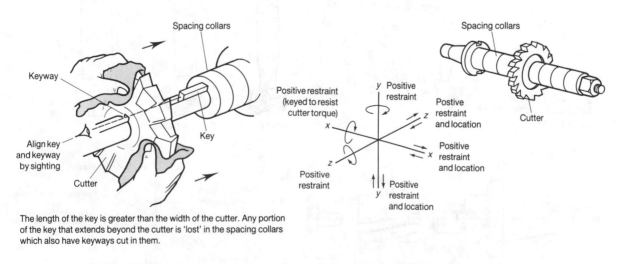

The length of the key is greater than the width of the cutter. Any portion of the key that extends beyond the cutter is 'lost' in the spacing collars which also have keyways cut in them.

(a) Keying the cutter to the arbor

(b) Restraints acting on the cutter when mounted on an arbor

Fig. 7.31 Cutter restraints

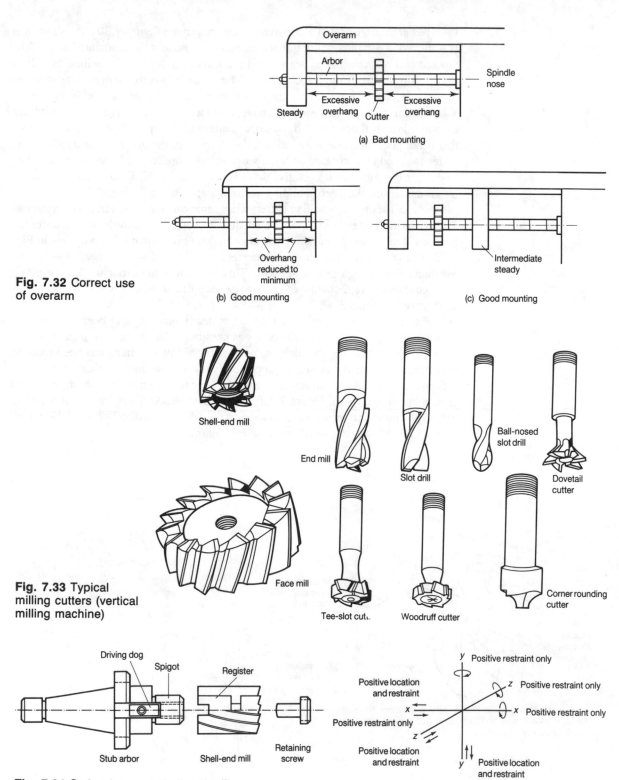

Fig. 7.32 Correct use of overarm

(a) Bad mounting

(b) Good mounting

(c) Good mounting

Fig. 7.33 Typical milling cutters (vertical milling machine)

Shell-end mill

End mill

Slot drill

Ball-nosed slot drill

Dovetail cutter

Face mill

Tee-slot cutter

Woodruff cutter

Corner rounding cutter

Fig. 7.34 Stub arbor and shell-end mill

Driving dog

Spigot

Register

Stub arbor

Shell-end mill

Retaining screw

Positive restraint only

Positive location and restraint

Positive restraint only

Positive restraint only

Positive restraint only

Positive location and restraint

Positive location and restraint

7.13 Toolholding applications (vertical milling machine)

Like the horizontal milling machine, the vertical milling machine can also be fitted with a wide variety of cutters. Some of these are shown in Fig. 7.33. These cutters can be attached to the spindle of a vertical milling machine in a variety of ways. Large face mills may be bolted directly to the machine nose, shell-end mills may be mounted on a stub arbor, and a wide variety of end-mills, slot drills and specialist cutters such as T-slot cutters may be held in collet chucks.

Stub-arbor

Figure 7.34 shows an 'exploded' view of a stub arbor and a shell-end milling cutter. The cutter is located on a cylindrical spigot and is driven positively by dogs. It is retained in position by a bolt. Because the location is cylindrical there is no compensation for wear. Therefore the spigot on the arbor and the register in the cutter have to be ground to a precision fit during manufacture. To maintain this accuracy and keep wear to a minimum, the register and the spigot must be cleaned carefully each time the cutter is changed. The appropriate restraints are also shown.

Collet chuck

Basically a collet is a hardened and tempered sleeve with a parallel bore on the inside and a tapered nose on the outside. It is slit at regular intervals around its circumference so that it can close onto the shank of the cutter when the outer sleeve is tightened. Again concentric tapers are used to ensure true running and to compensate for manufacturing tolerances and wear. The restraints appropriate to such an arrangement are shown in Fig. 7.35. The basic collet arrangement shown suffers from two main disadvantages.

(i) As the locking sleeve is closed, most of the closure of the collet on the cutter occurs at its nose. This leaves the 'tail' of the cutter shank free to move slightly within the collet, depending upon the degree of clearance present.

(ii) The cutter is only secured by friction and the cutting forces, acting upon the spiral flutes of the cutter, will tend to draw the cutter out of collet.

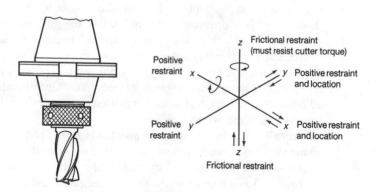

Fig. 7.35 Collet chuck

Figure 7.36 shows a proprietary make of collet chuck designed to overcome these problems. Firstly, the 'tail' of the cutter shank is located by a hardened and ground centre. Secondly, the cutter shank is screwed into the collet so that the cutter can not be drawn out by the cutting forces acting on the flutes.

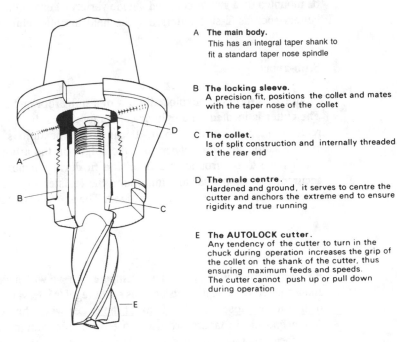

A **The main body.**
This has an integral taper shank to fit a standard taper nose spindle

B **The locking sleeve.**
A precision fit, positions the collet and mates with the taper nose of the collet

C **The collet.**
Is of split construction and internally threaded at the rear end

D **The male centre.**
Hardened and ground, it serves to centre the cutter and anchors the extreme end to ensure rigidity and true running

E **The AUTOLOCK cutter.**
Any tendency of the cutter to turn in the chuck during operation increases the grip of the collet on the shank of the cutter, thus ensuring maximum feeds and speeds. The cutter cannot push up or pull down during operation

Fig. 7.36 Mounting of screwed shank, solid end mills

7.14 Toolholding applications (single-point lathe tools)

The toolholding device of a centre lathe is called the *tool post*. The purpose of the tool post is to locate the turning tool in the correct position relative to the machine and the work, to ensure that the point of the tool is at the same height as the axis of the workpiece, and to restrain the tool against the forces acting on it during cutting. Figure 7.37 shows three types of toolpost you will find in common use.

The simple clamp-type, as shown in Fig. 7.37(a), is mostly found on small model-maker's lathes. It relies largely on frictional restraint and it is difficult to adjust the height of the tool point. Keep lots of assorted packing handy!

The pillar-type as shown in Fig. 7.37(b) is widely used on light duty lathes. It is easy to set as the tool height is readily adjustable by the rocking action of the 'boat piece'. Unfortunately adjustment tilts the tool and alters the cutting angles. Also it tends to lack rigidity due to the tool overhang inherent with this design.

The four-way turret type tool post shown in Fig. 7.37(c) is one of the most widely used on industrial centre lathes. It is robust and holds up to four tools which can be quickly swung into position as required. Unfortunately there is no height adjustment, and packing has to be resorted to in order to bring the tool point height into line with the workpiece axis.

Figure 7.37(d) shows a quick change toolholder. The tools are premounted in quick change holders. These, in turn, are located on a dovetail slide machined in the face of the toolpost and retrained by means of a cam type locking device operated by the handle. To change a tool the handle is released and the tool and holder is slipped

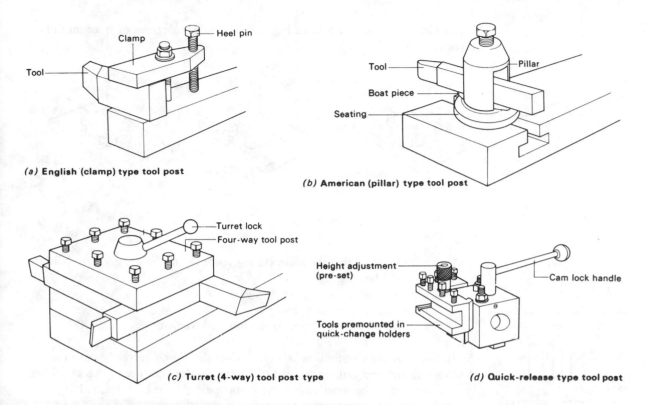

(a) **English (clamp) type tool post**

(b) **American (pillar) type tool post**

(c) **Turret (4-way) tool post type**

(d) **Quick-release type tool post**

Fig. 7.37 Centre lathe tool posts

off. The next tool and holder is simply slipped into the vacant position and clamped by means of the cam locking lever. The height of the tool can also be pre-set in a suitable fixture by a micrometer adjustment. This arrangement is more costly than the more common toolposts but the time saved in tool changing during small batch production justifies the cost.

Exercises

1 The metal block shown in Fig. 7.38 is completely unrestrained. That is, it is free
   (a) to move along the X, Y and Z axes in one direction only
   (b) to move along the X, Y and Z axes in both directions
   (c) to rotate around the X, Y and Z axes in one direction only
   (d) to rotate around the X, Y and Z axes in both directions and move along these axes in both directions

2 Wherever possible, the main cutting force acting on a workpiece should
   (a) be resisted by a positive restraint
   (b) be resisted by a frictional restraint
   (c) not be resisted in order to reduce tool wear
   (d) not be resisted in order to avoid distortion of the workpiece

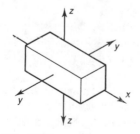

Fig. 7.38

3 In which of the illustrations in Fig 7.39 are the six degrees of freedom fully restrained?

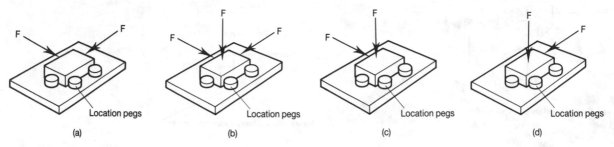

Fig. 7.39

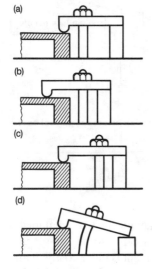

Fig. 7.40

4 It is good practice that the main cutting force acting on a workpiece held in a vice should be directed
    (a) parallel to the vice jaws
    (b) towards the moving jaw
    (c) in which ever direction is the most convenient
    (d) towards the fixed jaw

5 In which of the illustrations in Fig. 7.40 is the clamp correctly positioned?

6 When facing and drilling the end of a long slender component in a chuck on a centre lathe, the outer end of the component should be supported
    (a) using a centre in the tailstock
    (b) in a travelling steady
    (c) on a V-block
    (d) in a fixed steady

7 When cylindrically turning a long component between centres, the tailstock centre should be eased from time in order to
    (a) allow for expansion of the work as it heats up during cutting
    (b) check the condition of the centre
    (c) check the conditon of the centre hole
    (d) allow work to be carried out on the end of the component

8 Figure 7.41 shows a cylindrical component in which three holes are to be drilled parallel to the axis. The most satisfactory way to hold the component is
    (a) in a machine vice
    (b) in a machine vice with a V-block between the work and the fixed jaw of the vice
    (c) clamped directly to the machine table
    (d) by hand because of its awkward shape

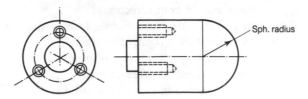

Fig. 7.41

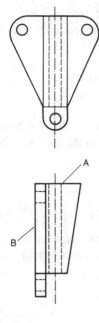

Fig. 7.42

9 Figure 7.42 shows a component in which a hole A must be drilled parallel to a datum surface B. The most satisfactory way to hold the component is
   (a) by clamping it to an angle plate
   (b) in a machine vice with face B against the fixed jaw
   (c) by clamping it with face B located against the machine table
   (d) by hand because of its awkward shape

10 When cylindrically turning a component between centres, its diameter should be checked at each end after the first cut to ensure that
   (a) the ends are perpendicular to the axis
   (b) it is not oval
   (c) it is parallel throughout its length
   (d) it has the correct taper

11 When a piece of hexagon bar is held in a three-jaw, self-centring chuck on a centre lathe, the work is driven against
   (a) the main cutting force and the feed force by frictional restraints
   (b) the main cutting force and the feed force by positive restraints
   (c) the main cutting force by positive restraint and the feed force by frictional restraint
   (d) the main cutting force by frictional restraint and the feed force by positive restraint

12 The bore of a drilling machine spindle usually has a morse taper. This is because it
   (a) will run true even if it becomes scored
   (b) will grip on the tang of the drill
   (c) is self-locking so the drill will not fall out
   (d) will accept both taper and parallel shank drills

13 A drill chuck is usually fitted to a drill machine spindle to hold
   (a) taper shank drills
   (b) slot drills
   (c) tapping attachments
   (d) parallel shank drills

14 Large taper shank drills are driven
   (a) by the tang on the end of the drill
   (b) by friction between the taper shank and the taper bore of the machine spindle
   (c) by a combination of (a) and (b)
   (d) positively by a cotter inserted through the drift hole in the spindle

15 Figure 7.43 shows four ways of clamping a plate so that it can be drilled. Which is the correct way of positioning the clamps and parallel strips?

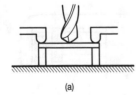
(a)

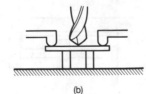
(b)

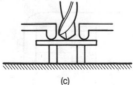
(c)

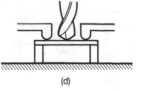
(d)

Fig. 7.43

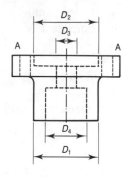

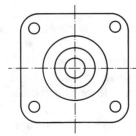

Fig. 7.44

16 The casting shown in Fig. 7.44 is to be chucked on the diameter D_1 whilst the diameters D_2, D_3 and face AA are turned. To ensure the diameters D_2 and D_3 are concentric they should be
    (a) reset after each diameter is turned
    (b) set with the aid of a DTI when first mounted in the chuck
    (c) set with a lathe test indicator
    (d) turned at the same setting

17 The casting shown in Fig 7.44 has to be reversed and held so that the bore, diameter D_4 can be turned with its axis truly perpendicular to the face AA. To do this the casting should be mounted:
    (a) in a self-centring chuck
    (b) on an angle-plate
    (c) on a surface plate
    (d) on a face plate

18 With reference to Fig. 7.44, the casting has to be set so that diameter D_4 can be bored truly concentric with diameter D_3. To ensure this concentricity, the casting should be set with the aid of a
    (a) dial test indicator (DTI)
    (b) universal surface gauge
    (c) lathe test indicator
    (d) centre finder

19 Taper shank drills should be removed from a drilling machine spindle by using a
    (a) taper drift acting on the tang of the drill
    (b) pair of grips clamped round the drill
    (c) knock-out bar passed down the hollow spindle
    (d) chuck key

20 Milling cutter arbors are located in the taper nose of the machine spindle and
    (a) driven by the draw bar
    (b) restrained by dogs on the spindle nose
    (c) driven by dogs on the spindle nose and restrained by the draw bar
    (d) driven by friction between the taper on the arbor and the taper in the machine spindle

21 Shell end mills are usually mounted
    (a) in a collet chuck
    (b) on a stub arbor
    (c) directly onto the spindle nose
    (d) on a long arbor

22 Figure 7.45 shows four ways in which a milling machine cutter can be mounted on a milling machine arbor. Which is the *least* desirable?

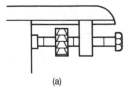

(a)

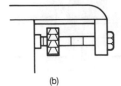

(b)

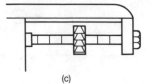

(c)

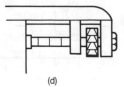

(d)

Fig. 7.45

23 When milling small workpieces they
    (a) should be securely clamped to the machine table
    (b) should be held in a vice
    (c) can be held by hand
    (d) should always be held in a milling fixture

24 Turning tools are usually held
    (a) in a chuck
    (b) in the tailstock
    (c) in a tool post
    (d) by clamping to the cross-slide

25 When drilling on a centre lathe, the drill is usually held in
    (a) a chuck or directly in the taper bore located in the tailstock barrel (poppet)
    (b) a chuck mounted on the headstock spindle
    (c) the toolpost
    (d) a steady

8 Removing material

8.1 Factors affecting penetration by the cutting edge

There are a number of basic factors which affect the penetration of the workpiece material by the cutting tool. We will now consider the more important of these.

Hardness of the workpiece material

It is easier to cut wood than it is to cut metal. It is easier to cut a soft metal such as lead than it is to cut a harder metal such as steel. Therefore, the harder the material, the more difficult it is to cut. This is because it is more difficult for the cutting tool to penetrate a hard material than it is for the cutting tool to penetrate a soft material.

Hardness of the cutting tool

You can cut wood with a steel tool, but you cannot cut steel (or any other common metal) with wood. For the cutting tool to penetrate the workpiece material, the cutting tool must be made from a material that is harder than the material to be cut. Since heat is generated by the cutting process, the cutting tool must retain its hardness as its temperature rises. Some materials are better at retaining their hardness at high temperatures than others. This is shown in Fig. 8.1. You can see that high-carbon steel is harder than high-speed steel at room temperature but loses its hardness quickly as its temperature rises. We say that its 'temper' is easily drawn. On the other hand, high-speed steel keeps its hardness up to red heat. This is why hand tools and fine edge tools are made from high-carbon steel to benefit from its superior hardness, and why metal cutting tools are made from high-speed steel so that they can resist the higher temperatures associated with machining. Where tools have to operate at even higher temperatures, materials such as stellite alloy, metal carbides and metal oxides are used.

Sharpness

Tools that are sightly blunt will cut, but the surface finish will be poor and the heat generated will be greater than that for a sharp tool so that the tool will quickly become soft and rendered useless. The increased cutting forces acting on the blunt tool may even break it. Cutting tools should be sharpened before use and the cutting conditions should be such that the tool will remain sharp for an economical period of time. To achieve this, the tool material must be selected to suit the workpiece material. The cutting speeed must be chosen so that the tool is not overheated. This is a

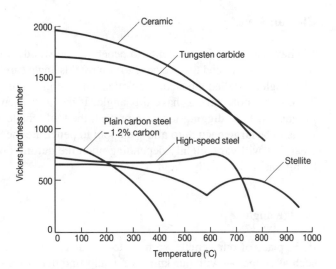

Fig. 8.1 Hardness/temperature curves for cutting tool materials

compromise between tool-life and rate of production. For economy of production, material must be removed as quickly as possible. On the other hand, too high a cutting speed may result in time lost through frequent tool changing and the cost of frequent tool refurbishment and replacement must also be taken into account.

Wedge form of the cutting tool

I expect that one of the first controlled cutting operations you performed must have been the sharpening of a pencil with a penknife. It is unlikely you will have received any formal instruction before your first attempt but, most likely, you soon found out (by trial and error) that the knife blade had to be presented to the wood at a definite angle if success was to be achieved. This is shown in Fig. 8.2. If the blade is laid flat on the wood it just slides along without cutting. If you tilt it at a slight angle, it will bite into the wood and start to cut. If you tilt it at too steep an angle, it will bite into the wood too deeply and it will not cut properly. You will also find that the best angle will vary between a knife which is sharp and a knife which is blunt. A sharp knife will penetrate the wood more easily, at a shallower angle, and you will have more control. But look at that knife blade. It is the shape of a wedge. In fact all cutting tools are wedge shaped (more or less), so let's now look at the angles of a typical metal cutting tool.

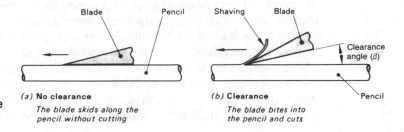

Fig. 8.2 The clearance angle

(a) **No clearance**
The blade skids along the pencil without cutting

(b) **Clearance**
The blade bites into the pencil and cuts

8.2 The angles of a wedge-shaped cutting tool

Clearance angle

We have seen that for our knife to penetrate the wood, we need to incline it to the surface being cut, and that we have to control this angle carefully for effective cutting. This angle, is called the *clearance angle* and we give it the Greek letter 'beta' (β). All cutting tools have to have this angle. It has to be kept as small as possible to prevent the tool 'digging-in' or to prevent the tool 'chattering'. On the other hand, it has to be large enough to allow the tool to penetrate the workpiece material. The clearance will vary slightly depending upon the cutting operation and the material being cut. It is usually about 5° to 7°.

Wedge angle

If, in place of our pencil, we tried to sharpen a point on a piece of soft metal — such as copper — with our knife we would find that it very quickly becomes blunt. If you examine this blunt edge under a magnifying glass, you will see that the cutting edge has crumbled away. To cut metal successfully, the cutting edge must be ground to a less acute angle to give greater strength. This is shown in Fig. 8.3. The angle to which the tool is ground is called the *wedge angle* or the *tool angle* and it is given the Greek letter 'gamma' (γ).

The greater the wedge angle, the stronger will be the tool. Also, the greater the wedge angle the quicker the heat of cutting will be conducted away from the cutting edge. This will prevent the tool overheating and softening, and help to prolong the tool life. Unfortunately, the greater the wedge angle is made, the greater will be the force required to make the tool penetrate the workpiece material. The choice of the wedge angle becomes a compromise between all these factors.

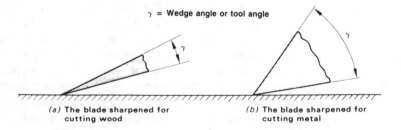

γ = Wedge angle or tool angle

(a) The blade sharpened for cutting wood

(b) The blade sharpened for cutting metal

Fig. 8.3 The wedge angle

Rake angle

To complete the angles associated with cutting tools, reference must be made to the *rake angle*. This is given the Greek letter alpha (α). The rake angle is very important, for it alone controls the geometry of the chip formation for any given material and, therefore, it controls the mechanics of the cutting action of the tool. The relationship of the rake angle to the angles previously discussed is shown in Fig. 8.4. Increasing the rake angle increases the cutting efficiency of the tool and makes cutting easier. Since increasing the rake angle reduces the wedge angle, increased cutting efficiency is gained at the expense of tool strength. Again a

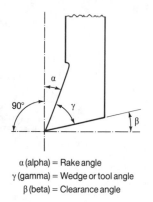

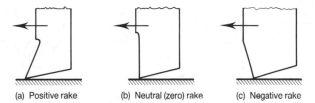

Some typical rake angles for high speed steel tools	
Material being cut	Rake
Cast iron	0°
Free-cutting brass	0°
Ductile brass	14°
Tin bronze	8°
Aluminium alloy	30°
Mild steel	25°
Medium carbon steel	20°
High carbon steel	12°
'Tufnol' plastic	0°

Fig. 8.4 Cutting tool angles

α (alpha) = Rake angle
γ (gamma) = Wedge or tool angle
β (beta) = Clearance angle

Fig. 8.5 Rake angles

(a) Positive rake   (b) Neutral (zero) rake   (c) Negative rake

compromise has to be reached in achieving a balance between cutting efficiency and tool strength and life.

So far only a single point tool with *positive* rake has been considered. Tools may also have *neutral rake* and *negative rake*. The meaning of these terms is explained in Fig. 8.5. It can be seen that the wedge angles for such tools is much more robust and it should come as no surprise that they are used for heavy cutting conditions. However, the cutting action of tools with neutral and negative rake angles is somewhat different to the positive rake geometry considered so far and is beyond the scope of this book.

8.3 Chip formation and cutting lubricants

Discontinuous chip

When a tool is cutting, the metal being cut is sheared away from the body of the workpiece as shown in Fig. 8.6(a). If the material is brittle, such as cast iron, the chips will break up into individual granules as shown in Fig. 8.6(b). These are called *discontinuous chips*.

Continuous chip

This is the long ribbon-like chip (swarf) which is produced when machining ductile materials such as mild steel, copper and aluminium. The metal behaves like a rigid plastic and, although the chip shears from the workpiece along the shear plane, it does not break up into individual 'plates' or granules as shown in Fig. 8.6(a). The formation of a continuous chip is shown in Fig. 8.7. Continuous chips have a razor

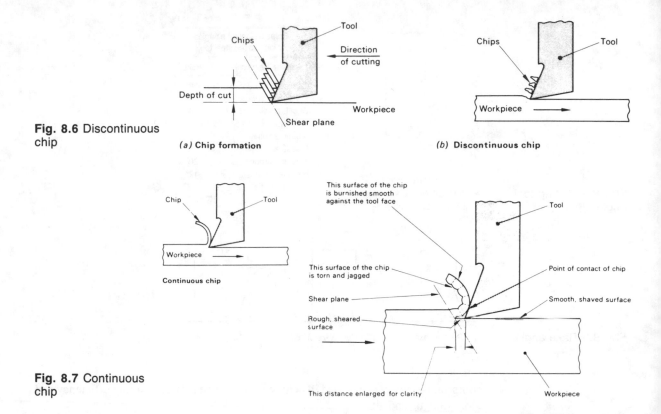

Fig. 8.6 Discontinuous chip

(a) Chip formation

(b) Discontinuous chip

Fig. 8.7 Continuous chip

sharp edge and can be very dangerous to handle. Where large quantities of chips (swarf) are being created under production conditions, the tools are usually fitted with a 'chip-breaker' to curl the chips up tightly. This causes the chips to break up into short lengths for easier disposal.

Continuous chips with a built-up edge

Under some conditions the friction between the chip and the tool face is very great. This can result in metal from the chip becoming pressure welded to the rake face of the tool making it rough. This increases the friction which, in turn, leads to the building up of layer upon layer of chip material as shown in Fig. 8.8(a). This is referred to as a *built-up edge*. Eventually the amount of material builds up to such an extent that it becomes unstable and breaks down. The particles of built-up material that flake away weld themselves to the chip and the workpiece as shown in Fig. 8.8(b). This produces a dangerously jagged chip and a rough surface on the workpiece. This formation of a built-up edge is called chip welding.

Prevention of chip welding

Since chip welding has a considerable and adverse effect on the cutting process and also upon the surface finish of the workpiece, we must make every attempt to prevent

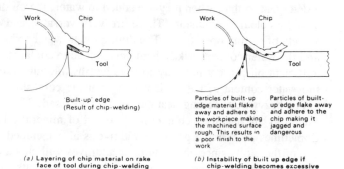

Fig. 8.8 Chip welding (built up edge)

(a) Layering of chip material on rake face of tool during chip-welding

(b) Instability of built up edge if chip-welding becomes excessive

it occurring. Usually this is achieved by reversing one or more of the factors which cause chip welding.

(a) *Reducing friction*. This can be achieved by increasing the rake angle, polishing the rake face, and introducing a lubricant between the chip and the rake face to prevent metal to metal contact.

(b) *Reducing the temperature*. This can be achieved by reducing the friction as described above and by flooding the cutting zone with a coolant. As a last resort, since it lowers productivity, the cutting speed has to be reduced.

(c) *Reducing the pressure* between the chip and the tool. This can be achieved by increasing the rake angle, reducing the feed rate, or by reducing the chip thickness by using oblique instead of orthogonal cutting as described in section 8.5.

(d) *Preventing metal-to-metal contact*. This can be achieved by the use of a lubricant including an extreme pressure additive. Such additives include sulphur and chlorine compounds in order to build up a non-metallic film on the tool face. The use of non-metallic tool materials such as carbides and ceramics also helps to prevent chip welding.

Lubricants and coolants

Cutting lubricants and coolants have already been mentioned above. Correctly selected and applied they are one of the most economical means of increasing the efficiency of any cutting process. They are designed to fulfil one or more of the following functions:

(a) to cool the tool and the workpiece
(b) to lubricate the chip/tool interface
(c) to flush away the chips formed by cutting
(d) to help to prevent chip welding
(e) to improve the surface finish of the workpiece
(f) to prevent corrosion of the work and the machine.

Ordinary lubricating oils are useless as cutting fluids. They cannot withstand the high pressures that exist between the chip and the tool. They also break down and give off noxious fumes at the temperatures that exist at the chip/tool interface.

For general purpose machining we use emulsified oils (suds). These are also called (wrongly) soluble oils. Normally oil and water will not mix but cutting oils contain a detergent so that, when they are added to water, the oil droplets disperse to form a milky coloured emulsion. These are very versatile and can be used for a wide variety of cutting operations. The dilution with water reduces the cost substantially and the water content makes them very effective coolants. Properly mixed there is sufficient oil present not only to give worthwhile lubrication, but also to prevent the water content of the coolant from causing corrosion.

For heavy duty cutting neat cutting oils are used. That is, the oil is not diluted. Such oils are usually a compound or blend of mineral oils and organic fatty oils. Sometimes an extreme pressure additive is also included. Care is required in the use of these oils since active sulphur additives will attack and corrode copper and copper alloys. Since they are not diluted, these lubricants are costly to use. Although very much more effective as lubricants than emulsified oils, they are less effective coolants.

Synthetic coolants are more expensive than coolants based on naturally occurring lubricants. However, they have a number of advantages.

(a) They are more efficient since they can be 'tailored' to suit a particular cutting situation.
(b) They are non-flammable. This is very important as large quantities of cutting oil can be present in a workshop.
(c) They are non-toxic, whereas constant exposure to mineral oils can cause skin cancer.
(d) They combine all the lubricating properties of neat blended oils with all the cooling properties of emulsified oils.
(e) They do not give off noxious and toxic fumes.
(f) They form stable emulsions which do not break down due to bacterial attack as do mineral oil based emulsions.

8.4 The application of cutting angles to different types of cutting tools

Cold chisels

The basic wedge angle (see section 8.2) applies to all metal-cutting tools. Figure 8.9(a) shows how the point of a cold chisel forms a metal-cutting wedge with rake and clearance angles, and how the angle at which you present the chisel work (angle of inclination) affects these angles. In Fig. 8.9(b) the chisel is presented to the work so that the angle of inclination is too small. As a result, the rake angle becomes larger and the clearance angle disappears. This prevents the chisel's cutting edge from biting into the work and the chisel 'lifts off' so that the cut becomes progressively shallower. In Fig. 8.9(c) the chisel is presented to the work so that the angle of

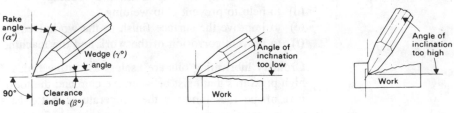

Fig. 8.9 The chisel — correct use

Cutting angles applied to a cold chisel

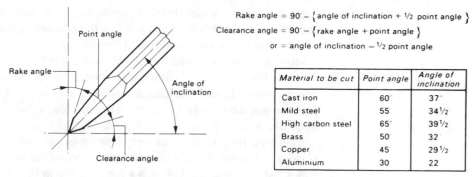

Rake angle = 90° − { angle of inclination + ½ point angle }

Clearance angle = 90° − { rake angle + point angle }

or = angle of inclination − ½ point angle

Material to be cut	Point angle	Angle of inclination
Cast iron	60°	37°
Mild steel	55°	34½°
High carbon steel	65°	39½°
Brass	50°	32°
Copper	45°	29½°
Aluminium	30°	22°

Fig. 8.10 Chisel angles

The point angle of a chisel is equivalent to the wedge angle of a lathe or shaping machine tool. The point angle together with the angle of inclination forms the rake and clearance angles

inclination is too large. This reduces the rake angle and increases the clearance angle. This results in the chisel's cutting edge 'digging in' so that the cut becomes progressively deeper.

The skilled craftsperson will control the angle of inclination of the chisel, to maintain a constant depth of cut, by eye and by the feel of the chisel as it cuts. As a start, however, Fig. 8.10 shows the correct wedge angles and angles of inclination for a variety of materials.

Files

Like any other cutting tool a file tooth must have correctly applied cutting angles. File teeth are formed by a chisel type cutter hitting the file blank at an angle as shown in Fig. 8.11(a). The tooth is formed partly by the cutting action of the cutter and partly by the displaced metal piling up ahead of the cutter.

This first or 'over-cut' produces a single cut file or 'float', as shown in Fig. 8.11(b).

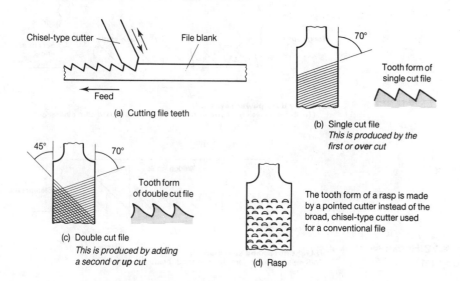

(a) Cutting file teeth

(b) Single cut file
This is produced by the first or over cut

(c) Double cut file
This is produced by adding a second or up cut

(d) Rasp

The tooth form of a rasp is made by a pointed cutter instead of the broad, chisel-type cutter used for a conventional file

Fig. 8.11 File teeth

Such files are not widely used except on soft materials such as brass, copper and aluminium. The tooth form is less likely to become clogged up than the tooth form of the more commonly used double-cut file.

Most files have a second or 'up-cut' and are referred to as 'double-cut' files as shown in Fig. 8.11(c). Up-cutting gives the teeth a positive rake angle and a smoother cutting action. Double cut files are suitable for use on tougher materials such as plain carbon steels and alloy steels. They are also suitable for use on cast iron and most non-ferrous metals.

Rasp type files are used on very soft materials such as pure aluminium, some plastics and wood. Individual teeth are raised on the blank by means of a pointed cutter and the appearance of such a file is shown in Fig. 8.11(d). The rows of teeth are staggered to produce a smoother cutting action.

Special files such as 'Millencut' and 'Dreadnought' type files are also available for use on soft materials. Their material removal rates are high but the finish is relatively rough and they are not suitable for precision work.

Hacksaw blades

The teeth of a heavy duty hacksaw blade suitable for use on a power driven sawing machine is shown in Fig. 8.12(a). You will see that the teeth form a series of metal cutting wedges. Since there are a series of metal cutting edges this is called a *multi-tooth* cutting tool, compared with a chisel or a lathe tool which are called *single-point* cutting tools. Like all multi-tooth cutting tools designed to work in a slot, the power hacksaw blade has to be provided with chip (secondary) clearance as well as cutting (primary) clearance. The secondary clearance provides room for the chips to be carried out of the slot without clogging the teeth whilst, at the same time, maintaining a strong cutting edge.

The finer teeth of a hand saw blade have only a simple wedge shape as shown in Fig. 8.12(b). Chip clearance is provided by exaggerating the primary clearance.

(a) **Heavy duty power saw blade**
(Tooth form gives high strength coupled with adequate chip clearance)

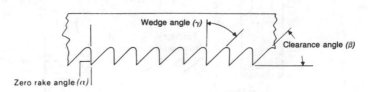

Fig. 8.12 Hacksaw blade teeth

(b) **Light duty hand saw blade**
(Simplified tooth form for fine tooth blades)

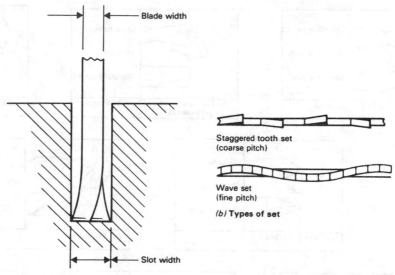

Fig. 8.13 Tooth set   *(a)* **The effect of set**

Although this weakens the teeth, their strength is adequate for a hand saw. In addition side clearance has to be provided to prevent the blade binding in the slot being cut. The way this is done is by staggering the teeth as shown in Fig. 8.13(a). This is called the 'set' of the teeth. For blades with very fine teeth it is not possible to set each tooth and the teeth are given a 'wave' set as shown in Fig. 8.13(b).

Twist drills

Figure 8.14 shows a typical twist drill and names its more important features. The application of the basic cutting angles to a twist drill is shown in Fig. 8.14(a). The rake angle is formed by the helical groove (flute) and is fixed at the time of manufacture and cannot be changed. The rake angle varies from point to point along the lip of the drill as shown in Fig. 8.14(b). It varies from negative rake at the chisel

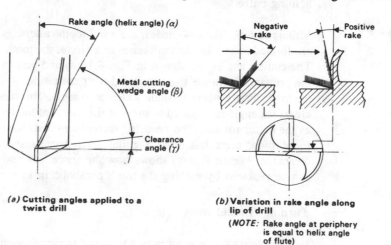

(a) **Cutting angles applied to a twist drill**

(b) **Variation in rake angle along lip of drill**

(NOTE: Rake angle at periphery is equal to helix angle of flute)

Fig. 8.14 Cutting angles applied to a twist drill

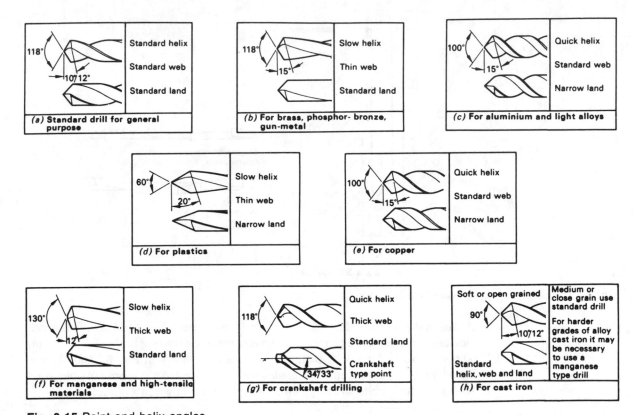

Fig. 8.15 Point and helix angles

point to positive rake at the outer corners. For most applications the standard 'jobber' type drill is used. However, for special applications, drills are available with different point and helix angles. Figure 8.15 shows some typical point and helix angles for a variety of materials.

Milling cutters

Milling cutters, like saw-blades, are multi-tooth cutters. However, because the teeth are formed round the circumference of a circle, the tooth form is slightly different. The cutting angles are shown in Fig. 8.16(a) and you can see that, in addition to the primary clearance angle required for penetration of the workpiece material by the tooth, there is also a secondary clearance angle. This time, however, the secondary clearance angle is required to prevent the 'heel' of the tooth fouling the workpiece as the cutter rotates. The need for secondary clearance is shown in Fig. 8.16(b). In addition, there has to be a gullet or tertiary clearance angle to provide chip clearance. Figure 8.16(c) shows how the secondary and tertiary clearance angles can be replaced by making the tooth parabolic in form.

Turning (Lathe) tools

Lathe tools are single-point cutting tools and the application of the basic cutting angles

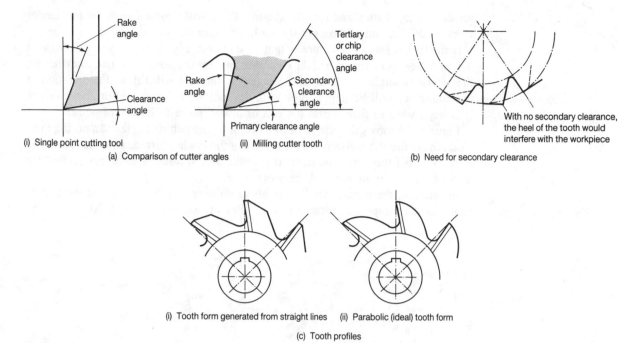

(i) Single point cutting tool

(ii) Milling cutter tooth

(a) Comparison of cutter angles

With no secondary clearance, the heel of the tooth would interfere with the workpiece

(b) Need for secondary clearance

(i) Tooth form generated from straight lines   (ii) Parabolic (ideal) tooth form

(c) Tooth profiles

Fig. 8.16 Milling cutter tooth form

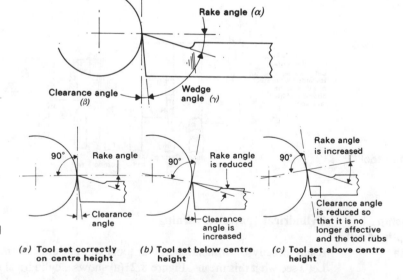

Fig. 8.17 Cutting angles applied to a single-point lathe tool

Rake angle (α)

Clearance angle (β)

Wedge angle (γ)

Fig. 8.18 Effect of tool height on turning tool angles

90° Rake angle

Clearance angle

(a) Tool set correctly on centre height

90° Rake angle is reduced

Clearance angle is increased

(b) Tool set below centre height

90° Rake angle is increased

Clearance angle is reduced so that it is no longer affective and the tool rubs

(c) Tool set above centre height

is shown in Fig. 8.17. Because the cutting edge is in contact with a curved surface the angles are referenced to imaginary planes at the point of contact.

Tool height is very important to turning tools. Normally you set the tool so that the point is in line with the axis of the workpiece as shown in Fig. 8.18(a). If the tool is set below centre height as shown in Fig. 8.18(b), you can see that the rake angle is decreased and the clearance angle is increased. There will be a tendency for the tool to 'chatter' and for it to 'dig-in'. There will also be a tendency for slender work to deflect and climb over the tool. *This can be very dangerous.*

If the tool is set above centre height as shown in Fig. 8.18(c), you can see that the rake angle is increased and the clearance angle is decreased. Carried to extremes, the clearance angle will disappear altogether, the tool will rub and penetration of the workpiece will be impossible. With the tool set either below or above centre it is impossible to face across the end of a workpiece to its centre point.

Figure 8.19 shows the effects of tool height on the cutting angles of a boring tool. You can see that these effects are the reverse of those when turning external diameters. Also note that this time you have to give the tool secondary clearance so that the heel of the tool does not foul the workpiece.

In practice, these basic angles are also influenced by the profile of the cutting tool. Some examples of turning tool profiles are shown in Fig. 8.20.

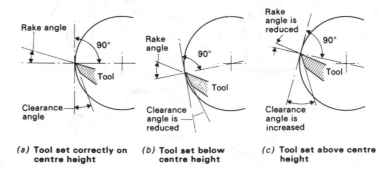

Fig. 8.19 Effect of tool height on boring tool angles

(a) **Tool set correctly on centre height** *(b)* **Tool set below centre height** *(c)* **Tool set above centre height**

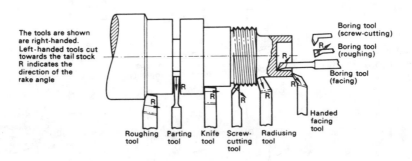

Fig. 8.20 Lathe tool profiles

8.5 Relationship between depth of cut and feed rate

Cylindrical (parallel) turning

It has already been mentioned that tools can cut either *orthogonally* or *obliquely*. Let's see what this means. Figure 8.21(a) shows a cylindrical turning operation being performed by moving the tool parallel to the axis of the workpiece. Since the cutting edge of the tool is at right angles (perpendicular) to the direction of feed, the tool is said to be cutting *orthogonally*. The shaded area represents the cross-sectional area (shear area) of the chip. This area is calculated by multiplying the feed per revolution of the workpiece by the depth of cut (A = d × f). Figure 8.21(b) shows the same turning operation using a tool in which the cutting edge is inclined away

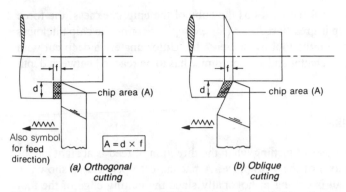

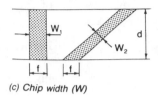

(i) Depth of cut (d) is constant for both figures.
(ii) Feed/rev (f) is constant for both figures.
(iii) Chip area (A = d × f) is constant for both figures.
(iv) Chip thickness (W) varies.
(v) Oblique cutting reduces (W) without reducing (A).

(c) Chip width (W)

Fig. 8.21 Orthogonal and oblique cutting (parallel turning)

from the direction of feed. Such a tool is said to be cutting *obliquely*. The cross-sectional area of the chip produced is the same as when cutting orthogonally since again A = d × f. However, when cutting obliquely, the chip thickness (W) is reduced as shown in Fig. 8.21(c), where it can be seen that:

(a) the depth of cut 'd' is constant in both examples;
(b) the feed/rev 'f' is constant in both examples;
(c) the chip area (A = d × f) is constant for both examples (parallelogram theory);
(d) the chip thickness is less when cutting obliquely because $W_1 > W_2$.

Since the chip is thinner when cutting obliquely the chip is more easily deflected over the rake face of the tool and the force it exerts on the tool is correspondingly less. This reduces wear on the tool and lessens the chance of chip welding without reducing the rate of material removal since the area of the cut is unaltered.

The same area of cut can be achieved using a shallow cut with a high rate of feed or by using a deep cut with a low rate of feed. So, which is the better? Figure 8.22(a) shows what happens when a shallow cut at a high rate of feed is chosen. The chip is being bent across its deepest section. This not only requires considerable force, but the high rate of feed will lead to a rough finish. In Fig. 8.22(b) a deep cut at a low rate of feed is being used. This time the chip is being bent across its thinnest

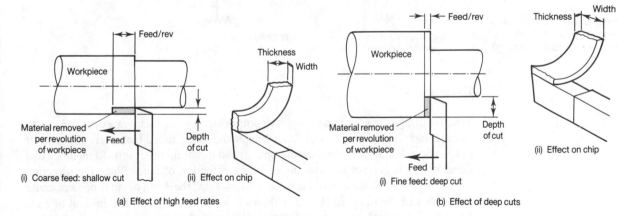

Fig. 8.22 Effect of rate of feed and depth of cut on chip thickness

section. Since the bending force varies as the cube of the chip thickness, the force required to bend the chip is greatly reduced (for example: halving the chip thickness reduces the force acting on the tool by one-eighth). Unfortunately a deep cut with a shallow feed can lead to chatter and a compromise has to be reached between depth of cut and rate of feed.

Perpendicular turning

Figure 8.23 shows examples of turning when the direction of feed is at right angles (perpendicular) to the axis of the workpiece. A parting-off operation is shown in Fig.8.23(a), and the tool is cutting orthogonally since the cutting edge of the tool is at right angles to the direction of feed. You may find it strange that the depth of cut is controlled by the width of the tool, but look at it this way. Depth of cut is always at right angles to the direction of feed. Since the feed is perpendicular to the workpiece axis, it follows that the depth of cut must be parallel to the workpiece axis and this is the width of the tool.

A facing operation is shown in Fig 8.23(b). This time the tool is cutting obliquely since the cutting edge is inclined to the direction of feed. In both examples the area of cut is the depth of cut multiplied by the feed per revolution (A = d × f).

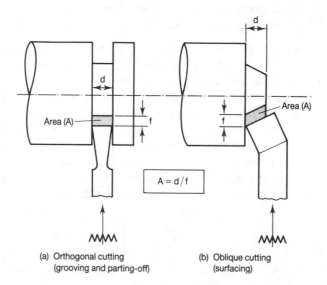

Fig. 8.23 Orthogonal and oblique cutting (perpendicular turning)

(a) Orthogonal cutting (grooving and parting-off)

(b) Oblique cutting (surfacing)

Drilling

When drilling, the situation is slightly complicated by the fact that a drill is a multi-tooth cutter. That is, it cuts on both lips at the same time. However, the area of cut can be calculated by considering one lip and doubling the result. Remember that depth of cut is always at right angles to the direction of feed. Since the direction of feed is parallel to the axis of the drill, it follows that the depth of cut is perpendicular to the axis of the drill. In fact, it is the radius of the drill 'd'. The in-feed of each lip is half the total feed per revolution ($\frac{1}{2}$f), and the area of cut is calculated as shown in Fig. 8.24.

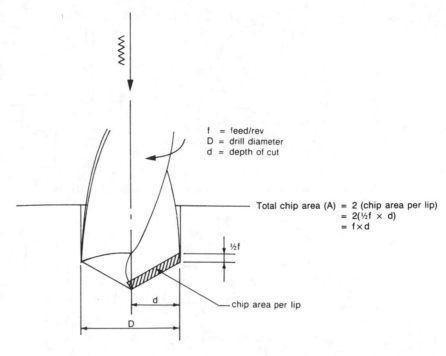

f = feed/rev
D = drill diameter
d = depth of cut

Total chip area (A) = 2 (chip area per lip)
= 2(½f × d)
= f × d

½f

chip area per lip

d

D

Fig. 8.24 Area of cut when drilling

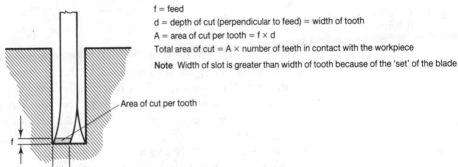

f = feed
d = depth of cut (perpendicular to feed) = width of tooth
A = area of cut per tooth = f × d
Total area of cut = A × number of teeth in contact with the workpiece

Note Width of slot is greater than width of tooth because of the 'set' of the blade

Area of cut per tooth

f

d

Fig. 8.25 Area of cut when hacksawing

Hacksaw

Again life is complicated since the hacksaw blade is also a multi-tooth cutter. The calculation of area of cut is similar to that for a twist drill. The direction of feed is into the work as shown in Fig. 8.25. Since the depth of cut is perpendicular to the direction of feed, it follows that the depth of cut equals the width of each cutting tooth. The in-feed is stated as being the feed per cutting stroke of the blade. Therefore the feed per tooth equals the feed per cutting stroke divided by the number of teeth involved in cutting. The formula for the total cutting area per cutting stroke is also derived (see Fig. 8.25).

8.6 Cutting forces

Figure 8.26(a) shows the main cutting forces acting on a turning tool. The tool is shown cutting orthogonally for simplicity. Additional forces are present when the tool is cutting obliquely as shown in Fig. 8.26(b).

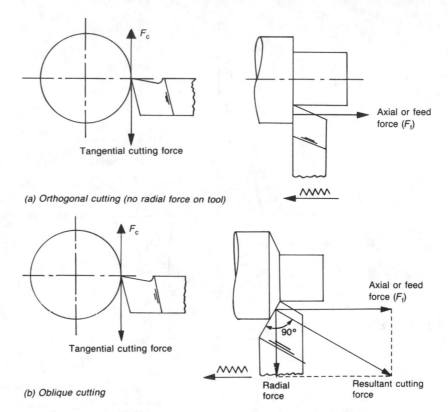

F_c

Tangential cutting force

(a) Orthogonal cutting (no radial force on tool)

Axial or feed force (F_f)

F_c

Tangential cutting force

Axial or feed force (F_f)

90°

Radial force

Resultant cutting force

Fig. 8.26 Forces acting on turning tools   *(b) Oblique cutting*

(a) The main cutting force F_c is caused by the resistance of the workpiece material to the cutting process. It is a reaction force equal to, but never greater than, the downward force of the chip on the tool. For any given material the cutting force is approximately proportional to the area of cut but it is unaffected by the speed of cutting.

(b) The feed force F_f is also a reaction force and is caused by the resistance of the material being cut to the penetration of the cutting tool.

We call these forces reaction forces because the size of the forces depends upon how the workpiece material reacts to the cutting action of the tool. If the lathe is operated without the workpiece in place the tool would not be cutting and there would be no cutting or feed force acting on the tool. If the workpiece is a relatively weak material such as aluminium then modest cutting and feed forces would be exerted on the cutting tool. However, if a strong material such as alloy steel is cut with the same depth of cut and rate of feed then the forces acting on the tool would be very much greater. The limiting forces are those which are so great that the tool cannot withstand them and it breaks.

Figure 8.27(a) shows how these forces act on a twist drill. Being a multi-tooth cutter the cutting force is shared out between the two lips of the drill. In the case of a saw blade, the cutting force is shared out between the number of teeth in contact with the work at any one time. This is shown in Fig. 8.27(b). The work holding and toolholding devices described in Chapter 6 have to be capable of resisting these forces. They also have to support the work and the tool so that they are not distorted or deflected by these forces.

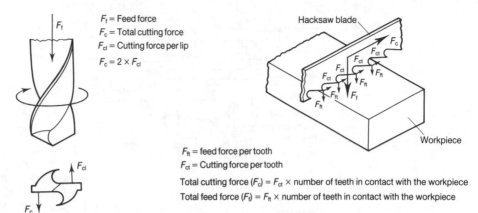

F_f = Feed force
F_c = Total cutting force
F_{cl} = Cutting force per lip
$F_c = 2 \times F_{cl}$

Hacksaw blade

Workpiece

Fig. 8.27 Cutting forces acting on multi-tooth cutters

(a) Forces acting on a twist drill

F_{ft} = feed force per tooth
F_{ct} = Cutting force per tooth

Total cutting force (F_c) = F_{ct} × number of teeth in contact with the workpiece
Total feed force (F_f) = F_{ft} × number of teeth in contact with the workpiece

(b) Forces on a hacksaw blade

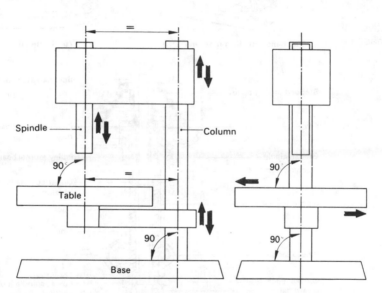

Spindle

Column

Table

Base

Fig. 8.28 Basic alignments of a drilling machine

8.7 Drilling machines

To remove material by drilling, the drilling machine has to rotate the drill and provide a means of feeding the drill into the workpiece. Usually the hole being drilled has to be perpendicular to the datum surface of the workpiece. Therefore the basic alignments of a drilling machine are as shown in Fig. 8.28. The *spindle* rotates and locates the drill and is itself located in precision bearings in a *sleeve* that can move within the body of the drilling machine. The sleeve slides vertically to or from the worktable so that, at all times, the axis of the spindle is perpendicular to the worktable.

Figure 8.29(a) shows a typical bench drilling machine incorporating the alignments and movements previously discussed. It is capable of accepting drills up to about 12.5 mm diameter either in a chuck or directly mounted in the taper bore of the spindle. Workholding and toolholding on the drilling machine have already been discussed in Chapter 7. As previously stated, for normal drilling operations the axis of the spindle must be perpendicular to the surface of the worktable. However, if the hole to be drilled is at an angle to the workpiece datum, you can tilt the worktable as shown in Fig. 8.29(b).

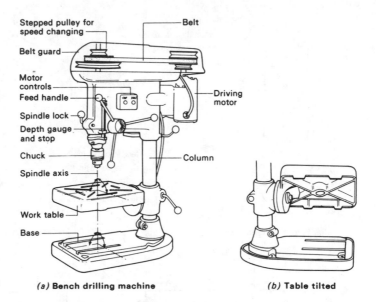

Fig. 8.29 Sensitive bench drilling machine

(a) **Bench drilling machine**   *(b)* **Table tilted**

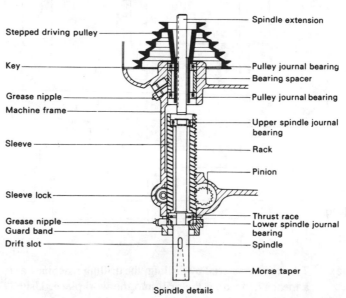

Fig. 8.30 Sensitive feed mechanism

Spindle details

You can also achieve variation of the spindle speed by altering the belt position on the stepped pulleys. *SAFETY: always switch off and isolate the machine before opening the guard and changing the speed.* The feed is operated by hand through a rack and pinion mechanism as shown in Fig. 8.30. This type of feed mechanism enables you to 'feel' the drill cutting into the workpiece material. Hence the name 'sensitive feed'. Figure 8.31 shows a heavier duty drilling machine. In this machine the spindle speed is changed by means of a gear box directly coupled to the drive motor. In addition to hand feed, power feed to the spindle is also provided. The rate of feed is also adjustable by means of a gear box.

Other operations which can be performed on the drilling machine are:

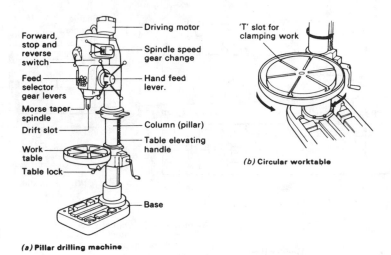

Fig. 8.31 Pillar drilling machine

(a) **Pillar drilling machine**

(b) **Circular worktable**

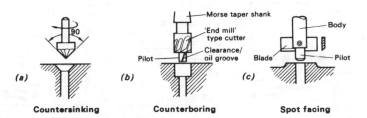

Fig. 8.32 Miscellaneous drilling operations

(a) **Countersinking** *(b)* **Counterboring** *(c)* **Spot facing**

countersinking, counter-boring, and spot facing. These operations are shown in Fig. 8.32.

Drilling operations can also be performed on the centre lathe. Here the work rotates and the drill is stationary. The drill is held in the tailstock barrel and fed into the work by the tailstock handwheel and screw.

8.8 Turning (centre lathe)

To remove material by turning, the lathe has to rotate the workpiece and guide the tool. The basic alignments and movements of the various elements of a centre lathe are shown in Fig. 8.33. You can see from Fig 8.33(a) that the common spindle and tailstock axis is parallel to the bed slideways in both the vertical and the horizontal planes.

The movement of the *carriage* alone is shown in Fig. 8.33(b). This moves the tool parallel to the spindle and workpiece axis and provides the movement required for *cylindrical* or *parallel* turning.

The *cross-slide* is mounted on top of the carriage as shown in Fig. 8.33(c) and provides movement of the tool perpendicular to the spindle and workpiece axis. This movement allows the depth of cut to be set when parallel turning. It also guides the tool when *facing* across the end of the workpiece.

The *compound slide* is mounted on the cross-slide and is sometimes called the top-slide because of its position. When set parallel to the spindle and workpiece axis it can be used for setting the depth of cut of the tool when facing the end of a

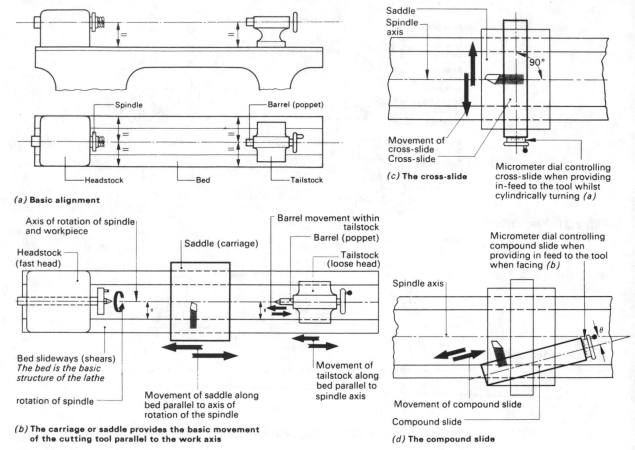

Fig. 8.33 Basic alignments of a centre lathe

component. When inclined to the spindle and workpiece axis as shown in Fig. 8.33(d) it guides the tool at an angle to the workpieces and enables a *taper* to be turned.

Figure 8.34 shows a complete centre lathe possessing all the features just discussed.

Parallel (cylindrical) turning

The work can be held between centre or in a chuck as shown in Fig. 8.35. The tool is fed into the work by the movement of the carriage along the bed and the depth of cut is controlled by the cross-slide. In the case of work held between centres the diameter of the workpiece should be checked at each end after the first cut. Any lack of parallelism can be corrected by adjusting the tailstock laterally across the bed of the lathe. This was described in section 7.7

Perpendicular (facing) turning

The work is usually held in a chuck as shown in Fig. 8.36. It can also be held on

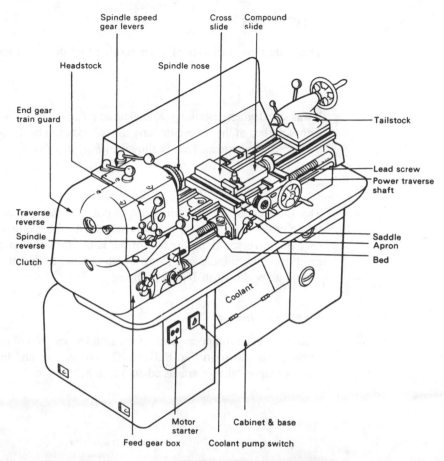

Fig. 8.34 Centre lathe

Fig. 8.35 Parallel (cylindrical) turning

Fig. 8.36 Perpendicular (facing) turning

a faceplate. The carriage is locked in position and the tool feed, perpendicular to the spindle axis, is provided by the cross slide. The compound slide controls the depth of cut. It is essential that the tool point is set in line with the axis of the spindle or a 'pip' will be left in the middle of the workpiece and it will not 'clean up'.

Taper turning

There are three methods of taper turning and these are shown in Fig 8.37.

Off-set tailstock

It was stated when describing parallel turning that the tailstock can be adjusted laterally across the bed of the lathe. Similarly the tailstock can be deliberately offset to provide a tapered component. This is shown in Fig. 8.37(a).

Taper turning attachment

This is an 'optional extra' which can be bolted to the back of the lathe and connected to the cross-slide. The guide bar is set over to the required half-angle and, as the carriage traverses along the bed of the lathe, the cross slide is moved towards or away from the spindle axis along a path parallel to the attachment guide bar. This technique is shown in Fig. 8.37(b).

Compound slide

Setting over the compound slide is the simplest method of producing tapers and this technique is shown in Fig. 8.37(c). The advantages and limitations of these three ways of taper turning are listed in Table 8.1.

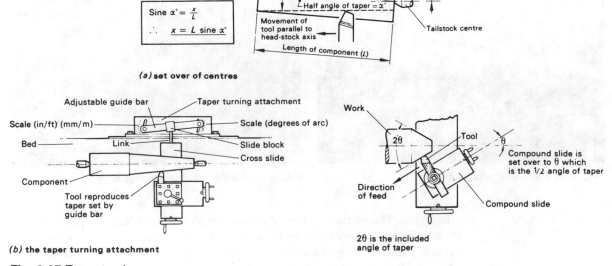

Fig. 8.37 Taper turning

Table 8.1 Comparison of taper turning techniques

Method	Advantages	Limitations
Set over of tailstock	1. Power traverse can be used 2. The full length of the bed used	1. Only small angles can be accommodated 2. Damage to the centre holes can occur 3. Difficulty in setting up 4. Only applies to work held between centres
Taper turning attachments	1. Power traverse can be used 2. Ease of setting 3. Can be applied to chucking and centre work	1. Only small angles can be accommodated 2. Only short lengths can be cut (304–547 mm (12–18 in) depending on make)
Compound slide	1. Very easy setting over a wide range of angles. (Usually used for short steep tapers and chamfers) 2. Can be applied to chucking and centre work	1. Only hand traverse available 2. Only very short lengths can be cut. Varies with m/c but is usually limited to about 76–101 mm (3–4 in)

8.9 Shaping

The shaping machine produces plane surfaces by 'ruling'. That is, it takes a series of cuts parallel to each other and lying in the same plane as shown in Fig. 8.38. The appearance of the machined surface is as though a series of lines have been ruled across it. The alignments and movements necessary for the generation of a plane surface by ruling are shown in Fig. 8.39.

A typical shaping machine is shown in Fig. 8.40. Cutting takes place on the forward stroke of the ram and the tool attached to it. The work is stationary during this cutting stroke. On the non-cutting or return stroke, the table moves across by one feed increment ready for the next cut. The clapper box allows the tool to lift over the uncut work on the return stroke and prevents damage to the cutting tool. Feed is provided by the table movement and the depth of cut is controlled by the tool slide on the ram. The drive to the ram is so designed that it has a slow forward and quick return action. This minimises the time wasted on the non-cutting return stroke. Some advantages and limitations of the shaping process are given in Table 8.2.

The workpiece can be held in a machine vice as shown in Fig. 8.41. Previously it has been stated that the main cutting force should be taken against a solid abutment such as the fixed jaw of a vice as shown in Fig. 8.41(a). However, on a shaping machine this rule is often broken and the work is mounted as shown in Fig 8.41(b). This is because the longer the stroke to which the ram driving mechanism can be set, the greater will be the ratio between the forward and return speeds, and the greater will be the cutting efficiency. Obviously, when the work is set as shown in Fig. 8.41(b), great care must be taken in tightening the vice to ensure that the work is held securely. The work may also be clamped directly to the machine table as shown in Fig. 8.42. The sequence of operations for squaring up a blank on a shaping machine is shown in Fig. 8.43.

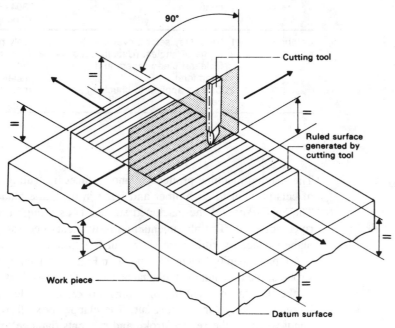

Cutting stroke

Return stroke

Cutting tool

Rough, unmachined surface

Machined plane surface

Component

Direction of feed

(a) Cutting action of the shaping machine

90°

Cutting tool

Ruled surface generated by cutting tool

Work piece

Datum surface

Fig. 8.38 Generation of a plane surface by ruling

(b) Generation of a plane surface by ruling

Table 8.2 The shaping process

Advantages	Limitations
Low cost machine compared to a milling machine.	Low rate of removal compared to horizontal or vertical milling.
Simple single-point tools can be used which can be ground 'off-hand'.	Much less versatile than the milling process.
Tools are much cheaper to buy and maintain than milling cutters.	
Simple to set and operate.	

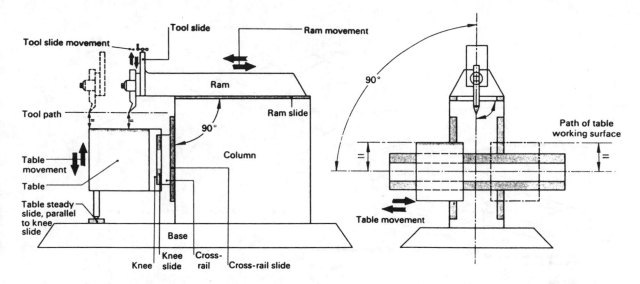

Fig. 8.39 Basic alignments of a shaping machine

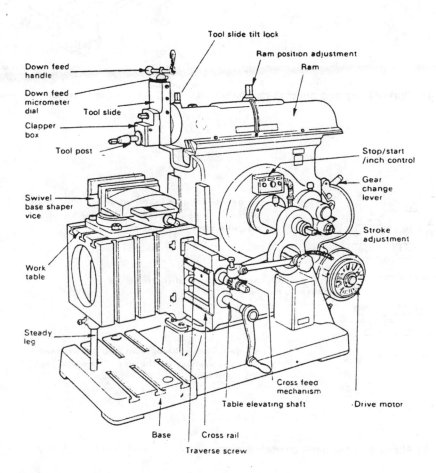

Fig. 8.40 Shaping machine

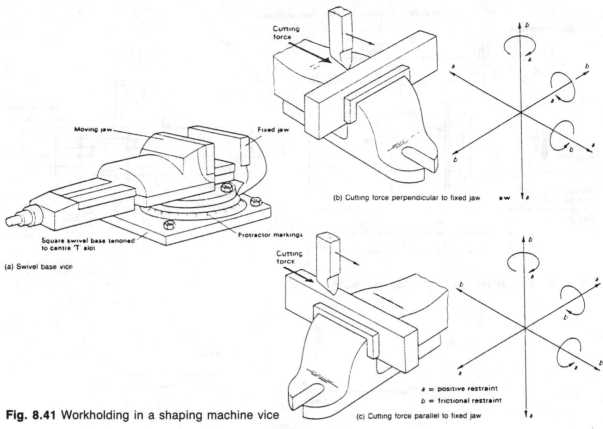

Fig. 8.41 Workholding in a shaping machine vice

(a) Swivel base vice

(b) Cutting force perpendicular to fixed jaw

(c) Cutting force parallel to fixed jaw

a = positive restraint
b = frictional restraint

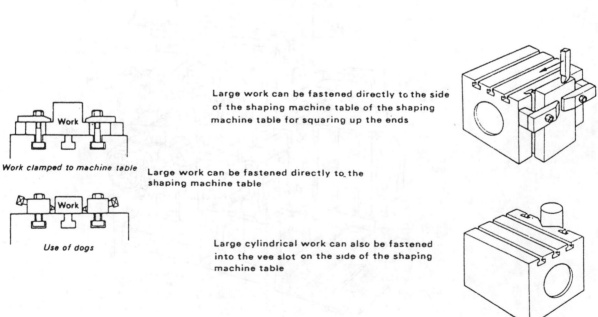

Large work can be fastened directly to the side of the shaping machine table of the shaping machine table for squaring up the ends

Work clamped to machine table

Large work can be fastened directly to the shaping machine table

Use of dogs

Large cylindrical work can also be fastened into the vee slot on the side of the shaping machine table

Fig. 8.42 Alternative methods of workholding

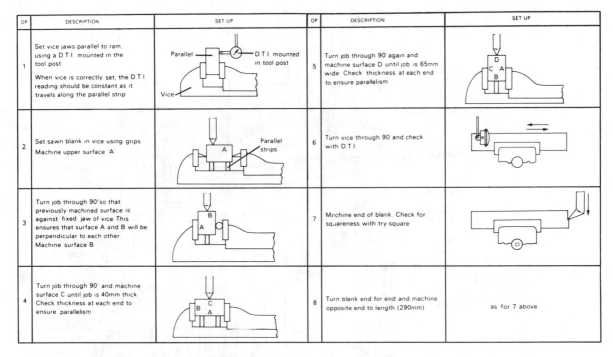

OP	DESCRIPTION	SET UP	OP	DESCRIPTION	SET UP
1	Set vice jaws parallel to ram, using a D.T.I. mounted in the tool post. When vice is correctly set, the D.T.I reading should be constant as it travels along the parallel strip		5	Turn job through 90° again and machine surface D until job is 65mm wide. Check thickness at each end to ensure parallelism	
2	Set sawn blank in vice using grips. Machine upper surface 'A'		6	Turn vice through 90° and check with D.T.I.	
3	Turn job through 90° so that previously machined surface is against fixed jaw of vice. This ensures that surface A and B will be perpendicular to each other. Machine surface B		7	Machine end of blank. Check for squareness with try-square	
4	Turn job through 90° and machine surface C until job is 40mm thick. Check thickness at each end to ensure parallelism		8	Turn blank end for end and machine opposite end to length (290mm)	as for 7 above

Fig. 8.43 Squaring up a blank on a shaping machine

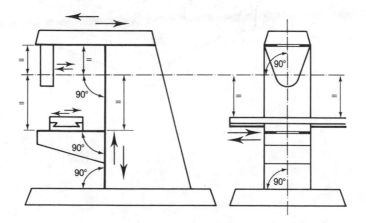

Fig. 8.44 Basic alignments of a horizontal milling machine

8.10 Milling machine (horizontal)

To remove material by milling, the machine has to rotate the cutter and guide the workpiece past it. The basic alignments and movements of a horizontal milling machine is shown in Fig. 8.44. The depth of cut is controlled by raising the knee and table subassembly. The position of the cut is controlled by the cross slide and the feed is provided by a lead screw and nut fitted to the table and separately driven to the spindle. Unlike the feed of a lathe which is directly related to the spindle speed and measured in mm/rev, the feed of a milling machine table is independent of the spindle and is measured in mm/min. A typical horizontal milling machine is shown in Fig. 8.45. There are two basic cutting techniques you can use when milling and these are:

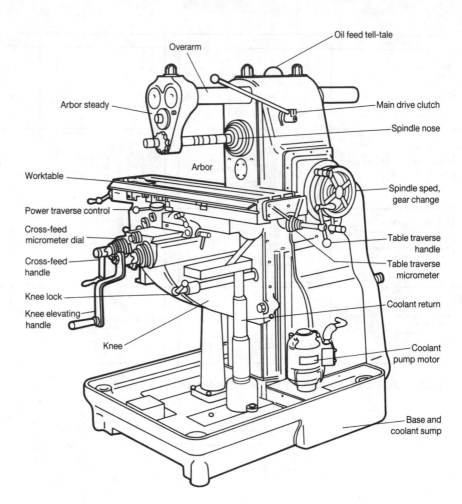

Fig. 8.45 Horizontal milling machine

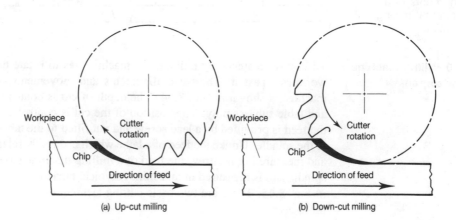

Fig. 8.46 Milling techniques

(a) Up-cut milling   (b) Down-cut milling

(i) *Up-cut* or *conventional milling* as shown in Fig. 8.46(a). You can see that the work is fed towards the cutter against the direction of rotation. This prevents the work being dragged into the cutter if there is any backlash in the feed mechanism. Unfortunately this technique causes the cutting edge to rub as each tooth starts to cut and this can lead to chatter and blunting of the cutting edge. Also the cutting action tends to lift the work off the machine table.

(ii) *Down-cut* or *climb milling* as shown in Fig. 8.46(b). Here you can see that the work is fed into the cutter in the same direction as the cutter is rotating. *SAFETY: this technique can only be used on machines fitted with a 'backlash eliminator' and which are designed for this technique*. If it can be used safely this technique has a number of advantages, particularly for heavy cutting operations. The cutter does not rub as each tooth starts to cut. This reduces the risk of chatter and prolongs the cutter life. Also the cutting forces keep the workpiece pressed down against the machine table. The action of the cutter helps to feed the work forward and takes most of the load off the feed mechanism.

Figure 8.47 shows various cutting operations using a horizontal milling machine and the types of cutter required. The sequence of operations for squaring up a blank on a horizontal milling machine is shown in Fig. 8.48.

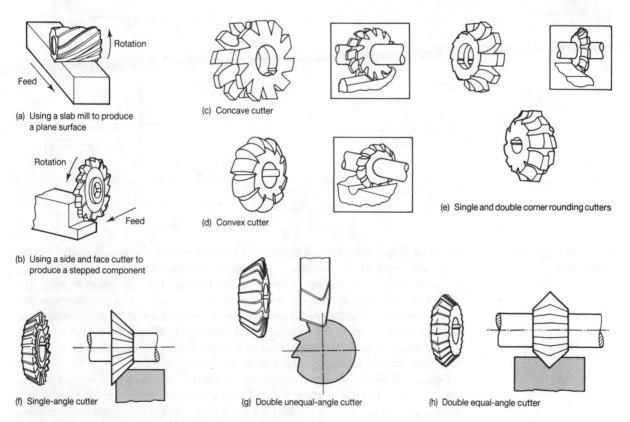

(a) Using a slab mill to produce a plane surface

(b) Using a side and face cutter to produce a stepped component

(c) Concave cutter

(d) Convex cutter

(e) Single and double corner rounding cutters

(f) Single-angle cutter

(g) Double unequal-angle cutter

(h) Double equal-angle cutter

Fig. 8.47 Some typical horizontal milling operations

Op.	Description	Set-up	Op.	Description	Set-up
1	Set vice jaws parallel to table using a DTI. When vice is correctly set the DTI reading should be constant as it travels along the parallel strip.		5	Turn job through 90° again and machine surface 'D' until job is 65 mm wide. Check width at each end to ensure paralellism.	
2	Set sawn blank in vice using grips. Mill surface 'A' using a slab (roller) mill.		6	Turn vice through 90° and check with DTI parallel to spindle axis.	
3	Turn job through 90° so that previously machined surface (A) is against fixed jaw of vice. This ensures surface (A) and (B) are perpendicular to each other. Machine surface 'B'.		7	Use side and face milling cutter to machine and square.	
4	Turn job through 90° and machine surface 'C' until 40 mm thick. Check thickness at each end of job to ensure parallelism.		8	Wind table across and machine to length. Check length with vernier caliper.	

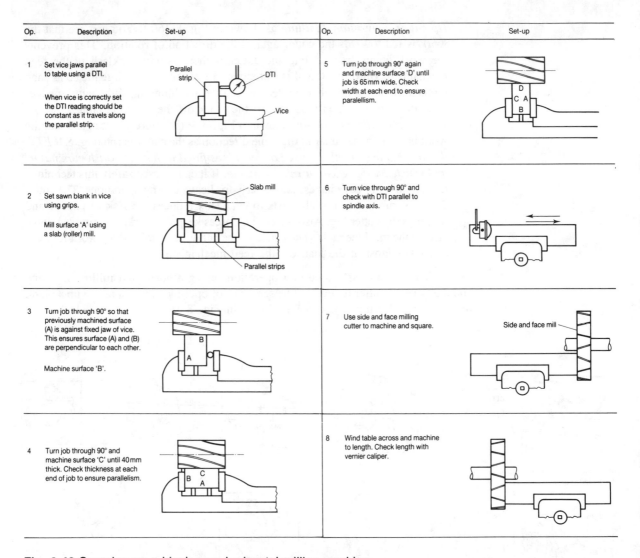

Fig. 8.48 Squaring up a blank on a horizontal milling machine

8.11 Milling machine (vertical)

The basic alignments and movements of a vertical milling machine is shown in Fig. 8.49. The depth of cut is controlled by raising the knee and table subassembly or, for some operations, raising or lowering the spindle. For maximum rigidity, the spindle is normally raised as far as possible. The position of the cut is controlled by the cross-slide and the feed is provided by a lead screw and nut fitted to the table and separately driven to the spindle. As for horizontal milling, the feed of a vertical milling machine table is independent of the spindle and is measured in mm/min. A typical vertical milling machine is shown in Fig. 8.50.

Figure 8.51 shows some typical cutting operations performed on a vertical milling machine and the types of cutter used. The sequence of operations for squaring up a blank on a vertical milling machine is similar to those used for the horizontal milling machine, but the cutters are different. Suitable cutters are shown in Fig.8.52.

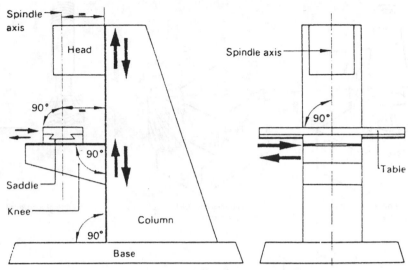

Spindle axis

Head

90°

90°

Saddle

Knee

Column

90°

Base

Spindle axis

90°

Table

Fig. 8.49 Basic
alignments of a
vertical milling
machine

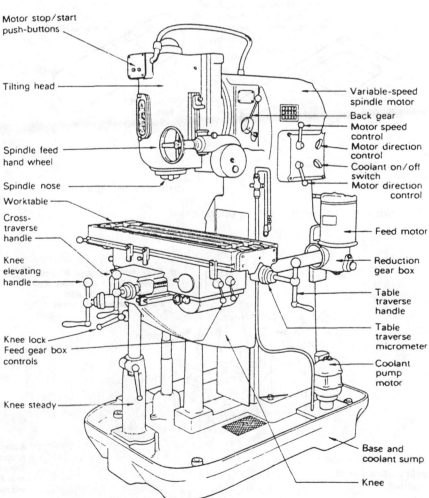

Motor stop/start
push-buttons

Tilting head

Spindle feed
hand wheel

Spindle nose

Worktable

Cross-
traverse
handle

Knee
elevating
handle

Knee lock

Feed gear box
controls

Knee steady

Variable-speed
spindle motor

Back gear

Motor speed
control

Motor direction
control

Coolant on/off
switch

Motor direction
control

Feed motor

Reduction
gear box

Table
traverse
handle

Table
traverse
micrometer

Coolant
pump
motor

Base and
coolant sump

Knee

Fig. 8.50 Vertical
milling machine

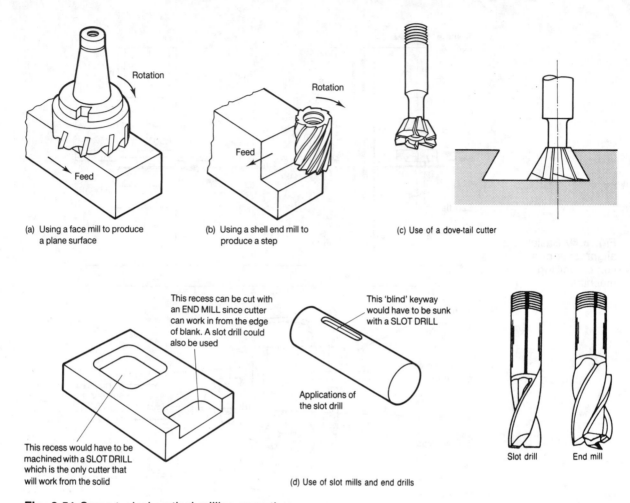

(a) Using a face mill to produce a plane surface

(b) Using a shell end mill to produce a step

(c) Use of a dove-tail cutter

This recess can be cut with an END MILL since cutter can work in from the edge of blank. A slot drill could also be used

This recess would have to be machined with a SLOT DRILL which is the only cutter that will work from the solid

This 'blind' keyway would have to be sunk with a SLOT DRILL

Applications of the slot drill

Slot drill   End mill

(d) Use of slot mills and end drills

Fig. 8.51 Some typical vertical milling operations

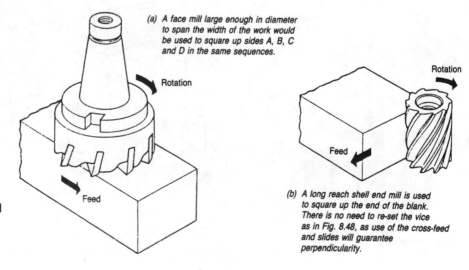

(a) A face mill large enough in diameter to span the width of the work would be used to square up sides A, B, C and D in the same sequences.

Fig. 8.52 Cutters used to square up a blank (vertical milling machine)

(b) A long reach shell end mill is used to square up the end of the blank. There is no need to re-set the vice as in Fig. 8.48, as use of the cross-feed and slides will guarantee perpendicularity.

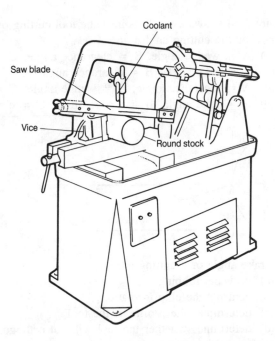

Coolant

Saw blade

Vice

Round stock

Fig. 8.53 Power hacksaw

8.12 Mechanical hacksawing

A typical machine is shown in Fig. 8.53. Unlike hand hacksaws, where cutting takes place on the forward stroke and the teeth of the blade face forward, in most hacksawing machines cutting takes place on the return stroke and the teeth of the blade face backwards. By pulling the blade through the work, the blade is kept in a state of tension. This prevents it buckling and snapping.

The blade is raised on the forward (non-cutting) stroke to prevent it rubbing. If the blade were allowed to rub it would quickly become blunt. A dashpot is also provided to prevent the blade being dropped onto the work. There is no power feed mechanism and the rate of in-feed is dependent on the force of gravity acting on the bow and blade assembly, the resistance of the material to cutting, and the area of the cut under the blade.

You should use a coolant in order to keep the blade cool and to flush away the chips. These might otherwise clog in the cut causing the blade to jam and break. The work should be fastened securely in the machine vice provided before cutting commences.

Exercises

1 The metal cutting wedge forms the basic geometry of
   (a) hand tools only
   (b) machine tools only
   (c) sheet metal cutting tools only
   (d) all cutting tools

2 The clearance angle of a cutting tool
   (a) prevents the point rubbing
   (b) controls the chip formation
   (c) determines the profile of the tool
   (d) determines whether the tool will cut orthogonally or obliquely

3 Figure 8.54 shows a single point lathe tool cutting orthogonally. The correct names for the cutting angles are
    (a) A = wedge angle, B = clearance angle, C = rake angle
    (b) A = rake angle, B = clearance angle, C = wedge angle
    (c) A = clearance angle, B = wedge angle, C = rake angle
    (d) A = rake angle, B = wedge angle, C = clearance angle

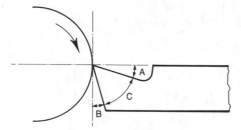

Fig. 8.54

4 The rake angle of a cutting tool
    (a) prevents rubbing
    (b) controls the chip formation
    (c) determines the profile of the tool
    (d) determines whether the tool will cut orthogonally or obliquely
5 Continuous chips may be formed when cutting
    (a) ductile materials
    (b) brittle materials
    (c) free-cutting (leaded) brass
    (d) grey cast iron
6 The 'suds' used as a general purpose cutting lubricant/coolant in machine shops consists of
    (a) water plus a detergent
    (b) an emulsion of water and oil
    (c) a solution of sodium carbonate in water
    (d) an undiluted (neat) mineral oil
7 Figure 8.55 shows a number of cutting tools. Which one has a *negative* rake angle?

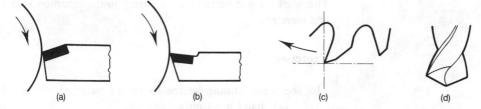

Fig. 8.55
    (a)   (b)   (c)   (d)

8 If you keep the clearance angle constant, any increase in the rake angle will result in
    (a) increased cutting efficiency and increased tool strength
    (b) decreased cutting efficiency and increased tool strength
    (c) increased cutting efficiency and decreased tool strength
    (d) decreased cutting efficiency and decreased tool strength

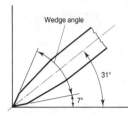

Fig. 8.56

9 The wedge angle for the chisel point shown in Fig. 8.56 is
   (a) 35°
   (b) 38°
   (c) 42°
   (d) 48°

10 Metal cutting files are usually
   (a) cross cut (double cut)
   (b) single cut
   (c) rasp cut
   (d) millencut

11 If you break a hacksaw blade part way through a cut it is usual to
   (a) continue in the same cut with a new blade
   (b) continue in the same cut with a new blade but use plenty of cutting oil
   (c) start a new cut to one side of the old one
   (d) start a new cut at an angle across the old cut

12 When hacksawing through thin metal, choose a blade whose pitch will give a minimum of
   (a) one tooth in contact with the metal at all times
   (b) three teeth in contact with the metal at all times
   (c) five teeth in contact with the metal at all times
   (d) ten teeth in contact with the metal at all times

13 If a turning tool cutting externally is set below centre it results in an effective
   (a) increase in rake angle and decrease in clearance angle
   (b) increase in both rake and clearance angles
   (c) decrease in both rake angle and clearance angles
   (d) decrease in rake angle and increase in clearance angle

14 It is normal practice to prevent the heel of a boring tool from fouling the surface of the bore by using
   (a) using more clearance angle
   (b) using secondary clearance
   (c) raising the tool
   (d) tilting the tool

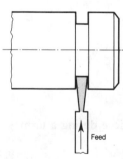

Fig. 8.57

15 The turning tool shown in Fig. 8.57 is cutting
   (a) acutely
   (b) obliquely
   (c) orthogonally
   (d) obtusely

16 The rake angle of the lip of a twist drill is controlled by
   (a) the helix angle of the flute
   (b) the included angle of the point
   (c) the chisel edge angle
   (d) the land width

17 The secondary clearance angle of a milling cutter tooth
   (a) makes the regrinding of a blunt cutter easier
   (b) prevents the heel of the tooth fouling the workpiece surface
   (c) prevents the sides of the teeth rubbing when cutting a slot
   (d) provides chip clearance

18 Figure 8.58 shows three types of turning tool. If the feed per revolution and the depth of cut is constant for each tool, the chip area
    (a) for A is the greatest
    (b) for B is the greatest
    (c) for C is the greatest
    (d) is also constant for all the tools

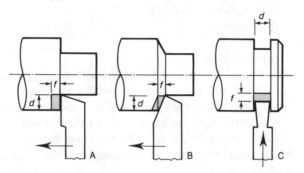

Fig. 8.58

f = feed/rev d = depth of cut

19 To produce a hole of accurate size and roundness with a good surface finish, it should be drilled
    (a) undersize and finished with another drill which is the correct size
    (b) undersize and opened up with a core drill
    (c) undersize and finished with a reamer
    (d) the correct size and finished with a reamer

20 To correct the position of a drilled pilot hole which has 'wandered', it should be
    (a) reamed to size
    (b) single point bored
    (c) opened up with a core drill
    (d) opened up with a piloted counterbore cutter

21 The spindle axis of a drilling machine is normally
    (a) perpendicular to the surface of the worktable
    (b) parallel to the surface of the worktable
    (c) inclined to the surface of the worktable
    (d) unrelated to the position of the worktable

22 If a lathe tool moves at an angle to the axis of a workpiece during a turning operation, the surface produced will be
    (a) plane
    (b) oval
    (c) conical
    (d) cylindrical

23 A shaping machine produces plane surfaces by the use of a
    (a) reciprocating multi-tooth cutter
    (b) rotating multi-tooth cutter
    (c) reciprocating single-point tool
    (d) rotating single-point tool

24 The clapper box of a shaping machine allows the
    (a) tool to lift on the cutting stroke
    (b) tool to lift on the return stroke
    (c) tool feed to be applied automatically
    (d) table traverse to be applied automatically

25 Milling machines are classified as vertical or horizontal according to the
    (a) plane in which the surface of the worktable lies
    (b) plane in which the spindle axis lies
    (c) direction of movement of the worktable
    (d) direction of feed of the cutter

26 The milling technique shown in Fig. 8.59 is called
    (a) downcut (climb) milling
    (b) conventional milling
    (c) upcut milling
    (d) fly-milling

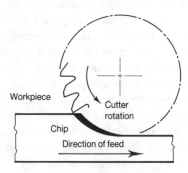

Fig. 8.59

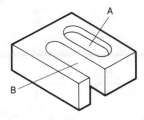

Fig. 8.60

27 For the component shown in Fig. 8.60, the pocket (A) should be milled using
    (a) an end mill
    (b) a face mill
    (c) a shell-end mill
    (d) a slot drill

28 For the component shown in Fig. 8.60, the slot (B) would normally be milled using
    (a) an end mill
    (b) a face mill
    (c) a shell-end mill
    (d) a slot drill

29 Power hacksaws are usually designed to cut on the back-stroke so that the blade is in tension and won't buckle. Therefore the bade should be fitted with the teeth facing
    (a) backwards
    (b) either way
    (c) forward
    (d) upwards

30 A coolant is generally flooded over the cutting zone of a power hacksaw in order to
    (a) cool the blade and workpiece only
    (b) cool the workpiece only
    (c) cool the blade and flush away the chips
    (d) flush away the chips only

9 Joining

9.1 Purpose of joining

A washing machine is an assembly of a great many individual components. Some of the components, such as the pressed steel panels forming the outer casing, are joined together *permanently* by spot welding or riveting. Other components need to be removed for servicing from time to time, or they need to be replaced because they have worn out. These components and subassemblies are attached by *temporary* fastenings such as bolts and nuts. Some components are attached by *flexible* fastenings such as the hinges which hold the door in place. Adhesives are also used to join components together, particularly where fluid-tight joints are required. Wherever components need to be joined together some form of fastening will be required, and that fastening must be correctly chosen and engineered so that it performs correctly at minimum cost to the manufacturer and to the user.

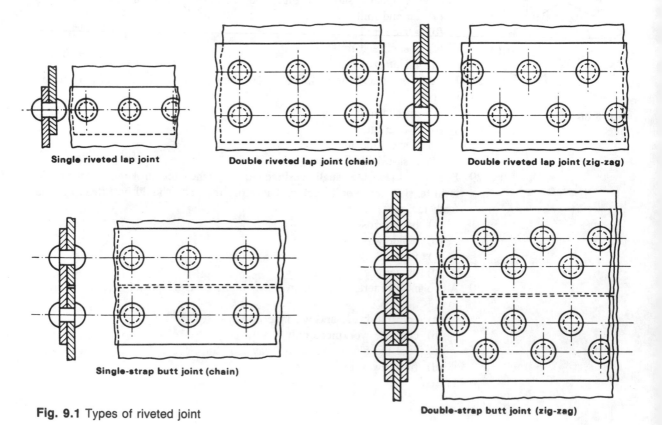

Single riveted lap joint

Double riveted lap joint (chain)

Double riveted lap joint (zig-zag)

Single-strap butt joint (chain)

Double-strap butt joint (zig-zag)

Fig. 9.1 Types of riveted joint

9.2 Permanent joints (riveting)

Permanent joints are those where one or more of the components, and/or the fastening itself has to be destroyed to dismantle the assembly. For example, consider the starter ring gear which is shrunk onto the flywheel of a motor car engine. The only way you can remove a worn out ring gear is to destroy it by splitting it. Again, the only way you can separate two components that have been riveted together is by chiselling the head off the rivet or by drilling it out.

Riveting is a method of making permanent joints. This process consists of drilling or punching holes in the components to be joined, inserting a rivet through the holes and, finally, closing the rivet by forming a second head. Some typical riveted joints are shown in Fig. 9.1. When choosing a rivet you must consider the following factors.

(a) The strength of the rivet (size and material).
(b) The material from which the rivet is made must not react with the components being joined, causing corrosion.

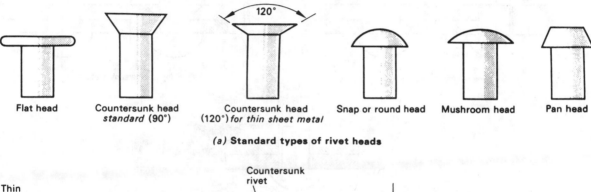

Flat head   Countersunk head *standard* (90°)   Countersunk head (120°) *for thin sheet metal*   Snap or round head   Mushroom head   Pan head

(a) **Standard types of rivet heads**

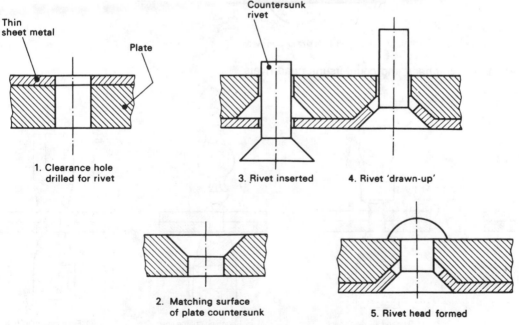

1. Clearance hole drilled for rivet

2. Matching surface of plate countersunk

3. Rivet inserted

4. Rivet 'drawn-up'

5. Rivet head formed

(b) **Countersunk riveting of thin material to thick material**

Fig. 9.2 Rivet heads and applications

(c) The ease with which the rivet can be closed.

(d) The appearance of the rivet when the joint is complete.

Some typical rivet heads are shown in Fig. 9.2. Where strength alone is required the snap head or the pan head is normally used.

The success of a riveted joint depends upon the correct riveting procedure being used. The hole clearance will depend upon the diameter of the rivet specified. You should drill or punch the rivet hole so that its diameter is 1.0625 times the rivet shank diameter. If you are going to close the rivet with a snap head, the length of

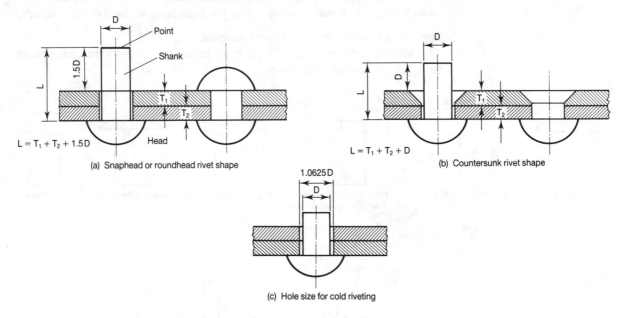

$L = T_1 + T_2 + 1.5D$

(a) Snaphead or roundhead rivet shape

$L = T_1 + T_2 + D$

(b) Countersunk rivet shape

(c) Hole size for cold riveting

Fig. 9.3 Proportions for snaphead and countersunk head rivets

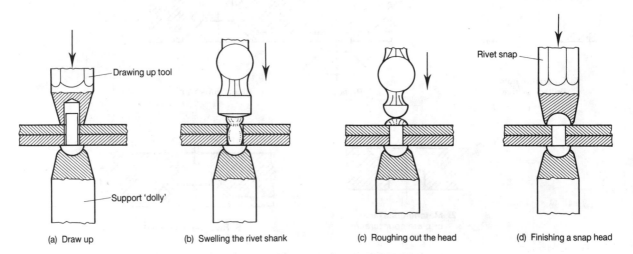

(a) Draw up

(b) Swelling the rivet shank

(c) Roughing out the head

(d) Finishing a snap head

Fig. 9.4 Correct procedure for closing a riveted joint

the rivet should be 1.5 times the diameter of the rivet plus the combined thicknesses of the components being joined. These proportions are shown in Fig. 9.3 together with those for a countersunk rivet. The correct procedure for closing a rivet with a snap head is shown in Fig. 9.4, and the more common defects that occur in riveted joints together with their causes are shown in Fig. 9.5. Even if the rivet is correctly closed, the joint may still fail if it has not been correctly proportioned. Some common causes of failure are shown in Fig. 9.6.

CAUSE OF RIVETING DEFECT	RESULTANT EFFECT
Rivet too long	Too much shank protruding to form required head 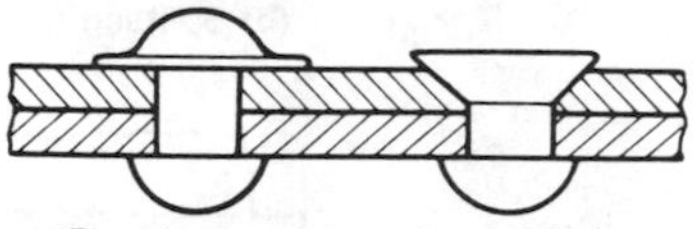 'Flash' formed around head (Jockey cap) Countersinking over-filled
Rivet set or dolly not struck square	Badly shaped head - off centre 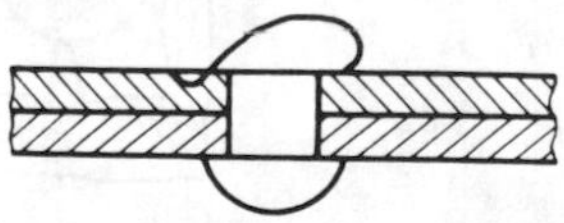 Sheet damaged by riveting tool
Drilling burrs not removed	Not enough shank protruding to form the correct size head 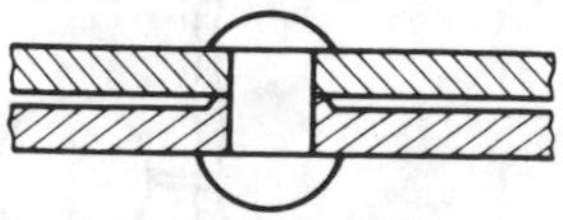 Plates or sheets not closed together Unequal heads
Sheets not closed together — rivet not drawn up sufficiently	Weak joint. Rivet shank swells between the plates  Not enough shank protruding to form correctly shaped head
Rivet holes not matched	Weak mis-shapened head  Rivet deformed and does not completely fill the hole

Fig. 9.5 Common defects in riveting

(a) Crushing of the metal

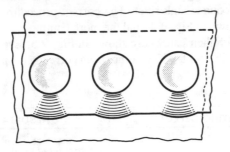

Cause Diameter of rivet too large compared with thickness of plate. The rivets when driven tend to bulge and crush the metal in front of them.

Prevention Select the correct diameter rivet for the thickness of the metal plate.

(b) Splitting of the metal

Cause Rivet holes punched or drilled too near edge of plate. Metal is likely to fail by splitting in front of the rivets.

Prevention Drill or punch the rivet holes at the correct edge distance, and use the correct lap allowance for the diameter of rivet selected.

(c) Tearing of the plate

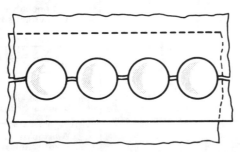

Cause Plates weakened by rivet holes being too close together. Plates tend to rupture along the centre line of the rivets.

Prevention Punch or drill rivet holes at the correct spacing or 'pitch'. In addition remove all burrs from the holes before final assembly.

Fig. 9.6 Common causes of failure in riveted joints

Hollow components present special problems when riveting because of the difficulty of getting a hold-up or 'dolly' behind the rivet being headed. Cylindrical components can be riveted using a *bench mandrel* as shown in Fig. 9.7(a). Box shaped components, where a hold-up cannot be inserted, can be joined using *'POP' rivets*. The principle of 'POP' riveting is shown in Fig. 9.7(b). (POP® is a registered trademark of Tucker Fasteners Ltd.)

Despite the fact that welding is a more skilful process and despite the fact that it requires much more costly equipment, welding has largely superseded riveted joints for many applications because:

(a) it is difficult to make riveted joints fluid tight;
(b) welded joints are lighter than riveted joints;

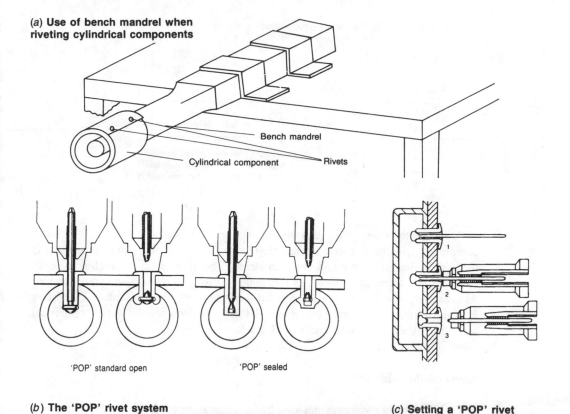

(a) **Use of bench mandrel when riveting cylindrical components**

Bench mandrel

Cylindrical component — Rivets

'POP' standard open

'POP' sealed

(b) **The 'POP' rivet system**

(c) **Setting a 'POP' rivet**

Fig. 9.7 Riveting hollow components (POP® is a registered trademark of Tucker Fasteners Ltd)

(c) the joint stresses are uniformally distributed in a welded joint whereas they are concentrated around each rivet in a riveted joint;

(d) riveting is slower than welding;

(e) the components don't have to have rivet holes drilled or punched in them. This is not only time consuming but the reduction in cross-sectional area at each hole weakens the components being joined.

9.3 Permanent joints (compression)

Mechanical

Compression joints rely upon the elasticity of components being joined to secure one component to another. No additional fastenings, such as bolts or rivets, are required. Basically, a mechanical compression joint consists of an oversize peg being forced into an undersize hole so that the peg is compressed and the hole is stretched. In a lightly compressed joint, friction will be generated between the two components as they try to spring back to their original dimensions. This friction, alone, secures the components together. Where the size difference is greater, the one component may actually 'bite' into the other giving some degree of positive locking. Figure 9.8 shows a typical pressed or 'staked' compression joint.

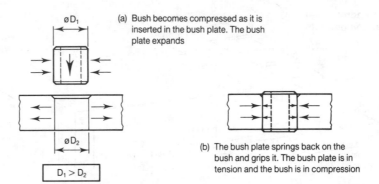

Fig. 9.8 Compression joint (mechanical)

You have to choose the materials for compression joints with care. The outer component is subjected to considerable tensile stress and the inner component is subjected to considerable compression stress. Therefore steel is suitable for both the inner and outer components as it is equally strong in tension and compression. Alternatively you could use cast iron for the inner component because it is strong in compression. However, you should not use cast iron for the outer component since it is weak in tension and would crack.

Thermal (hot-shrunk)

Instead of forming a compression joint by mechanical pressing, the thermal expansion of the outer component is exploited. You may remember that, when metals are heated, they expand. So, if the outer component is heated sufficiently it expands to a size where it can be slipped easily over the inner component. As the outer component cools it shrinks back to its original size and forms a compression joint on the inner component as shown in Fig. 9.9(a). This technique is used for shrinking the rolled steel tyres onto the hubs of locomotive wheels. Heating must be uniform to prevent distortion and the temperature has to be closely controlled. Too low a temperature results in insufficient expansion for the components to be assembled, too high a temperature can result in changes in the properties and structure of the material used for the outer (heated) component.

Thermal (cold expansion)

In a cold expansion joint, the inner component is cooled down until it will slip easily into the hole in the outer component. As it warms up to room temperature, it expands and forms a compression joint with the outer component as shown in Fig. 9.9(b). This technique requires the use of such coolants as solid carbon dioxide (dry ice) or liquid nitrogen. These are best used under carefully controlled workshop conditions as such low temperatures are potentially dangerous and special equipment is required in their use. Care must be taken when handling heated or cooled components. The appropriate codes of practice and safety regulations must be rigidly adhered to. You should always wear the protective clothing provided. Cooling has the advantage that it does not affect the physical properties of the material, whereas heating may do so. For example, heating a ring gear to slip it over a flywheel may soften the teeth of the gear. The precautions concerning the choice of materials for thermal compression joints are the same as those for mechanical compression joints.

9.4 Permanent joints (soldered)

Soft soldering

The process of soft soldering involves the use of a suitable low melting temperature range alloy of tin and lead which is 'bonded' to an unmelted parent metal by the application of heat and a suitable flux. The parent metal is the metal from which

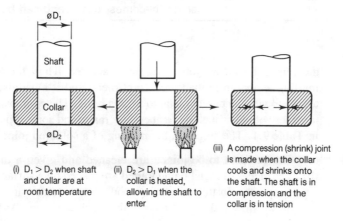

(i) $D_1 > D_2$ when shaft and collar are at room temperature

(ii) $D_2 > D_1$ when the collar is heated, allowing the shaft to enter

(iii) A compression (shrink) joint is made when the collar cools and shrinks onto the shaft. The shaft is in compression and the collar is in tension

(a) Hot shrink compression joint

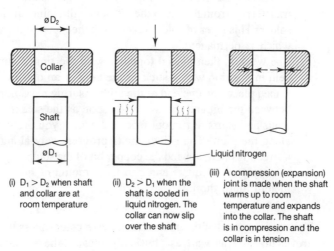

(i) $D_1 > D_2$ when shaft and collar are at room temperature

(ii) $D_2 > D_1$ when the shaft is cooled in liquid nitrogen. The collar can now slip over the shaft

(iii) A compression (expansion) joint is made when the shaft warms up to room temperature and expands into the collar. The shaft is in compression and the collar is in tension

(b) Cold expansion compression joint

Fig. 9.9 Compression joint (thermal)

Table 9.1 Types of soft solder

BS solder	Composition(%)			Melting range (°C)	Remarks
	Tin	Lead	Antimony		
A	65	34.4	0.6	183–185	Free running solder ideal for soldering electronic and instrument assemblies. Commonly referred to as *electrician's solder*
K	60	39.5	0.5	183–188	Used for high-class tinsmith's work, and is known as *tinman's solder*
F	50	49.5	0.5	183–212	Used for general soldering work in coppersmithing and sheet metal work
G	40	59.6	0.4	183–234	*Blow-pipe solder.* This is supplied in strip form with a D cross-section 0.3 mm wide
J	30	69.7	0.3	183–255	*Plumber's solder.* Because of its wide melting range this solder becomes 'pasty' and can be moulded and wiped.

the components being joined are manufactured. Thus, the solder must have a lower melting temperature than the parent metal and it must also be capable of reacting together with the parent metal to form a bond. The composition of some soft solders together with their melting temperature range and some typical applications are listed in Table 9.1. The stages in the making of a soldered joint are shown in Fig. 9.10.

(a) The surfaces to be joined are cleaned and given a thin film of flux.

(b) The pieces of metal being joined are placed on a surface which will not conduct away heat. In this case it is wood. A hot, tinned and loaded soldering iron is drawn slowly along the ends of the work as shown. As heat energy is conducted from the copper 'bit' to the work, the temperature of the work is raised. When it reaches the melting temperature of the solder being used, the solder is transferred from the bit to the work and the joint surfaces become 'tinned' with solder. This layer of solder reacts with the metal of the work to form an amalgam which is permanent.

(c) The work is then placed together with the tinned surfaces in contact and are held in position with a stick or the tang of an old file. A heated soldering iron is then placed on one end of the joint ensuring maximum surface contact is made between the bit and the work. As soon as the solder from the pre-tinned work melts and starts to run out from the edges, you draw the soldering iron slowly along the joint. The solder melts progressively along the joint. This is called a sweating operation and the copper bit of the soldering iron must be large enough to supply an adequate and constant amount of heat energy to ensure uniform melting until the joint is complete.

The tinning action of the solder cannot take place unless the two surfaces to be joined are chemically as well as physically clean. The surfaces of the joint should be degreased and then scoured with 'steel wool' to make them physically clean. They are then chemically cleaned and prepared for tinning by the action of the flux. The purpose of a flux is to:

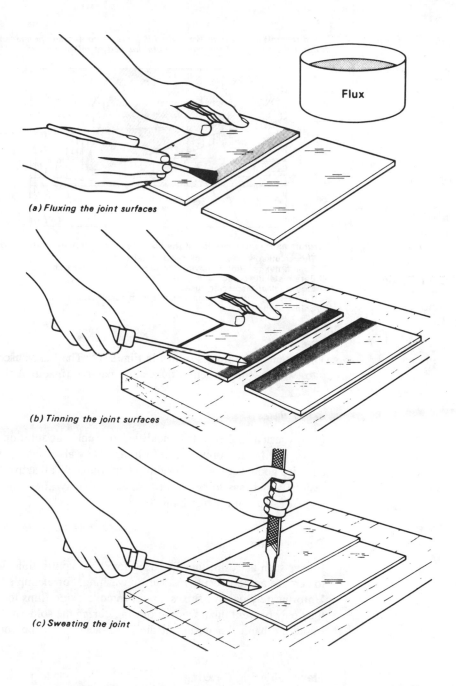

(a) Fluxing the joint surfaces

(b) Tinning the joint surfaces

(c) Sweating the joint

Fig. 9.10 Soft soldering

(a) remove the oxide film from the surfaces to be soldered
(b) prevent the oxide film from reforming during the soldering process
(c) 'wet' the surfaces being joined so that the molten solder will run out into an even film
(d) allow itself to be easily displaced by the molten solder so that a metal-to-metal contact is achieved

A molten solder is said to 'wet' when it leaves a continuous permanent film on the surface of the parent metal instead of rolling over it.

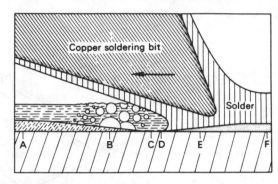

Diagrammatic representation of the displacement of flux by molten solder.
A Flux solution lying above oxidised metal surface.
B Boiling flux solution removing the film of oxide (e.g. as chloride).
C Bare metal in contact with fused flux.
D Liquid solder displacing fused flux.
E Tin reacting with the basis metal to form compound.
F Solder solidifying.

Fig. 9.11 Essential functions of a soldering flux

The action of the flux is shown in Fig. 9.11. The fluxes used for soft soldering fall into two categories, active fluxes and passive (inactive) fluxes.

Active fluxes

Fluxes such as Baker's fluid (acidified zinc chloride solution); they quickly dissolve the oxide film and prevent it reforming. They also etch the surface to be soldered, ensuring good wetting and bonding. Unfortunately all active fluxes leave a corrosive residue which has to be washed off immediately after soldering and the joint has to be treated with a rust inhibitor.

Passive fluxes

Fluxes such as resin; they are used for those applications where it is not possible to remove any corrosive residue by washing, for example, electrical connections. Unfortunately passive fluxes do not remove oxide films to any appreciable extent, they only prevent them from reforming during the soldering process. Therefore the initial mechanical scouring of the joint faces has to be very thorough.

Hard soldering (brazing)

Hard soldering is the general term used for silver soldering and brazing, and it can be defined as:

a process of joining metals in which a molten filler metal is drawn by capillary attraction into the space between closely adjacent surfaces of the parts to be joined.

As in soft soldering only the filler metal (solder) becomes molten and the parent

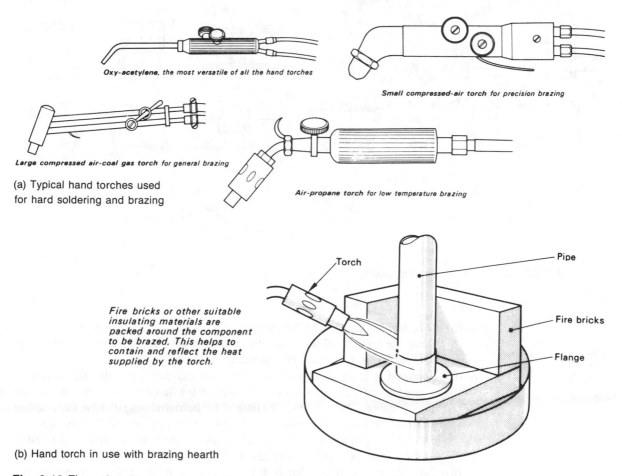

Oxy-acetylene, the most versatile of all the hand torches

Small compressed-air torch for precision brazing

Large compressed air-coal gas torch for general brazing

(a) Typical hand torches used for hard soldering and brazing

Air-propane torch for low temperature brazing

Torch

Pipe

Fire bricks or other suitable insulating materials are packed around the component to be brazed. This helps to contain and reflect the heat supplied by the torch.

Fire bricks

Flange

(b) Hand torch in use with brazing hearth

Fig. 9.12 Flame brazing

metal remains solid throughout the process. Therefore, like soft solders, hard solders also have a melting temperature range below that of the parent metal. However, this melting temperature range is well above that of soft solder (generally above 500°C) and a soldering iron cannot be used. The heat required for the process is provided by some form of gas blow-pipe. Natural gas from the main supply or bottled gas (propane) may be used. Some typical hand torches for flame bazing are shown in Fig. 9.12(a) and a typical set-up for flame brazing is shown in Fig. 9.12(b).

A hard soldered joint is much stronger than a soft soldered joint. You require special fluxes for hard soldering processes and the flux must match the filler alloy being used. Such fluxes are supplied by the manufacturers of hard solders and brazing spelters and you should follow their instructions carefully. Hard soldering fluxes are usually supplied as powders and have to be mixed into a paste with water before applying to the joint. Some typical hard soldered joints are shown in Fig. 9.13. The success of all hard soldering processes depends upon the following conditions.

(a) Selection of a suitable filler alloy which has a melting range appreciably lower than the parent metals being joined.

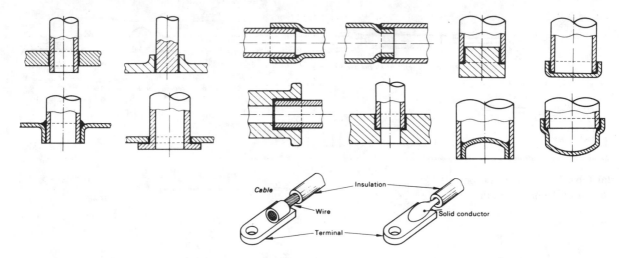

Fig. 9.13 Types of hard soldered and brazed joints

(b) Thorough cleanliness of the surface to be joined by hard soldering.

(c) Complete removal of the oxide film from the joint surfaces before and during hard soldering by means of a suitable flux.

(d) Complete 'wetting' of the joint surfaces by the molten filler alloy. When a surface is 'wetted' by a liquid, a continuous film of the liquid remains on that surface after draining. This condition is essential for hard soldering and the flux, having removed the oxide film, must completely wet the joint surfaces. This 'wetting' action by the flux assists the spreading and feeding of the molten filler alloy into the joint by capillary attraction. This ensures a completely filled joint.

(e) Since the molten filler alloy is drawn into the joint by capillary attraction, the space between the joint surfaces must be kept to a minimum and it must also be kept *constant*. Any local increase in the gap can present a barrier to the feeding of the filler alloy. This will prevent the joint from being uniformly filled, resulting in serious loss of strength.

(f) Melting the filler alloy alone is not sufficient to produce a sound joint. The parent metal must itself be raised to the brazing temperature so that the filler alloy melts on coming into contact with the joint surfaces even after the flame has been withdrawn.

Unlike welding, dissimilar metals and alloys may be joined by hard soldering. For example: copper to brass, steel to brass, mild steel to malleable cast iron, etc. The groups of filler material most widely used for hard soldering are summarised in Table 9.2.

Silver solders

These are expensive materials since they contain the precious metal silver. However, they produce strong and ductile joints and are used for the finest work as the melting temperature range is sufficiently low not to affect the parent metal, and a very neat joint can be made.

Table 9.2 Composition of hard solders and brazing spelters

BS 1845 type No.	Category	Composition percentage by weight					Approximate melting range (°C)
		Silver	Copper	Zinc	Cadmium	Phosphorus	
3	Silver solders	49–51	14–16	15–17	18–20	—	620–640
4		60–62	27.5–29.5	9–11	—	—	690–735
5		42–44	36–38	18.5–20.5	—	—	700–775
6	Self-fluxing brazing alloys	13–15	Balance	—	—	4–6	625–780
7	containing phosphorus	—	Balance	—	—	7–7.5	705–800
8	Brazing spelters (brass	—	49–51	Balance	—	—	860–870
9	alloys)	—	53–55	Balance	—	—	870–880
10		—	59–61	Balance	—	—	885–890

Type 3 is extremely fluid at brazing temperatures and is, therefore, ideal when brazing dissimilar metals. It is a low melting range alloy.

Type 4 has high electrical conductivity and is, therefore, very suitable for joining electrical conductors. It is the most expensive because of its high silver content.

Type 5 is a general purpose silver solder which can be employed at much higher brazing temperatures. It is the strongest of the silver solders.

Brazing alloys containing phosphorus

These are usually referred to as 'self-fluxing' alloys. These alloys contain silver, phosphorus and copper. They are cheaper and stronger than the silver solders, but they can only be used to braze copper and copper alloy components in air. No separate flux is needed. The phosphorus content reacts with the oxygen in the air to form a compound which acts as a flux. These filler alloys must not be used for brazing nickel, nickel alloys or copper-based alloys containing more than 10 per cent nickel. Neither must they be used for brazing ferrous metals and alloys.

Brazing spelters

These are brass alloys and are the oldest filler alloys used. It is from the use of these brass alloys that 'brazing' gets its name. These 'spelters' make the strongest joints but they also have the highest melting temperatures. They are mainly used for brazing copper, steel and malleable cast iron components.

9.5 Permanent joints (fusion-welding)

In the soldering and brazing processes previously described in section 9.4, the joints are made by a thin film of metal that has a lower melting point and inferior strength than the metals being joined. In *fusion welding* any additional material added to the joint has a similar composition and strength to the metals being joined. Figure 9.14 shows the principle of fusion welding where not only the filler metal but also the edges of the components being joined are melted. The molten metals fuse together and, when solid, form a homogeneous joint whose strength is equal to the metals being joined.

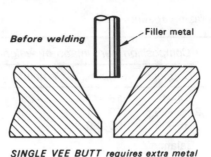

Before welding

Filler metal

After welding

Fig. 9.14 Fusion welding

SINGLE VEE BUTT requires extra metal

The edges of vee are melted and fused together with the molten filler metal

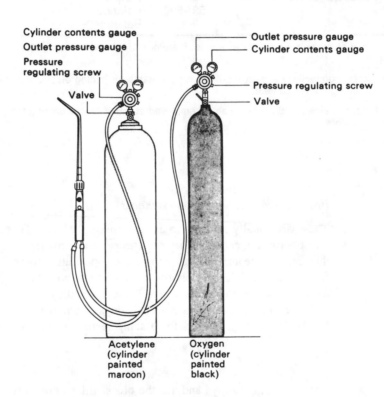

Fig. 9.15 Oxy-acetylene welding equipment

Cylinder contents gauge
Outlet pressure gauge
Pressure regulating screw
Valve

Outlet pressure gauge
Cylinder contents gauge

Pressure regulating screw
Valve

Acetylene (cylinder painted maroon)

Oxygen (cylinder painted black)

Oxy-acetylene welding

In this process the heat source is a mixture of oxygen and acetylene burning to produce a flame whose temperature can reach 3250°C and this is above the melting point of most metals. Figure 9.15 shows a typical set of welding equipment. Since the gases are stored under high pressure and form highly flammable and even explosive mixtures, you must handle this equipment with great care. Further, oxy-acetylene welding equipment must only be used by persons who have been fully instructed in the operating and safety procedures recommended by the Home Office and by the equipment suppliers, or by trainees under close supervision by such a qualified person. Figure 9.16 shows the two basic techniques for fusion welding using an

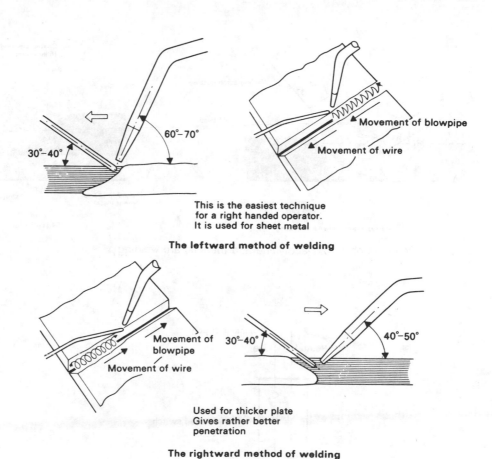

Fig. 9.16 Oxy-acetylene welding techniques

60°–70°

30°–40°

← (arrow)

Movement of blowpipe

Movement of wire

This is the easiest technique
for a right handed operator.
It is used for sheet metal

The leftward method of welding

Movement of
blowpipe

Movement of wire

30°–40°

40°–50°

→ (arrow)

Used for thicker plate
Gives rather better
penetration

The rightward method of welding

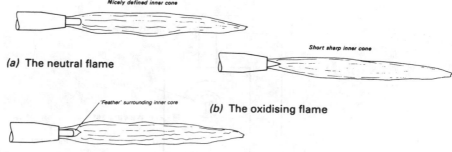

Fig. 9.17 Oxy-acetylene welding flame conditions

Nicely defined inner cone

(a) The neutral flame

Short sharp inner cone

(b) The oxidising flame

'Feather' surrounding inner core

(c) The carburising flame

oxy-acetylene torch. No flux is required when welding ferrous metals as the products of combustion from the burnt gases protect the molten weld pool from atmospheric oxygen. The three types of flame produced by a welding torch are shown in Fig. 9.17, and the neutral flame is the one normally used when welding ferrous metals.

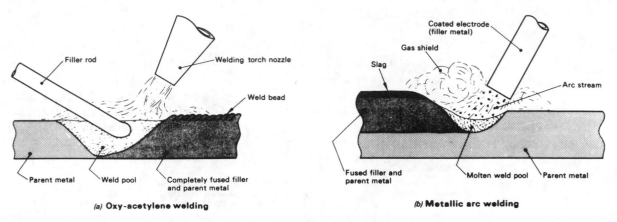

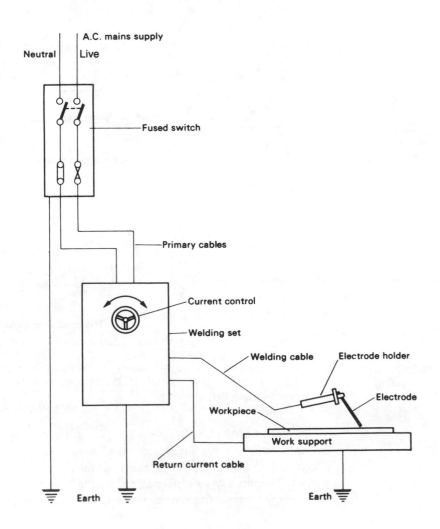

Fig. 9.18 Comparison of oxy-acetylene and metallic arc welding

Fig. 9.19 Manual metal-arc welding circuit diagram

Metallic arc welding

This is a fusion welding process where the heat energy required to melt the edges of the components being joined and also the filler rod is supplied by an electric arc. The *arc* is the name given to the prolonged spark struck between two electrodes. In this process the filler rod forms one electrode and the work forms the other electrode. The filler rod/electrode is coated with a flux which melts and shields the joint from atmospheric oxygen at the very high temperatures involved. (Average arc temperature is about 6000°C.) The flux also stabilises the arc and prevents the rod from short circuiting against the sides of the joint when welding thick metal. Figure 9.18 compares the principles of gas and metallic arc welding. A transformer is used to reduce the mains voltage to a low voltage, heavy current supply which is not only safe but suitable for arc welding. As with gas welding, arc-welding equipment must not be used by untrained persons except under the closest supervision. The dangers with arc welding arise from the very high temperatures and very heavy electric currents involved. Also high voltages are present in the primary circuit (supply side) of the transformer, and these can lead to accidents involving electrocution. Figure 9.19 shows the general arrangement of a metallic arc welding installation.

Table 9.3 Advantages and limitations of bonded joints

Advantages
1. The ability to join dissimilar materials, and materials of widely different thicknesses
2. The ability to join components of difficult shape that would restrict the application of welding or riveting equipment
3. Smooth finish to the joint which will be free from voids and protrusions such as weld beads, rivet and bolt heads, etc.
4. Uniform distribution of stress over entire area of joint. This reduces the chances of the joint failing in fatigue
5. Elastic properties of many adhesives allow for flexibility in the joint and give it vibration damping characteristics
6. The ability to electrically insulate the adherends and prevent corrosion due to galvanic action between dissimilar metals
7. The join may be sealed against moisture and gases
8. Heat-sensitive materials can be joined

Limitations
1. The bonding process is more complex than mechanical and thermal processes, i.e. the need for surface preparation, temperature and humidity control of the working atmosphere, ventilation and health problems caused by the adhesives and their solvents. The length of time that the assembly must be jigged up whilst setting (curing) takes place
2. Inspection of the joint is difficult
3. Joint design is more critical than for many mechanical and thermal processes
4. Incompatibility with the adherends. The adhesive itself may corrode the materials it is joining
5. Degradation of the joint when subject to high and low temperatures, chemical atmospheres, etc.
6. Creep under sustained loads

For both gas and electric arc welding, you must use suitable eye protection equipment. This was discussed in section 2.6.

9.6 Permanent joints (adhesive bonding)

Naturally occurring adhesives fall into two categories:

(i) *Glues*. These are made from the bones, hooves and horns of animals and the bones of fishes. Derivatives of milk and blood are also used. Glues were largely used for joining wood and were used in the furniture and toy manufacturing industries. They have now been almost totally replaced with modern high strength synthetic adhesives, but they are still used where their non-toxic and non-narcotic properties are important.

(ii) *Gums*. These are still made from vegetable matter, resins and rubbers being extracted from trees and starches from the by-products of flour milling. Since

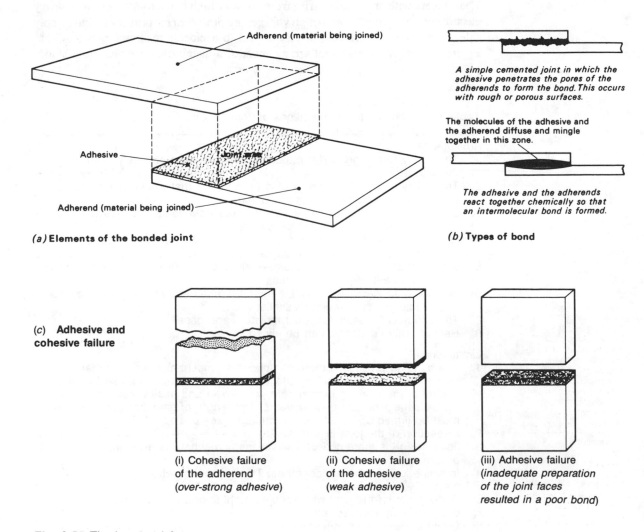

(a) Elements of the bonded joint

A simple cemented joint in which the adhesive penetrates the pores of the adherends to form the bond. This occurs with rough or porous surfaces.

The molecules of the adhesive and the adherend diffuse and mingle together in this zone.

The adhesive and the adherends react together chemically so that an intermolecular bond is formed.

(b) Types of bond

(c) Adhesive and cohesive failure

(i) Cohesive failure of the adherend (*over-strong adhesive*)

(ii) Cohesive failure of the adhesive (*weak adhesive*)

(iii) Adhesive failure (*inadequate preparation of the joint faces resulted in a poor bond*)

Fig. 9.20 The bonded joint

they are non-toxic they are used for such low strength applications as stamp adhesives and envelope flap adhesives which have to be licked.

Modern high strength synthetic adhesives have been developed by the plastics industry. Table 9.3 lists some of the more important advantages and limitations of such adhesives compared with the mechanical and thermal jointing processes discussed earlier in this chapter.

Figure 9.20(a) shows a typical bonded joint and explains the terminology used for the various features of the joint. The strength of the joint depends upon the two following factors.

Table 9.4 Selection of adhesives

Adhesive groups — *Natural:* Animal glues, Starch, Dextrine, Casein · *Elastomers:* Acrylonitrile butadiene, Polychloroprene, Polyurethane, Silicone rubber, Polybutadiene, Natural rubber, Butyl · *Thermoplastics:* Cellulose nitrate, Polyvinyl alcohol, Polyvinyl acetate, Polyarylate, Silicone resin, Cyanoacrylate · *Thermosets:* Phenolic formaldehyde, Urea formaldehyde, Resorcinol formaldehyde, Melamine formaldehyde, Polyesters (unsaturated), Epoxy resins, Polyimides, Phenolic-vinyl formal, Phenolic-polyvinylacetal, Phenolic nitrile, Phenolic epoxy · *Inorganic:* Sodium silicate

Adherends	Animal glues	Starch	Dextrine	Casein	Acrylonitrile butadiene	Polychloroprene	Polyurethane	Silicone rubber	Polybutadiene	Natural rubber	Butyl	Cellulose nitrate	Polyvinyl alcohol	Polyvinyl acetate	Polyarylate	Silicone resin	Cyanoacrylate	Phenolic formaldehyde	Urea formaldehyde	Resorcinol formaldehyde	Melamine formaldehyde	Polyesters (unsaturated)	Epoxy resins	Polyimides	Phenolic-vinyl formal	Phenolic-polyvinylacetal	Phenolic nitrile	Phenolic epoxy	Sodium silicate
Metals					•	•				•				•			•						•	•			•	•	
Glass, Ceramics	•					•											•						•			•			•
Wood			•							•			•				•	•	•	•	•		•			•			
Paper	•	•	•	•									•	•															
Leather					•	•			•				•	•															
Textiles, felt	•					•				•			•	•															
Elastomers																													
Polychloroprene (Neoprene)						•																							
Nitrile					•												•												
Natural					•		•										•												
Silicone								•																	•				
Butyl					•						•																		
Polyurethane					•	•	•																						
Thermoplastics																													
Polyvinyl chloride (flexible)					•	•	•																						
Polyvinyl chloride (rigid)					•	•																	•						
Cellulose acetate							•					•					•												
Cellulose nitrate												•					•												
Ethyl cellulose												•																	
Polyethylene (film)							•		•														•						
Polyethylene (rigid)														•									•						
Polypropylene (film)							•							•									•						
Polypropylene (rigid)																							•						
Polycarbonate							•																•						
Fluorocarbons										•												•	•						
Polystyrene																						•	•						
Polyamides (nylon)							•																•						
Polyformaldehyde (acetals)							•										•						•		•				
Methyl pentene					•																								
Thermosets																													
Epoxy																	•						•						
Phenolic						•												•		•			•						
Polyester																						•		•					
Melamine																						•							
Polyethylene terephthalate					•	•											•												
Diallyl phthalate					•																	•							
Polyimide																							•	•					

Note: In general, any two adherends may be bonded together if the chart shows that they are compatible with the same adhesive.

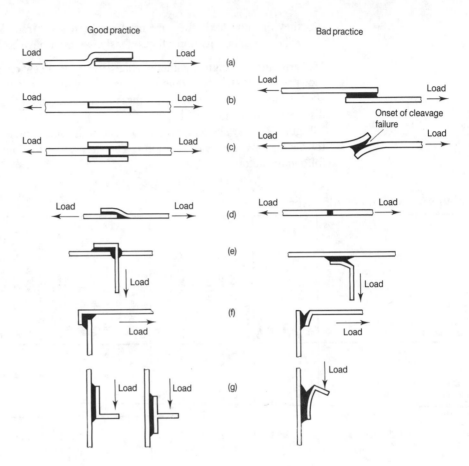

Fig. 9.21 Suitable joints for bonding

(i) *Adhesion* is the ability of the bonding material (adhesive) to stick (adhere) to the materials being joined (adherends). There are two ways in which the bond can occur. These are shown in Fig. 9.20(b).

(ii) *Cohesion* is the ability of the adhesive film itself to resist the applied forces acting on the joint. Figure 9.20(c) shows the three ways in which a bonded joint may fail under load. These failures can be prevented by careful joint design and their correct selection of the adhesive. Table 9.4 lists some typical adhesives and the adherend materials for which they can be used. Careful preparation of the joint surfaces is essential for a sound joint. The surfaces must be chemically and physically clean. Also the atmospheric temperature and humidity of the working environment must be closely controlled.

No matter how effective the adhesive, and how carefully you apply it, the joint will be a failure if it is not correctly designed. It is bad practice to apply adhesive to a joint which was originally proportioned for bolting, riveting, or welding. You must design the joint to exploit the special properties of adhesives. Some typical adhesive joint designs are shown in Fig. 9.21. Most adhesives are relatively strong in *tension* and *shear* but weak in *cleavage* and *peel*. These terms are explained in Fig. 9.22. The adhesive must 'wet' the joint surfaces thoroughly or voids will occur and the actual bonded area will be substantially less than the design area. This will result in a weak joint. Figure 9.23 shows the effect of wetting on the adhesive film.

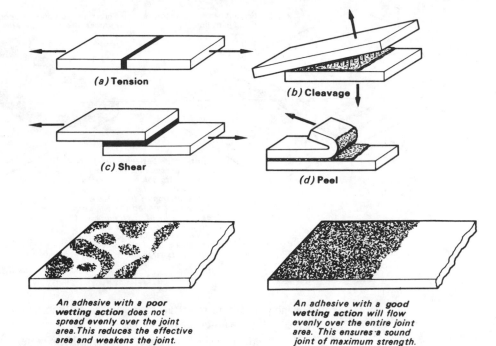

Fig. 9.22 The stressing of bonded joints

(a) Tension

(b) Cleavage

(c) Shear

(d) Peel

Fig. 9.23 Wetting capacity of an adhesive

An adhesive with a *poor*
wetting action does not
spread evenly over the joint
area. This reduces the effective
area and weakens the joint.

An adhesive with a *good*
wetting action will flow
evenly over the entire joint
area. This ensures a sound
joint of maximum strength.

Thermoplastic adhesives

Thermoplastic materials are those plastic materials, like polystyrene washing-up bowls, which soften when heated and harden again when cooled. The adhesives derived from this group of synthetic materials may be applied in two ways.

(i) *Heat activated* where the adhesive is softened by heating until fluid enough to spread freely over the joint surfaces. These are brought into contact immediately, whilst the adhesive is still soft, and pressure is applied until the adhesive has cooled to room temperature and set.

(ii) *Solvent activated* where the adhesive is softened by a volatile solvent. The dissolved adhesive is applied to the joint and a bond is achieved by the solvent evaporating. The cellulose adhesive (balsa cement) used by aero-modellers is an example of a solvent activated adhesive. Because the evaporation is essential to the setting of the adhesive, a sound bond is almost impossible to achieve at the centre of a large joint area when joining impervious materials. This is shown in Fig. 9.24.

Impact adhesives

These are solvent-based adhesives which are spread separately on the joint faces and left to dry. Because the coated joint faces are open to the atmosphere, evaporation of the solvent is rapid and total. When dry, the coated joint faces are brought into contact whereupon they instantly bond together by intermolecular attraction. This

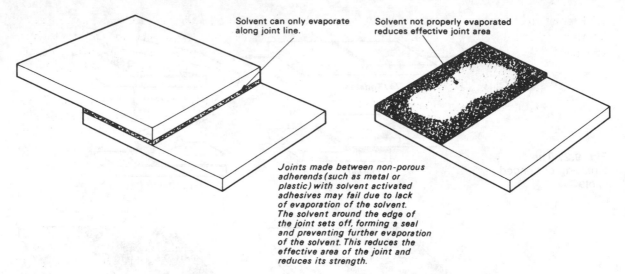

Solvent can only evaporate along joint line.

Solvent not properly evaporated reduces effective joint area

Joints made between non-porous adherends (such as metal or plastic) with solvent activated adhesives may fail due to lack of evaporation of the solvent. The solvent around the edge of the joint sets off, forming a seal and preventing further evaporation of the solvent. This reduces the effective area of the joint and reduces its strength.

Fig. 9.24 Solvent activated adhesive fault

enables non-absorbent materials to be successfully joined over large contact areas. A typical joint is shown in Fig. 9.25.

Thermoplastic adhesives are based upon synthetic materials such as polyamides, vinyl and acrylic polymers and cellulose derivatives. They are also based upon naturally occurring materials such as resins, shellac, mineral waxes and rubber. Such adhesives are not as strong as the thermosetting adhesives but, being generally more flexible, they are more suitable for joining non-rigid materials. Unfortunately they are heat sensitive and they lose their strength rapidly as the temperature rises. For example, natural glues become liquid at the temperature of boiling water.

1. The impact adhesive is spread thinly and evenly on both joint surfaces.
2. The adhesive is then left to dry be evaporation. This avoids the problem in Fig. 9.24.

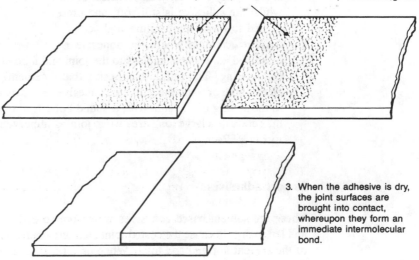

3. When the adhesive is dry, the joint surfaces are brought into contact, whereupon they form an immediate intermolecular bond.

Fig. 9.25 The use of an impact adhesive

9.7 Permanent joints (thermosetting adhesives)

Thermosetting plastic materials change chemically when heated (cured) and can never again be softened. This makes them less heat sensitive than thermoplastic adhesives. The heat necessary to cure the adhesive can be applied externally as when phenolic resins are used or the heat may be generated internally by chemical reaction (addition of a chemical hardener) as when epoxy and polystyrene resins are used.

Since the setting process is a chemical reaction and is not dependent on the evaporation of a solvent, the area of the joint does not affect the setting process. Thermosetting adhesives can be very strong and are used to make structural joints between high strength materials such as metals. Joints in the body shells of motor cars and stressed components in aircraft are increasingly dependent upon high strength adhesives in place of welding and riveting. The stresses are more uniformly transmitted from one component of the joint to the other. The joints are sealed against corrosion. Dissimilar materials can be joined without the risk of electro-chemical attack. The relatively low curing temperatures, compared with welding temperatures, do not adversely affect the structure and properties of the materials being joined. Unfortunately thermosetting materials tend to be rigid when cured, so they are unsuitable for joining flexible materials or structures, or for making joints which are subjected to high levels of vibration.

9.8 Safety in the use of adhesives

One of the great advantages of naturally occurring glues and gums is that they are neither toxic nor narcotic. Further, they are not particularly flammable. Therefore they are widely used for labelling and packaging food stuffs, and for the adhesives on stamps and envelope flaps which have to be licked. Unfortunately most synthetic adhesives and their solvents, hardeners, catalysts, etc., are toxic, and narcotic to some degree. Also their solvents are invariably highly flammable. Therefore these adhesives, together with their solvents, hardeners and catalysts must be stored and used only in well-ventilated conditions and the working area must be declared a *no-smoking zone*. The health hazards associated with these materials range from dermatitis and sensitisation of your skin, to permanent damage to your brain, liver, kidneys and other internal organs if inhaled or accidently swallowed. All safety regulations concerning these materials must be rigidly adhered to (if you'll excuse the pun) and any protective clothing provided must be worn.

Precautions

(a) Use only in well-ventilated areas.
(b) Wear protective clothing that is appropriate to the process, no matter how inconvenient.
(c) If you don't wear gloves, protect your hands with a barrier cream.
(d) After use, wash thoroughly in soap and water; *do not use solvents* except under medical supervision.
(e) Do not smoke in the presence of solvents. Not only are they highly flammable but, when the vapours are drawn in through a cigarette or a pipe, some of the vapours change chemically into highly poisonous gases.

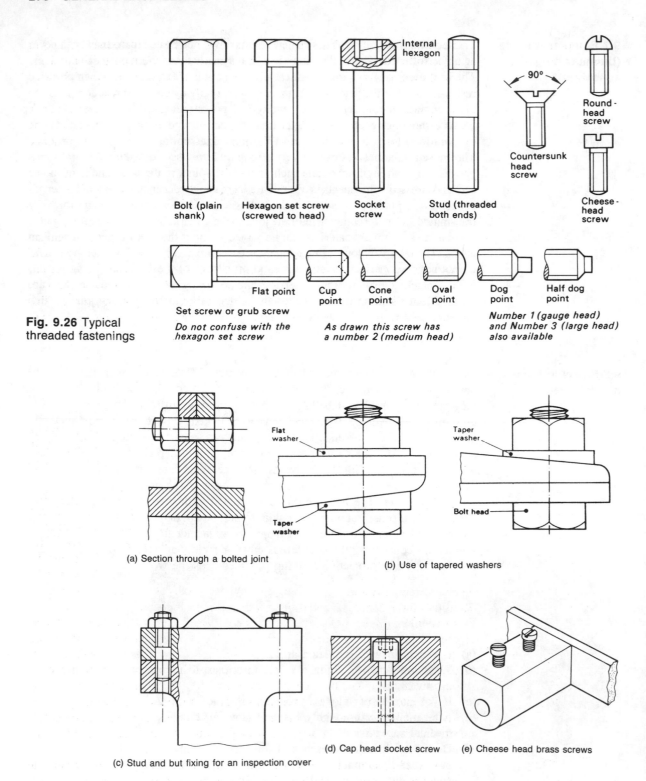

Fig. 9.26 Typical threaded fastenings

Bolt (plain shank)

Hexagon set screw (screwed to head)

Socket screw

Stud (threaded both ends)

Internal hexagon

90°

Countersunk head screw

Round-head screw

Cheese-head screw

Flat point

Set screw or grub screw

Do not confuse with the hexagon set screw

Cup point

Cone point

As drawn this screw has a number 2 (medium head)

Oval point

Dog point

Half dog point

Number 1 (gauge head) and Number 3 (large head) also available

(a) Section through a bolted joint

(b) Use of tapered washers

Flat washer

Taper washer

Taper washer

Bolt head

(c) Stud and but fixing for an inspection cover

(d) Cap head socket screw

(e) Cheese head brass screws

Fig. 9.27 Use of threaded fastenings

9.9 Temporary joints (threaded fastenings)

Various threaded (screw) fastenings are used where components have to be assembled and dismantled from time to time. Such fastenings are designed so that they are equally strong in shear across the bolt and in tension. Figure 9.26 shows some typical threaded fastenings and Fig. 9.27 shows some typical applications.

Figure 9.27(a) shows a section through a *bolted joint*. Note that the plain shank of the bolt extends beyond the joint face so that no shearing forces are carried by the screw threads. The head of the bolt and the nut should pull down onto machined seatings to provide a flat surface perpendicular to the axis of the bolt. This prevents bending and twisting which could weaken the bolt and also prevent the nut from pulling up tight, causing it to work loose in service. You should put a washer under the nut not only to give it a smooth surface to bed down onto, but to prevent the component being damaged by the corners of the nut.

Figure 9.27(b) shows a *taper washer* as used when bolting fitments onto girders. These again allow the nut to pull down tight without bending or twisting the bolt.

Figure 9.27(c) shows a *stud and nut fixing* for an inspection cover. You use this type of fixing where a joint is regularly dismantled. Most of the wear occurs on the stud and nut which can eventually be replaced cheaply and easily. This avoids wear falling on screw threads of the expensive component to which the cover is fixed.

Figure 9.27(d) shows a *cap head socket screw*. Although more expensive than machine cut hexagon head screws and bolts, socket screws are much stronger since they are made from forged, high-tensile alloy steels toughened by heat treatment. The threads are rolled instead of being cut which also increases their strength and wear resistance. They are widely used in the manufacture of machine tools, jigs and fixtures and other devices where strength and reliability are more important than initial cost. As shown, the head of the bolt is recessed so as to provide a flush surface. This not only reduces the risk of accidents but makes cleaning easier as well.

Figure 9.27(e) shows *cheese head screws*. These are used for light duties where cost is important and where the use of a screwdriver is more convenient than a spanner. In this example they are being used to clamp an electric cable into a terminal.

All the above fastenings are used in conjunction with a nut or with a thread which has previously been cut into the component. *Self-tapping* screws are often used with soft materials such as plastics and also in sheet metal. As their name implies, self-tapping screws cut their own thread as they are driven into the tapping-size hole. There are three basic types and these are shown in Fig. 9.28.

Figure 9.28(a) shows a typical *thread-forming screw*. These produce a screw thread by displacing the material round the pilot hole. They are used for joining components made from non-ferrous sheet metal and also from thermoplastics. Both of these materials will flow readily to a thread form under the influence of the screw.

Figure 9.28(b) shows a typical *thread-cutting screw*. These generate a screw thread by cutting into the pilot hole of the component as the screw is driven home. They are more suitable for use with harder and more rigid materials such as thermosetting plastic and sheet steel which will not flow adequately for use with thread forming screws.

Figure 9.28(c) shows a typical *drive-screw*. These are designed to be driven into a hole by hammering or pressing. They can be made from a variety of materials and, although cheap to install, they can only be used once.

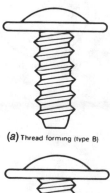

(a) Thread forming (type B)

(b) Thread cutting (type T)

(c) Drive (type U)

Fig. 9.28 Self-tapping screws

Locking devices

Locking devices are employed to prevent threaded fastenings from slacking-off in use as a result of vibration. A selection of locking devices are shown in Fig. 9.29. You will see that they are divided into two categories: those which depend upon friction and those whose locking action is positive. Positive locking devices are more time consuming to fit, so they are only used for critical joints where failure could cause serious accidents; for example, the control systems of vehicles and aircraft. The correct tightening of threaded fasteners is described in section 10.6.

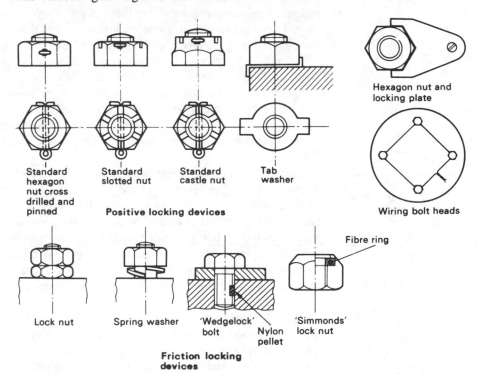

Fig. 9.29 Locking devices

9.10 Temporary joints (miscellaneous)

Dowels

Threaded fastenings such as screws, bolts and nuts are usually inserted through clearance holes, the exception being 'fitted' bolts which have turned or ground shanks and are inserted through reamed holes. Where clearance holes are used it is necessary to use parallel dowels to provide a positive location between two components. The dowel is manufactured to be a light drive fit in a reamed hole. It is given a slight taper lead so that as it is driven into the hole the metal of the component expands slightly and that of the dowel compresses slightly. The elastic 'spring-back' holds the dowel rigidly in place and ensures positive location (see mechanical compression joints: section 9.3). Dowels are case-hardened and ground, not only for precision, but to prevent them 'picking-up' as they are driven into their holes. An example is shown in Fig. 9.30(a). Dowels should never be fitted into blind holes since it would be impossible to drive them out should the joint have to be dismantled.

Taper pins

Taper pins are used for fastening components such as collars or handles onto shafts. When the collar or handle has been correctly located on the shaft, a parallel hole is drilled through the component and the shaft. This hole is then opened up using a taper pin reamer of the appropriate size. The taper pin is then driven home in the tapered hole. An example is shown in Fig. 9.30(b). Any wear which takes place during assembly or dismantling is compensated for by driving the pin deeper into the hole. The taper is self-locking and the pin will not drop out since it has a morse type taper as used on twist drill shanks.

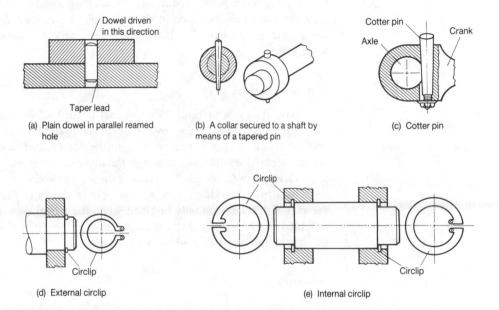

(a) Plain dowel in parallel reamed hole

(b) A collar secured to a shaft by means of a tapered pin

(c) Cotter pin

Fig. 9.30
Miscellaneous fastenings

(d) External circlip

(e) Internal circlip

Cotter pins

Cotter pins are taper pins with a screw thread at the smaller end. They are secured by the thread and nut which also pulls the cotter tightly against its seating. One side of the cotter has a flat which engages with a flat on the shaft to provide a positive drive. A typical example is the fixing of the pedal crank of your bicycle as shown in Fig 9.30(c).

Circlips

These are spring steel clips used for locating components against a shoulder as shown in Fig. 9.30(d) and (e). The clips can be opened or closed for fitting by specially shaped pliers which fit into the holes in the lugs at the end of the clips.

Keys

These are used to provide a positive drive between components such as wheels and shafts as shown in Fig. 9.31. The key transmits energy by being partly embedded in the shaft and partly embedded in the wheel or other component mounted on the shaft.

Feather key

This type of key fits into a pocket milled into a shaft. Generally the pocket is end milled as shown in Fig. 9.31(a). This enables the key and the wheel or other device it is driving to be positioned at any point along a shaft. The key is only fitted on its width and its clearance on its depth. It only drives the wheel or other device and these have to be secured to the shaft, positionally, by some arrangement such as a set screw.

Gib-head (tapered) key

This type of key is driven into a slot that is cut half into the wheel and half into the shaft. Being tapered, the key can be driven in tight and is secured by the spring-back of the metal as in a mechanical compression joint. The wheel, or other device, is only secured by friction, although the drive is positive. For safety, a set screw is also sometimes provided. The point of the set screw bites into the shaft and prevents the wheel from working loose. An example is shown in Fig. 9.31(b) and you can see that such a key can only be fitted when the wheel it is securing and driving is mounted on the end of a shaft. The key can be removed by driving a wedge between the wheel hub and the gib-head of the key.

Woodruff key

This is fitted into a segmental socket which is milled into the shaft. Since the key can 'float', it is self-aligning and is widely used in conjunction with tapered mountings as shown in Fig. 9.31(c). A special milling cutter is used to cut the pocket in the shaft. The key is used to provide a positive drive. It does not secure the wheel or other device on the shaft. In the example shown, you can see that a nut is used to secure the wheel in place.

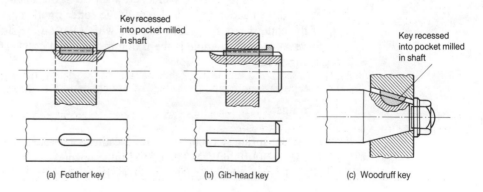

Fig. 9.31 Keys   (a) Feather key   (b) Gib-head key   (c) Woodruff key

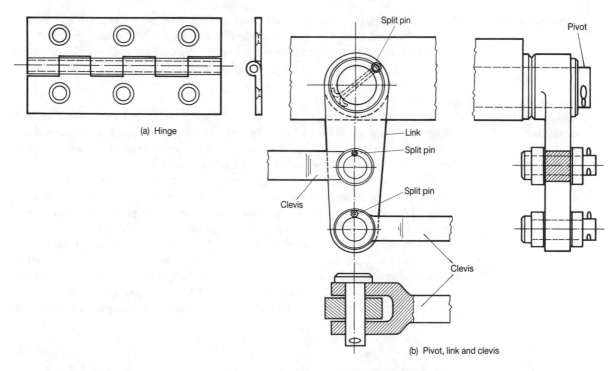

(a) Hinge

(b) Pivot, link and clevis

Fig. 9.32 Flexible joints

Table 9.5 Equipment and consumables

Joining process	Equipment and consumables required (This list assumes components have been prepared for joining)
Riveting (cold)	Suitable rivets, hold up (dolly), drawing up tool, rivet snap, ball pein hammer, ear protectors
Riveting (pop)	Suitable rivets, riveting tool
Compression (mechanical)	Suitable press for assembling the component
Compression (thermal)	Heating or cooling equipment, tongs for handling heated or cooled components, protective clothing and goggles
Soldering (soft)	Soldering iron, means of heating soldering iron, soft-solder, suitable flux, means of washing corrosive residue from work if an active flux is used
Hard-soldering (brazing)	Suitable grade of solder or spelter for the job, recommended flux for the solder or spelter being used, brazing hearth, brazing torch, bottled gas
Fusion-welding (gas)	Cylinder of acetylene fitted with regulator and gauges, cylinder of oxygen fitted with regulator and gauges, appropriate hoses fitted with flash-back arrestors, welding torch with nozzle appropriate for the job, supply of filler rods appropriate for the job, protective clothing, appropriate welding goggles
Fusion-welding (arc)	Welding set, high and low voltage cables, electrode-holder, electrodes appropriate for the job, screens, protective clothing, visor with appropriate filter glass, chipping hammer and clear goggles
Temporary fastenings	(i) Nut, bolts and washers as specified, spanners as appropriate (ii) cotter pins, hammer, drift, spanner (iii) Dowels, plain or tapered reamers as required, tap wrench, hammer (iv) Circlips, circlip pliers (internal and external) (v) keys, files for fitting keys, taper draft to remove gib-head keys, hammer

9.11 Flexible joints

These provide positive or frictional restraint in five of the six degrees of freedom (section 7.2), but allow the components to rotate about one of the axes. For example, such a device can be a hinge as shown in Fig. 9.32(a), or a pivot, or a clevis. These last two devices are shown in Fig. 9.32(b).

9.12 Equipment and consumables

Before you go out on a shopping expedition, the first thing I expect you do is to make a shopping list. This will prevent you from forgetting anything important and will also enable you to arrange the order in which you intend to buy the goods so that you don't waste time having to go back to shops you've visited previously. Similarly, before starting on any engineering procedure, you should always make a list of equipment and consumables you require so that you do not have to keep going back to the stores for things which you have forgotten. This is particularly important when you are working on site at some distance from the stores. Table 9.5 lists the joining techniques we have considered in this chapter and the main items of equipment and consumables you will require. Remember, some jobs will require additional equipment, so check the details carefully before making your stores requisition out. Also check the condition of the tools and equipment. It is no use getting to the site only to find that some essential piece of equipment is worn out or faulty.

Exercises

1 A temporary joint is one which
   (a) holds two components together until a permanent joint can be made
   (b) can be dismantled and reassembled repeatedly
   (c) allows one part to move relative to another
   (c) can only be dismantled by the destruction of one or more of the components forming the joint
2 A permanent joint is one which
   (a) can only be made by soldering, welding or brazing
   (b) can only be made by riveting
   (c) can only be dismantled by the destruction of one or more components forming the joint
   (d) can only be dismantled by the use of an extractor
3 For maximum strength a riveted joint should be designed so that the rivet is in
   (a) shear
   (b) tension
   (c) compression
   (d) no way stressed
4 The riveted joint shown in Fig. 9.33 is called a
   (a) butt joint
   (b) butt joint with a cover plate
   (c) double row lap joint
   (d) single row lap joint
5 The outer component of a compression joint should be made from a material having a high
   (a) tensile strength

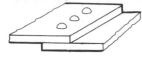

Fig. 9.33

(b) compression strength

(c) shear strength

(d) hardness number

6 For the riveted joint shown in Fig. 9.34

    (a) $L = 14$ mm and $D = 4$ mm diameter

    (b) $L = 14$ mm and $D = 4.25$ mm diameter

    (c) $L = 12$ mm and $D = 4$ mm diameter

    (d) $L = 12$ mm and $D = 4.25$ mm diameter

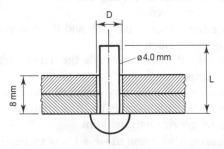

Fig. 9.34

7 When riveting closed box sections the only suitable type of rivet is a

    (a) 'pop' rivet

    (b) tinman's rivet

    (c) pan head rivet

    (d) bifurcated rivet

8 In a compression joint, the components are secured by the

    (a) tensile strength of the component materials

    (b) compression strength of the component materials

    (c) shear strength of the component materials

    (d) elasticity of the component materials

9 In a mechanical compression joint the components have to be machined to give a

    (a) clearance fit

    (b) transition fit

    (c) interference fit

    (d) running fit

10 In a thermal compression joint it becomes possible to assemble the components by

    (a) heating the outer component only

    (b) heating both the inner and outer components

    (c) cooling both the inner and outer components

    (d) cooling the outer component only

11 When soft-soldering, the solder adheres to the parent metal by

    (a) roughing the metal surfaces to provide a mechanical 'key'

    (b) the adhesive properties of the flux

    (c) the solder shrinking as it cools to form a compression joint

    (d) the solder forming intermetallic compounds with the parent metal

12 The soldering flux known as 'killed spirits' or 'Baker's fluid' is

    (a) non-corrosive

    (b) passive

    (c) active

    (d) suitable for electronic circuit building

13 Soft-solder is an alloy of
  (a) tin and lead
  (b) tin and silver
  (c) copper and tin
  (d) silver and lead

14 When brazing, the joint is at the correct temperature when
  (a) the edges of the parent metal start to melt
  (b) the heat source can melt the spelter
  (c) the spelter melts on coming into contact with joint even when the heat source is removed
  (d) the combined heat of the joint and the heat source will melt the spelter

15 When brazing, the molten spelter
  (a) flows into the joint through the large clearance left between the components
  (b) is drawn into the joint by capillary attraction
  (c) is drawn into the joint as the flux contracts
  (d) flows by gravity into the joint

16 A suitable brazing flux when using a brass spelter is
  (a) resin
  (b) tallow
  (c) acidified zinc chloride
  (d) borax/water paste

17 Fusion welding differs from brazing in that
  (a) both the edges of the parent metal and the filler material melt
  (b) no melting takes place but the edges of the parent metals are forged together
  (c) the components are sweated together
  (d) electric resistance heating is used

18 No flux is required when welding mild steel using the oxy-acetylene process because the
  (a) temperature is not high enough to cause oxidation
  (b) filler material is a self-fluxing alloy
  (c) burnt gases from the welding flame displace the oxygen of the air and prevent oxidation of the joint
  (d) any oxides formed float to the surface of the weld pool and can be removed by wire brushing

19 The flux coating surrounding electric arc welding electrodes
  (a) prevents heat loss from the electrodes
  (b) reduces the risk of electric shock
  (c) stabilises the arc and protects the weld pool from oxidation
  (d) makes it easier to strike the arc

20 Most adhesives are relatively strong in
  (a) tension and shear
  (b) cleavage and peel
  (c) tension and cleavage
  (d) shear and peel

21 The strongest adhesives are based upon
    (a) natural glues
    (b) natural gums
    (c) thermoplastic materials
    (d) thermosetting resins

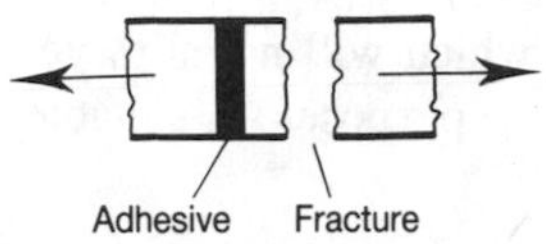

22 Figure 9.35 shows an adhesive joint which has failed. This is the result of
    (a) adhesive failure
    (b) cohesive failure
    (c) failure of the adherend
    (d) failure of the adhesive

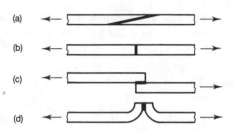

Adhesive Fracture

Fig. 9.35

23 Which of the joints shown in Fig. 9.36 is the most suitable for use with adhesives?

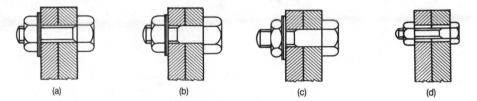

Fig. 9.36

24 Which of the screwed joints shown in Fig. 9.37 is correctly proportioned?

Fig. 9.37

(a)   (b)   (c)   (d)

25 To hold two components tightly together by means of a screwed fastening, the bolt material must have the property of
    (a) toughness
    (b) malleability
    (c) ductility
    (d) elasticity

26 When maximum clamping and locking effects are required a screw with a
    (a) coarse pitch thread is used
    (b) fine pitch thread is used
    (c) square thread form is used
    (d) buttress thread form is used

27 A spring washer can be used under a nut
    (a) as a frictional locking device
    (b) as a positive locking device
    (c) as an anti-vibration mounting
    (d) to prevent the bolt breaking when subject to shock loads

28 A castle nut and split pin are used
    (a) as a frictional locking device
    (b) as a positive locking device
    (c) to prevent the bolt dropping out if the nut works loose
    (d) to prevent the threads stripping if overloaded

29 A collar has to be attached to a shaft with a fastening which will not slip, yet which can be removed from time to time for maintenance purposes. A suitable fastening is a
    (a) grub screw
    (b) cap head screw
    (c) dowel
    (d) taper pin

30 Figure 9.38 shows a gear wheel mounted on a taper nose shaft. The most suitable type of self-aligning key to drive this gear would be a
    (a) gib-head key
    (b) woodruff key
    (c) feather key
    (d) saddle key

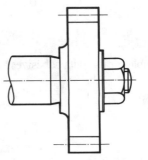

Fig. 9.38

10 Assembly and dismantling

10.1 The purpose of assembly

In engineering, the term *assembly* refers to the putting together of a number of individual components or subassemblies to build up a total system, or a device such as a machine, or a structure such as a bridge. Successful assembly depends upon careful planning at the design stage.

Sequence of assembly

This must be planned so that as each component is added its position in the assembly and the position of its fastenings are accessible. Further, that the addition of one component does not render the position of the next component inaccessible.

Joining

The methods used for joining the components together must be selected so that:

(a) They are suitable for the materials from which the individual components are made.
(b) They are suitable for the components themselves. For example, components which need to be removed or replaced for maintenance purposes must not be permanently fastened by such processes as welding, riveting or adhesive bonding.
(c) They are suitable for the loads which will be imposed upon them in service.
(d) They do not adversely affect adjacent components. For example, welding components in place should not take place near components made from low melting point materials such as thermoplastics or near to heat sensitive components such as transistors.

Various methods of joining have been described in Chapter 9.

Position of joints

Engineering equipment should be designed for ease and speed of assembly and ease of subsequent maintenance. There must be adequate room for the components to be installed and adequate room for spanners and keys to be turned. The need for special tools should be avoided. The design should allow you to use standard tools for assembly and dismantling during the initial construction and subsequent maintenance. Components which have to be regularly replaced during maintenance must be readily accessible. You would find it most inconvenient to have to remove the engine from your motorbike in order to change a sparking plug.

Interrelationship and identification of parts

General arrangement drawings similar to Fig. 4.11 can be used to identify parts. Such drawings also show the position of each of the parts and their interrelationship with adjacent parts of the assembly. To avoid incorrect assembly, interrelationship markings are often provided. For example, the various members and joints of structural steelwork are given a number and letter code. This makes identification and correct assembly easier. Bolts and dowels are often offset (asymmetric) so components can only be assembled one way round. When a new camshaft drive belt has to be fitted to a car engine, care has to be taken to ensure that the marks on the pulleys are in line with the marks provided on the cylinder-block and cylinder-head castings with the belt fitted. This ensures that the engine is correctly timed.

Tolerances

The method of assembly must take the accuracy and finish of the individual components into account. The assembly techniques used when erecting structural steelwork are very different to those used when assembling a machine tool of high precision. Sometimes drawings are given assembly tolerances and the fitter has to ensure that the finished assembly lies within these tolerances. This may entail:

(a) *selective assembly* where several combinations of components have to be tried until the required tolerance is attained;
(b) the joint faces have a fitting allowance so that they can be hand fitted by scraping at the time of assembly.

Obviously this is slow and costly and, for volume production, *non-selective assembly* is required. Here the individual components are manufactured to tolerances which will give the correct assembly tolerance without selection or hand-fitting.

Protection of parts

Parts awaiting assembly require protection against corrosion and accidental physical damage. In the case of structural steelwork this may only entail painting with a suitable primer and careful stacking. In the case of motor car bodies, great care is now taken to ensure that the individual panels are treated against corrosion during storage and that they are stored and issued on a first in, first out (FIFO) basis. Further, the assembled bodies are often now carefully cleaned and zinc galvanised before painting to delay corrosion in service. Precision components are treated with a removable anti-corrosion coating such as a lanolin compound. To prevent mechanical damage, small components are often dipped into a molten synthetic wax which provides a tough coating (you will often see this around new milling cutters). Larger components are supported on special wooden pallets and cradles. Bores should be sealed with plastic plugs and external screwthreads with plastic caps. Heavy components and subassemblies should be provided with integral lifting lugs and eye-bolts so that precision ground surfaces are not damaged by the use of slings and other lifting gear.

10.2 The purpose of dismantling

There are various reasons why assemblies and structures have to be dismantled. One of the most obvious is because the assembly or structure is no longer required and it needs to be broken down into smaller units so that it can be removed. The techniques involved will depend upon whether the dismantled units are to be scrapped or whether they are to be reclaimed for subsequent use eleswhere. We will now consider some other reasons for dismantling assemblies, structures and systems.

Periodic inspection and maintenance

Assemblies often have to be opened up in order to carry out routine inspection and maintenance. For example, steam boilers, air receivers and other pressure vessels have to be inspected internally for corrosion; the gearbox driving the rotor of a helicopter has to be opened up for inspection and maintenance at regular intervals since a failure in service could cause considerable loss of life; and the cylinder heads of internal combustion engines need to be removed from time to time for decarbonising and valve grinding as well as inspection of the cylinder bores. In all these examples great care is required in dismantling the components so that their joint faces are not damaged. Any damage to the joint faces will make it impossible to reassemble the components with fluid-tight joints.

Repair

When a breakdown occurs, the failed component has to be removed for repair or replacement. In either case, great care must be taken in dismantling the equipment and removing the failed component or subassembly so as not to damage any other components to which it is attached and with which it is interrelated. Sometimes the failed component is not immediately accessible and the assembly may have to be extensively dismantled in order to reach the failed component. Since all the parts, other than the one which has failed will be re-used, care must be taken not to damage them during dismantling or whilst they are being stored prior to re-assembly.

Replacement of worn components

Many of the comments in the preceding paragraph apply equally to the replacement of worn components. However, where the routine replacement of worn components can be planned in advance, provision can be made to ease the process of dismantling and re-assembly. For example, the circulating pump in a central heating system is much more likely to wear out than the pipework and radiators. For this reason, full-flow stop valves are fitted either side of the pump. In the event of failure, the valves can be closed and the pump removed without having to drain the system down. The pump is also connected into the system using flanged joints or nut and union joints so that it can be removed without disturbing the associated pipework.

Trial assemblies

It would be an impossible task to transport an oil refinery to its site ready assembled. In fact it would be impossible even to transport many of its subassemblies. Therefore the component parts have to be delivered separately for assembly on site. It would be most embarrassing if, on arrival, it was found that they did not fit together. Therefore a trial assembly is often carried out in the erection shop. This enables any snags to be corrected prior to delivery. After the trial assembly the structure has to be carefully dismantled so that none of the components are lost or damaged.

10.3 Methods of assembly and dismantling

On-site assembly: no prefabrication

This is likely to occur when a fitter is called upon to adapt or alter an existing piece of equipment; for example, to replace a defective electric motor of obsolete design with a new one. For a given power output, the new one will most likely be more compact. The fitter then has to use his/her ingenuity to adapt the motor mounting to suit the hole centres of the feet of the new motor and also to bring the shaft centre into alignment with the existing equipment. Packing plates and, possibly, new mountings will have to be fabricated or adapted on-site to the design of the fitter who will most likely have to manufacture them as well.

On-site assembly: partial prefabrication

Prefabricated and manufactured components are often used to build up systems which are assembled and fitted on site; for example, heating systems, plumbing systems, and electrical installations. In all these examples standard fittings and components are available. The larger items are mounted in place and then connected together using standard piping, couplings, conduit, etc. Ventilating systems are designed for a specific installation. They are then fabricated from sheet metal in a workshop and taken to the site where the final fitting and erection takes place.

Large structure assembly

Large engineering projects such as ships, oil rigs and refineries, power stations, bridges, etc., involve many components and assembly techniques. The components and subassemblies are large and heavy and cranes will have to be used. There will be many teams of fitters at work on different parts of the assembly at the same time. Therefore the work has to be carefully planned so that it progresses in the correct sequence without the teams getting in each other's way. Because of its size and weight the work is potentially hazardous. Great care has to be taken by individual workers, not only for their own safety but for the safety of other workers on the site.

Trial assembly

Large structures and assemblies are often too big to be transported from the maufacturer to the customer completely built up. In order that they may be checked and tested before delivery a trial assembly is carried out on the manufacturer's premises. Once any adjustments have been made and the assembly has been proved to be satisfactory, it is dismantled into convenient sized units for transportation to the customer.

One-off assembly

An example of this type of work would be the assembly of a milling fixture such as that shown in Fig. 10.1. The individual components would be supplied to the fitter from the machine shop. Some of the components will be supplied only partly finished and the fitter may need to drill and tap screw holes and ream dowel holes after the components have been correctly positioned according to the assembly drawing. Under these conditions the fitter has a considerable influence on the accuracy and performance of the finished assembly.

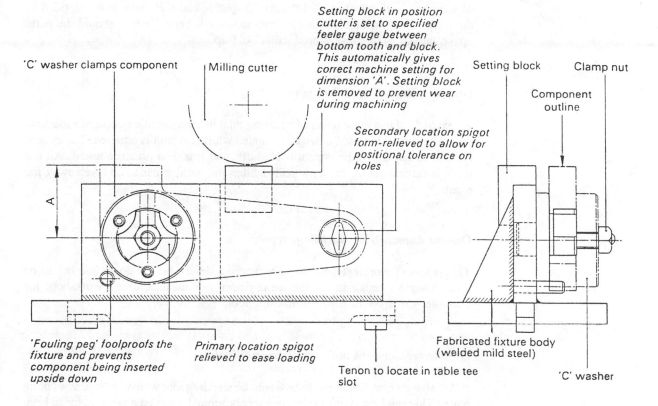

'C' washer clamps component   Milling cutter

Setting block in position cutter is set to specified feeler gauge between bottom tooth and block. This automatically gives correct machine setting for dimension 'A'. Setting block is removed to prevent wear during machining

Setting block   Clamp nut

Component outline

Secondary location spigot form-relieved to allow for positional tolerance on holes

'Fouling peg' toolproofs the fixture and prevents component being inserted upside down

Primary location spigot relieved to ease loading

Tenon to locate in table tee slot

Fabricated fixture body (welded mild steel)

'C' washer

Fig. 10.1 Milling fixture

Batch assembly

This refers to the assembly of a small or medium number of devices of the same type; for example, the assembly of a batch of self-centring lathe chucks. The assembler would be supplied with the chuck bodies, jaws, scrolls, backplates and key sockets/bevel gears, bevel gear retaining clips, and screw, all finished machined and ready for assembly. These components would then be assembled together and no skilled fitting would be involved. Upon completion they should all function satisfactorily without further adjustment.

Line assembly

This refers to the mass production of cars and washing machines or any other devices which are manufactured in very large quantities. No single, highly skilled fitter is involved in total assembly. Assembly is by a team, with the work being passed from one individual to the next along a conveyor belt. Each individual adds one part or subassembly. No skilled fitting is involved and the components are simply fastened together like a Meccano set. Minimum adjustment should be required on completion and costs are minimised by the use of only semi-skilled labour or robotised and automated assembly cells. All the components have to be made to a high standard of accuracy so that they are fully interchangeable and they have to be supplied to the factory 'just-in-time' so that no excess stock is kept. Neither should the parts arrive late so as to cause a production hold-up.

On-site dismantling and repair

An example of this is the repair of a leaking joint in the hydraulic system of a machine tool. The system is closed down and emptied whilst the joint is repaired. The system is refilled, any air in the system is bled off, and it is then pressure tested. All the work is carried out on-site by a skilled fitter and nothing has to be taken away for repair.

On-site dismantling: workshop repair

This refers to more extensive repairs where a device breaks down and has to be taken away for repair in the service engineer's or manufacturer's workshop; for example, the drive motor of a machine tool.

On-site replacement and works reconditioning

In the above example the machine would be standing idle whilst the repair is taking place. This can be avoided by fitting a reconditioned, or even a new, motor to keep the machine running and producing goods. Such interchangeability is one of the benefits of using standardised equipment. When the original motor has been repaired, it can be kept as a spare for use in the event of the next breakdown.

10.4 Selection of methods of assembly and dismantling

A number of factors influence the choice of the method of assembly or dismantling and some of the more important ones will now be considered.

Size

The size of the components in an assembly or system will influence the means of assembly and dismantling. Figure 10.2(a) shows a small bush being knocked out using a hammer and drift. Figure 10.2(b) shows how a new bush can be pressed into place using a bench vice. For larger components presses are used. Figure 10.2(c) shows an arbor press and Fig. 10.2(d) shows a hydraulic press. The force required to remove or replace a component gets greater as the components get bigger. Correspondingly the equipment used by the fitter is designed to exert an ever greater force on the component in each example.

Whilst you can lift small items of equipment manually and strip it and reassemble it on the bench, large components and assemblies require cranes and special lifting and handling equipment.

This is potentially more dangerous and you should not work unaided. There should be someone always available to assist you, and who can summon help in the event of an accident. Standard safety procedures must be observed at all times when using power operated lifting equipment. Never work on or under equipment whilst it is suspended from a crane. The equipment must be lowered onto suitable supports (see section 3.4).

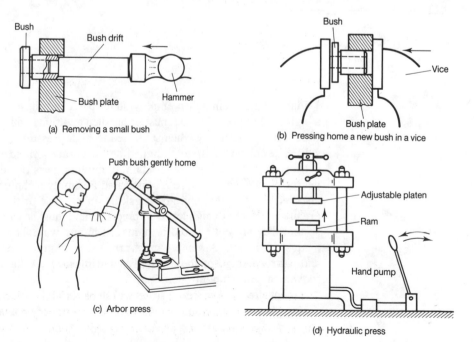

(a) Removing a small bush

(b) Pressing home a new bush in a vice

(c) Arbor press

(d) Hydraulic press

Fig. 10.2 Influence of size on equipment required

Static and moving parts

Static equipment can be considered as assemblies and structures containing no moving parts; for example, storage tanks and the steel framework for buildings. Providing the components have been properly prefabricated and numbered, no problems should arise during erection and no adjustment should be necessary. Figure 10.3 shows a roof truss and the numbering of detail 1. The other joints will be numbered similarly; for example, detail 2 would have components numbered 2.0, 2.1, 2.2, etc. Apart from cranes to lift the parts into position, the only tools required will be drifts to align the holes and spanners to tighten the nuts and bolts. Riveting on site is rarely used these days and, where a permanent fixing is required, welding is resorted to.

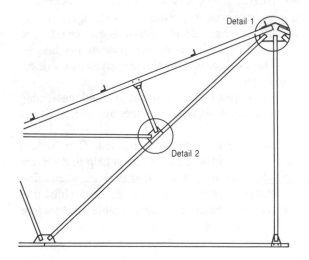

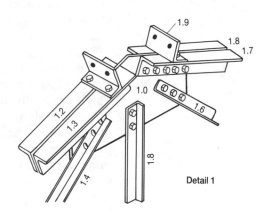

Fig. 10.3 Numbering structural elements

Flanged pipe joints also employ static parts but these must be manufactured to a high level of precision and must be handled and fitted with care if they are to remain fluid tight, particularly when subjected to high pressures. Jointing compound is no substitute for an accurately aligned and accurately fitted joint.

More complex assemblies containing moving parts (for example, a machine tool gearbox) will require more sophisticated assembly techniques and tools. They will also require different and greater skills on the part of the fitter. The components are manufactured to high levels of precision and must be carefully stored and handled so that they are not bruised or damaged in any way. They must also be protected against corrosion. Assembly must proceed with great care to avoid misalignment and, at each stage of the assembly, you must check the components for correct movement and smooth operation.

Except after trial erection, structural steelwork rarely has to be dismantled except during general demolition. However, most machinery containing moving parts will

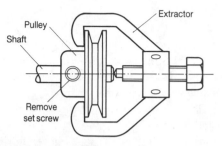
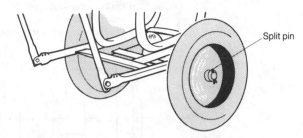

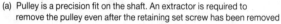

(a) Pulley is a precision fit on the shaft. An extractor is required to remove the pulley even after the retaining set screw has been removed

(b) Wheel is easy clearance fit on shaft and can be slid off by hand after removing the split pin

Fig. 10.4 Removing close and coarsely toleranced components

have to be dismantled from time to time for maintenance, routine replacement of worn components, and to carry out repairs. The same care must be taken in dismantling precision equipment as is used in re-assembling it. The parts must be cleaned as they are removed and they must be laid out in trays in the order in which they were removed so that they can be rebuilt in the same order. Although when first assembled some of the components would have been interchangeable, interrelated parts 'bed down' in service and will need to be kept and re-assembled as 'sets' if smooth running is to be maintained.

Accuracy

The assembly skills required depend largely upon the accuracy of the components being joined together and upon their functional requirements in service. Any jobbing gardener should be able to fit a new wheel to his or her barrow, but very high levels of skill are required, together with special equipment, when assembling an aircraft jet engine. Similarly great skill and, often, special equipment is required when dismantling a precision assembly; for example, Fig. 10.4(a) shows an extractor being used to draw a pulley wheel off a shaft without causing damage to either the wheel or the shaft. By contrast, the coarsely toleranced wheel shown in Fig. 10.4(b) can be removed by hand after withdrawing the split pin.

Accessibility

It has already been stated that components which have to be removed for maintenance need accessible fixings. This makes assembly and dismantling easier and avoids the need to remove a number of components to get at the part you want. Unfortunately the current design tendency is towards increasingly compact designs and miniaturisation. This often dictates the need for special assembly and dismantling tools. Where a complex assembly is being built up, the stages must be carefully planned in advance so that all the fixings at each stage are accessible. When dismantling such an assembly it is often necessary to remove components that are functioning correctly in order to gain access to the failed component. In this case

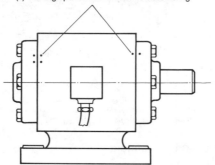

(1) Dot or number punch mating components before dismantling

(2) Re-align punch marks when re-assembling

Fig. 10.5 Marking parts to ensure correct positioning

the components should be arranged in the order in which they were removed so that they can be put back in the same order.

Number of parts

Where an assembly is built up from a great number of parts, a parts list should be made. This not only makes the ordering of parts easier, but ensures that assembly has been carried out correctly. As the components are assembled they are crossed off the list. The parts should be laid out on a clean and cleared bench so that they are conveniently to hand as assembly proceeds. Components that are liable to roll off the bench should be laid in shallow trays or boxes. If assembly is correct there should be no parts left over and no shortages. In any assembly it is unlikely that all the components will fail at the same time. Therefore many of the parts dismantled will be used again. To ensure they go back in the same position, they should be marked before dismantling as shown in Fig. 10.5.

Transport

Large equipment often has to be partly dismantled so that it can be transported from one site to another. When this is required the following factors should be taken into account.

(a) The size of the individual units should be as large as possible so that the equipment suffers the minimum disturbance.

(b) The size of the individual units is governed by:
   - the capacity of the transport available;
   - any traffic regulations along the route (e.g. low bridges, weight restrictions, etc.);
   - the size of the cranes available at the point of loading and the point of off-loading. The smallest crane is the limiting factor.

Nature of repair

The method of dismantling will depend upon the requirements of the repair. If the component or subassembly being removed is to be scrapped and replaced, then it does not matter if it is damaged during dismantling. However, care must be taken not to damage any interrelated components to which the replacement is to be attached. This particularly applies to the faces of fluid tight joints. Where components are to be reclaimed then considerable care is necessary in their removal, particularly if they have not been disturbed for a number of years and have become virtually immovable.

On-site assembly conditions

On-site assembly is required where plant has had to be partly dismantled because of transportation and loading/off-loading restrictions. A number of factors will have to be considered before assembly is commenced.

(a) Are there any restrictions of access and height?
(b) If portable cranes are required is the load-bearing capacity of the ground suitable?
(c) Are the lifting facilities adequate for off-loading and handling the units into the position where they are to be re-assembled?
(d) Are the lifting facilities sufficiently flexible so that the units can be positioned together correctly whilst alignment and fixing is carried out?
(e) Are the environmental conditions suitable or do the units/assembly need to be protected against corrosion until the installation is complete?
(f) Are all the services in place ready for coupling up to the installation so that it can be tested?

Ease of dismantling

Earlier in this section it was stated that when joints have been undisturbed for a long time they may become corroded and difficult to undo. This applies particularly to screwed fastenings.

(a) First apply a penetrating oil and leave it to soak into the threads, then try again to unscrew the fastening.
(b) Next, if the application of penetrating oil fails to ease the threads, the next line of attack is to heat up the nut with an oxy-acetylene or propane torch. The uneven expansion of the nut and bolt usually breaks the corrosion seal and loosens the nut. It also allows any further application of a lubricant to penetrate the threads.
(c) Finally if all else fails the nut has to be cut off with a nut splitter. An example of a nut splitter is shown later in section 10.8.

The only way to remove rivets is either to chisel the heads off or carefully centre the heads and drill the rivets out. Either way great care has to be taken not to damage the surrounding metal.

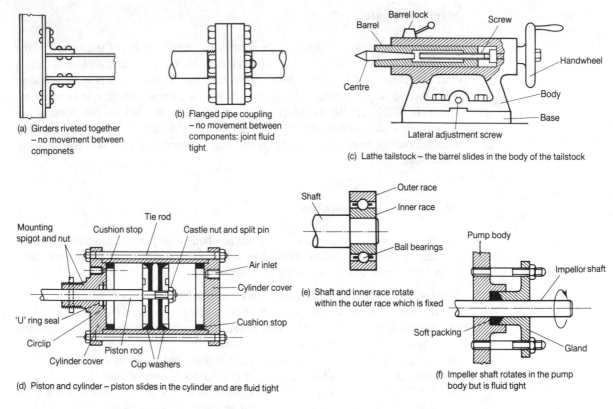

(a) Girders riveted together – no movement between componets

(b) Flanged pipe coupling – no movement between components: joint fluid tight

(c) Lathe tailstock – the barrel slides in the body of the tailstock

(d) Piston and cylinder – piston slides in the cylinder and are fluid tight

(e) Shaft and inner race rotate within the outer race which is fixed

(f) Impeller shaft rotates in the pump body but is fluid tight

Fig. 10.6 Relationship between assembled components

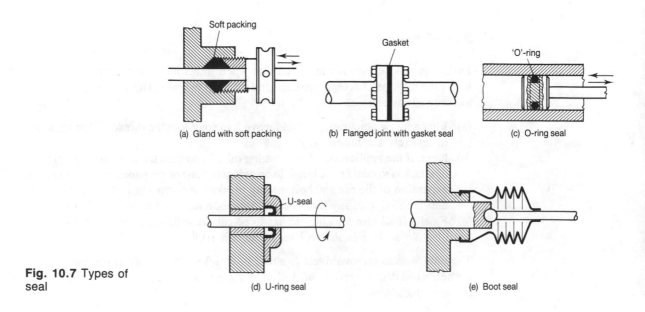

(a) Gland with soft packing

(b) Flanged joint with gasket seal

(c) O-ring seal

(d) U-ring seal

(e) Boot seal

Fig. 10.7 Types of seal

10.5 Relationship between assembled components

When components are assembled the following relationships can exist between them.

(a) There is no movement between the components.
(b) The joint between the non-moving components is fluid tight.
(c) One component slides relative to another.
(d) The joint between the sliding and fixed components is fluid tight.
(e) One part rotates against another.
(f) The joint between the rotating and fixed component is fluid tight.

Examples of these various types of joint are shown in Fig. 10.6.

In view of the number of instances in the above examples where fluid tight joints are required, some examples of *seals* will now be considered. Where possible, you should design seals so that the fluid pressure helps to keep the seal tight on its seating. For engineering purposes seals are usually made from a synthetic rubber such as neoprene which is wear resistant and unaffected by mineral oils. Some examples of seals are shown in Fig. 10.7. The boot seal is used to keep dirt out of the joint rather than provide a fluid tight seal.

10.6 Forces used in assembly and dismantling

The forces acting on joints and the components associated with joints can be summarised as shown in Fig. 10.8 and the effects of these forces on nuts, bolts, pins and rivets are shown in Fig 10.9. *Note*: it is not good practice to load rivets in tension so that the main load is taken by their heads. Wherever possible rivets should be loaded in shear.

It is important when assembling and dismantling threaded components that they are not over stressed. When a threaded fastening, such as a bolt, is tightened it stretches slightly. Since the material from which the bolt is made is elastic, this slight stretching causes it to act like a powerful spring pulling the joint faces together.

If you overtighten a threaded fastening, it will stretch so far that it takes on a permanent set and no longer holds the joint faces in close contact. If the overtightening

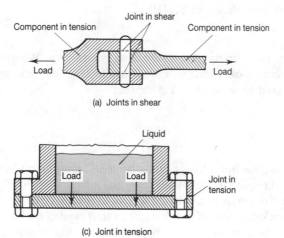

(a) Joints in shear

(c) Joint in tension

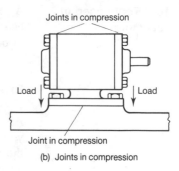

(b) Joints in compression

Fig. 10.8 Forces acting on joints

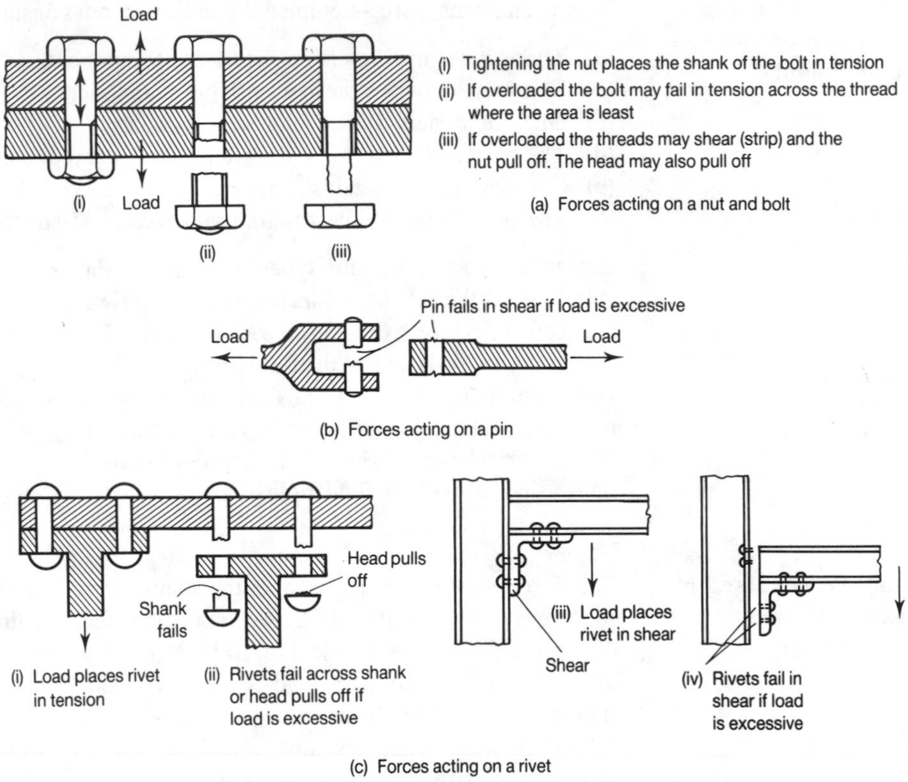

Load

(i) Tightening the nut places the shank of the bolt in tension

(ii) If overloaded the bolt may fail in tension across the thread where the area is least

(iii) If overloaded the threads may shear (strip) and the nut pull off. The head may also pull off

(i) Load

(ii)　(iii)

(a) Forces acting on a nut and bolt

Pin fails in shear if load is excessive

Load　Load

(b) Forces acting on a pin

Head pulls off

Shank fails

(iii) Load places rivet in shear

Shear

(i) Load places rivet in tension

(ii) Rivets fail across shank or head pulls off if load is excessive

(iv) Rivets fail in shear if load is excessive

(c) Forces acting on a rivet

Fig. 10.9 Forces acting on fastenings

is extreme, the fastening will break. To prevent either of these happening, a torque spanner is used. This only allows the correct tightness to be achieved. Spanners will be discussed in the next section. Over-tightening can also cause components to distort and break as shown in Fig 10.10.

10.7 Tools used in assembly

A very wide variety of tools are used in assembly. Wherever possible these should be standard tools which are readily available. Sometimes special-purpose tools have to be used because of lack of space.

Riveted joints

Assuming the holes have already been drilled in the components being joined, then you will require the following tools and materials. A 'dolly' or 'hold-up' to support the head of the rivet, a drawing up tool to ensure the components are properly seated, a ball-pein hammer of suitable size to start closing the rivet, and a rivet set to finish closing the rivet with a properly formed head. Also required are the rivets themselves. These must be of the correct material, correctly heat-treated. They must also be of the correct diameter and the correct length. Rivets, riveted joints and riveting

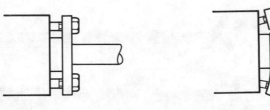

Fig. 10.10 Effects of overtightening

(a) Correctly and evenly tightened gland

(b) Effects of over-tightening and uneven tightening

1 Spring retainer
2 Bush
3 Cylinder
4 Piston
5 Exhaust shield
6 Dowel
7 Handle
8 Valve chest assembly comprising:
   Valve chest
   Bottom valve seat
9 Valve chest plug
10 Valve
11 Grubscrew
12 Body
13 Valve
14 'O' ring
15 Nipple (standard)
16 Nipple (alternative)
17 Plug
18 Spring
19 Valve
20 Bush
21 Rod
22 Pin
23 Link
24 Pin
25 Button
26 Pin

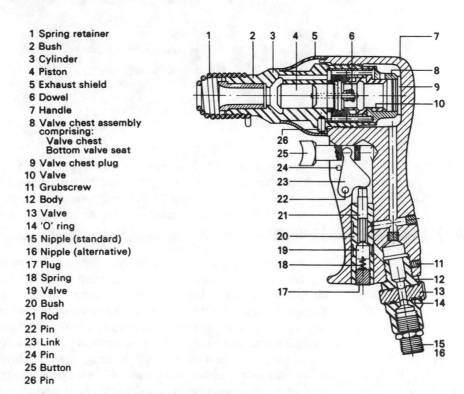

Fig. 10.11 Portable pneumatic riveting machine

tools were considered in Chapter 9. For hot-riveting you would also require a solid-fuel or gas-fired hearth to heat the rivets and tongs to handle the red-hot rivets. Where a large quantity of rivets are to be used a pneumatic riveting gun should be used to reduce operator fatigue and ensure uniformity of the closing process. An example is shown in Fig. 10.11. For sheet metal work, 'POP' riveting is often used. 'POP' riveting was described in Chapter 9. (POP® is a registered trademark of Tucker Fasteners Ltd.)

Threaded fastenings

Examples of joining techniques using threaded (screwed) fastenings were shown in Fig. 9.26. To turn the nut or the bolt you have to use various types of spanners,

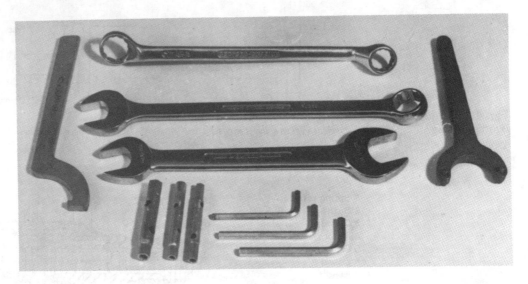

Fig. 10.12 Keys and spanner

keys and wrenches. A selection are shown in Fig. 10.12. Spanners are proportioned so that the length of the spanner provides sufficient leverage for a person of average strength to be able to tighten the fastening correctly. It has already been stated in section 10.6 that the spanner must not be extended to gain more leverage. Extending the spanner will overstress the fastening and weaken it. Further, it will also result in damage to the spanner jaws so that they will not fit properly and this can give rise to injuries. Figure 10.13 shows you the correct way to use spanners.

Where the tightening of a screwed fastening is critical, the designer will specify the torque to be used. Torque is the force exerted on the spanner multiplied by the leverage distance. That is, the distance from the point of application of the force on the spanner, to the axis of the fastening. To ensure that the correct torque is applied a torque wrench is used. An example is shown in Fig. 10.14. As the fastening becomes tighter the arm of the wrench (which is springy) starts to bend. The amount of bend is indicated by the pointer on the scale. When the pointer indicates the correct torque no further tightening is required. Other types of wrench employ a slipping clutch

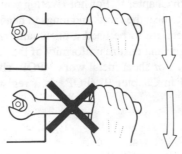

Pull towards your body whenever possible. Do not extend the spanner with lengths of tube, etc., to obtain extra leverage. Use a steady pull, not a jerky action. Do not hit the spanner with a hammer. Ensure that your hands will not strike obstructions if the nut turns unexpectedly. Make sure the jaws of the spanner are a good fit on the nut.

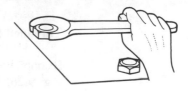

Fig. 10.13 Correct use of spanners

Tighten a nut as shown in the upper illustration above. The force exerted on the spanner tends to keep the jaws on the nut. Used as shown in the lower illustration, the jaws tend to slip of the nut.

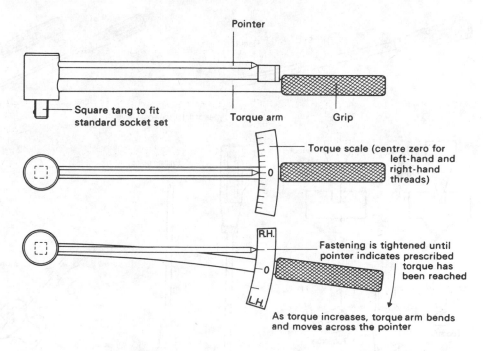

Fig. 10.14 Typical torque spanner

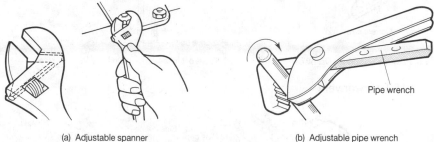

Fig. 10.15 Adjustable spanner and pipe wrench

(a) Adjustable spanner

(b) Adjustable pipe wrench

which can be pre-set so that when the correct torque is reached the clutch slips and the fastening cannot be overtightened.

An adjustable spanner and pipe wrench are shown in Fig. 10.15. You use these mostly for electrical conduit fitting, pipe-fitting and plumbing. They should only be used as a last resource when assembling or dismantling precision joints. Because the arms of the spanners and wrenches are of a fixed length, small fastenings may be over-tightened, and large fastenings may not be securely fastened. As they become worn, the jaws of adjustable spanners tend to slip and damage the corners of hexagon nuts and bolts. This can also lead to accidents.

Screwdrivers must also be chosen with care so that they fit the head of the screw correctly. A variety of screwdrivers are shown in Fig. 10.16.

Pliers are also used for assembly and dismantling. They are mostly used by electricians but are also used for holding small components and for inserting and removing split pins. Pliers with special jaws are used for removing *circlip* type fastenings as shown in Fig. 10.17. On no account should they be used for tightening or loosening hexagon nuts and bolts as the serrated jaws would damage the corners of the hexagons.

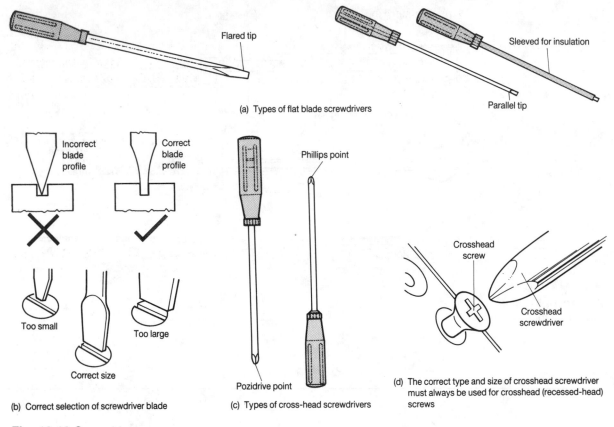

(a) Types of flat blade screwdrivers

Flared tip

Sleeved for insulation

Parallel tip

Incorrect blade profile

Correct blade profile

Too small

Too large

Correct size

(b) Correct selection of screwdriver blade

Phillips point

Pozidrive point

(c) Types of cross-head screwdrivers

Crosshead screw

Crosshead screwdriver

(d) The correct type and size of crosshead screwdriver must always be used for crosshead (recessed-head) screws

Fig. 10.16 Screwdrivers

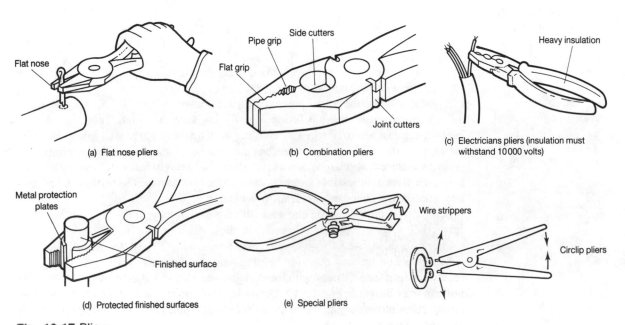

Flat nose

(a) Flat nose pliers

Pipe grip

Side cutters

Flat grip

Joint cutters

(b) Combination pliers

Heavy insulation

(c) Electricians pliers (insulation must withstand 10 000 volts)

Metal protection plates

Finished surface

(d) Protected finished surfaces

Wire strippers

Circlip pliers

(e) Special pliers

Fig. 10.17 Pliers

Compression joints

These were described in Chapter 8 and also earlier in this chapter. They rely on the shrinkage of the outer component or the expansion of the inner component to produce an interference fit between the components and this locks them together by friction.

Hammers

The use of hammers has already been introduced when discussing riveted joints. Whatever they are being used for, the correct type and size of hammer must be carefully chosen. If the hammer is too big it will be clumsy to use and proper control cannot be exercised. If the hammer is too small it has to be wielded with so much effort that, again, proper control cannot be exercised. In both these instances the use of the incorrect size of hammer will result in an unsatisfactory job and possible injury to the user.

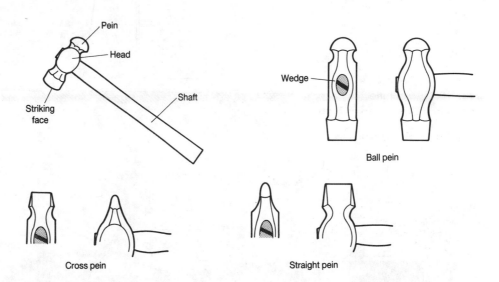

Fig. 10.18 Hammers

Some different types of hammer are shown in Fig. 10.18. Like any other tool, it is important that hammers are kept in good condition. Before using a hammer you must make sure that:

(a) the handle is not split;
(b) the head is securely fitted;
(c) the head is not cracked or chipped.

You must be careful, when using a hammer, that the components being struck are not bruised. Soft faced hammers should be used when machined surfaces have to be struck. Alternatively a soft metal drift should be placed between the hammer head and the component being struck.

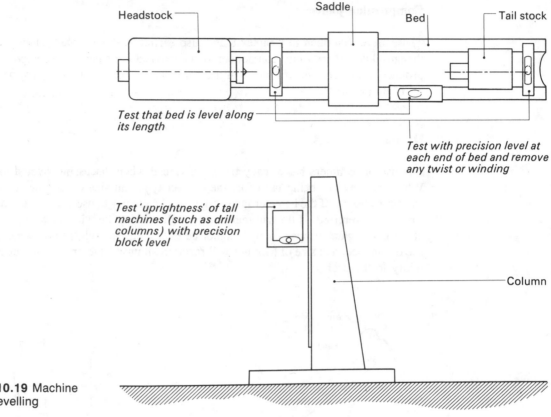

Headstock

Saddle

Bed

Tail stock

Test that bed is level along its length

Test with precision level at each end of bed and remove any twist or winding

Test 'uprightness' of tall machines (such as drill columns) with precision block level

Column

Fig. 10.19 Machine tool levelling

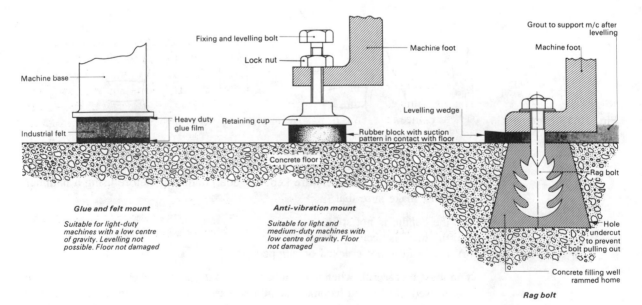

Machine base

Industrial felt

Heavy duty glue film

Fixing and levelling bolt

Lock nut

Machine foot

Retaining cup

Rubber block with suction pattern in contact with floor

Concrete floor

Levelling wedge

Grout to support m/c after levelling

Machine foot

Rag bolt

Hole undercut to prevent bolt pulling out

Concrete filling well rammed home

Glue and felt mount

Suitable for light-duty machines with a low centre of gravity. Levelling not possible. Floor not damaged

Anti-vibration mount

Suitable for light and medium-duty machines with low centre of gravity. Floor not damaged

Rag bolt

Suitable for all machines where a permanent fixing is required

Fig. 10.20 Machinery mounts and fixings

Measuring equipment

Measuring and checking equipment is generally the same as that used in the manufacture of components as described in Chapter 4. Figure 10.19 shows how a spirit (bubble) level is used for the installation of plant on site. It is essential when installing a machine to make sure that the bed or frame is not being warped in any way as this would upset the fundamental accuracy of the machine. An example of machinery mounts and fixings are shown in Fig. 10.20.

10.8 Tools for dismantling

Mostly, the tools you use for dismantling are the same as those you use for assembly. However, because fastenings often become tight with age, generally through corrosion, there are some additional requirements. For example, a sharp blow will often loosen a joint when a steady pressure has no effect. It is bad practice to hit an ordinary spanner and a specially designed *impact spanner* should be used as shown in Fig. 10.21.

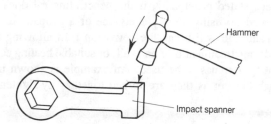

Fig. 10.21 Impact spanner

Cleansing agents

These have to be used when equipment has not been dismantled for a long time and particularly equipment which has been used in dirty environments such as foundries. Cleansing is necessary not only to make the job of dismantling more pleasant, but also so that the position of joints and defects in the components can be located. On site, the simplest method of cleaning down is swabbing with paraffin. Care must be taken since paraffin is highly flammable. Plastic or rubber gloves should be worn so that the paraffin does not get on your skin. Large assemblies such as structural steel work, chemical plant, storage tanks, etc., are often cleaned down with high-pressure steam jets prior to dismantling. For workshop repairs, small assemblies and components can be cleaned down using solvents such as trichloroethylene. These are highly toxic and are used in enclosed degreasing equipment so that the fumes cannot escape. Such solvents must only be used under supervision by trained persons using approved equipment. Emergency breathing apparatus must be available.

Dyes and markers

When assemblies are dismantled it is frequently necessary to put distinguishing marks on the components so that they can be reassembled in the correct sequence and in the correct relationship to each other. To do this paint and aerosol dye sprays are used together with stencils. Where permanent marking is required number and letter punches and even centre punch dots can be used. An example of the latter technique was shown in Fig. 10.5.

Penetrating oils

Once the assembly has been cleaned and marked up ready for dismantling it is often necessary to apply a penetrating oil to the screwed fastenings to assist in loosening and easing corroded threads. Penetrating oils are not suitable for general lubrication. The penetrating oil is very thin and seeps into the threads by capillary attraction, carrying with it a small amount of a lubricant such as graphite.

Nut splitter

As has been stated previously, if the penetrating oil does not work, then the nut can be heated up using an oxy-acetylene or a propane torch. This will cause the nut to expand and will break the corrosion film allowing the nut to be turned. If even this drastic treatment is of no avail, or suitable heating equipment is not available, then a nut splitter has to be used. An example is shown in Fig. 10.22. The jaws cut through the nut as they are forced together by tightening the bolt.

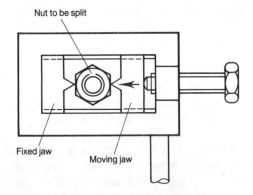

Fig. 10.22 Nut splitter

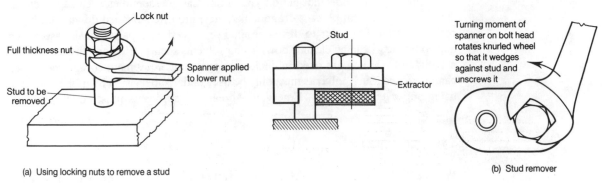

(a) Using locking nuts to remove a stud

(b) Stud remover

Fig. 10.23 Stud removal

Stud remover

Studs can be removed by tightening two nuts together on the exposed end of the stud as shown in Fig. 10.23(a). The spanner is applied to the lower nut so that the act of unscrewing the stud tightens the nuts together. Alternatively a stud remover can be used as shown in Fig. 10.23(b). An eccentrically mounted hardened and knurled roller is wedged against the stud by the action of the spanner. This affords sufficient grip to remove the stud.

'Easy-out'

Broken screws and studs can be removed by an 'easy out'. This is, essentially, a coarse-thread left-handed tap. A pilot hole is drilled down the centre of the broken bolt or stud and the tap is screwed in. Being left-handed the force exerted on the tap as it is screwed home tends to unscrew the bolt or stud which will have a conventional right-handed thread.

Chisel

Permanent fastenings such as rivets can only be removed by destruction of the rivet. The head can be removed as shown in Fig. 10.24. Drilling the rivet reduces the thickness of metal to be cut through with the cold chisel.

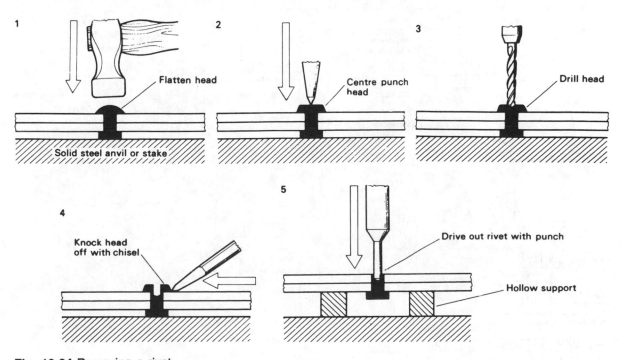

Fig. 10.24 Removing a rivet

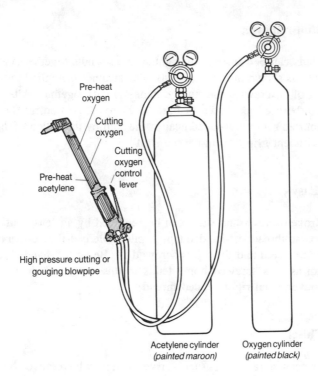

Fig. 10.25 Flame
cutting equipment

Pre-heat
oxygen

Cutting
oxygen

Cutting
oxygen
control
lever

Pre-heat
acetylene

High pressure cutting or
gouging blowpipe

Acetylene cylinder
(*painted maroon*)

Oxygen cylinder
(*painted black*)

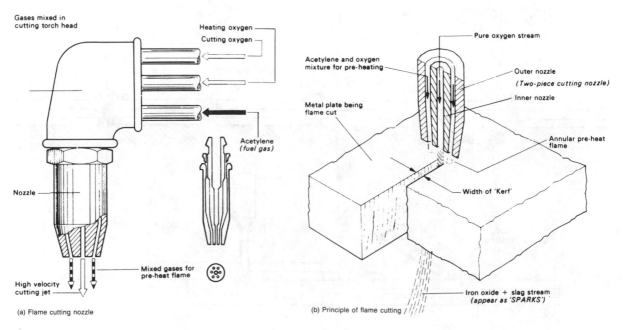

Gases mixed in
cutting torch head

Heating oxygen

Cutting oxygen

Acetylene
(*fuel gas*)

Nozzle

Mixed gases for
pre-heat flame

High velocity
cutting jet

(a) Flame cutting nozzle

Pure oxygen stream

Acetylene and oxygen
mixture for pre-heating

Outer nozzle
(*Two-piece cutting nozzle*)

Inner nozzle

Metal plate being
flame cut

Annular pre-heat
flame

Width of 'Kerf'

Iron oxide + slag stream
(*appear as 'SPARKS'*)

(b) Principle of flame cutting

Fig. 10.26 Flame cutting nozzle

Flame-cutting

This is also destructive dismantling. It is a quick way of cutting up large assemblies, pipework, and structural steelwork into pieces which can be easily transported away. Flame-cutting can only be used for ferrous metals. A set of flame-cutting equipment is shown in Fig. 10.25. This is *not* the same as welding equipment although it looks similar. The oxygen regulator must be capable of passing a much larger volume of gas and a special torch is used. A cutting nozzle is shown in Fig. 10.26. You can see that it provides a ring of flames to preheat the metal being cut. When the metal reaches its ignition temperature, a powerful jet of pure oxygen is released into the centre of the preheated area. The hot metal immediately oxidises and burns away. The oxygen stream blows the metal oxides through the cut in a shower of sparks. The oxidising reaction also helps to heat up the metal being cut and the process becomes continuous. The cutting torch is moved forward along the line of the cut as shown in Fig. 10.27.

10.9 Precautions   Assemblies and structures should not be dismantled until all the potential hazards have been considered.

Forces

The precautions that should be taken when lifting and moving heavy loads have already been discussed in Chapter 3. The forces acting on a piece of equipment must also be assessed so that it cannot fall during dismantling. For example, the pipework

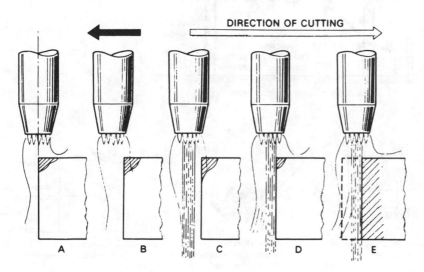

DIRECTION OF CUTTING

A   Pre-heat to ignition temperature
B   Move the cutting torch backwards, just clear of edge
C   Open the cutting oxygen valve
D   Commence cutting
E   Continue cutting

Fig. 10.27 Flame cutting technique

and the steam valve shown in Fig. 10.28(a) must be supported before the flanges are unbolted.

You must also take care to ensure that the forces required to tighten or loosen fastenings do not dislodge the equipment upon which you are working.

Containers should be drained before moving them. This is because any liquids they contain may start to surge and make the containers unstable as shown in Fig. 10.28(b). A spreader should be used to balance the load as shown in Fig. 10.28(c).

Contents

You must always find out what a pipework system contains, or has contained, before attempting to dismantle it. This is because the contents of pipes may be flammable, toxic, under high pressure and/or hot. Even pipework which has been drained can still be dangerous, For example, pipework which has contained a flammable substance, such as petrol, will still contain highly flammable and potentially explosive petrol vapour long after the original liquid has been drained off. Such pipework would need to be 'purged' with a non-flammable, non-toxic fuid to displace the petrol vapour and render the pipework safe. The BS colour code (Fig. 4.40) helps to identify the contents of pipework and containers.

A '*permit-to-work*' must be obtained before work commences. Closing down the system and rendering it safe is the responsibility of the senior supervisory staff and should not be attempted by a fitter, however, experienced. Valves should be locked so that they cannot be inadvertently opened whilst work is in progress.

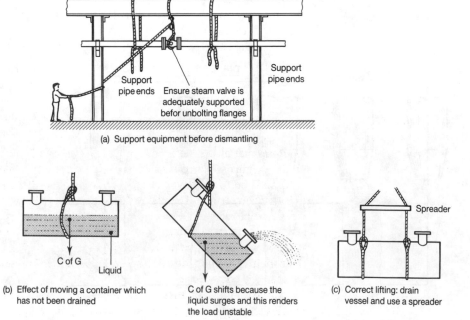

(a) Support equipment before dismantling

Fig. 10.28 Precautions when dismantling

(b) Effect of moving a container which has not been drained

C of G shifts because the liquid surges and this renders the load unstable

(c) Correct lifting: drain vessel and use a spreader

Electricity

Assembling and dismantling electrically powered plant and equipment must not be attempted until the electrical supply has been disconnected by a qualified and authorised electrician. The fuses should be drawn and the supply locked off so that it cannot be inadvertently reinstated whilst work is in progress. Once the supply has been locked off the fitter should keep the key until the work is complete. If a lock is not provided then the fitter should keep the fuses until the work is complete.

Temperature

High temperature devices such as furnaces, pumps, pipework and valves may have to undergo emergency repairs before they have fully cooled down. Suitable protective clothing must be worn, and breathing apparatus may be necessary. The maintenance fitter should be closely supervised so that he or she can be rescued if overcome by the heat.

Chemicals

Codes of practice must be rigorously observed when working on plant associated with dangerous and radio-active chemicals. The work must only be carried out under the strictest supervision by qualified and authorised persons. Appropriate protective clothing must be worn together with breathing apparatus if necessary. In the latter case the fitter must be properly trained in the use of such equipment and the equipment itself must be thoroughly tested by an authorised person before use. Precautions must be taken against accidental leakage of dangerous substances, since these could cause a health hazard over a wide area.

10.10 Material properties

The designer selects the material for a component with great care, taking into account such factors as strength, hardness, wear-resistance and corrosion resistance. It is essential that all replacement components must be made to the same specification as the originals. For example, if a high-tensile bolt was replaced by an ordinary mild-steel bolt for convenience, then a serious accident could occur if the weaker bolt failed in service. The properties of the material must be reflected in the treatment the material receives. For example, brittle material such as cast iron must not be struck with a hard hammer; a hide-faced mallet would be more appropriate. If components have to be heated during assembly or dismantling, then not only must their melting temperatures be taken into account but also the melting temperatures of adjacent components.

Sealing compounds must be suitable for the joint being made. You must always check that they are capable of withstanding the temperatures and pressures present in the system, and they must not be dissolved or degraded in any way by the fluids flowing in the system.

Corrosion must be minimised by careful choice of materials. Wherever possible you should use replacements made to the original equipment specification. If this is not possible, then the following rules should be observed.

(a) The fixings should be made from the same type of metal as the component. That is, steel nuts, bolts and rivets for joining steel and cast-iron components (steel and cast-iron are both *ferrous* metals).

(b) Do not mix dissimilar metals, for example, steel and copper. These will react together in the presence of moisture and corrode.

(c) Structural steelwork should be painted with a suitable primer containing a rust inhibitor before and after assembly to prevent moisture seeping into the joints and causing rusting.

10.11 General rules for dismantling and assembling

When assembling machines, plant, structures and systems from new, or when reassembling after maintenance and repair, the following rules must be observed.

(a) Upon completion each assembly or subassembly must operate correctly. For example, the table of a milling machine must slide freely on the cross-slide for its full length without binding or sloppiness at any point which could affect its accuracy.

(b) If available, the assembly drawings and specifications must be strictly adhered to.

(c) Before commencing assembly, the sequence of operations must be carefully planned and any components and tools required must be made available.

(d) Check that all the parts and tools are in good condition before commencing work.

(e) Dirt and any other undesirable substances must be kept out of the work during assembly.

(f) All joints must be made using the correct fastenings.

(g) Tightening tools must be of the correct type and size so that they not only fit correctly, but also provide the correct degree of tightness.

(h) Components must be assembled in accordance with any identification marks, and any components bearing alignment marks must be assembled so that such markings are correctly positioned.

(i) Checking and inspection should be carried out as frequently as the work permits so that, in the event of an error, the minimum amount of work has to be corrected before assembly can again proceed.

The following rules should be observed when dismantling machines, structures, plant and systems.

(a) Ensure that the system to be dismantled has been made safe and that a 'permit to work' has been issued.

(b) If they are available, assembly drawings and specifications must be followed in reverse order.

(c) If such information is not available, then careful notes and sketches must be made as the work is dismantled so that re-assembly can proceed in the correct sequence.

(d) Always plan the sequence in which dismantling is to be carried out before commencing work.

(e) Select and list the tools and equipment required so that you can check that they are all available. This is particularly important if you are working on site and you are isolated from the stores.

(f) Burrs and corrosive deposits should be removed to ease the dismantling process and to prevent further damage.

(g) To avoid further damage tools such as hammers, drifts, levers and extractors must be carefully selected and used.

At all times during assembly and dismantling you must observe the correct safety practices. This is especially important where large and heavy objects are involved and power-operated lifting equipment is being used. Carefully observe any special procedures which apply when flammable fluids, dangerous chemicals, steam, compressed air, and hydraulic or electrical services are involved. Cooperate fully with the supervisory staff as they are responsible both for your safety and the safety of others working in the same vicinity.

10.12 Assembling pipework systems	The design of pipework systems carrying fluids must take into acount a number of factors. For example:

(a) working pressure
(b) steady or pulsating flow
(c) volume of fluid flowing
(d) rate of flow
(e) temperature
(f) type of fluid being conducted (corrosion)
(g) viscosity (thickness)
(h) whether any solids will be carried in the fluid (erosion, silting-up, etc.)

Valves for bleeding off the system must be provided at strategic points in both the pipework and the fittings so that the air in the system can be released as the liquid is fed in initially. Without such facilities it would be impossible to fill the system and impossible for the liquid to circulate correctly. These valves also allow the system to be bled off from time to time in service as dissolved gases in the liquid are released. System carrying gases do not require such comprehensive bleed-off facilities.

Pipework systems also require valves to be provided for draining the system down. The system has to be drained down before repairs or alterations can be carried out.

Plumbing services providing hot and cold water, and removing effluents require a totally different approach to the hydraulic system of a machine tool. The former will be involved with large volumes of water at low or relatively low pressures, whilst the latter will be involved in relatively low volumes of oil at very high pressures.

Fatal and serious accidents are liable to occur in badly installed or badly maintained high-pressure and high temperature installations. As a result, stringent safety codes of practice have been drawn up which are enforceable at law. Installations operating at high temperatures and pressures, such as pneumatic, hydraulic and steam systems must meet the following requirements.

(a) They must be designed by expert, specialist engineers to meet the requirements of the Health and Safety at Work Act, and the Factory Acts, plus any special legislation appropriate to a particular type of installation.

(b) Such installations must only be constructed from equipment which has been tested and certified, and which is in accordance with the recommendations of the British Standards Institution.

(c) Upon completion such installations must be inspected by the appropriate authorities. For example, specialist insurance surveyors and, where appropriate, local authority engineers and the fire service, before the installation is taken into service.

(d) Such installations must be regularly and expertly maintained. They must also be inspected at regular intervals (annually) by an authorised person such as a specialist insurance surveyor and its certification renewed.

(e) The pipework should be colour coded to indicate its contents.

Electrical conduit and its associated fittings require a rather different approach. The purpose of the conduit is to provide:

(a) mechanical protection for electrical conductors
(b) earth continuity

Because of this latter requirement no jointing compounds are used in the screwed joints which must maintain a metal-to-metal contact to ensure electrical continuity. Electrical installations in hazardous environments require specialised conduit, fittings and installation, for example: quarries, mines and petrol stations. The regulations governing the installation of electrical systems are to be found in publications issued by the Institution of Electrical Engineers, as well as various Acts of Parliament.

There are many different type of pipe and tube used and they are made from a variety of materials.

Copper: solid-drawn

This is used for installations where the pressure does not exceed 150 bars when the tube has been annealed, or 350 bars when the tube is in the 'as-drawn' (half-hard) condition. The safe working pressure becomes less as the temperature increases. Copper tubes and pipes are corrosion resistant and are widely used for low- and medium-pressure fluids such as water, hydraulic oil and compressed air and natural gas.

Steel: hot finished seamless

This is solid-drawn pipe made in a wide range of sizes. It can be used at the highest temperatures and pressures (up to 600 bars). Unfortunately it has a rough and scaly finish and it cannot be used with compression fittings. It is used in conjunction with screwed and welded joints.

Steel: cold finished seamless

This is also a solid-drawn pipe. However, it has a smooth finish and can be used with compression joint fittings. Unfortunately it is more difficult to manufacture and this is reflected in its very much higher price.

Steel: electric resistance welded

This is produced from steel strip, edge-welded. It is widely used for electrical conduit. Resistance welded *stainless steel* tube is used as an alternative to copper for low pressure installations such as domestic plumbing and heating services. It is less costly than copper but harder to cut, bend and joint.

Cast iron

This is used for large-diameter pipes for high-volume, low-pressure services such as waste water and effluent disposal. Cast iron pipes are also used for water supply mains.

Plastic

Extruded plastic pipes are used increasingly for underground domestic water and gas supplies. It is also used for effluent disposal (soil) pipes. Plastic pipes are unaffected by water, oil and many normally corrosive chemicals. Flexible plastic tubing is used for low- and medium-pressure coolant, oil, and compressed air systems on machine tools. Special plastic hoses are also used for high-pressure hydraulic services, for example, on machine tools, earth-moving equipment and road vehicles. To prevent the hoses from bursting and to protect them from mechanical damage, they are contained within a high-tensile steel braid outer sheath.

Ceramic pipes

These are the traditional earthenware drain pipes. They are still widely used for underground effluent disposal. It is important that they are carefully laid and supported or they will crack. They are also liable to crack as the result of ground heave and subsidence and as a result of heavy loads passing over the ground above them.

10.13 Pipe jointing

Screwed joints

These can only be used with thick walled steel tubes since the strength of the joint is reduced to that of the metal remaining at the bottom of the thread as shown in Fig. 10.29(a). There are two systems of screwed joint in common use.

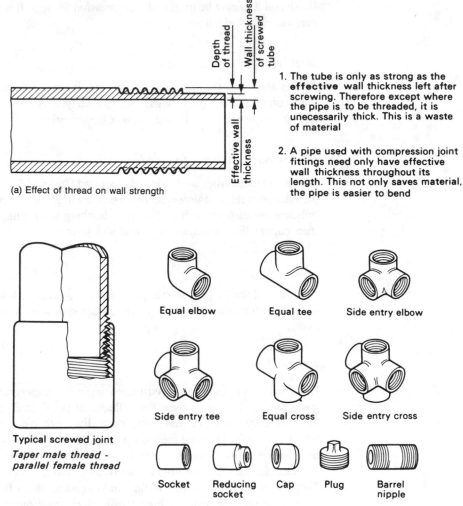

Depth of thread

Wall thickness of screwed tube

Effective wall thickness

(a) Effect of thread on wall strength

1. The tube is only as strong as the **effective** wall thickness left after screwing. Therefore except where the pipe is to be threaded, it is unecessarily thick. This is a waste of material

2. A pipe used with compression joint fittings need only have effective wall thickness throughout its length. This not only saves material, the pipe is easier to bend

Equal elbow   Equal tee   Side entry elbow

Side entry tee   Equal cross   Side entry cross

Typical screwed joint
Taper male thread - parallel female thread

Socket   Reducing socket   Cap   Plug   Barrel nipple

Fig. 10.29 Threaded pipe joints

(b) Typical screwed fittings

British Standard pipe thread

This is also a fine-thread, constant-pitch system. The thread on the end of the pipe is tapered and the thread in the fitting is parallel. This enables you to screw home the pipe tightly into the fitting to make a fluid-tight joint. A jointing compound can be put on the threads before assembly or, alternatively, PTFE tape can be wrapped around the threads before assembly. A typical screwed pipe joint, together with some fittings, is shown in Fig. 10.29(b).

Conduit thread

This is a fine, constant pitch, parallel thread system. That is, the pitch remains the same irrespective of the diameter of the thread. Therefore, if the pitch is constant,

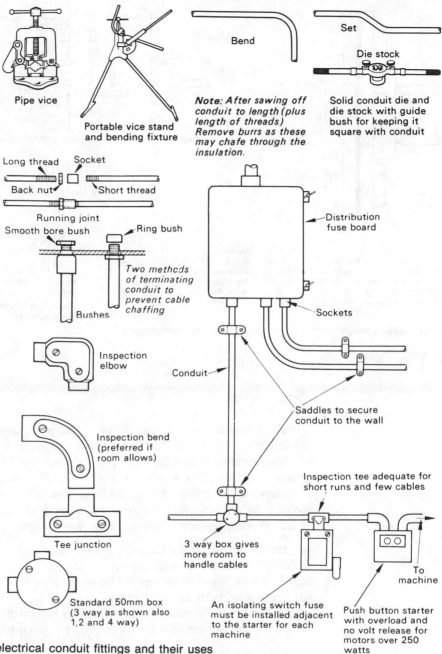

Fig. 10.30 Some typical electrical conduit fittings and their uses

so is the depth of thread and the wall thickness of the conduit tube itself can also be kept constant irrespective of its diameter. Since, as has already been stated, the conduit often forms an earth return path, the joints must be tight but NO jointing compound may be used. To be electrically conductive the joint must have a metal-to-metal contact. Figure 10.30 shows some typical conduit fittings and their uses.

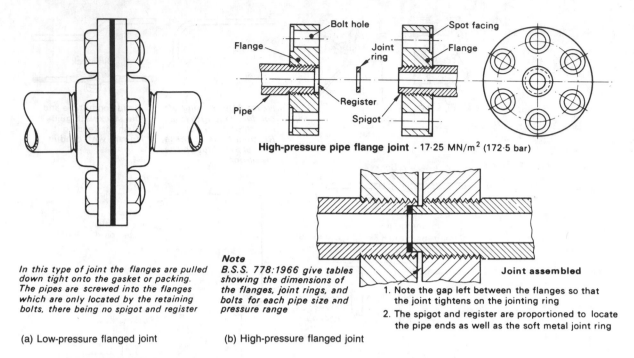

High-pressure pipe flange joint - 17·25 MN/m^2 (172·5 bar)

In this type of joint the flanges are pulled down tight onto the gasket or packing. The pipes are screwed into the flanges which are only located by the retaining bolts, there being no spigot and register

Note
B.S.S. 778:1966 give tables showing the dimensions of the flanges, joint rings, and bolts for each pipe size and pressure range

Joint assembled

1. Note the gap left between the flanges so that the joint tightens on the jointing ring
2. The spigot and register are proportioned to locate the pipe ends as well as the soft metal joint ring

(a) Low-pressure flanged joint

(b) High-pressure flanged joint

Fig. 10.31 Flanged joints

Flanged joints

These are used for medium and high-pressure joints and examples of these joints are shown in Fig. 10.31. The flanges my be attached to the pipes by screwing or welding. Welding is now the more popular since there is no reduction in the wall thickness and loss of strength in the pipe run. Flanged joints are required where the joints may have to be dismantled from time to time and where the pipe run is too rigid for a union joint to be used. An example of a union joint is shown in Fig. 10.32. When assembling flanged joints, it is essential to ensure that:

(a) the flanges are aligned axially to each other;
(b) they are parallel to each other;
(c) their joint faces are perpendicular to the pipe axis;
(d) the bolting holes are in alignment;
(e) no bolt lies on the bottom centre-line. Any bolt on the bottom centre-line would be subject to corrosion from any seepage which might occur.

Compression and capillary joints

These are being used increasingly in place of screwed joints for smaller diameter tubes and pipes. Not only do they save installation time (and cost) but they allow lighter gauge tubing to be used since the wall thickness will not be reduced by threading with the associated loss of strength. However, compression joints tend

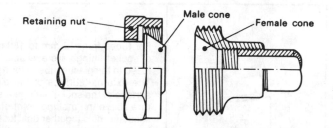

Fig. 10.32 Union joint

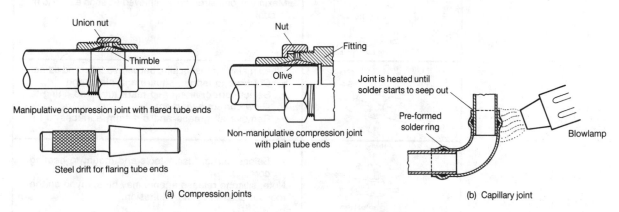

Fig. 10.33 Compression and capillary pipe joints

to be bulky and expensive to manufacture. For plumbing installations, involving copper pipe and fittings, soldered capillary joints are now widely used where the joint is unlikely to have to be dismantled. An example of each type of joint is shown in Fig 10.33.

Sleeve joints

These are used with cast iron pipes and ceramic pipes. A number of proprietary systems are available and two examples of typical joints are shown in Fig 10.34.

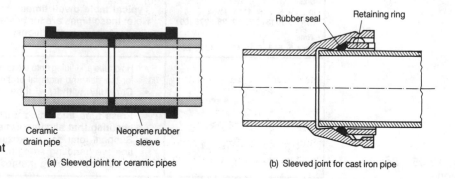

Fig. 10.34 Sleeve joint for ceramic pipes

(a) Sleeved joint for ceramic pipes

(b) Sleeved joint for cast iron pipe

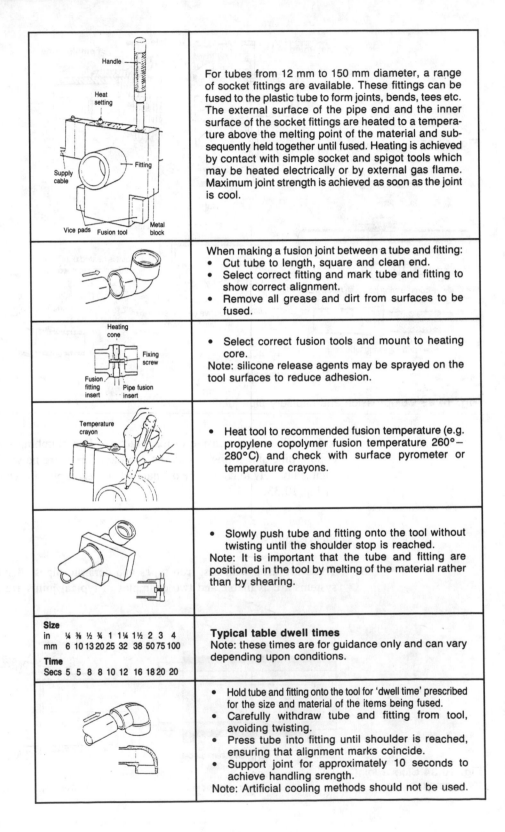

For tubes from 12 mm to 150 mm diameter, a range of socket fittings are available. These fittings can be fused to the plastic tube to form joints, bends, tees etc. The external surface of the pipe end and the inner surface of the socket fittings are heated to a temperature above the melting point of the material and subsequently held together until fused. Heating is achieved by contact with simple socket and spigot tools which may be heated electrically or by external gas flame. Maximum joint strength is achieved as soon as the joint is cool.

When making a fusion joint between a tube and fitting:
- Cut tube to length, square and clean end.
- Select correct fitting and mark tube and fitting to show correct alignment.
- Remove all grease and dirt from surfaces to be fused.

- Select correct fusion tools and mount to heating core.
Note: silicone release agents may be sprayed on the tool surfaces to reduce adhesion.

- Heat tool to recommended fusion temperature (e.g. propylene copolymer fusion temperature 260°–280°C) and check with surface pyrometer or temperature crayons.

- Slowly push tube and fitting onto the tool without twisting until the shoulder stop is reached.
Note: It is important that the tube and fitting are positioned in the tool by melting of the material rather than by shearing.

Size

in	¼	⅜	½	¾	1	1¼	1½	2	3	4
mm	6	10	13	20	25	32	38	50	75	100

Time

Secs	5	5	8	8	10	12	16	18	20	20

Typical table dwell times
Note: these times are for guidance only and can vary depending upon conditions.

- Hold tube and fitting onto the tool for 'dwell time' prescribed for the size and material of the items being fused.
- Carefully withdraw tube and fitting from tool, avoiding twisting.
- Press tube into fitting until shoulder is reached, ensuring that alignment marks coincide.
- Support joint for approximately 10 seconds to achieve handling srength.
Note: Artificial cooling methods should not be used.

Fig. 10.35 Socket fusion

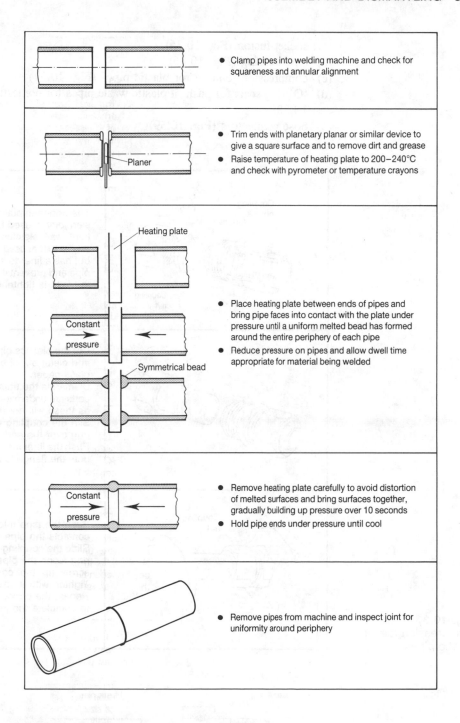

- Clamp pipes into welding machine and check for squareness and annular alignment

- Trim ends with planetary planar or similar device to give a square surface and to remove dirt and grease
- Raise temperature of heating plate to 200–240°C and check with pyrometer or temperature crayons

Heating plate

Constant pressure

Symmetrical bead

- Place heating plate between ends of pipes and bring pipe faces into contact with the plate under pressure until a uniform melted bead has formed around the entire periphery of each pipe
- Reduce pressure on pipes and allow dwell time appropriate for material being welded

Constant pressure

- Remove heating plate carefully to avoid distortion of melted surfaces and bring surfaces together, gradually building up pressure over 10 seconds
- Hold pipe ends under pressure until cool

- Remove pipes from machine and inspect joint for uniformity around periphery

Fig. 10.36 Butt-welding plastic pipe

Plastic pipes

There are a wide variety of jointing techniques used in conjunction with plastic pipes depending upon whether they are rigid or flexible and what fluid will be flowing through them. Jointing techniques include:

(a) socket-fusion (Fig. 10.35)

(b) butt-welding (Fig. 10.36)

(c) compression jointing for plastic pipes (Fig. 10.37)

(d) 'O' ring seals for push fit plastic waste pipes for domestic sanitary ware (Fig. 10.38)

(e) hose connectors (Fig. 10.39)

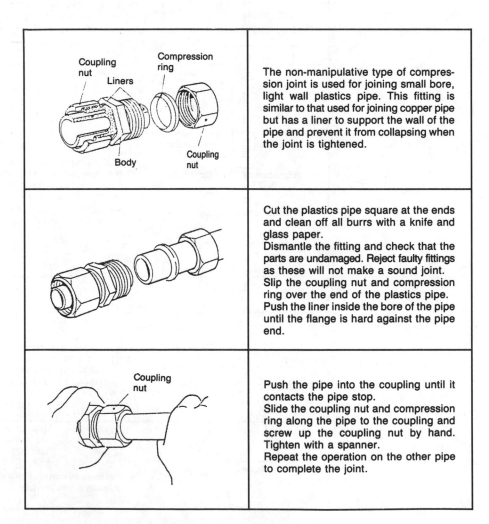

The non-manipulative type of compression joint is used for joining small bore, light wall plastics pipe. This fitting is similar to that used for joining copper pipe but has a liner to support the wall of the pipe and prevent it from collapsing when the joint is tightened.

Cut the plastics pipe square at the ends and clean off all burrs with a knife and glass paper.
Dismantle the fitting and check that the parts are undamaged. Reject faulty fittings as these will not make a sound joint.
Slip the coupling nut and compression ring over the end of the plastics pipe.
Push the liner inside the bore of the pipe until the flange is hard against the pipe end.

Push the pipe into the coupling until it contacts the pipe stop.
Slide the coupling nut and compression ring along the pipe to the coupling and screw up the coupling nut by hand. Tighten with a spanner.
Repeat the operation on the other pipe to complete the joint.

Fig. 10.37
Compression joining
plastic pipes

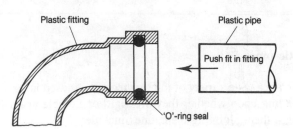

Fig. 10.38 Sleeve joint
for plastic pipe

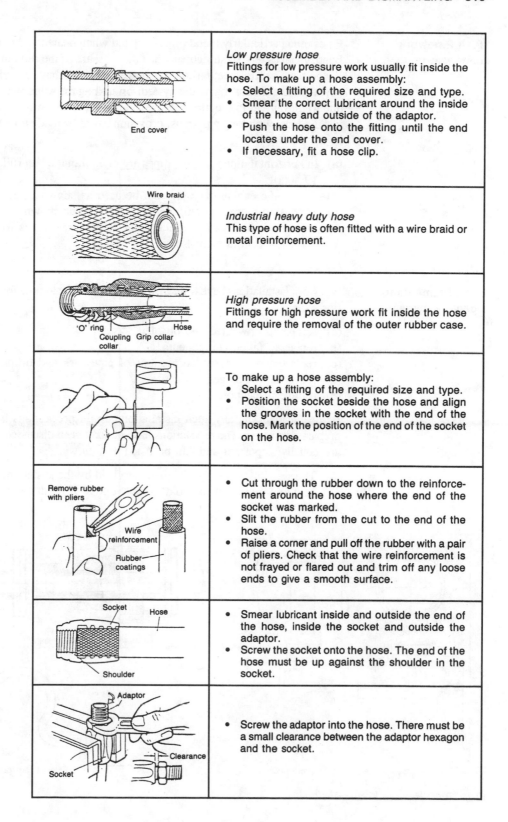

Low pressure hose
Fittings for low pressure work usually fit inside the hose. To make up a hose assembly:
- Select a fitting of the required size and type.
- Smear the correct lubricant around the inside of the hose and outside of the adaptor.
- Push the hose onto the fitting until the end locates under the end cover.
- If necessary, fit a hose clip.

Industrial heavy duty hose
This type of hose is often fitted with a wire braid or metal reinforcement.

High pressure hose
Fittings for high pressure work fit inside the hose and require the removal of the outer rubber case.

To make up a hose assembly:
- Select a fitting of the required size and type.
- Position the socket beside the hose and align the grooves in the socket with the end of the hose. Mark the position of the end of the socket on the hose.

- Cut through the rubber down to the reinforcement around the hose where the end of the socket was marked.
- Slit the rubber from the cut to the end of the hose.
- Raise a corner and pull off the rubber with a pair of pliers. Check that the wire reinforcement is not frayed or flared out and trim off any loose ends to give a smooth surface.

- Smear lubricant inside and outside the end of the hose, inside the socket and outside the adaptor.
- Screw the socket onto the hose. The end of the hose must be up against the shoulder in the socket.

- Screw the adaptor into the hose. There must be a small clearance between the adaptor hexagon and the socket.

Fig. 10.39 Hose connectors

10.14 Pipework suspension

Pipes, and particularly metal pipes, expand when heated and contract when cooled. Bends in pipes tend to straighten when the pressure of the fluid in the pipes increases. If you have central heating in your home, you may have heard the pipes creaking when the thermostat turns the system on and again when it is turned off. This is due to movement in the pipes, often referred to as the system 'breathing'. In large installations, with long pipe runs, provision has to be made for substantial movement in the pipes.

(a) In horizontal pipe runs, the pipes are often mounted on rollers as shown in Fig. 10.40(a).

(b) Telescopic expansion joints can be used as shown in Fig. 10.40(b).

(c) Expansion loops can be formed in the pipe as shown in Fig. 10.40(c). Such loops must lie in a horizontal plane to avoid air locks forming which would prevent the fluid from flowing.

10.15 Dismantling pipework systems

Pipework installations have to be dismantled from time to time for a variety of reasons. For example:

(a) scrapping unwanted and obsolete systems

(b) replacing failed components

(c) replacement of corroded sections of pipework and fittings

(d) removing blockages

(e) routine inspection

Before dismantling any such installation certain precautions have to be taken and preparations made. The precautions have already been discussed, but the preparations are equally important and can be listed as follows.

(a) The shutdown time for the plant serviced by the system must be estimated and kept to a minimum to avoid excessive loss of production. The start date must

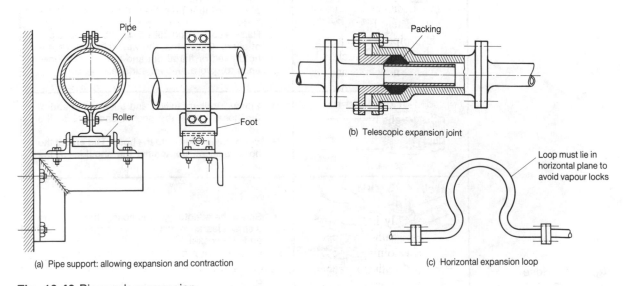

(a) Pipe support: allowing expansion and contraction

(b) Telescopic expansion joint

(c) Horizontal expansion loop

Fig. 10.40 Pipework suspension

be discussed with all the management services involved and all supervisory staff must be kept fully aware of what is involved.

(b) The correct procedure and sequence for shutdown must be strictly observed (section 10.7). This is particularly important when dangerous chemicals, high temperatures and fluids at high-pressures are involved.

(c) Replacement sections should be prefabricated to minimise down-time.

(d) All tools, equipment and materials must be available before draining down, purging, and dismantling commences.

The shutdown procedures are as follows.

(a) The contents of the pipes and fittings to be dismantled must be identified.

(b) Pipes must be depressurised and drained. They may also have to be purged of any residual and potentially dangerous contents, such as toxic, corrosive or flammable chemicals. Expert advise and supervision must be sought.

(c) Pipe runs and fittings may have to have additional and temporary supports so that they do not fall or collapse when key components are removed.

(d) Alternative routing of services may be necessary to maintain production if the operation is to take an unacceptably long time. Also, some processes by their very nature have to run continuously.

(e) The safety procedures and codes of practice in force at the plant must be strictly adhered to. Not only on the site whilst the work is in progress, but also in the administrative preplanning and paperwork leading up to the actual work of dismantling. The persons normally working on the plant, the fitters involved in its dismantling, the supervisors and the managers concerned with the operation, must all be properly notified and given prior warning of the work that is to be undertaken. This also applies to the managers whose departments will be affected by the operation.

Pipework which has screwed joints or union couplings must be capable of being separated lengthways for the couplings to be disconnected. If the pipework is rigid and this cannot be achieved then a section of pipe may have to be destroyed by cutting out a sufficient length of pipe to allow the joints to be separated. The replacement length of pipe and its associated fittings will have to be re-assembled with parallel flanged joints. No reclaimed jointing materials may be used when re-assembling. Always use new bolts and gaskets. Joint faces must be cleaned of old jointing materials and checked for flatness before re-assembling. Joint faces which have become corroded or distorted may have to be scraped or remachined to ensure a correct and fluid-tight fit.

Exercises

1 Assembly is the
    (a) gathering together of individual components ready for joining
    (b) joining together of individual components to make a total device
    (c) gathering together of employees during a fire-drill
    (d) preparation of components ready for joining together

2 Figure 10.41 shows a number of components to be assembled on to the shaft. The correct sequence of assembly is
    (a) 1, 2, 3, 4, 5
    (b) 5, 4, 3, 2, 1
    (c) 4, 3, 5, 2, 1
    (d) 3, 5, 2, 4, 1

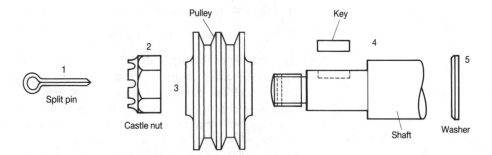

Fig. 10.41

3 Figure 10.42 shows an inspection cover. Before removing the cover the fitter has added the dot punch marks. The reason for doing this is to
    (a) ensure that the cover is re-assembled in its original position
    (b) mark the position for drilling an additional bolt hole
    (c) identify the fitter carrying out the work
    (d) indicate the sequence of assembly

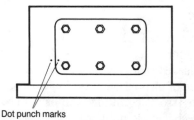

Fig. 10.42   Dot punch marks

4 When assembling or dismantling, the term 'accessibility' means
    (a) the issue of a permit to work on the equipment
    (b) the necessary tools are available in the store
    (c) the site has been cleared round the equipment ready for the fitter to work
    (d) all parts and fastenings of the assembly can be easily reached and manipulated using standard tools

5 Components from batch 'A' have to be assembled to components from batch 'B'. 'Selective assembly' means that
    (a) the fitter has the right to choose which job to do next
    (b) several combinations of components from each batch have to be tried together until the desired fit is obtained
    (c) any component from batch 'A' will fit any component from batch 'B'
    (d) none of the components will fit until they have been re-machined as pairs

6 To carry out routine maintenance and repairs, it should only be necessary to
  (a) partially dismantle and re-assemble a machine
  (b) completely dismantle and re-assemble a machine
  (c) dismantle and carry out a trial assembly of the machine
  (d) make adjustments

7 Pneumatic and hydraulic fittings are usually supplied with plastic seals covering any holes. This is to
  (a) prevent dirt entering the holes and to protect the seatings whilst the fittings are in use
  (b) prevent any leaks whilst the fittings are in use
  (c) prevent dirt entering the holes and to protect the seatings whilst the fittings are in the stores
  (d) provide easily removable inspection covers for maintenance

8 The gland packing shown in Fig. 10.43 will allow the valve spindle to
  (a) rotate without leaking
  (b) slide without leaking
  (c) rotate and slide without leaking
  (d) rotate and slide with reduced friction

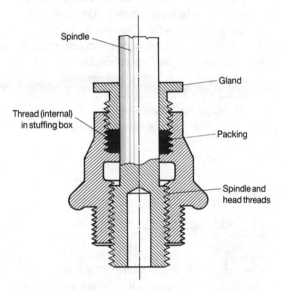

Fig. 10.43

9 A self-contained boiler, control sytem and circulating pump has been supplied as a single unit for a heating system which is being installed in a building. This is known as
  (a) large structure assembly
  (b) trial assembly
  (c) one-off assembly
  (d) on-site assembly with partial prefabrication

10 A coolant pump with a burnt-out motor is returned to the makers for a rewind. To avoid loss of production a replacement pump is fitted whilst the repair is carried out. This is known as

      (a) on-site dismantling and workshop repair

      (b) on-site dismantling and repair

      (c) on-site dismantling and works reconditioning

      (d) one-off dismantling and repair

11 Trial assemblies are often carried out on large structures before they are fully or partially dismantled for delivery to site. This is to

      (a) make transportation easier

      (b) ensure that there will be no problems during assembly under site conditions

      (c) train the assembly fitters before they go out to the site

      (d) work out the cost of assembly

12 Torque wrenches are used to

      (a) tighten up screwed fastenings as much as possible

      (b) provide a fitter with increased leverage

      (c) control the tightness of a screwed fastening and prevent over-stressing

      (d) remove the need for any locking device

13 When tightening a screwed fastening it is bad practice to

      (a) extend the spanner to get more leverage

      (b) use a socket wrench fitted with a ratchet

      (c) place a mild steel washer under the nut

      (d) use an open-ended spanner

14 When re-assembling a high pressure pipejoint all the fastenings and gaskets must comply with the original specification in order to

      (a) avoid infringement of any patents

      (b) make sure the fastenings fit the tools available

      (c) minimise the cost of materials

      (d) ensure the joint is safe and reliable

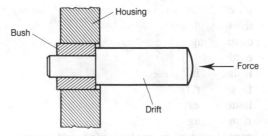

Fig. 10.44

15 The bush drift shown in Fig 10.44 is being used to

      (a) insert the bush in its housing

      (b) drive the bush out of its housing

      (c) open up the bore of an over-tight bush

      (d) swell the bush so that it will not move in its housing

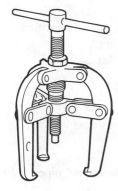

Fig. 10.45

16 The device shown in Fig 10.45 can be used for
(a) extracting a wheel from its shaft
(b) centring a wheel on its shaft
(c) pressing a wheel onto its shaft
(d) fastening a wheel to its shaft

17 Impact spanners are used for
(a) tightening high tensile bolts and nuts
(b) tightening screwed fastenings on site
(c) loosening tight and corroded nuts
(d) loosening lock nuts

18 To assist in dismantling obstinate screwed fastenings a
(a) penetrating oil should be used in preference to a lubricating oil
(b) cleansing solvent should be used
(c) lubricating oil should be used in preference to a penetrating oil
(d) degreasing solvent should be used

19 An 'easy-out' can be used for removing
(a) tight nuts
(b) broken studs
(c) tight studs
(d) broken screw-thread taps

20 Tight and corroded screwed fastenings can often be loosened by heating them up. This exploits the thermal property of
(a) conduction
(b) radiation
(c) contraction
(d) expansion

21 Heavy equipment not resting on the ground must be secured before dismantling commences. This is to prevent
(a) difficulty in removing the equipment when dismantling is complete
(b) the equipment slipping and injuring the fitter
(c) the equipment being stolen when it is separated from the rest of the system
(d) the equipment being re-assembled in the wrong position

22 Before dismantling electrically powered equipment, a qualified electrician must
(a) earth it
(b) isolate it from the supply
(c) fit smaller fuses
(d) issue a 'permit-to-work'

23 Before dismantling pipework it is essential that
(a) penetrating oil is applied to all the screwed fastenings
(b) the fitter isolates and drains down the system
(c) the system is isolated, drained down and purged by an authorised and competent person
(d) the system is thoroughly cleaned so that no dirt can get into it during dismantling

24 Flanged pipe joints must be assembled so that there is no screwed fastening on the bottom centre line because

    (a) this will weaken the joint

    (b) seepage from the joint could corrode a fastening in this position

    (c) it is difficult to inspect a fastening in this position

    (d) it is difficult to properly tighten a fastening in this position

25 When re-assembling flanged joints always use

    (a) new bolts and the original gasket

    (b) the original bolts and a new gasket

    (c) new bolts and a new gasket

    (d) the original bolts and the original gasket

26 Compression joints and capillary joints are used

    (a) as an alternative to screwed joints for smaller tubes and pipes at low and medium pressures

    (b) when fitting oversize pipes into standard fittings

    (c) when fitting undersize pipes into standard fittings

    (d) only for very high pressure hydraulic systems

27 The joint shown in Fig. 10.46 is suitable for

    (a) mains water pipes made of plastic

    (b) earthenware drain pipes

    (c) plastic waste pipes

    (d) chemical plant

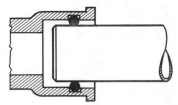

Fig. 10.46

28 Plastic pipes for gas mains are usually joined by

    (a) fusion welding

    (b) sleeved joints

    (c) compression fittings

    (d) butt welding

29 Expansion fittings are used in pipework systems to allow for

    (a) extensions to the system

    (b) expansion and contraction of the length of the pipe runs due to changes of temperature

    (c) expansion and contraction of the diameter of the pipes due to changes of temperature

    (d) pipes to be withdrawn during dismantling

30 When installing electrical equipment the metal conduit should be screwed into the fittings

    (a) tightly so that there is good metal to metal contact

    (b) using a jointing compound to keep out water

    (c) using PTFE tape so as to keep out water

    (d) after painting the threads to prevent corrosion

Answers to exercises

Chapter 1		
1. a	16. c
2. c	17. a
3. b	18. d
4. d	19. b
5. c	20. b
6. b	
7. a	
8. c	
9. b	
10. b	
11. d	
12. a	
13. b	
14. c	
15. b	

Chapter 2		
1. d	16. c
2. c	17. d
3. a	18. d
4. d	19. b
5. c	20. a
6. d	21. b
7. a	22. b
8. d	23. d
9. b	24. c
10. d	25. c
11. a	26. c
12. c	27. a
13. d	28. a
14. a	29. a
15. a	30. d

Chapter 3		
1. a	16. d
2. c	17. d
3. b	18. d
4. c	19. b
5. c	20. b
6. b	
7. d	
8. c	
9. d	
10. b	
11. d	
12. a	
13. a	
14. a	
15. b	

Chapter 4		
1. c	16. a
2. c	17. b
3. d	18. d
4. a	19. b
5. c	20. a
6. a	
7. b	
8. a	
9. b	
10. a	
11. d	
12. a	
13. c	
14. d	
15. b	

Chapter 5		
1. c	16. a
2. c	17. d
3. a	18. c
4. a	19. b
5. d	20. d
6. d	21. a
7. a	22. d
8. b	23. d
9. c	24. b
10. b	25. b
11. b	26. a
12. d	27. d
13. c	28. c
14. d	29. c
15. a	30. b

Chapter 6		
1. c	
2. b	
3. d	
4. a	
5. c	
6. b	
7. a	
8. c	
9. d	
10. c	
11. a	
12. b	
13. a	
14. a	
15. c	

Chapter 7		
1. d	16. d
2. a	17. d
3. b	18. a
4. d	19. a
5. a	20. c
6. d	21. b
7. a	22. c
8. b	23. b
9. a	24. c
10. c	25. a
11. c	
12. c	
13. d	
14. b	
15. c	

Chapter 8		
1. d	16. a
2. a	17. b
3. b	18. d
4. b	19. c
5. a	20. b
6. b	21. a
7. a	22. c
8. c	23. c
9. d	24. b
10. a	25. b
11. c	26. a
12. b	27. d
13. d	28. a
14. b	29. a
15. c	30. c

Chapter 9		
1. b	16. d
2. c	17. a
3. a	18. c
4. d	19. c
5. a	20. a
6. b	21. d
7. a	22. c
8. d	23. a
9. c	24. b
10. a	25. d
11. d	26. b
12. c	27. a
13. a	28. b
14. c	29. d
15. b	30. b

Chapter 10		
1. b	16. a
2. c	17. c
3. a	18. a
4. d	19. b
5. b	20. d
6. a	21. b
7. c	22. b
8. c	23. c
9. d	24. b
10. c	25. c
11. b	26. a
12. c	27. c
13. a	28. d
14. d	29. b
15. b	30. a

Index